ENGLISH ESSAYS

ENGLISH ESSAYS

SELECTED AND EDITED BY

WALTER C. BRONSON

Essay Index Reprint Series

BOOKS FOR LIBRARIES PRESS
FREEPORT, NEW YORK

First Published 1905
Reprinted 1970

STANDARD BOOK NUMBER:
8369-1595-X

LIBRARY OF CONGRESS CATALOG CARD NUMBER:
74-111817

PRINTED IN THE UNITED STATES OF AMERICA

PREFACE.

THIS book has been made with a definite, practical object in view, which has set certain limits to it and determined its nature and method. It is intended for use with college classes in introductory courses in literature; and the chief purpose of it is to cultivate in the undergraduate a liking for good English prose, and to give him some knowledge of English thought as it has found expression in English essays of the last three hundred years, by putting into his hands a not too bulky collection of interesting texts by some of the greater essayists from Bacon to Stevenson. In selecting material, therefore, chief regard has been paid to intrinsic interest of thought and style, and entire essays or chapters have been given whenever that was possible; when it was not, only such extracts are presented as have a certain completeness in themselves. The title *English Essays,* which best indicates the nature of the collection as a whole, has been interpreted liberally, in order to include some interesting and valuable matter which is not strictly of the essay type. On the other hand, there has been no attempt to include all the good essayists since Bacon, for that would have swelled the volume unduly unless the selections were unduly short. It has not been a main object, either, to afford illustrations of the historical development of English prose style, although to a certain extent the book may be so used, and to increase its value in this respect specimens of English prose before Bacon have been added in the Appendix.

In furtherance of intelligibility and interest, the spelling, capitalization, punctuation, and sometimes the paragraphing have been modernized, except in the earlier extracts in the Appendix and in the essays of Lamb and Carlyle, where the peculiarities of capitalization and punctuation have special charm or significance. Much care has been taken to secure a correct text; and whenever it has been advisable, for any reason, to omit portions of the original, the omission has been indicated by a row of points.

Biographies of the essayists represented, exposition of the thought, and literary criticism have been excluded from the Notes, in the belief that such matters are better conveyed by histories of literature and by lectures. The explanatory notes are perhaps fuller and more precise than some teachers will care for. These may be reminded of Hazlitt's remark about the allegory in *The Faerie Queene;* if one lets the notes alone, they won't bite him. In many cases the more precise form of statement has been used because it is more concise, as well as more valuable for reference; thus it takes less space to give the dates of a man's birth and death than to say that he lived in the latter part of such-and-such a century, but it does not follow that the student should be required to learn the exact dates. As to number of notes, I cannot be alone in my experience that most college undergraduates, in the earlier years of their course, are lamentably ignorant, not only of literature, but of history, biography, and art, and that if they are to understand what they read considerable annotation is necessary. Furthermore, although the text may often be intelligible, in a general way, without the reader's knowing the significance of an allusion or the source of a quotation, it may well be one of the secondary benefits of reading essays like those here contained that the student should widen, if only superficially and at second hand, his knowledge of the world of letters and men. I hope, however, that all teachers who use the book will urge their classes to read each essay through, at first, without looking at a note, in order to get the thought as a whole and the general effect; but also that they will then adopt the apostolic method of St. Philip, and put to the rider in these literary chariots that embarrassing but profitable question, "Understandest thou what thou readest?"

In conclusion I wish to express my indebtedness to Miss Elsie Marion Straffin, A. M., Fellow in English in Brown University, for valuable aid in collating texts, verifying references, and reading proof.

WALTER C. BRONSON.

BROWN UNIVERSITY,
May 17, 1905.

CONTENTS

PAGE

PREFACE iii

FRANCIS BACON
Of Truth 1
Of Innovations 3
Of Nature in Men 4
Of Youth and Age 6
Of Negotiating 7
Of Studies 9

JOHN MILTON
Freedom of the Press 11

SIR THOMAS BROWNE
Vanity of Earthly Monuments 25

JOHN DRYDEN
Preface to the Fables 33

JONATHAN SWIFT
The Battle of the Books 56

SIR RICHARD STEELE
The Club at "The Trumpet" 81

JOSEPH ADDISON
A Very Pretty Poet 85
True and False Humor 89
The Vision of Mirzah 92
Dissection of a Coquet's Heart 97

DANIEL DEFOE
An Academy for Women 101

SAMUEL JOHNSON
Shakespeare 109

OLIVER GOLDSMITH
Beau Tibbs, a Character 120

PAGE

EDMUND BURKE
England and the French Revolution 127

WILLIAM HAZLITT
On Reading Old Books 140

CHARLES LAMB
New Year's Eve 152
A Dissertation upon Roast Pig 159
Poor Relations 166

WALTER SAVAGE LANDOR
Petrarch Attends the Parish Church 174

THOMAS DE QUINCEY
Levana and Our Ladies of Sorrow 180
Literature of Knowledge and Literature of Power 187

THOMAS CARLYLE
Biography 192
Heroes and Hero-Worship 208

THOMAS BABINGTON MACAULAY
Oliver Goldsmith 222

WILLIAM MAKEPEACE THACKERAY
Oliver Goldsmith 238

JOHN RUSKIN
Selections from Modern Painters 250
An Idealist's Arraignment of the Age 259

JOHN HENRY NEWMAN
The Roman Catholic Church 273

MATTHEW ARNOLD
Hebraism and Hellenism 286

THOMAS HENRY HUXLEY
On a Piece of Chalk 300

WALTER PATER
Dionysus 323

ROBERT LOUIS STEVENSON
Æs Triplex 337

PAGE

EARLY TRANSLATIONS OF THE BIBLE
The Lord's Prayer 347
The Parable of the Prodigal Son 348

SIR JOHN MANDEVILLE
Of the Hilles of Gold 350

SIR THOMAS MALORY
The Parting of Launcelot and Guinevere . . . 351

HUGH LATIMER
An Arraignment of London 354

JOHN LYLY
The Character of Euphues 355

SIR PHILIP SIDNEY
Her Lovers Describe Urania 356

RICHARD HOOKER
The Majesty and Beneficence of Law 359

NOTES 363

ENGLISH ESSAYS.

Francis Bacon.

1561–1626.

OF TRUTH.

(From *Essays or Counsels, Civil and Moral*, 1625.)

"What is truth?" said jesting Pilate; and would not stay for an answer. Certainly there be that delight in giddiness, and count it a bondage to fix a belief, affecting free will in thinking as well as in acting. And though the sects of philosophers of that kind be gone, yet there remain certain discoursing wits which are of the same veins, though there be not so much blood in them as was in those of the ancients. But it is not only the difficulty and labor which men take in finding out of truth, nor again that when it is found it imposeth upon men's thoughts, that doth bring lies in favor, but a natural though corrupt love of the lie itself. One of the later school of the Grecians examineth the matter, and is at a stand to think what should be in it that men should love lies where neither they make for pleasure, as with poets, nor for advantage, as with the merchant, but for the lie's sake. But I cannot tell: this same truth is a naked and open daylight, that doth not show the masks and mummeries and triumphs of the world half so stately and daintily as candlelights. Truth may perhaps come to the price of a pearl, that showeth best by day; but it will not rise to the price of a diamond or carbuncle, that showeth best in varied lights. A mixture of a lie doth ever add pleasure. Doth any man doubt that if there were taken out of men's minds vain opinions, flattering hopes, false valuations, imaginations as one would, and the like, but it would leave the minds of a number of men poor shrunken things, full of melancholy and indisposition, and unpleasing to themselves? One of the fathers, in great severity, called poesy "vinum daemonum" because it filleth the imagination, and yet it is but with the shadow of a lie. But it is not the lie that passeth through the mind, but the lie that sinketh in and settleth in it, that doth the hurt, such as we spake of before. But howsoever these things are thus in men's depraved judgments and affections, yet truth, which only doth judge itself, teacheth that the inquiry of truth, which is the love-making or wooing of it, the knowledge of truth, which is the presence of it, and the belief of truth, which is the enjoying of it, is the sovereign good of human nature. The first creature of God, in the works of the days, was the light of the sense; the last was the light of reason; and His sabbath work ever since is the illumination of His Spirit. First He breathed light upon the face of the matter, or chaos; then He breathed light into the face of man; and still He breatheth and inspireth light into the face of His chosen. The poet that beautified the sect that was otherwise inferior to the rest saith yet excellently well: "It is a pleasure to stand upon the shore and to see ships tossed upon the sea; a pleasure to stand in the window of a castle and to see a battle and the adventures thereof below: but no pleasure is comparable to the standing upon the vantage ground of truth" (a hill not to be commanded, and where the air is always clear and serene) "and to see the errors and wanderings, and mists and tempests, in the vale below"—so always that this prospect be with pity, and not with swelling or pride. Certainly it is heaven upon earth to have a man's mind move in charity, rest in Providence, and turn upon the poles of truth.

To pass from theological and philosophical truth to the truth of civil business: it will be acknowledged, even by those that practise it not, that clear and round dealing is the honor of man's nature, and that mixture of falsehood is like allay in coin of gold and silver, which may make the metal work the better but it embaseth it; for these winding and crooked courses are the goings of the serpent, which goeth basely upon the belly and not upon the feet. There is no vice that doth so cover a man with shame as to be found false and perfidious: and therefore Montaigne saith prettily, when he inquired the reason why the word of the lie should be such a disgrace and such an odious charge, saith he, "If it be well weighed, to say that a man lieth is as much to say as that he is brave towards God and a coward towards men." For a lie faces God and shrinks from man. Surely the wickedness of falsehood and breach of faith cannot possibly be so highly expressed as in that it shall be the last peal to call the judgments of God upon the generations of men, it being foretold that when Christ cometh "He shall not find faith upon the earth."

OF INNOVATIONS.

(From the same.)

As the births of living creatures at first are ill-shapen, so are all innovations, which are the births of time; yet, notwithstanding, as those that first bring honor into their family are commonly more worthy than most that succeed, so the first precedent (if it be good) is seldom attained by imitation: for ill, to man's nature as it stands perverted, hath a natural motion strongest in continuance; but good, as a forced motion, strongest at first. Surely every medicine is an innovation; and he that will not apply new remedies must expect new evils: for time is the greatest innovator; and if time of course alter things to the worse, and wisdom and counsel shall not alter them to the better, what shall be the end? It is true that what is settled by custom, though it be not good, yet at least it is fit; and those things which have long gone together are, as it were, confederate within themselves: whereas new things piece not so well; but though they help by their utility, yet they trouble by their inconformity; besides, they are like strangers, more admired and less favored. All this is true, if time stood still; which, contrariwise, moveth so round that a froward retention of custom is as turbulent a thing as an innovation; and they that reverence too much old times are but a scorn to the new. It were good, therefore, that men in their innovations would follow the example of time itself, which indeed innovateth greatly, but quietly and by degrees scarce to be perceived: for otherwise whatsoever is new is unlooked for, and ever it mends some and pairs other; and he that is holpen takes it for a fortune and thanks the time; and he that is hurt, for a wrong and imputeth it to the author. It is good also not to try experiments in States, except the necessity be urgent or the utility evident: and well to beware that it be the reformation that draweth on the change, and not the desire of change that pretendeth the reformation: and lastly, that the novelty, though it be not rejected, yet be held for a suspect; and as the Scripture saith, "That we make a stand upon the ancient way, and then look about us, and discover what is the straight and right way, and so to walk in it."

OF NATURE IN MEN.

(From the same.)

Nature is often hidden, sometimes overcome, seldom extinguished. Force maketh nature more violent in the return; doctrine and discourse maketh nature less importune; but custom only doth alter and subdue nature. He that seeketh victory over his nature, let him not set himself too great nor too small tasks; for the first will make him dejected by often failings, and the second will make him a small proceeder though by often prevailings. And, at the first, let him practise with helps, as swimmers do with bladders or rushes; but, after a time, let him practise with disadvantages, as dancers do with thick shoes, for it breeds great perfection if the practice be harder than the use. When nature is mighty, and therefore the victory hard, the degrees had need be, first, to stay and arrest nature in time, like to him that would say over the four and twenty letters when he was angry; then to go less in quantity, as if one should, in forbearing wine, come from drinking healths to a draught at a meal; and, lastly, to discontinue altogether. But if a man have the fortitude and resolution to enfranchise himself at once, that is the best:

> "Optimus ille animi vindex lædentia pectus
> Vincula qui rupit, dedoluitque semel."

Neither is the ancient rule amiss, to bend nature as a wand to a contrary extreme, whereby to set it right; understanding it, where the contrary extreme is no vice. Let not a man force a habit upon himself with a perpetual continuance, but with some intermission: for both the pause reinforceth the new onset; and if a man that is not perfect be ever in practice, he shall as well practise his errors as his abilities and induce one habit of both, and there is no means to help this but by seasonable intermissions. But let not a man trust his victory over his nature too far, for nature will lay buried a great time and yet revive upon the occasion or temptation; like as it was with Æsop's damsel, turned from a cat to a woman, who sat very demurely at the board's end till a mouse ran before her: therefore let a man either avoid the occasion altogether, or put himself often to it that he may be little moved with it. A man's nature is best perceived in privateness, for there is no affectation; in passion, for that putteth a man out of his precepts; and in a new case or experiment, for there custom leaveth him. They are happy men whose natures sort with their vocations; otherwise they may say, "Multum incola fuit anima mea," when they converse in those things they do not affect. In studies, whatsoever a man commandeth upon himself, let him set hours for it; but whatsoever is agreeable to his nature, let him take no care for any set times, for his thoughts will fly to it of themselves, so as the spaces of other business or studies will suffice. A man's nature runs either to herbs or weeds; therefore let him seasonably water the one and destroy the other.

OF YOUTH AND AGE.

(From the same.)

A man that is young in years may be old in hours, if he have lost no time; but that happeneth rarely. Generally, youth is like the first cogitations, not so wise as the second, for there is a youth in thoughts as well as in ages; and yet the invention of young men is more lively than that of old, and imaginations stream into their minds better, and, as it were, more divinely. Natures that have much heat, and great and violent desires and perturbations, are not ripe for action till they have passed the meridian of their years; as it was with Julius Cæsar and Septimius Severus, of the latter of whom it is said, "Juventutem egit erroribus, immo furoribus plenam"; and yet he was the ablest emperor, almost, of all the list. But reposed natures may do well in youth, as it is seen in Augustus Cæsar, Cosmos Duke of Florence, Gaston de Foix, and others. On the other side, heat and vivacity in age is an excellent composition for business. Young men are fitter to invent than to judge, fitter for execution than for counsel, and fitter for new projects than for settled business; for the experience of age, in things that fall within the compass of it, directeth them, but in new things abuseth them. The errors of young men are the ruin of business; but the errors of aged men amount but to this, that more might have been done or sooner.

Young men, in the conduct and manage of actions, embrace more than they can hold; stir more than they can quiet; fly to the end without consideration of the means and degrees; pursue some few principles which they have chanced upon, absurdly; care not to innovate, which draws unknown inconveniences; use extreme remedies at first, and, that which doubleth all errors, will not acknowledge or retract them—like an unready horse, that will neither stop nor turn. Men of age object too much, consult too long, adventure too little, repent too soon, and seldom drive business home to the full period but content themselves with a mediocrity of success.

Certainly it is good to compound employments of both: for that will be good for the present, because the virtues of either age may correct the defects of both; and good for succession, that young men may be learners, while men in age are actors; and, lastly, good for extern accidents, because authority followeth old men, and favor and popularity youth. But for the moral part perhaps youth will have the pre-eminence, as age hath for the politic. A certain rabbin, upon the text, "Your young men shall see visions, and your old men shall dream dreams," inferreth that young men are admitted nearer to God than old, because vision is a clearer revelation than a dream. And, certainly, the more a man drinketh of the world the more it intoxicateth; and age doth profit rather in the powers of understanding than in the virtues of the will and affections.

There be some have an over-early ripeness in their years, which fadeth betimes. These are, first, such as have brittle wits, the edge whereof is soon turned; such as was Hermogenes the rhetorician, whose books are exceeding subtle, who afterwards waxed stupid. A second sort is of those that have some natural dispositions which have better grace in youth than in age, such as is a fluent and luxuriant speech, which becomes youth well but not age; so Tully saith of Hortensius, "Idem manebat, neque idem decebat." The third is of such as take too high a strain at the first, and are magnanimous more than tract of years can uphold; as was Scipio Africanus, of whom Livy saith in effect, "Ultima primis cedebant."

OF NEGOTIATING.

(From the same.)

It is generally better to deal by speech than by letter, and by the mediation of a third than by a man's self. Letters are good when a man would draw an answer by letter back again, or when it may serve for a man's justification afterwards to produce his own letter, or where it may be danger to be interrupted or heard by pieces. To deal in person is good when a man's face breedeth regard, as commonly with inferiors; or in tender cases, where a man's eye upon the countenance of him with whom he speaketh may give him a direction how far to go; and generally, where a man will reserve to himself liberty either to disavow or to expound. In choice of instruments it is better to choose men of a plainer sort, that are like to do that that is committed to them and to report back again faithfully the success, than those that are cunning to contrive out of other men's business somewhat to grace themselves, and will help the matter in report for satisfaction sake. Use also such persons as affect the business wherein they are employed, for that quickeneth much; and such as are fit for the matter, as bold men for expostulation, fair-spoken men for persuasion, crafty men for inquiry and observation, froward and absurd men for business that doth not well bear out itself. Use also such as have been lucky and prevailed before in things wherein you have employed them; for that breeds confidence, and they will strive to maintain their prescription.

It is better to sound a person with whom one deals, afar off, than to fall upon the point at first, except you mean to surprise him by some short question. It is better dealing with men in appetite than with those that are where they would be. If a man deal with another upon conditions, the start, or first performance, is all; which a man cannot reasonably demand, except either the nature of the thing be such which must go before, or else a man can persuade the other party that he shall still need him in some other thing, or else that he be counted the honester man. All practice is to discover or to work. Men discover themselves in trust, in passion, at unawares, and of necessity when they would have somewhat done and cannot find an apt pretext. If you would work any man, you must either know his nature and fashions and so lead him, or his ends and so persuade him, or his weakness and disadvantages and so awe him, or those that have interest in him and so govern him. In dealing with cunning persons we must ever consider their ends to interpret their speeches; and it is good to say little to them, and that which they least look for. In all negotiations of difficulty a man may not look to sow and reap at once, but must prepare business and so ripen it by degrees.

OF STUDIES.

(From the same.)

Studies serve for delight, for ornament, and for ability. Their chief use for delight is in privateness and retiring; for ornament, is in discourse; and for ability, is in the judgment and disposition of business: for expert men can execute, and perhaps judge of particulars one by one; but the general counsels and the plots and marshalling of affairs come best from those that are learned. To spend too much time in studies is sloth; to use them too much for ornament is affectation; to make judgment wholly by their rules is the humor of a scholar. They perfect nature and are perfected by experience: for natural abilities are like natural plants, that need pruning by study; and studies themselves do give forth directions too much at large, except they be bounded in by experience. Crafty men contemn studies, simple men admire them, and wise men use them; for they teach not their own use, but that is a wisdom without them and above them, won by observation. Read not to contradict and confute, nor to believe and take for granted, nor to find talk and discourse, but to weigh and consider. Some books are to be tasted, others to be swallowed, and some few to be chewed and digested; that is, some books are to be read only in parts, others to be read but not curiously, and some few to be read wholly and with diligence and attention. Some books also may be read by deputy, and extracts made of them by others; but that would be only in the less important arguments and the meaner sort of books; else, distilled books are like common distilled waters, flashy things. Reading maketh a full man, conference a ready man, and writing an exact man; and therefore if a man write little, he had need have a great memory; if he confer little, he had need have a present wit; and if he read little, he had need have much cunning, to seem to know that he doth not. Histories make men wise; poets, witty; the mathematics, subtile; natural philosophy, deep; moral, grave; logic and rhetoric, able to contend. "Abeunt studia in mores." Nay, there is no stand or impediment in the wit but may be wrought out by fit studies, like as diseases of the body may have appropriate exercises. Bowling is good for the stone and reins, shooting for the lungs and breast, gentle walking for the stomach, riding for the head, and the like. So, if a man's wit be wandering, let him study the mathematics, for in demonstrations, if his wit be called away never so little, he must begin again; if his wit be not apt to distinguish or find differences, let him study the schoolmen, for they are *cymini sectores;* if he be not apt to beat over matters, and to call up one thing to prove and illustrate another, let him study the lawyers' cases: so every defect of the mind may have a special receipt.

John Milton.

1608–1674.

FREEDOM OF THE PRESS.

(From *Areopagitica,* 1644.)

I deny not but that it is of greatest concernment in the Church and Commonwealth to have a vigilant eye how books demean themselves as well as men, and thereafter to confine, imprison, and do sharpest justice on them as malefactors: for books are not absolutely dead things, but do contain a potency of life in them to be as active as that soul was whose progeny they are; nay, they do preserve as in a vial the purest efficacy and extraction of that living intellect that bred them. I know they are as lively, and as vigorously productive, as those fabulous dragon's teeth; and being sown up and down, may chance to spring up armed men. And yet, on the other hand, unless wariness be used, as good, almost, kill a man as kill a good book: who kills a man kills a reasonable creature, God's image; but he who destroys a good book kills reason itself, kills the image of God, as it were, in the eye. Many a man lives a burden to the earth; but a good book is the precious life-blood of a master spirit, embalmed and treasured up on purpose to a life beyond life. 'Tis true, no age can restore a life, whereof perhaps there is no great loss; and revolutions of ages do not oft recover the loss of a rejected truth, for the want of which whole nations fare the worse. We should be wary, therefore, what persecution we raise against the living labors of public men, how we spill that seasoned life of man, preserved and stored up in books, since we see a kind of homicide may be thus committed, sometimes a martyrdom, and if it extend to the whole impression a kind of massacre, whereof the execution ends not in the slaying of an elemental life, but strikes at that ethereal and fifth essence, the breath of reason itself, slays an immortality rather than a life.

. . . .

Good and evil, we know, in the field of this world grow up together almost inseparably; and the knowledge of good is so involved and interwoven with the knowledge of evil, and in so many cunning resemblances hardly to be discerned, that those confused seeds, which were imposed on Psyche as an incessant labor to cull out and sort asunder, were not more intermixed. It was from out the rind of one apple tasted that the knowledge of good and evil, as two twins cleaving together, leaped forth into the world. And perhaps this is that doom which Adam fell into of knowing good and evil, that is to say, of knowing good by evil. As, therefore, the state of man now is, what wisdom can there be to choose, what continence to forbear, without the knowledge of evil? He that can apprehend and consider vice with all her baits and seeming pleasures, and yet abstain, and yet distinguish, and yet prefer that which is truly better, he is the true wayfaring Christian. I cannot praise a fugitive and cloistered virtue, unexercised and unbreathed, that never sallies out and sees her adversary, but slinks out of the race where that immortal garland is to be run for, not without dust and heat. Assuredly we bring not innocence into the world, we bring impurity much rather; that which purifies us is trial, and trial is by what is contrary. That virtue therefore which is but a youngling in the contemplation of evil, and knows not the utmost that vice promises to her followers, and rejects it, is but a blank virtue, not a pure; her whiteness is but an excremental whiteness; which was the reason why our sage and serious poet Spenser, whom I dare be known to think a better teacher than Scotus or Aquinas, describing true temperance under the person of Guyon, brings him in with his palmer through the cave of Mammon and the bower of earthly bliss, that he might see and know and yet abstain. Since, therefore, the knowledge and survey of vice is in this world so necessary to the constituting of human virtue, and the scanning of error to the confirmation of truth, how can we more safely and with less danger scout into the regions of sin and falsity than by reading all manner of tractates and hearing all manner of reason? And this is the benefit which may be had of books promiscuously read.

. . . .

Well knows he who uses to consider, that our faith and knowledge thrives by exercise, as well as our limbs and complexion. Truth is compared in Scripture to a streaming fountain: if her waters flow not in a perpetual progression, they sicken into a muddy pool of conformity and tradition. A man may be a heretic in the truth; and if he believe things only because his pastor says so or the assembly so determines, without knowing other reason, though his belief be true yet the very truth he holds becomes his heresy. There is not any burden that some would gladlier post off to another than the charge and care of their religion. There be—who knows not that there be?—of Protestants and professors who live and die in as arrant an implicit faith as any lay Papist of Loretto. A wealthy man addicted to his pleasure and to his profits finds religion to be a traffic so entangled, and of so many piddling accounts, that of all mysteries he cannot skill to keep a stock going upon that trade. What should he do? Fain he would have the name to be religious, fain he would bear up with his neighbors in that. What does he, therefore, but resolves to give over toiling, and to find himself out some factor, to whose care and credit he may commit the whole managing of his religious affairs; some divine of note and estimation, that must be. To him he adheres, resigns the whole warehouse of his religion, with all the locks and keys, into his custody; and indeed makes the very person of that man his religion, esteems his associating with him a sufficient evidence and commendatory of his own piety. So that a man may say his religion is now no more within himself, but is become a dividual movable, and goes and comes near him according as that good man frequents the house. He entertains him, gives him gifts, feasts him, lodges him: his Religion comes home at night, prays, is liberally supped and sumptuously laid to sleep, rises, is saluted, and after the malmsey or some well-spiced brewage, and better breakfasted than He whose morning appetite would have gladly fed on green figs between Bethany and Jerusalem, his Religion walks abroad at eight, and leaves his kind entertainer in the shop trading all day without his Religion.

. . . .

There is yet behind, of what I purposed to lay open, the incredible loss and detriment that this plot of licensing puts us to. More than if some enemy at sea should stop up all our havens and ports and creeks, it hinders and retards the importation of our richest merchandise, Truth: nay, it was first established and put in practice by anti-Christian malice and mystery on set purpose to extinguish, if it were possible, the light of Reformation, and to settle falsehood, little differing from that policy wherewith the Turk upholds his *Alcoran* by the prohibition of printing. 'Tis not denied, but gladly confessed, we are to send our thanks and vows to Heaven, louder than most of nations, for that great measure of truth which we enjoy, especially in those main points between us and the Pope, with his appurtenances the prelates; but he who thinks we are to pitch our tent here, and have attained the utmost prospect of reformation that the mortal glass wherein we contemplate can show us, till we come to beatific vision, that man by this very opinion declares that he is yet far short of Truth.

Truth indeed came once into the world with her Divine Master, and was a perfect shape most glorious to look on: but when He ascended, and His apostles after Him were laid asleep, then straight arose a wicked race of deceivers, who, as that story goes of the Egyptian Typhon with his conspirators, how they dealt with the good Osiris, took the virgin Truth, hewed her lovely form into a thousand pieces, and scattered them to the four winds. From that time ever since, the sad friends of Truth, such as durst appear, imitating the careful search that Isis made for the mangled body of Osiris, went up and down gathering up limb by limb still as they could find them. We have not yet found them all, Lords and Commons, nor ever shall do till her Master's second coming; He shall bring together every joint and member, and shall mould them into an immortal feature of loveliness and perfection. Suffer not these licensing prohibitions to stand at every place of opportunity, forbidding and disturbing them that continue seeking, that continue to do our obsequies to the torn body of our martyred saint. We boast our light; but if we look not wisely on the sun itself, it smites us into darkness. Who can discern those planets that are oft combust, and those stars of brightest magnitude that rise and set with the sun, until the opposite motion of their orbs bring them to such a place in the firmament where they may be seen evening or morning? The light which we have gained was given us, not to be ever staring on, but by it to discover onward things more remote from our knowledge. It is not the unfrocking of a priest, the unmitring of a bishop, and the removing him from off the Presbyterian shoulders, that will make us a happy nation; no, if other things as great in the Church and in the rule of life, both economical and political, be not looked into and reformed, we have looked so long upon the blaze that Zuinglius and Calvin hath beaconed up to us that we are stark blind. There be who perpetually complain of schisms and sects, and make it such a calamity that any man dissents from their maxims. 'Tis their own pride and ignorance which causes the disturbing, who neither will hear with meekness nor can convince, yet all must be suppressed which is not found in their *Syntagma*. They are the troublers, they are the dividers of unity, who neglect and permit not others to unite those dissevered pieces which are yet wanting to the body of Truth. To be still searching what we know not by what we know, still closing up truth to truth as we find it (for all her body is homogeneal and proportional), this is the golden rule in theology as well as in arithmetic, and makes up the best harmony in a church, not the forced and outward union of cold and neutral and inwardly divided minds.

Lords and Commons of England, consider what nation it is whereof ye are and whereof ye are the governors: a nation not slow and dull, but of a quick, ingenious, and piercing spirit, acute to invent, subtle and sinewy to discourse, not beneath the reach of any point the highest that human capacity can soar to. Therefore the studies of Learning in her deepest sciences have been so ancient and so eminent among us that writers of good antiquity and ablest judgment have been persuaded that even the school of Pythagoras and the Persian wisdom took beginning from the old philosophy of this island. And that wise and civil Roman, Julius Agricola, who governed once here for Cæsar, preferred the natural wits of Britain before the labored studies of the French. Nor is it for nothing that the grave and frugal Transylvanian sends out yearly from as far as the mountainous borders of Russia and beyond the Hercynian wilderness, not their youth, but their staid men, to learn our language and our theologic arts. Yet that which is above all this, the favor and the love of Heaven we have great argument to think in a peculiar manner propitious and propending towards us. Why else was this nation chosen before any other, that out of her as out of Sion should be proclaimed and sounded forth the first tidings and trumpet of Reformation to all Europe? And had it not been the obstinate perverseness of our prelates against the divine and admirable spirit of Wiclif, to suppress him as a schismatic and innovator, perhaps neither the Bohemian Huss and Jerome, no, nor the name of Luther or of Calvin, had been ever known: the glory of reforming all our neighbors had been completely ours. But now, as our obdurate clergy have with violence demeaned the matter, we are become hitherto the latest and the backwardest scholars of whom God offered to have made us the teachers. Now once again, by all concurrence of signs, and by the general instinct of holy and devout men as they daily and solemnly express their thoughts, God is decreeing to begin some new and great period in His Church, even to the reforming of Reformation itself: what does He, then, but reveal Himself to His servants, and, as His manner is, first to His Englishmen? I say, as His manner is, first to us, though we mark not the method of His counsels and are unworthy. Behold now this vast city: a city of refuge, the mansion house of liberty, encompassed and surrounded with His protection; the shop of war hath not there more anvils and hammers waking, to fashion out the plates and instruments of armed Justice in defence of beleaguered Truth, than there be pens and heads there, sitting by their studious lamps, musing, searching, revolving new notions and ideas wherewith to present, as with their homage and their fealty, the approaching Reformation, others as fast reading, trying all things, assenting to the force of reason and convincement. What could a man require more from a nation so pliant and so prone to seek after knowledge? What wants there to such a towardly and pregnant soil but wise and faithful laborers, to make a knowing people, a nation of prophets, of sages, and of worthies? We reckon more than five months yet to harvest: there need not be five weeks; had we but eyes to lift up, the fields are white already. Where there is much desire to learn, there of necessity will be much arguing, much writing, many opinions; for opinion in good men is but knowledge in the making. Under these fantastic terrors of sect and schism, we wrong the earnest and zealous thirst after knowledge and understanding which God hath stirred up in this city. What some lament of we rather should rejoice at, should rather praise this pious forwardness among men to reassume the ill-deputed care of their religion into their own hands again. A little generous prudence, a little forbearance of one another, and some grain of charity might win all these diligences to join and unite in one general and brotherly search after truth, could we but forego this prelatical tradition of crowding free consciences and Christian liberties into canons and precepts of men. I doubt not, if some great and worthy stranger should come among us, wise to discern the mould and temper of a people and how to govern it, observing the high hopes and aims, the diligent alacrity of our extended thoughts and reasonings in the pursuance of truth and freedom, but that he would cry out as Pyrrhus did, admiring the Roman docility and courage, "If such were my Epirots, I would not despair the greatest design that could be attempted to make a church or kingdom happy!" Yet these are the men cried out against for schismatics and sectaries; as if, while the temple of the Lord was building, some cutting, some squaring the marble, others hewing the cedars, there should be a sort of irrational men who could not consider there must be many schisms and many dissections made in the quarry and in the timber, ere the house of God can be built. And when every stone is laid artfully together, it cannot be united into a continuity, it can but be contiguous in this world; neither can every piece of the building be of one form; nay, rather, the perfection consists in this, that, out of many moderate varieties and brotherly dissimilitudes that are not vastly disproportional, arises the goodly and the graceful symmetry that commends the whole pile and structure. Let us, therefore, be more considerate builders, more wise in spiritual architecture, when great reformation is expected. For now the time seems come wherein Moses, the great prophet, may sit in heaven rejoicing to see that memorable and glorious wish of his fulfilled, when not only our seventy Elders, but all the Lord's people, are become prophets. No marvel, then, though some men, and some good men, too, perhaps, but young in goodness, as Joshua then was, envy them. They fret, and out of their own weakness are in agony, lest those divisions and subdivisions will undo us. The adversary again applauds, and waits the hour: "When they have branched themselves out," saith he, "small enough into parties and partitions, then will be our time." Fool! he sees not the firm root out of which we all grow, though into branches; nor will beware until he see our small divided maniples cutting through at every angle of his ill-united and unwieldy brigade. And that we are to hope better of all these supposed sects and schisms, and that we shall not need that solicitude, honest perhaps though over-timorous, of them that vex in this behalf, but shall laugh in the end at those malicious applauders of our differences, I have these reasons to persuade me.

First, when a city shall be as it were besieged and blocked about, her navigable river infested, inroads and incursions round, defiance and battle oft rumored to be marching up even to her walls and suburb trenches, that then the people, or the greater part, more than at other times, wholly taken up with the study of highest and most important matters to be reformed, should be disputing, reasoning, reading, inventing, discoursing, even to a rarity and admiration, things not before discoursed or written of, argues first a singular goodwill, contentedness, and confidence in your prudent foresight and safe government, Lords and Commons; and from thence derives itself to a gallant bravery and well-grounded contempt of their enemies, as if there were no small number of as great spirits among us as his was who, when Rome was nigh besieged by Hannibal, being in the city, bought that piece of ground, at no cheap rate, whereon Hannibal himself encamped his own regiment. Next, it is a lively and cheerful presage of our happy success and victory. For as in a body, when the blood is fresh, the spirits pure and vigorous, not only to vital but to rational faculties, and those in the acutest and the pertest operations of wit and subtlety, it argues in what good plight and constitution the body is, so when the cheerfulness of the people is so sprightly up as that it has, not only wherewith to guard well its own freedom and safety, but to spare, and to bestow upon the solidest and sublimest points of controversy and new invention, it betokens us not degenerated nor drooping to a fatal decay, but casting off the old and wrinkled skin of corruption to outlive these pangs and wax young again, entering the glorious ways of truth and prosperous virtue destined to become great and honorable in these latter ages. Methinks I see in my mind a noble and puissant nation rousing herself like a strong man after sleep and shaking her invincible locks. Methinks I see her as an eagle mewing her mighty youth, and kindling her undazzled eyes at the full midday beam, purging and unscaling her long-abused sight at the fountain itself of heavenly radiance; while the whole noise of timorous and flocking birds, with those also that love the twilight, flutter about, amazed at what she means, and in their envious gabble would prognosticate a year of sects and schisms.

What should ye do, then, should ye suppress all this flowery crop of knowledge and new light sprung up and yet springing daily in this city, should ye set an oligarchy of twenty engrossers over it, to bring a famine upon our minds again, when we shall know nothing but what is measured to us by their bushel? Believe it, Lords and Commons, they who counsel ye to such a suppressing do as good as bid ye suppress yourselves; and I will soon show how. If it be desired to know the immediate cause of all this free writing and free speaking, there cannot be assigned a truer than your own mild and free and humane government: it is the liberty, Lords and Commons, which your own valorous and happy counsels have purchased us, liberty which is the nurse of all great wits; this is that which hath rarefied and enlightened our spirits like the influence of heaven; this is that which hath enfranchised, enlarged, and lifted up our apprehensions degrees above themselves. Ye cannot make us now less capable, less knowing, less eagerly pursuing of the truth, unless ye first make yourselves, that made us so, less the lovers, less the founders, of our true liberty. We can grow ignorant again, brutish, formal, and slavish, as ye found us; but you then must first become that which ye cannot be, oppressive, arbitrary, and tyrannous, as they were from whom ye have freed us. That our hearts are now more capacious, our thoughts more erected to the search and expectation of greatest and exactest things, is the issue of your own virtue propagated in us; ye cannot suppress that unless ye reinforce an abrogated and merciless law, that fathers may despatch at will their own children. And who shall, then, stick closest to ye, and excite others? not he who takes up arms for cote and conduct and his four nobles of Danegelt—although I dispraise not the defence of just immunities, yet love my peace better if that were all. Give me the liberty to know, to utter, and to argue freely, according to conscience, above all liberties.

. . . .

And now the time in special is, by privilege, to write and speak what may help to the further discussing of matters in agitation. The temple of Janus with his two controversal faces might now not unsignificantly be set open. And though all the winds of doctrine were let loose to play upon the earth, so Truth be in the field, we do injuriously by licensing and prohibiting to misdoubt her strength. Let her and Falsehood grapple; who ever knew Truth put to the worse in a free and open encounter? Her confuting is the best and surest suppressing. He who hears what praying there is for light and clearer knowledge to be sent down among us would think of other matters to be constituted beyond the discipline of Geneva, framed and fabricked already to our hands. Yet when the new light which we beg for shines in upon us, there be who envy and oppose if it come not first in at their casements. What a collusion is this, whenas we are exhorted by the Wise Man to use diligence, to seek for wisdom as for hidden treasures early and late, that another order shall enjoin us to know nothing but by statute! When a man hath been laboring the hardest labor in the deep mines of knowledge, hath furnished out his findings in all their equipage, drawn forth his reasons as it were a battle ranged, scattered and defeated all objections in his way, calls out his adversary into the plain, offers him the advantage of wind and sun if he please, only that he may try the matter by dint of argument, for his opponents then to skulk, to lay ambushments, to keep a narrow bridge of licensing where the challenger should pass, though it be valor enough in soldiership, is but weakness and cowardice in the wars of Truth. For who knows not that Truth is strong next to the Almighty? She needs no policies, no stratagems, nor licensings to make her victorious; those are the shifts and the defences that Error uses against her power. Give her but room, and do not bind her when she sleeps, for then she speaks not true, as the old Proteus did, who spake oracles only when he was caught and bound; but then rather she turns herself into all shapes except her own, and perhaps tunes her voice according to the time, as Micaiah did before Ahab, until she be adjured into her own likeness. Yet is it not impossible that she may have more shapes than one. What else is all that rank of things indifferent, wherein Truth may be on this side or on the other, without being unlike herself? What but a vain shadow else is the abolition of those ordinances, that handwriting nailed to the Cross, what great purchase is this Christian liberty which Paul so often boasts of? His doctrine is that he who eats or eats not, regards a day or regards it not, may do either to the Lord. How many other things might be tolerated in peace and left to conscience, had we but charity, and were it not the chief stronghold of our hypocrisy to be ever judging one another. I fear yet this iron yoke of outward conformity hath left a slavish print upon our necks; the ghost of a linen decency yet haunts us. We stumble and are impatient at the least dividing of one visible congregation from another, though it be not in fundamentals; and through our forwardness to suppress, and our backwardness to recover any enthralled piece of truth out of the gripe of custom, we care not to keep truth separated from truth, which is the fiercest rent and disunion of all. We do not see that while we still affect by all means a rigid external formality, we may as soon fall again into a gross conforming stupidity, a stark and dead congealment of wood and hay and stubble forced and frozen together, which is more to the sudden degenerating of a church than many subdichotomies of petty schisms. Not that I can think well of every light separation, or that all in a church is to be expected gold and silver and precious stones: it is not possible for man to sever the wheat from the tares, the good fish from the other fry; that must be the angels' ministry at the end of mortal things. Yet if all cannot be of one mind—as who looks they should be?—this doubtless is more wholesome, more prudent, and more Christian: that many be tolerated rather than all compelled. I mean not tolerated Popery and open superstition, which, as it extirpates all religions and civil supremacies, so itself should be extirpate, provided first that all charitable and compassionate means be used to win and regain the weak and misled: that also which is impious or evil absolutely, either against faith or manners, no law can possibly permit that intends not to unlaw itself: but those neighboring differences, or rather indifferences, are what I speak of, whether in some point of doctrine or of discipline, which, though they may be many, yet need not interrupt the unity of spirit if we could but find among us the bond of peace. In the meanwhile, if any one would write, and bring his helpful hand to the slow-moving Reformation which we labor under, if Truth have spoken to him before others, or but seemed at least to speak, who hath so bejesuited us that we should trouble that man with asking licence to do so worthy a deed? and not consider this, that if it come to prohibiting there is not aught more likely to be prohibited than truth itself, whose first appearance to our eyes, bleared and dimmed with prejudice and custom, is more unsightly and unplausible than many errors, even as the person is of many a great man slight and contemptible to see to? And what do they tell us vainly of new opinions, when this very opinion of theirs, that none must be heard but whom they like, is the worst and newest opinion of all others, and is the chief cause why sects and schisms do so much abound and true knowledge is kept at distance from us? Besides yet a greater danger which is in it: for when God shakes a kingdom with strong and healthful commotions to a general reforming, 'tis not untrue that many sectaries and false teachers are then busiest in seducing; but yet more true it is that God then raises to His own work men of rare abilities and more than common industry, not only to look back and revise what hath been taught heretofore, but to gain further and go on some new enlightened steps in the discovery of truth. For such is the order of God's enlightening His Church, to dispense and deal out by degrees His beam so as our earthly eyes may best sustain it. Neither is God appointed and confined, where and out of what place these His chosen shall be first heard to speak: for He sees not as man sees, chooses not as man chooses, lest we should devote ourselves again to set places and assemblies and outward callings of men, planting our faith one while in the old Convocation House and another while in the Chapel at Westminster; when all the faith and religion that shall be there canonized is not sufficient, without plain convincement and the charity of patient instruction, to supple the least bruise of conscience, to edify the meanest Christian who desires to walk in the Spirit and not in the letter of human trust, for all the number of voices that can be there made, no, though Harry the Seventh himself there, with all his liege tombs about him, should lend them voices from the dead to swell their number. And if the men be erroneous who appear to be the leading schismatics, what withholds us but our sloth, our self-will, and distrust in the right cause that we do not give them gentle meetings and gentle dismissions, that we debate not and examine the matter thoroughly with liberal and frequent audience, if not for their sakes yet for our own, seeing no man who hath tasted learning but will confess the many ways of profiting by those who, not contented with stale receipts, are able to manage and set forth new positions to the world? And were they but as the dust and cinders of our feet, so long as in that notion they may serve to polish and brighten the armory of Truth, even for that respect they were not utterly to be cast away. But if they be of those whom God hath fitted for the special use of these times with eminent and ample gifts, and those perhaps neither among the priests nor among the Pharisees, and we in the haste of a precipitant zeal shall make no distinction, but resolve to stop their mouths, because we fear they come with new and dangerous opinions, as we commonly fore-judge them ere we understand them, no less than woe to us, while, thinking thus to defend the Gospel, we are found the persecutors.

Sir Thomas Browne.

1605–1682.

VANITY OF EARTHLY MONUMENTS.

(*Hydriotaphia: Urn Burial*, Chapter V., 1658.)

Now since these dead bones have already out-lasted the living ones of Methuselah, and in a yard underground, and thin walls of clay, out-worn all the strong and specious buildings above it, and quietly rested under the drums and tramplings of three conquests, what prince can promise such diuturnity unto his relics, or might not gladly say,

"Sic ego oomponi versus in ossa velim"?

Time, which antiquates antiquities, and hath an art to make dust of all things, hath yet spared these minor monuments.

In vain we hope to be known by open and visible conservatories, when to be unknown was the means of their continuation, and obscurity their protection. If they died by violent hands and were thrust into their urns, these bones become considerable, and some old philosophers would honor them, whose souls they conceived most pure which were thus snatched from their bodies, and to retain a stronger propension unto them; whereas they weariedly left a languishing corpse, and with faint desires of re-union. If they fell by long and aged decay, yet, wrapt up in the bundle of time, they fall into indistinction and make but one blot with infants. If we begin to die when we live, and long life be but a prolongation of death, our life is a sad composition; we live with death, and die not in a moment. How many pulses made up the life of Methuselah, were work for Archimedes: common counters sum up the life of Moses his man. Our days become considerable, like petty sums, by minute accumulations, where numerous fractions make up but small round numbers; and our days of a span long make not one little finger.

If the nearness of our last necessity brought a nearer conformity into it, there were a happiness in hoary hairs and no calamity in half senses. But the long habit of living indisposeth us for dying; when avarice makes us the sport of death, when even David grew politicly cruel, and Solomon could hardly be said to be the wisest of men. But many are too early old, and before the date of age. Adversity stretcheth our days, misery makes Alcmena's nights, and time hath no wings unto it. But the most tedious being is that which can unwish itself, content to be nothing or never to have been, which was beyond the mal-content of Job, who cursed not the day of his life but his nativity, content to have so far been as to have a title to future being, although he had lived here but in an hidden state of life, and, as it were, an abortion.

What song the Sirens sang, or what name Achilles assumed when he hid himself among women, though puzzling questions, are not beyond all conjecture. What time the persons of these ossuaries entered the famous nations of the dead, and slept with princes and counsellors, might admit a wide solution. But who were the proprietaries of these bones, or what bodies these ashes made up, were a question above antiquarism; not to be resolved by man, nor easily perhaps by spirits, except we consult the provincial guardians or tutelary observators. Had they made as good provision for their names as they have done for their relics, they had not so grossly erred in the art of perpetuation. But to subsist in bones, and be but pyramidally extant, is a fallacy in duration. Vain ashes, which in the oblivion of names, persons, times, and sexes, have found unto themselves a fruitless continuation, and only arise unto late posterity as emblems of mortal vanities, antidotes against pride, vain-glory, and madding vices! Pagan vain-glories, which thought the world might last forever, had encouragement for ambition; and, finding no *Atropos* unto the immortality of their names, were never dampt with the necessity of oblivion. Even old ambitions had the advantage of ours, in the attempts of their vain-glories, who, acting early and before the probable meridian of time, have by this time found great accomplishment of their designs, whereby the ancient heroes have already out-lasted their monuments and mechanical preservations. But in this latter scene of time we cannot expect such mummies unto our memories, when ambition may fear the prophecy of Elias, and Charles the Fifth can never hope to live within two Methuselahs of Hector.

And, therefore, restless inquietude for the diuturnity of our memories unto present considerations seems a vanity almost out of date and superannuated piece of folly. We cannot hope to live so long in our names as some have done in their persons. One face of Janus holds no proportion unto the other. 'Tis too late to be ambitious. The great mutations of the world are acted, or time may be too short for our designs. To extend our memories by monuments whose death we daily pray for, and whose duration we cannot hope without injury to our expectations in the advent of the Last Day, were a contradiction to our beliefs. We whose generations are ordained in this setting part of time are providentially taken off from such imaginations; and, being necessitated to eye the remaining particle of futurity, are naturally constituted unto thoughts of the next world, and cannot excusably decline the consideration of that duration which maketh pyramids pillars of snow and all that 's past a moment.

Circles and right lines limit and close all bodies, and the mortal right-lined circle must conclude and shut up all. There is no antidote against the opium of time, which temporally considereth all things: our fathers find their graves in our short memories, and sadly tell us how we may be buried in our survivors. Grave-stones tell truth scarce forty years. Generations pass while some trees stand, and old families last not three oaks. To be read by bare inscriptions like many in Gruter, to hope for eternity by enigmatical epithets or first letters of our names, to be studied by antiquaries, who we were, and have new names given us like many of the mummies, are cold consolations unto the students of perpetuity, even by everlasting languages.

To be content that times to come should only know there was such a man, not caring whether they knew more of him, was a frigid ambition in Cardan, disparaging his horoscopal inclination and judgment of himself. Who cares to subsist like Hippocrates's patients, or Achilles's horses in Homer, under naked nominations, without deserts and noble acts, which are the balsam of our memories, the *entelechia* and soul of our subsistences? To be nameless in worthy deeds exceeds an infamous history. The Canaanitish woman lives more happily without a name than Herodias with one. And who had not rather have been the good thief than Pilate?

But the iniquity of oblivion blindly scattereth her poppy, and deals with the memory of men without distinction to merit of perpetuity. Who can but pity the founder of the pyramids? Herostratus lives that burnt the temple of Diana; he is almost lost that built it. Time hath spared the epitaph of Adrian's horse, confounded that of himself. In vain we compute our felicities by the advantage of our good names, since bad have equal durations and Thersites is like to live as long as Agamemmon. Who knows whether the best of men be known, or whether there be not more remarkable persons forgot than any that stand remembered in the known account of time? Without the favor of the everlasting register, the first man had been as unknown as the last, and Methuselah's long life had been his only chronicle.

Oblivion is not to be hired. The greater part must be content to be as though they had not been, to be found in the register of God, not in the record of man. Twenty-seven names make up the first story before the Flood, and the recorded names ever since contain not one living century. The number of the dead long exceedeth all that shall live. The night of time far surpasseth the day, and who knows when was the equinox? Every hour adds unto that current arithmetic, which scarce stands one moment. And since death must be the *Lucina* of life, and even Pagans could doubt whether thus to live were to die; since our longest sun sets at right descensions and makes but winter arches, and therefore it cannot be long before we lie down in darkness and have our light in ashes; since the brother of death daily haunts us with dying mementos, and time, that grows old in itself, bids us hope no long duration; diuturnity is a dream and folly of expectation.

Darkness and light divide the course of time, and oblivion shares with memory a great part even of our living beings; we slightly remember our felicities, and the smartest strokes of affliction leave but short smart upon us. Sense endureth no extremities, and sorrows destroy us or themselves. To weep into stones are fables. Afflictions induce callosities; miseries are slippery, or fall like snow upon us, which notwithstanding is no unhappy stupidity. To be ignorant of evils to come and forgetful of evils past is a merciful provision in nature, whereby we digest the mixture of our few and evil days, and, our delivered senses not relapsing into cutting remembrances, our sorrows are not kept raw by the edge of repetitions. A great part of antiquity contented their hopes of subsistency with a transmigration of their souls —a good way to continue their memories, while, having the advantage of plural successions, they could not but act something remarkable in such variety of beings, and, enjoying the fame of their passed selves, make accumulation of glory unto their last durations. Others, rather than be lost in the uncomfortable night of nothing, were content to recede into the common being and make one particle of the public soul of all things, which was no more than to return into their unknown and divine original again. Egyptian ingenuity was more unsatisfied, contriving their bodies in sweet consistencies, to attend the return of their souls. But all was vanity, feeding the wind, and folly. The Egyptian mummies, which Cambyses or time hath spared, avarice now consumeth. Mummy is become merchandise, Mizraim cures wounds, and Pharaoh is sold for balsams.

In vain do individuals hope for immortality or any patent from oblivion, in preservations below the moon; men have been deceived even in their flatteries, above the sun, and studied conceits to perpetuate their names in heaven. The various cosmography of that part hath already varied the names of contrived constellations; Nimrod is lost in Orion, and Osiris in the Dog-star. While we look for incorruption in the heavens, we find they are but like the earth—durable in their main bodies, alterable in their parts; whereof, beside comets and new stars, perspectives begin to tell tales, and the spots that wander about the sun, with Phaeton's favor, would make clear conviction.

There is nothing strictly immortal but immortality. Whatever hath no beginning may be confident of no end; which is the peculiar of that necessary essence that cannot destroy itself, and the highest strain of omnipotency, to be so powerfully constituted as not to suffer even from the power of itself: all others have a dependent being and within the reach of destruction. But the sufficiency of Christian immortality frustrates all earthly glory, and the quality of either state, after death, makes a folly of posthumous memory. God, Who can only destroy our souls and hath assured our resurrection, either of our bodies or names hath directly promised no duration. Wherein there is so much of chance that the boldest expectants have found unhappy frustration; and to hold long subsistence seems but a scape in oblivion. But man is a noble animal, splendid in ashes and pompous in the grave, solemnizing nativities and deaths with equal lustre, nor omitting ceremonies of bravery in the infamy of his nature.

Life is a pure flame, and we live by an invisible sun within us. A small fire sufficeth for life; great flames seemed too little after death, while men vainly affected precious pyres and to burn like Sardanapalus: but the wisdom of funeral laws found the folly of prodigal blazes, and reduced undoing fires unto the rule of sober obsequies, wherein few could be so mean as not to provide wood, pitch, a mourner, and an urn.

Five languages secured not the epitaph of Gordianus. The man of God lives longer without a tomb than any by one, invisibly interred by angels and adjudged to obscurity, though not without some marks directing human discovery. Enoch and Elias, without either tomb or burial, in an anomalous state of being, are the great examples of perpetuity, in their long and living memory, in strict account being still on this side death and having a late part yet to act upon this stage of earth. If in the decretory term of the world we shall not all die but be changed, according to received translation, the Last Day will make but few graves; at least, quick resurrections will anticipate lasting sepultures. Some graves will be opened before they be quite closed, and Lazarus be no wonder. When many that feared to die shall groan that they can die but once, the dismal state is the second and living death, when life puts despair on the damned, when men shall wish the coverings of mountains, not of monuments, and annihilations shall be courted.

While some have studied monuments, others have studiously declined them, and some have been so vainly boisterous that they durst not acknowledge their graves; wherein Alaricus seems most subtle, who had a river turned to hide his bones at the bottom. Even Sylla, that thought himself safe in his urn, could not prevent revenging tongues, and stones thrown at his monument. Happy are they whom privacy makes innocent, who deal so with men in this world that they are not afraid to meet them in the next, who, when they die, make no commotion among the dead, and are not touched with that poetical taunt of Isaiah.

Pyramids, arches, obelisks were but the irregularities of vain-glory, and wild enormities of ancient magnanimity. But the most magnanimous resolution rests in the Christian religion, which trampleth upon pride and sits on the neck of ambition, humbly pursuing that infallible perpetuity unto which all others must diminish their diameters and be poorly seen in angles of contingency.

Pious spirits who passed their days in raptures of futurity made little more of this world than the world that was before it, while they lay obscure in the chaos of pre-ordination and night of their fore-beings. And if any have been so happy as truly to understand Christian annihilation, ecstasies, exolution, liquefaction, transformation, the kiss of the spouse, gustation of God, and ingression into the divine shadow, they have already had an handsome anticipation of heaven; the glory of the world is surely over, and the earth in ashes unto them.

To subsist in lasting monuments, to live in their productions, to exist in their names and predicament of chimæras, was large satisfaction unto old expectations, and made one part of their Elysiums. But all this is nothing in the metaphysics of true belief. To live indeed is to be again ourselves, which being not only an hope, but an evidence, in noble believers, 'tis all one to lie in St. Innocent's churchyard as in the sands of Egypt; ready to be anything, in the ecstasy of being ever, and as content with six foot as the *moles* of Adrianus.

. . . "tabesne cadavera solvat,
An rogus, haud refert."

LUCAN.

John Dryden.

1631–1700.

PREFACE TO THE FABLES.

(1700.)

'Tis with a poet as with a man who designs to build, and is very exact, as he supposes, in casting up the cost beforehand; but, generally speaking, he is mistaken in his account, and reckons short of the expense he first intended: he alters his mind as the work proceeds, and will have this or that convenience more, of which he had not thought when he began. So has it happened to me. I have built a house where I intended but a lodge; yet with better success than a certain nobleman, who, beginning with a dog-kennel, never lived to finish the palace he had contrived.

From translating the first of Homer's *Iliads* (which I intended as an essay to the whole work) I proceeded to the translation of the twelfth book of Ovid's *Metamorphoses*, because it contains, among other things, the causes, the beginning, and ending of the Trojan War. Here I ought in reason to have stopped; but the speeches of Ajax and Ulysses lying next in my way, I could not balk them. When I had compassed them, I was so taken with the former part of the fifteenth book (which is the masterpiece of the whole *Metamorphoses*) that I enjoined myself the pleasing task of rendering it into English. And now I found, by the number of my verses, that they began to swell into a little volume; which gave me an occasion of looking backward on some beauties of my author, in his former books: there occurred to me the Hunting of the Boar, Cinyras and Myrrha, the good-natured story of Baucis and Philemon, with the rest, which I hope I have translated closely enough, and given them the same turn of verse which they had in the original; and this, I must say without vanity, is not the talent of every poet. He who has arrived the nearest to it is the ingenious and learned Sandys, the best versifier of the former age, if I may properly call it by that name, which was the former part of this concluding century. For Spenser and Fairfax both flourished in the reign of Queen Elizabeth; great masters in our language, and who saw much farther into the beauties of our numbers than those who immediately followed them. Milton was the poetical son of Spenser, and Mr. Waller of Fairfax, for we have our lineal descents and clans as well as other families. Spenser more than once insinuates that the soul of Chaucer was transfused into his body, and that he was begotten by him two hundred years after his decease. Milton has acknowledged to me that Spenser was his original, and many besides myself have heard our famous Waller own that he derived the harmony of his numbers from the *Godfrey of Bulloigne*, which was turned into English by Mr. Fairfax.

But to return. Having done with Ovid for this time, it came into my mind that our old English poet, Chaucer, in many things resembled him, and that with no disadvantage on the side of the modern author, as I shall endeavor to prove when I compare them; and as I am, and always have been, studious to promote the honor of my native country, so I soon resolved to put their merits to the trial by turning some of the *Canterbury Tales* into our language as it is now refined; for by this means, both the poets being set in the same light and dressed in the same English habit, story to be compared with story, a certain judgment may be made betwixt them by the reader, without obtruding my opinion on him. Or if I seem partial to my countryman, and predecessor in the laurel, the friends of antiquity are not few; and besides many of the learned, Ovid has almost all the beaux, and the whole fair sex, his declared patrons. Perhaps I have assumed somewhat more to myself than they allow me, because I have adventured to sum up the evidence; but the readers are the jury, and their privilege remains entire, to decide according to the merits of the cause, or, if they please, to bring it to another hearing before some other court.

In the meantime, to follow the thread of my discourse (as thoughts, according to Mr. Hobbes, have always some connection), so from Chaucer I was led to think on Boccace, who was not only his contemporary but also pursued the same studies; wrote novels in prose, and many works in verse; particularly is said to have invented the octave rhyme, or stanza of eight lines, which ever since has been maintained by the practice of all Italian writers who are, or at least assume the title of, heroic poets. He and Chaucer, among other things, had this in common, that they refined their mother tongues; but with this difference, that Dante had begun to file their language, at least in verse, before the time of Boccace, who likewise received no little help from his master, Petrarch. But the reformation of their prose was wholly owing to Boccace himself, who is yet the standard of purity in the Italian tongue, though many of his phrases are become obsolete, as in process of time it must needs happen. Chaucer (as you have formerly been told by our learned Mr. Rymer) first adorned and amplified our barren tongue from the Provençal, which was then the most polished of all the modern languages; but this subject has been copiously treated by that great critic, who deserves no little commendation from us his countrymen. For these reasons of time and resemblance of genius in Chaucer and Boccace, I resolved to join them in my present work; to which I have added some original papers of my own, which, whether they are equal or inferior to my other poems, an author is the most improper judge, and therefore I leave them wholly to the mercy of the reader. I will hope the best, that they will not be condemned; but if they should, I have the excuse of an old gentleman, who, mounting on horseback before some ladies, when I was present, got up somewhat heavily, but desired of the fair spectators that they would count fourscore and eight before they judged him. By the mercy of God I am already come within twenty years of his number, a cripple in my limbs; but what decays are in my mind the reader must determine. I think myself as vigorous as ever in the faculties of my soul, excepting only my memory, which is not impaired to any great degree; and if I lose not more of it, I have no great reason to complain. What judgment I had increases rather than diminishes; and thoughts, such as they are, come crowding in so fast upon me that my only difficulty is to choose or to reject, to run them into verse or to give them the other harmony of prose. I have so long studied and practised both that they are grown into a habit and become familiar to me. In short, though I may lawfully plead some part of the old gentleman's excuse, yet I will reserve it till I think I have greater need, and ask no grains of allowance for the faults of this my present work but those which are given of course to human frailty. I will not trouble my reader with the shortness of time in which I writ it, or the several intervals of sickness: they who think too well of their own performances are apt to boast in their prefaces how little time their works have cost them, and what other business of more importance interfered; but the reader will be as apt to ask the question, Why they allowed not a longer time to make their works more perfect, and why they had so despicable an opinion of their judges as to thrust their indigested stuff upon them, as if they deserved no better.

With this account of my present undertaking, I conclude the first part of this discourse: in the second part, as at a second sitting, though I alter not the draught, I must touch the same features over again and change the dead coloring of the whole. In general, I will only say that I have written nothing which savors of immorality or profaneness; at least, I am not conscious to myself of any such intention. If there happen to be found an irreverent expression or a thought too wanton, they are crept into my verses through my inadvertency; if the searchers find any in the cargo, let them be staved or forfeited, like contrabanded goods; at least, let their authors be answerable for them, as being but imported merchandise and not of my own manufacture. On the other side, I have endeavored to choose such fables, both ancient and modern, as contain in each of them some instructive moral; which I could prove by induction, but the way is tedious, and they leap foremost into sight without the reader's trouble of looking after them. I wish I could affirm with a safe conscience that I had taken the same care in all my former writings; for it must be owned that, supposing verses are never so beautiful or pleasing, yet if they contain anything which shocks religion or good manners, they are at best, what Horace says of good numbers without good sense "Versus inopes rerum, nugæque canoræ." Thus far, I hope, I am right in court, without renouncing my other right of self-defence where I have been wrongfully accused and my sense wire-drawn into blasphemy or bawdry, as it has often been by a religious lawyer in a late pleading against the stage, in which he mixes truth with falsehood, and has not forgotten the old rule of calumniating strongly that something may remain.

I resume the thrid of my discourse with the first of my translations, which was the first *Iliad* of Homer. If it shall please God to give me longer life and moderate health, my intentions are to translate the whole *Ilias*, provided still that I meet with those encouragements from the public which may enable me to proceed in my undertaking with some cheerfulness. And this I dare assure the world beforehand, that I have found by trial Homer a more pleasing task than Virgil, though I say not the translation will be less laborious. For the Grecian is more according to my genius than the Latin poet. In the works of the two authors we may read their manners and natural inclinations, which are wholly different. Virgil was of a quiet, sedate temper; Homer was violent, impetuous, and full of fire. The chief talent of Virgil was propriety of thoughts and ornament of words; Homer was rapid in his thoughts, and took all the liberties, both of numbers and of expressions, which his language and the age in which he lived allowed him. Homer's invention was more copious, Virgil's more confined; so that if Homer had not led the way, it was not in Virgil to have begun heroic poetry, for nothing can be more evident than that the Roman poem is but the second part of the *Ilias*—a continuation of the same story, and the persons already formed; the manners of Æneas are those of Hector superadded to those which Homer gave him. The adventures of Ulysses in the *Odysseis* are imitated in the first six books of Virgil's *Æneis;* and though the accidents are not the same (which would have argued him of a servile copying and total barrenness of invention), yet the seas were the same in which both the heroes wandered, and Dido cannot be denied to be the poetical daughter of Calypso. The six latter books of Virgil's poem are the four and twenty *Iliads* contracted—a quarrel occasioned by a lady, a single combat, battles fought, and a town besieged. I say not this in derogation to Virgil, neither do I contradict anything which I have formerly said in his just praise: for his episodes are almost wholly of his own invention; and the form which he has given to the telling makes the tale his own, even though the original story had been the same. But this proves, however, that Homer taught Virgil to design; and if invention be the first virtue of an epic poet, then the Latin poem can only be allowed the second place. Mr. Hobbes, in the preface to his own bald translation of the *Ilias* (studying poetry, as he did mathematics, when it was too late), Mr. Hobbes, I say, begins the praise of Homer where he should have ended it. He tell us that the first beauty of an epic poem consists in diction, that is, in the choice of words and harmony of numbers. Now, the words are the coloring of the work, which in the order of nature is last to be considered: the design, the disposition, the manners, and the thoughts are all before it; where any of those are wanting or imperfect, so much wants or is imperfect in the imitation of human life, which is in the very definition of a poem. Words indeed, like glaring colors, are the first beauties that arise and strike the sight; but if the draught be false or lame, the figures ill-disposed, the manners obscure or inconsistent, or the thoughts unnatural, then the finest colors are but daubing, and the piece is a beautiful monster at the best. Neither Virgil nor Homer were deficient in any of the former beauties; but in this last, which is expression, the Roman poet is at least equal to the Grecian, as I have said elsewhere, supplying the poverty of his language by his musical ear and by his diligence. But to return: our two great poets, being so different in their tempers, one choleric and sanguine, the other phlegmatic and melancholic, that which makes them excel in their several ways is that each of them has followed his own natural inclination, as well in forming the design as in the execution of it. The very heroes show their authors: Achilles is hot, impatient, revengeful—"Impiger, iracundus, inexorabilis, acer," etc.; Æneas, patient, considerate, careful of his people and merciful to his enemies, ever submissive to the will of Heaven —"quo fata trahunt retrahuntque sequamur." I could please myself with enlarging on this subject, but am forced to defer it to a fitter time. From all I have said I will only draw this inference, that the action of Homer being more full of vigor than that of Virgil, according to the temper of the writer, is of consequence more pleasing to the reader. One warms you by degrees; the other sets you on fire all at once, and never intermits his heat. 'Tis the same difference which Longinus makes betwixt the effects of eloquence in Demosthenes and Tully. One persuades, the other commands. You never cool while you read Homer, even not in the second book (a graceful flattery to his countrymen); but he hastens from the ships, and concludes not that book till he has made you an amends by the violent playing of a new machine. From thence he hurries on his action with variety of events, and ends it in less compass than two months. This vehemence of his, I confess, is more suitable to my temper, and therefore I have translated his first book with greater pleasure than any part of Virgil; but it was not a pleasure without pains: the continual agitations of the spirits must needs be a weakening of any constitution, especially in age; and many pauses are required for refreshment betwixt the heats, the *Iliad* of itself being a third part longer than all Virgil's works together.

This is what I thought needful in this place to say of Homer. I proceed to Ovid and Chaucer, considering the former only in relation to the latter. With Ovid ended the golden age of the Roman tongue; from Chaucer the purity of the English tongue began. The manners of the poets were not unlike: both of them were well-bred, well-natured, amorous, and libertine—at least in their writings, it may be also in their lives. Their studies were the same, philosophy and philology. Both of them were knowing in astronomy, of which Ovid's books of the Roman feasts and Chaucer's treatise of the astrolabe are sufficient witnesses; but Chaucer was likewise an astrologer, as were Virgil, Horace, Persius, and Manilius. Both writ with wonderful facility and clearness: neither were great inventors; for Ovid only copied the Grecian fables, and most of Chaucer's stories were taken from his Italian contemporaries or their predecessors. Boccace his *Decameron* was first published, and from thence our Englishman has borrowed many of his *Canterbury Tales;* yet that of Palamon and Arcite was written in all probability by some Italian wit in a former age, as I shall prove hereafter. The tale of Grizild was the invention of Petrarch, by him sent to Boccace, from whom it came to Chaucer. *Troilus and Cressida* was also written by a Lombard author, but much amplified by our English translator, as well as beautified, the genius of our countrymen in general being rather to improve an invention than to invent themselves, as is evident, not only in our poetry, but in many of our manufactures. I find I have anticipated already, and taken up from Boccace before I come to him; but there is so much less behind, and I am of the temper of most kings, who love to be in debt, are all for present money, no matter how they pay it afterwards; besides, the nature of a preface is rambling, never wholly out of the way nor in it. This I have learnt from the practice of honest Montaigne; and return at my pleasure to Ovid and Chaucer, of whom I have little more to say. Both of them built on the inventions of other men; yet since Chaucer had something of his own, as *The Wife of Bath's Tale, The Cock and the Fox,* which I have translated, and some others, I may justly give our countryman the precedence in that part, since I can remember nothing of Ovid which was wholly his. Both of them understood the manners, under which name I comprehend the passions and in a larger sense the descriptions of persons and their very habits. For an example, I see Baucis and Philemon as perfectly before me as if some ancient painter had drawn them; and all the pilgrims in the *Canterbury Tales*, their humors, their features, and the very dress, as distinctly as if I had supped with them at the Tabard in Southwark: yet even there too the figures in Chaucer are much more lively and set in a better light, which, though I have not time to prove, yet I appeal to the reader, and am sure he will clear me from partiality. The thoughts and words remain to be considered in the comparison of the two poets: and I have saved myself one half of that labor by owning that Ovid lived when the Roman tongue was in its meridian, Chaucer in the dawning of our language; therefore that part of the comparison stands not on an equal foot, any more than the diction of Ennius and Ovid, or of Chaucer and our present English. The words are given up as a post not to be defended in our poet, because he wanted the modern art of fortifying. The thoughts remain to be considered, and they are to be measured only by their propriety, that is, as they flow more or less naturally from the persons described, on such and such occasions. The vulgar judges, which are nine parts in ten of all nations, who call conceits and jingles wit, who see Ovid full of them and Chaucer altogether without them, will think me little less than mad for preferring the Englishman to the Roman; yet, with their leave, I must presume to say that the things they admire are only glittering trifles, and so far from being witty that in a serious poem they are nauseous because they are unnatural. Would any man who is ready to die for love describe his passion like Narcissus? Would he think of "inopem me copia fecit," and a dozen more of such expressions, poured on the neck of one another and signifying all the same thing? If this were wit, was this a time to be witty, when the poor wretch was in the agony of death? This is just John Littlewit in *Bartholomew Fair*, who had a conceit (as he tells you) left him in his misery; a miserable conceit. On these occasions the poet should endeavor to raise pity; but, instead of this, Ovid is tickling you to laugh. Virgil never made use of such machines when he was moving you to commiserate the death of Dido: he would not destroy what he was building. Chaucer makes Arcite violent in his love and unjust in the pursuit of it; yet when he came to die he made him think more reasonably: he repents not of his love, for that had altered his character, but acknowledges the injustice of his proceedings and resigns Emilia to Palamon. What would Ovid have done on this occasion? He would certainly have made Arcite witty on his death-bed: he had complained he was farther off from possession by being so near, and a thousand such boyisms, which Chaucer rejected as below the dignity of the subject. They who think otherwise would, by the same reason, prefer Lucan and Ovid to Homer and Virgil, and Martial to all four of them. As for the turn of words, in which Ovid particularly excels all poets, they are sometimes a fault and sometimes a beauty, as they are used properly or improperly, but in strong passions always to be shunned, because passions are serious and will admit no playing. The French have a high value for them, and I confess they are often what they call delicate when they are introduced with judgment; but Chaucer writ with more simplicity, and followed nature more closely, than to use them.

I have thus far, to the best of my knowledge, been an upright judge betwixt the parties in competition, not meddling with the design or the disposition of it, because the design was not their own and in the disposing of it they were equal. It remains that I say somewhat of Chaucer in particular.

In the first place, as he is the father of English poetry, so I hold him in the same degree of veneration as the Grecians held Homer or the Romans Virgil. He is a perpetual fountain of good sense, learned in all sciences, and therefore speaks properly on all subjects. As he knew what to say, so he knows when to leave off; a continence which is practised by few writers, and scarcely by any of the ancients, excepting Virgil and Horace. One of our late great poets is sunk in his reputation because he could never forego any conceit which came in his way, but swept, like a drag-net, great and small. There was plenty enough, but the dishes were ill sorted; whole pyramids of sweetmeats for boys and women, but little of solid meat for men. All this proceeded, not from any want of knowledge, but of judgment. Neither did he want that in discerning the beauties and faults of other poets, but only indulged himself in the luxury of writing; and perhaps knew it was a fault but hoped the reader would not find it. For this reason, though he must always be thought a great poet, he is no longer esteemed a good writer; and for ten impressions, which his works have had in so many successive years, yet at present a hundred books are scarcely purchased once a twelvemonth; for, as my last Lord Rochester said, though somewhat profanely, "Not being of God, he could not stand."

Chaucer followed nature everywhere, but was never so bold to go beyond her, and there is a great difference of being *poeta* and *nimis poeta;* if we believe Catullus, as much as betwixt a modest behavior and affectation. The verse of Chaucer, I confess, is not harmonious to us; but is like the eloquence of one whom Tacitus commends, it was "auribus istius temporis accommodata": they who lived with him, and some time after him, thought it musical; and it continues so even in our judgment, if compared with the numbers of Lydgate and Gower, his contemporaries; there is the rude sweetness of a Scotch tune in it, which is natural and pleasing though not perfect. 'Tis true I cannot go so far as he who published the last edition of him, for he would make us believe the fault is in our ears, and that there were really ten syllables in a verse where we find but nine; but this opinion is not worth confuting; it is so gross and obvious an error that common sense (which is a rule in everything but matters of faith and revelation) must convince the reader that equality of numbers in every verse which we call heroic was either not known or not always practised in Chaucer's age. It were an easy matter to produce some thousands of his verses which are lame for want of half a foot and sometimes a whole one, and which no pronunciation can make otherwise. We can only say that he lived in the infancy of our poetry, and that nothing is brought to perfection at the first. We must be children before we grow men. There was an Ennius, and in process of time a Lucilius and a Lucretius, before

Virgil and Horace; even after Chaucer there was a Spenser, a Harrington, a Fairfax, before Waller and Denham were in being, and our numbers were in their nonage till these last appeared. I need say little of his parentage, life, and fortunes: they are to be found at large in all the editions of his works. He was employed abroad, and favored by Edward the Third, Richard the Second, and Henry the Fourth, and was poet, as I suppose, to all three of them. In Richard's time, I doubt, he was a little dipped in the rebellion of the Commons; and, being brother-in-law to John of Gaunt, it was no wonder if he followed the fortunes of that family, and was well with Henry the Fourth when he had deposed his predecessor. Neither is it to be admired that Henry, who was a wise as well as a valiant prince, who claimed by succession, and was sensible that his title was not sound but was rightfully in Mortimer, who had married the heir of York—it was not to be admired, I say, if that great politician should be pleased to have the greatest wit of those times in his interests and to be the trumpet of his praises. Augustus had given him the example, by the advice of Mæcenas, who recommended Virgil and Horace to him; whose praises helped to make him popular while he was alive, and after his death have made him precious to posterity. As for the religion of our poet, he seems to have some little bias towards the opinions of Wiclif, after John of Gaunt his patron; somewhat of which appears in the tale of *Piers Plowman;* yet I cannot blame him for inveighing so sharply against the vices of the clergy in his age: their pride, their ambition, their pomp, their avarice, their worldly interest deserved the lashes which he gave them, both in that and in most of his *Canterbury Tales.* Neither has his contemporary Boccace spared them. Yet both those poets lived in much esteem with good and holy men in orders; for the scandal which is given by particular priests reflects not on the sacred function: Chaucer's Monk, his Canon, and his Friar took not from the character of his Good Parson. A satirical poet is the check of the laymen on bad priests. We are only to take care that we involve not the innocent with the guilty in the same condemnation. The good cannot be too much honored nor the bad too coarsely used; for the corruption of the best becomes the worst. When a clergyman is whipped, his gown is first taken off, by which the dignity of his order is secured. If he be wrongfully accused, he has his action of slander; and it is at the poet's peril if he transgress the law. But they will tell us that all kind of satire, though never so well-deserved by particular priests, yet brings the whole order into contempt. Is, then, the peerage of England anything dishonored when a peer suffers for his treason? If he be libelled or any way defamed, he has his *Scandalum Magnatum* to punish the offender. They who use this kind of argument seem to be conscious to themselves of somewhat which has deserved the poet's lash, and are less concerned for their public capacity than for their private; at least there is pride at the bottom of their reasoning. If the faults of men in orders are only to be judged among themselves, they are all in some sort parties; for, since they say the honor of their order is concerned in every member of it, how can we be sure that they will be impartial judges? How far I may be allowed to speak my opinion in this case I know not, but I am sure a dispute of this nature caused mischief in abundance betwixt a king of England and an archbishop of Canterbury, one standing up for the laws of his land, and the other for the honor (as he called it) of God's Church, which ended in the murder of the prelate and in the whipping of his majesty from post to pillar for his penance. The learned and ingenious Dr. Drake has saved me the labor of inquiring into the esteem and reverence which the priests have had of old, and I would rather extend than diminish any part of it; yet I must needs say that when a priest provokes me without any occasion given him, I have no reason, unless it be the charity of a Christian, to forgive him. *Prior læsit* is justification sufficient in the Civil Law. If I answer him in his own language, self-defence, I am sure, must be allowed me; and if I carry it farther, even to a sharp recrimination, somewhat may be indulged to human frailty. Yet my resentment has not wrought so far but that I have followed Chaucer in his character of a holy man, and have enlarged on that subject with some pleasure, reserving to myself the right, if I shall think fit hereafter, to describe another sort of priests, such as are more easily to be found than the Good Parson, such as have given the last blow to Christianity in this age by a practice so contrary to their doctrine. But this will keep cold till another time. In the meanwhile I take up Chaucer where I left him.

He must have been a man of a most wonderful comprehensive nature, because, as it has been truly observed of him, he has taken into the compass of his *Canterbury Tales* the various manners and humors (as we now call them) of the whole English nation in his age. Not a single character has escaped him. All his pilgrims are severally distinguished from each other, and not only in their inclinations but in their very physiognomies and persons. Baptista Porta could not have described their natures better than by the marks which the poet gives them.

The matter and manner of their tales and of their telling are so suited to their different educations, humors, and callings that each of them would be improper in any other mouth. Even the grave and serious characters are distinguished by their several sorts of gravity: their discourses are such as belong to their age, their calling, and their breeding, such as are becoming of them and of them only. Some of his persons are vicious and some virtuous; some are unlearned, or (as Chaucer calls them) lewd, and some are learned. Even the ribaldry of the low characters is different: the Reeve, the Miller, and the Cook are several men, and distinguished from each other as much as the mincing Lady Prioress and the broad-speaking, gap-toothed Wife of Bath. But enough of this: there is such a variety of game springing up before me that I am distracted in my choice and know not which to follow. It is sufficient to say, according to the proverb, that here is God's plenty. We have our forefathers and great-grand-dames all before us as they were in Chaucer's days: their general characters are still remaining in mankind, and even in England, though they are called by other names than those of monks and friars and canons and lady abbesses and nuns; for mankind is ever the same, and nothing lost out of nature though everything is altered.

May I have leave to do myself the justice (since my enemies will do me none, and are so far from granting me to be a good poet that they will not allow me so much as to be a Christian or a moral man), may I have leave, I say, to inform my reader that I have confined my choice to such tales of Chaucer as savor nothing of immodesty? If I had desired more to please than to instruct, the Reeve, the Miller, the Shipman, the Merchant, the Summoner, and above all the Wife of Bath, in the prologue to her tale, would have procured me as many friends and readers as there are beaux and ladies of pleasure in the town. But I will no more offend against good manners; I am sensible, as I ought to be, of the scandal I have given by my loose writings, and make what reparation I am able by this public acknowledgment. If anything of this nature or of profaneness be crept into these poems, I am so far from defending it that I disown it. "Totum hoc indictum volo." Chaucer makes another manner of apology for his broad speaking, and Boccace makes the like; but I will follow neither of them. Our countryman, in the end of his characters, before the *Canterbury Tales*, thus excuses the ribaldry, which is very gross in many of his novels:—

"But first, I pray you of your courtesy,
That ye ne arrete it nought my villany,
Though that I plainly speak in this mattere
To tellen you her words, and eke her chere:
Ne though I speak her words properly,
For this ye knowen as well as I,
Who shall tellen a tale after a man
He mote rehearse as nye as ever he can
Everich word of it been in his charge,
All speke he, never so rudely, ne large.
Or else he mote tellen his tale untrue,
Or feine things, or find words new:
He may not spare, altho he were his brother
He mote as well say o word as another.
Christ spake himself full broad in holy writ,
And well I wote no villany is it.

> Eke Plato saith, who so can him rede,
> The words mote been cousin to the dede."

Yet if a man should have inquired of Boccace or of Chaucer what need they had of introducing such characters where obscene words were proper in their mouths but very undecent to be heard, I know not what answer they could have made; for that reason such tales shall be left untold by me. You have here a specimen of Chaucer's language, which is so obsolete that his sense is scarce to be understood; and you have likewise more than one example of his unequal numbers, which were mentioned before. Yet many of his verses consist of ten syllables, and the words not much behind our present English: as for example these two lines, in the description of the carpenter's young wife:—

> "Wincing she was, as is a jolly colt,
> Long as a mast, and upright as a bolt."

I have almost done with Chaucer when I have answered some objections relating to my present work. I find some people are offended that I have turned these tales into modern English, because they think them unworthy of my pains, and look on Chaucer as a dry, old-fashioned wit, not worth reviving. I have often heard the late Earl of Leicester say that Mr. Cowley himself was of that opinion; who, having read him over at my lord's request, declared he had no taste of him. I dare not advance my opinion against the judgment of so great an author; but I think it fair, however, to leave the decision to the public. Mr. Cowley was too modest to set up for a dictator; and, being shocked perhaps with his old style, never examined into the depth of his good sense. Chaucer, I confess, is a rough diamond, and must first be polished ere he shines. I deny not, likewise, that, living in our early days of poetry, he writes not always of a piece, but sometimes mingles trivial things with those of greater moment. Sometimes, also, though not often, he runs riot, like Ovid, and knows not when he has said enough. But there are more great wits besides Chaucer whose fault is their excess of conceits, and those ill-sorted. An author is not to write all he can but only all he ought. Having observed this redundancy in Chaucer (as it is an easy matter for a man of ordinary parts to find a fault in one of greater), I have not tied myself to a literal translation, but have often omitted what I judged unnecessary or not of dignity enough to appear in the company of better thoughts. I have presumed farther, in some places, and added somewhat of my own where I thought my author was deficient and had not given his thoughts their true lustre, for want of words in the beginning of our language. And to this I was the more emboldened, because (if I may be permitted to say it of myself) I found I had a soul congenial to his and that I had been conversant in the same studies. Another poet, in another age, may take the same liberty with my writings; if at least they live long enough to deserve correction. It was also necessary sometimes to restore the sense of Chaucer, which was lost or mangled in the errors of the press. Let this example suffice at present: in the story of Palamon and Arcite, where the temple of Diana is described, you find these verses in all the editions of our author:—

> "There saw I Danè, turned into a tree,
> I mean not the goddess Diane,
> But Venus daughter, which that hight Danè ;"

which, after a little consideration, I knew was to be reformed into this sense, that Daphne, the daughter of Peneus, was turned into a tree. I durst not make thus bold with Ovid, lest some future Milbourn should arise and say I varied from my author because I understood him not.

But there are other judges who think I ought not to have translated Chaucer into English, out of a quite contrary notion: they suppose there is a certain veneration due to his old language, and that it is little less than profanation and sacrilege to alter it. They are farther of opinion that somewhat of his good sense will suffer in this transfusion, and much of the beauty of his thoughts will infallibly be lost, which appear with more grace in their old habit. Of this opinion was that excellent person, whom I mentioned, the late Earl of Leicester, who valued Chaucer as much as Mr. Cowley despised him. My lord dissuaded me from this attempt (for I was thinking of it some years before his death), and his authority prevailed so far with me as to defer my undertaking while he lived, in deference to him: yet my reason was not convinced with what he urged against it. If the first end of a writer be to be understood, then, as his language grows obsolete, his thoughts must grow obscure:—

> "Multa renascentur quæ jam cecidere; cadentque
> Quæ nunc sunt in honore vocabula, si volet usus,
> Quem penes arbitrium est et jus et norma loquendi."

When an ancient word for its sound and significancy deserves to be revived, I have that reasonable veneration for antiquity to restore it. All beyond this is superstition. Words are not like landmarks, so sacred as never to be removed; customs are changed, and even statutes are silently repealed when the reason ceases for which they were enacted. As for the other part of the argument, that his thoughts will lose of their original beauty by the innovation of words, in the first place not only their beauty but their being is lost where they are no longer understood, which is the present case. I grant that something must be lost in all transfusion, that is, in all translations; but the sense will remain, which would otherwise be lost, or at least be maimed, when it is scarce intelligible and that but to a few. How few are there who can read Chaucer so as to understand him perfectly? And if imperfectly, then with less profit and no pleasure. It is not for the use of some old Saxon friends that I have taken these pains with him: let them neglect my version, because they have no need of it. I made it for their sakes who understand sense and poetry as well as they, when that poetry and sense is put into words which they understand. I will go farther, and dare to add that what beauties I lose in some places I give to others which had them not originally: but in this I may be partial to myself; let the reader judge, and I submit to his decision. Yet I think I have just occasion to complain of them who, because they understand Chaucer, would deprive the greater part of their countrymen of the same advantage, and hoard him up, as misers do their grandam gold, only to look on it themselves, and hinder others from making use of it. In sum, I seriously protest that no man ever had or can have a greater veneration for Chaucer than myself. I have translated some part of his works only that I might perpetuate his memory, or at least refresh it, amongst my countrymen. If I have altered him anywhere for the better, I must at the same time acknowledge that I could have done nothing without him. "Facile est inventis addere" is no great commendation, and I am not so vain to think I have deserved a greater. I will conclude what I have to say of him singly, with this one remark: A lady of my acquaintance, who keeps a kind of correspondence with some authors of the fair sex in France, has been informed by them that Mademoiselle de Scudery, who is as old as Sibyl, and inspired like her by the same god of poetry, is at this time translating Chaucer into modern French. From which I gather that he has been formerly translated into the old Provençal; for how she should come to understood old English, I know not. But the matter of fact being true, it makes me think that there is something in it like fatality that, after certain periods of time, the fame and memory of great wits should be renewed, as Chaucer is both in France and England. If this be wholly chance, 'tis extraordinary, and I dare not call it more for fear of being taxed with superstition.

Boccace comes last to be considered, who, living in the same age with Chaucer, had the same genius and followed the same studies: both writ novels, and each of them cultivated his mother tongue. But the greatest resemblance of our two modern authors being in their familiar style and pleasing way of relating comical adventures, I may pass it over, because I have translated nothing from Boccace of that nature. In the serious part of poetry the advantage is wholly on Chaucer's side; for though the Englishman has borrowed many tales from the Italian, yet it appears that those of Boccace were not generally of his own making but taken from authors of former ages and by him only modelled, so that what there was of invention in either of them may be judged equal. But Chaucer has refined on Boccace, and has mended the stories which he has borrowed in his way of telling, though prose allows more liberty of thought, and the expression is more easy when unconfined by numbers. Our countryman carries weight, and yet wins the race at disadvantage. I desire not the reader should take my word, and therefore I will set two of their discourses on the same subject, in the same light, for every man to judge betwixt them. I translated Chaucer first, and amongst the rest pitched on *The Wife of Bath's Tale*. . . . When I had closed Chaucer, I returned to Ovid and translated some more of his fables; and by this time had so far forgotten *The Wife of Bath's Tale* that, when I took up Boccace, unawares I fell on the same argument of preferring virtue to nobility of blood and titles, in the story of *Sigismonda*, which I had certainly avoided for the resemblance of the two discourses if my memory had not failed me. Let the reader weigh them both; and if he thinks me partial to Chaucer, 'tis in him to right Boccace.

I prefer in our countryman, far above all his other stories, the noble poem of *Palamon and Arcite*, which is of the epic kind, and perhaps not much inferior to the *Ilias* or the *Æneis*. The story is more pleasing than either of them, the manners as perfect, the diction as poetical, the learning as deep and various, and the disposition full as artful; only it includes a greater length of time, as taking up seven years at least; but Aristotle has left undecided the duration of the action, which yet is easily reduced into the compass of a year by a narration of what preceded the return of Palamon to Athens. I had thought for the honor of our nation, and more particularly for his whose laurel, though unworthy, I have worn after him, that this story was of English growth and Chaucer's own, but I was undeceived by Boccace; for, casually looking on the end of his seventh *Giornata*, I found Dioneo (under which name he shadows himself) and Fiametta (who represents his mistress, the natural daughter of Robert,

King of Naples), of whom these words are spoken: "Dioneo e la Fiametta gran pezza cantarono insieme d'Arcita, e di Palamone"; by which it appears that this story was written before the time of Boccace; but the name of its author being wholly lost, Chaucer is now become an original, and I question not but the poem has received many beauties by passing through his noble hands. Besides this tale there is another of his own invention, after the manner of the Provençals, called *The Flower and the Leaf*, with which I was so particularly pleased, both for the invention and the moral, that I cannot hinder myself from recommending it to the reader.

As a corollary to this preface, in which I have done justice to others, I owe somewhat to myself; not that I think it worth my time to enter the lists with one Milbourn and one Blackmore, but barely to take notice that such men there are who have written scurrilously against me without any provocation. Milbourn, who is in orders, pretends amongst the rest this quarrel to me, that I have fallen foul on priesthood; if I have, I am only to ask pardon of good priests, and am afraid his part of the reparation will come to little. Let him be satisfied that he shall not be able to force himself upon me for an adversary. I contemn him too much to enter into competition with him. His own translations of Virgil have answered his criticisms on mine. If (as they say he has declared in print) he prefers the version of Ogilby to mine, the world has made him the same compliment, for it is agreed on all hands that he writes even below Ogilby. That, you will say, is not easily to be done; but what cannot Milbourn bring about? I am satisfied, however, that while he and I live together I shall not be thought the worst poet of the age. It looks as if I had desired him underhand to write so ill against me; but, upon my honest word, I have not bribed him to do me this service, and am wholly guiltless of his pamphlet. 'Tis true I should be glad if I could persuade him to continue his good offices and write such another critique on anything of mine; for I find by experience he has a great stroke with the reader, when he condemns any of my poems, to make the world have a better opinion of them. He has taken some pains with my poetry, but nobody will be persuaded to take the same with his. If I had taken to the Church (as he affirms, but which was never in my thoughts), I should have had more sense, if not more grace, than to have turned myself out of my benefice by writing libels on my parishioners. But his account of my manners and my principles are of a piece with his cavils and his poetry; and so I have done with him forever.

As for the City Bard, or Knight Physician, I hear his quarrel to me is that I was the author of *Absalom and Achitophel*, which he thinks is a little hard on his fanatic patrons in London. But I will deal the more civilly with his two poems because nothing ill is to be spoken of the dead, and therefore peace be to the *manes* of his Arthurs. I will only say that it was not for this noble knight that I drew the plan of an epic poem on King Arthur, in my preface to the translation of Juvenal. The guardian angels of kingdoms were machines too ponderous for him to manage; and therefore he rejected them, as Dares did the whirl-bats of Eryx when they were thrown before him by Entellus. Yet from that preface he plainly took his hint; for he began immediately upon the story, though he had the baseness not to acknowledge his benefactor but instead of it to traduce me in a libel.

I shall say the less of Mr. Collier because in many things he has taxed me justly, and I have pleaded guilty to all thoughts and expressions of mine which can be truly argued of obscenity, profaneness, or immorality, and retract them. If he be my enemy, let him triumph; if he be my friend, as I have given him no personal occasion to be otherwise, he will be glad of my repentance. It becomes me not to draw my pen in the defence of a bad cause when I have so often drawn it for a good one. Yet it were not difficult to prove that in many places he has perverted my meaning by his glosses, and interpreted my words into blasphemy and bawdry of which they were not guilty—besides that he is too much given to horse-play in his raillery, and comes to battle like a dictator from the plough. I will not say the zeal of God's house has eaten him up, but I am sure it has devoured some part of his good manners and civility. . . . But I am not to prejudice the cause of my fellow poets, though I abandon my own defence; they have some of them answered for themselves, and neither they nor I can think Mr. Collier so formidable an enemy that we should shun him. He has lost ground at the latter end of the day by pursuing his point too far, like the Prince of Condé at the battle of Senneffe: from immoral plays to no plays, "ab abuso ad usum not valet consequentia." But, being a party, I am not to erect myself into a judge. As for the rest of those who have written against me, they are such scoundrels that they deserve not the least notice to be taken of them. Blackmore and Milbourn are only distinguished from the crowd by being remembered to their infamy.

"Demetri, teque Tigelli,
Discipularum inter jubeo plorare cathedras."

Jonathan Swift

1667–1745.

THE BATTLE OF THE BOOKS.

(1704.)

Whoever examines, with due circumspection, into the *Annual Records of Time*, will find it remarked that War is the child of Pride, and Pride the daughter of Riches:—the former of which assertions may be soon granted, but one cannot so easily subscribe to the latter; for Pride is nearly related to Beggary and Want, either by father or mother, and sometimes by both: and to speak naturally, it very seldom happens among men to fall out when all have enough, invasions usually travelling from north to south, that is to say, from poverty upon plenty. The most ancient and natural grounds of quarrels are Lust and Avarice; which, though we may allow to be brethren or collateral branches of Pride, are certainly the issues of Want. For, to speak in the phrase of writers upon the politics, we may observe in the Republic of Dogs (which, in its original, seems to be an institution of the many) that the whole state is ever in the profoundest peace after a full meal; and that civil broils arise among them when it happens for one great bone to be seized on by some leading dog, who either divides it among the few, and then it falls to an oligarchy, or keeps it to himself, and then it runs up to a tyranny. . . . Again, if we look upon any of these republics engaged in a foreign war, either of invasion or defence, we shall find the same reasoning will serve as to the grounds and occasions of each, and that poverty or want, in some degree or other (whether real or in opinion, which makes no alteration in the case), hath a great share, as well as pride, on the part of the aggressor.

Now, whoever will please to take this scheme, and either

reduce or adapt it to an intellectual state, or commonwealth of learning, will soon discover the first ground of disagreement between the two great parties at this time in arms, and may form just conclusions upon the merits of either cause. But the issue or events of this war are not so easy to conjecture at; for the present quarrel is so inflamed by the warm heads of either faction, and the pretensions somewhere or other so exorbitant, as not to admit the least overtures of accommodation. This quarrel first began, as I have heard it affirmed by an old dweller in the neighborhood, about a small spot of ground, lying and being upon one of the two tops of the hill Parnassus; the highest and largest of which had, it seems, been time out of mind in quiet possession of certain tenants, called the Ancients, and the other was held by the Moderns. But these, disliking their present station, sent certain ambassadors to the Ancients, complaining of a great nuisance, how the height of that part of Parnassus quite spoiled the prospect of theirs, especially towards the east; and therefore, to avoid a war, offered them the choice of this alternative—either that the Ancients would please to remove themselves and their effects down to the lower summity, which the Moderns would graciously surrender to them, and advance in their place; or else the said Ancients will give leave to the Moderns to come with shovels and mattocks, and level the said hill as low as they shall think it convenient. To which the Ancients made answer how little they expected such a message as this from a colony whom they had admitted, out of their own free grace, to so near a neighborhood; that, as to their own seat, they were aborigines of it, and therefore to talk with them of a removal or surrender was a language they did not understand; that if the height of the hill on their side shortened the prospect of the Moderns, it was a disadvantage they could not help, but desired them to consider whether that injury (if it be any) were not largely recompensed by the shade and shelter it afforded them; that, as to the levelling or digging down, it was either folly or ignorance to propose it, if they did or did not know how that side of the hill was an entire rock, which would break their tools and hearts, without any damage to itself; that they would therefore advise the Moderns rather to raise their own side of the hill than dream of pulling down that of the Ancients, to the former of which they would not only give license but also largely contribute. All this was rejected by the Moderns with much indignation, who still insisted upon one of the two expedients; and so this difference broke out into a long and obstinate war, maintained on the one part by resolution, and by the courage of certain leaders and allies; but, on the other, by the greatness of their number, upon all defeats affording continual recruits. In this quarrel whole rivulets of ink have been exhausted, and the virulence of both parties enormously augmented. Now, it must here be understood that ink is the great missive weapon in all battles of the learned, which, conveyed through a sort of engine called a quill, infinite numbers of these are darted at the enemy by the valiant on each side, with equal skill and violence, as if it were an engagement of porcupines. This malignant liquor was compounded, by the engineer who invented it, of two ingredients, which are gall and copperas; by its bitterness and venom to suit, in some degree, as well as to foment, the genius of the combatants. And as the Grecians, after an engagement, when they could not agree about the victory, were wont to set up trophies on both sides, the beaten party being content to be at the same expense, to keep itself in countenance (a laudable and ancient custom, happily revived of late, in the art of war), so the learned, after a sharp and bloody dispute, do, on both sides, hang out their trophies too, whichever comes by the worst. These trophies have largely inscribed on them the merits of the cause, a full impartial account of such a battle, and how the victory fell clearly to the party that set them up. They are known to the world under several names; as disputes, arguments, rejoinders, brief considerations, answers, replies, remarks, reflections, objections, confutations. For a very few days they are fixed up in all public places, either by themselves or their representatives, for passengers to gaze at; whence the chiefest and largest are removed to certain magazines they call libraries, there to remain in a quarter purposely assigned them, and from thenceforth begin to be called Books of Controversy.

In these books is wonderfully instilled and preserved the spirit of each warrior while he is alive; and after his death his soul transmigrates there to inform them. This at least is the more common opinion; but I believe it is with libraries as with other cemeteries, where some philosophers affirm that a certain spirit, which they call *brutum hominis*, hovers over the monument, till the body is corrupted and turns to dust or to worms, but then vanishes or dissolves. So, we may say, a restless spirit haunts over every book, till dust or worms have seized upon it—which to some may happen in a few days, but to others later; and therefore, books of controversy, being, of all others, haunted by the most disorderly spirits, have always been confined in a separate lodge from the rest, and, for fear of a mutual violence against each other, it was thought prudent by our ancestors to bind them to the peace with strong iron chains. Of which invention the original occasion was this: when the works of Scotus first came out, they were carried to a certain library and had lodgings appointed them; but this author was no sooner settled than he went to visit his master Aristotle; and there both concerted together to seize Plato by main force, and turn him out from his ancient station among the divines, where he had peaceably dwelt near eight hundred years. The attempt succeeded, and the two usurpers have reigned ever since in his stead; but, to maintain quiet for the future, it was decreed that all polemics of the larger size should be held fast with a chain.

By this expedient the public peace of libraries might certainly have been preserved if a new species of controversial books had not arose of late years, instinct with a most malignant spirit, from the war above mentioned between the learned, about the higher summity of Parnassus.

When these books were first admitted into the public libraries, I remember to have said, upon occasion, to several persons concerned, how I was sure they would create broils wherever they came, unless a world of care were taken; and therefore I advised that the champions of each side should be coupled together, or otherwise mixed, that, like the blending of contrary poisons, their malignity might be employed among themselves. And it seems I was neither an ill prophet nor an ill counsellor; for it was nothing else but the neglect of this caution which gave occasion to the terrible fight that happened on Friday last, between the Ancient and Modern books, in the King's Library. Now, because the talk of this battle is so fresh in everybody's mouth, and the expectation of the town so great to be informed in the particulars, I, being possessed of all qualifications requisite in an historian, and retained by neither party, have resolved to comply with the urgent importunity of my friends by writing down a full impartial account thereof.

The guardian of the regal library, a person of great valor, but chiefly renowned for his humanity, had been a fierce champion for the Moderns; and, in an engagement upon Parnassus, had vowed, with his own hands to knock down two of the Ancient chiefs, who guarded a small pass on the superior rock; but, endeavoring to climb up, was cruelly obstructed by his own unhappy weight and tendency towards his centre —a quality to which those of the Modern party are extremely subject, for, being light-headed, they have in speculation a wonderful agility and conceive nothing too high for them to mount, but in reducing to practice discover a mighty pressure about their posteriors and their heels. Having thus failed in his design, the disappointed champion bore a cruel rancor to the Ancients, which he resolved to gratify by showing all marks of his favor to the books of their adversaries and lodging them in the fairest apartments; when, at the same time, whatever book had the boldness to own itself for an advocate of the Ancients was buried alive in some obscure corner, and threatened, upon the least displeasure, to be turned out of doors. Besides, it so happened that about this time there was a strange confusion of place among all the books in the library, for which several reasons were assigned. Some imputed it to a great heap of learned dust, which a perverse wind blew off from a shelf of Moderns into the keeper's eyes. Others affirmed he had a humor to pick the worms out of the schoolmen and swallow them fresh and fasting, whereof some fell upon his spleen, and some climbed up into his head, to the great perturbation of both. And lastly, others maintained that, by walking much in the dark about the library, he had quite lost the situation of it out of his head; and therefore, in replacing his books, he was apt to mistake and clap Descartes next to Aristotle, poor Plato had got between Hobbes and the Seven Wise Masters, and Virgil was hemmed in with Dryden on one side and Wither on the other.

Meanwhile, those books that were advocates for the Moderns chose out one from among them to make a progress through the whole library, examine the number and strength of their party, and concert their affairs. This messenger performed all things very industriously, and brought back with him a list of their forces, in all fifty thousand, consisting chiefly of light-horse, heavy-armed foot, and mercenaries: whereof the foot were in general but sorrily armed and worse clad; their horses large but extremely out of case and heart; however, some few, by trading among the Ancients, had furnished themselves tolerably enough.

While things were in this ferment, discord grew extremely high; hot words passed on both sides, and ill blood was plentifully bred. Here a solitary Ancient, squeezed up among a whole shelf of Moderns, offered fairly to dispute the case, and to prove by manifest reasons that the priority was due to them, from long possession, and in regard of their prudence, antiquity, and, above all, their great merits toward the Moderns. But these denied the premises, and seemed very much to wonder how the Ancients could pretend to insist upon their antiquity, when it was so plain (if they went to that) that the Moderns were much the more ancient of the two. As for any obligations they owed to the Ancients, they renounced them all. "'Tis true," said they, "we are informed some few of our party have been so mean to borrow their subsistence from you; but the rest, infinitely the greater number (and especially we French and English), were so far from stooping to so base an example that there never passed, till this very hour, six words between us. For our horses are of our own breeding, our arms of our own forging, and our clothes of our own cutting out and sewing." Plato was by chance up on the next shelf, and observing those that spoke to be in the ragged plight mentioned a while ago—their jades lean and foundered, their weapons of rotten wood, their armor rusty, and nothing but rags underneath—he laughed loud, and in his pleasant way swore by G—— he believed them.

Now, the Moderns had not proceeded in their late negotiation with secrecy enough to escape the notice of the enemy. For those advocates who had begun the quarrel, by setting first on foot the dispute of precedency, talked so loud of coming to a battle that Temple happened to overhear them, and gave immediate intelligence to the Ancients, who thereupon drew up their scattered troops together, resolving to act upon the defensive; upon which several of the Moderns fled over to their party, and among the rest Temple himself. This Temple, having been educated and long conversed among the Ancients, was, of all the Moderns, their greatest favorite, and became their greatest champion.

Things were at this crisis, when a material accident fell out. For upon the highest corner of a large window there dwelt a certain spider, swollen up to the first magnitude by the destruction of infinite numbers of flies, whose spoils lay scattered before the gates of his palace like human bones before the cave of some giant. The avenues to his castle were guarded with turnpikes and palisadoes, all after the modern way of fortification. After you had passed several courts you came to the centre, wherein you might behold the constable himself in his own lodgings, which had windows fronting to each avenue, and ports to sally out, upon all occasions of prey or defence. In this mansion he had for some time dwelt in peace and plenty, without danger to his person by swallows from above, or to his palace by brooms from below; when it was the pleasure of fortune to conduct thither a wandering bee, to whose curiosity a broken pane in the glass had discovered itself, and in he went; where, expatiating a while, he at last happened to alight upon one of the outward walls of the spider's citadel, which, yielding to the unequal weight, sunk down to the very foundation. Thrice he endeavored to force his passage, and thrice the centre shook. The spider within, feeling the terrible convulsion, supposed at first that Nature was approaching to her final dissolution, or else that Beelzebub, with all his legions, was come to revenge the death of many thousands of his subjects, whom this enemy had slain and devoured. However, he at length valiantly resolved to issue forth and meet his fate. Meanwhile the bee had acquitted himself of his toils, and, posted securely at some distance, was employed in cleansing his wings and disengaging them from the ragged remnants of the cobweb. By this time the spider was adventured out, when, beholding the chasms, the ruins, and dilapidations of his fortress, he was very near at his wit's end; he stormed and swore like a madman, and swelled till he was ready to burst. At length, casting his eye upon the bee, and wisely gathering causes from events (for they knew each other by sight), "A plague split you!" said he; . . . "is it you, with a vengeance, that have made this litter here? Could not you look before you, and be d——d? Do you think I have nothing else to do (in the devil's name) but to mend and repair after you?"—"Good words, friend," said the bee (having now pruned himself, and being disposed to droll); "I'll give you my hand and word to come near your kennel no more; I was never in such a confounded pickle since I was born."—"Sirrah," replied the spider, "if it were not for breaking an old custom in our family never to stir abroad against an enemy, I should come and teach you better manners."—"I pray have patience," said the bee, "or you will spend your substance, and, for aught I see, you may stand in need of it all towards the repair of your house."—"Rogue! rogue!" replied the spider; "yet methinks you should have more respect to a person whom all the world allows to be so much your betters."—"By my troth," said the bee, "the comparison will amount to a very good jest; and you will do me a favor to let me know the reasons that all the world is pleased to use in so hopeful a dispute." At this the spider, having swelled himself into the size and posture of a disputant, began his argument in the true spirit of controversy, with a resolution to be heartily scurrilous and angry, to urge on his own reasons without the least regard to the answers or objections of his opposite, and fully predetermined in his mind against all conviction.

"Not to disparage myself," said he, "by the comparison with such a rascal, what art thou but a vagabond without house or home, without stock or inheritance, born to no possession of your own but a pair of wings and a drone-pipe? Your livelihood is an universal plunder upon nature; a freebooter over fields and gardens; and, for the sake of stealing, will rob a nettle as readily as a violet. Whereas I am a domestic animal, furnished with a native stock within myself. This large castle (to show my improvements in the mathematics) is all built with my own hands, and the materials extracted altogether out of my own person."

"I am glad," answered the bee, "to hear you grant at least that I am come honestly by my wings and my voice; for then, it seems, I am obliged to Heaven alone for my flights and my music, and Providence would never have bestowed on me two such gifts without designing them for the noblest ends. I visit, indeed, all the flowers and blossoms of the field and the garden; but whatever I collect from thence enriches myself without the least injury to their beauty, their smell, or their taste. Now, for you and your skill in architecture and other mathematics, I have little to say: in that building of yours there might, for aught I know, have been labor and method enough; but, by woeful experience for us both, 'tis too plain the materials are naught; and I hope you will henceforth take warning, and consider duration and matter as well as method and art. You boast, indeed, of being obliged to no other creature, but of drawing and spinning out all from yourself; that is to say, if we may judge of the liquor in the vessel by what issues out, you possess a good plentiful store of dirt and poison in your breast; and though I would by no means lessen or disparage your genuine stock of either, yet I doubt you are somewhat obliged, for an increase of both, to a little foreign assistance. Your inherent portion of dirt does not fail of acquisitions, by sweepings exhaled from below; and one insect furnishes you with a share of poison to destroy another. So that, in short, the question comes all to this: whether is the nobler being of the two, that which, by a lazy contemplation of four inches round, by an overweening pride, feeding and engendering on itself, turns all into excrement and venom, producing nothing at all but fly-bane and a cobweb; or that which, by an universal range, with long search, much study, true judgment, and distinction of things, brings home honey and wax?"

This dispute was managed with such eagerness, clamor, and warmth that the two parties of books, in arms below, stood silent a while, waiting in suspense what would be the issue, which was not long undetermined; for the bee, grown impatient at so much loss of time, fled straight away to a bed of roses, without looking for a reply, and left the spider, like an orator, collected in himself and just prepared to burst out.

It happened upon this emergency that Æsop broke silence first. He had been of late most barbarously treated by a strange effect of the regent's humanity, who had tore off his title-page, sorely defaced one half of his leaves, and chained him fast among a shelf of Moderns, where, soon discovering how high the quarrel was likely to proceed, he tried all his arts, and turned himself to a thousand forms. At length, in the borrowed shape of an ass, the regent mistook him for a Modern, by which means he had time and opportunity to escape to the Ancients, just when the spider and the bee were entering into their contest, to which he gave his attention with a world of pleasure; and when it was ended, swore in the loudest key that in all his life he had never known two cases so parallel and adapt to each other as that in the window and this upon the shelves. "The disputants," said he, "have admirably managed the dispute between them, have taken in the full strength of all that is to be said on both sides, and exhausted the substance of every argument *pro* and *con.* It is but to adjust the reasonings of both to the present quarrel, then to compare and apply the labors and fruits of each, as the bee hath learnedly deduced them, and we shall find the conclusion fall plain and close upon the Moderns and us. For, pray, gentlemen, was ever anything so modern as the spider in his air, his turns, and his paradoxes? He argues in the behalf of you his brethren and himself, with many boastings of his native stock and great genius; that he spins and spits wholly from himself, and scorns to own any obligation or assistance from without. Then he displays to you his great skill in architecture, and improvement in the mathematics. To all this the bee, as an advocate retained by us the Ancients, thinks fit to answer that, if one may judge of the great genius or inventions of the Moderns by what they have produced, you will hardly have countenance to bear you out in boasting of either. Erect your schemes with as much method and skill as you please; yet if the materials be nothing but dirt, spun out of your own entrails, . . . the edifice will conclude at last in a cobweb, the duration of which, like that of other spiders' webs, may be imputed to their being forgotten or neglected or hid in a corner. For anything else of genuine that the Moderns may pretend to I cannot recollect, unless it be a large vein of wrangling and satire, much of a nature and substance with the spider's poison, which, however they pretend to spit wholly out of themselves, is improved by the same arts, by feeding upon the insects and vermin of the age. As for us, the Ancients, we are content, with the bee, to pretend to nothing of our own beyond our wings and our voice, that is to say, our flights and our language. For the rest, whatever we have got hath been by infinite labor and search and ranging through every corner of nature; the difference is that instead of dirt and poison we have rather chose to fill our hives with honey and wax, thus furnishing mankind with the two noblest of things, which are sweetness and light."

It is wonderful to conceive the tumult arisen among the books upon the close of this long descant of Æsop: both parties took the hint, and heightened their animosities so on a sudden that they resolved it should come to a battle. Immediately the two main bodies withdrew, under their several ensigns, to the farthest parts of the library, and there entered into cabals and consults upon the present emergency. The Moderns were in very warm debates upon the choice of their leaders, and nothing less than the fear impending from their enemies could have kept them from mutinies upon this occasion. The difference was greatest among the horse, where every private trooper pretended to the chief command, from Tasso and Milton to Dryden and Wither. The light-horse were commanded by Cowley and Despreaux. There came the bowmen under their valiant leaders, Descartes, Gassendi, and Hobbes, whose strength was such that they could shoot their arrows behind the atmosphere, never to fall down again, but turn, like that of Evander, into meteors, or, like the cannon ball, into stars. Paracelsus brought a squadron of stink-pot-flingers from the snowy mountains of Rhætia. There came a vast body of dragoons, of different nations, under the leading of Harvey, their great *aga:* part armed with scythes, the weapons of death; part with lances and long knives, all steeped in poison; part shot bullets of a most malignant nature, and used white powder, which infallibly killed without report. There came several bodies of heavy-armed foot, all mercenaries, under the ensigns of Guicciardini, Davila, Polydore Virgil, Buchanan, Mariana, Camden, and others. The engineers were commanded by Regiomontanus and Wilkins. The rest were a confused multitude, led by Scotus, Aquinas, and Bellarmine; of mighty bulk and stature, but without either arms, courage, or discipline. In the last place came infinite swarms of *calones*, a disorderly rout led by L'Estrange; rogues and ragamuffins, that follow the camp for nothing but the plunder, all without coats to cover them.

The army of the Ancients was much fewer in number. Homer led the horse, and Pindar the light-horse; Euclid was chief engineer; Plato and Aristotle commanded the bowmen, Herodotus and Livy the foot, Hippocrates the dragoons; the allies, led by Vossius and Temple, brought up the rear.

All things violently tending to a decisive battle, Fame, who much frequented and had a large apartment formerly assigned her in the regal library, fled up straight to Jupiter, to whom she delivered a faithful account of all that passed between the two parties below (for among the gods she always tells truth). Jove, in great concern, convokes a council in the Milky Way. The senate assembled, he declares the occasion of convening them—a bloody battle just impendent between two mighty armies of Ancient and Modern creatures, called books, wherein the celestial interest was but too deeply concerned. Momus, the patron of the Moderns, made an excellent speech in their favor, which was answered by Pallas, the protectress of the Ancients. The assembly was divided in their affections; when Jupiter commanded the Book of Fate to be laid before him. Immediately were brought by Mercury three large volumes in folio, containing memoirs of all things past, present, and to come. The clasps were of silver double gilt, the covers of celestial turkey-leather, and the paper such as here on earth might almost pass for vellum. Jupiter, having silently read the decree, would communicate the import to none, but presently shut up the book.

Without the doors of this assembly there attended a vast number of light, nimble gods, menial servants to Jupiter: these are his ministering instruments in all affairs below. They travel in a caravan, more or less together, and are fastened to each other, like a link of galley-slaves, by a light chain, which passes from them to Jupiter's great toe; and yet, in receiving or delivering a message, they may never approach above the lowest step of his throne, where he and they whisper to each other through a long hollow trunk. These deities are called by mortal men accidents or events; but the gods call them second causes. Jupiter having delivered his message to a certain number of these divinities, they flew immediately down to the pinnacle of the regal library, and, consulting a few minutes, entered unseen, and disposed the parties according to their orders.

Meanwhile Momus, fearing the worst, and calling to mind an ancient prophecy which bore no very good face to his children the Moderns, bent his flight to the region of a malignant deity called Criticism. She dwelt on the top of a snowy mountain in Nova Zembla; there Momus found her extended in her den, upon the spoils of numberless volumes, half devoured. At her right hand sat Ignorance, her father and husband, blind with age; at her left, Pride, her mother, dressing her up in the scraps of paper herself had torn. There was Opinion, her sister, light of foot, hood-winked, and head-strong, yet giddy and perpetually turning. About her played her children, Noise and Impudence, Dulness and Vanity, Positiveness, Pedantry, and Ill-Manners. The goddess herself had claws like a cat; her head and ears and voice resembled those of an ass; her teeth fallen out before, her eyes turned inward, as if she looked only upon herself; her diet was the overflowing of her own gall; her spleen was so large as to stand prominent, like a dug of the first rate, nor wanted excrescencies in the form of teats, at which a crew of ugly monsters were greedily sucking; and, what is wonderful to conceive, the bulk of spleen increased faster than the sucking could diminish it. "Goddess," said Momus, "can you sit idly here while our devout worshippers, the Moderns, are this minute entering into a cruel battle, and perhaps now lying under the swords of their enemies? Who, then, hereafter will ever sacrifice, or build altars, to our divinities? Haste, therefore, to the British Isle, and if possible prevent their destruction; while I make factions among the gods, and gain them over to our party."

Momus, having thus delivered himself, stayed not for an answer, but left the goddess to her own resentments. Up she rose in a rage, and, as it is the form upon such occasions, began a soliloquy: "'Tis I," said she, "who give wisdom to infants and idiots; by me children grow wiser than their parents; by me beaux become politicians, and schoolboys judges of philosophy; by me sophisters debate, and conclude upon the depths of knowledge; and coffee-house wits, instinct by me, can correct an author's style and display his minutest errors, without understanding a syllable of his matter or his language; by me striplings spend their judgment, as they do their estate, before it comes into their hands. 'Tis I who have deposed Wit and Knowledge from their empire over poetry, and advanced myself in their stead. And shall a few upstart Ancients dare oppose me?—But come, my aged parents, and you, my children dear, and thou, my beauteous sister; let us ascend my chariot, and haste to assist our devout Moderns, who are now sacrificing to us a hecatomb, as I perceive by that grateful smell which from thence reaches my nostrils."

The goddess and her train, having mounted the chariot, which was drawn by tame geese, flew over infinite regions, shedding her influence in due places, till at length she arrived at her beloved island of Britain; but in hovering over its metropolis what blessings did she not let fall upon her seminaries of Gresham and Covent Garden! And now she reached the fatal plain of St. James's Library, at what time the two armies were upon the point to engage; where, entering with all her caravan unseen, and landing upon a case of shelves, now desert but once inhabited by a colony of virtuosos, she stayed awhile to observe the posture of both armies.

But here the tender cares of a mother began to fill her thoughts and move in her breast; for at the head of a troop of Modern bowmen she cast her eyes upon her son Wotton, to whom the Fates had assigned a very short thread. Wotton, a young hero, whom an unknown father of mortal race begot by stolen embraces with this goddess. He was the darling of his mother above all her children, and she resolved to go and comfort him. But first, according to the good old custom of deities, she cast about to change her shape, for fear the divinity of her countenance might dazzle his mortal sight and overcharge the rest of his senses. She therefore gathered up her person into an octavo compass; her body grew white and arid, and split in pieces with dryness; the thick turned into pasteboard, and the thin into paper, upon which her parents and children artfully strewed a black juice, or decoction of gall and soot, in form of letters; her head and voice and spleen kept their primitive form; and that which before was a cover of skin did still continue so. In which guise she marched on towards the Moderns, undistinguishable in shape and dress from the divine Bentley, Wotton's dearest friend. "Brave Wotton," said the goddess, "why do our troops stand idle here, to spend their present vigor and opportunity of the day? Away! let us haste to the generals, and advise to give the onset immediately." Having spoke thus, she took the ugliest of her monsters, full-glutted from her spleen, and flung it invisibly into his mouth, which, flying straight up into his head, squeezed out his eyeballs, gave him a distorted look, and half overturned his brain. Then she privately ordered two of her beloved children, Dulness and Ill-Manners, closely to attend his person in all encounters. Having thus accoutred him, she vanished in a mist, and the hero perceived it was the goddess his mother.

The destined hour of fate being now arrived, the fight began; whereof before I dare adventure to make a particular description, I must, after the example of other authors, petition for a hundred tongues and mouths and hands and pens, which would all be too little to perform so immense a work. Say, goddess that presidest over history, who it was that first advanced in the field of battle! Paracelsus, at the head of his dragoons, observing Galen in the adverse wing, darted his javelin with a mighty force, which the brave Ancient received upon his shield, the point breaking in the second fold.

* * * * * * * *Hic pauca*
* * * * * * * *desunt.*

They bore the wounded *aga* on their shields to his chariot

* * * * * * * *Desunt*
* * * * * * * *nonnulla.*

Then Aristotle, observing Bacon advance with a furious mien, drew his bow to the head and let fly his arrow, which missed the valiant Modern and went hizzing over his head. But Descartes it hit; the steel point quickly found a defect in his head-piece; it pierced the leather and the pasteboard, and went in at his right eye. The torture of the pain whirled the valiant bowman round, till death, like a star of superior influence, drew him into his own vortex.

Ingens hiatus * * * * * *
hic in MS. * * * * * *

* * * when Homer appeared at the head of the cavalry, mounted on a furious horse, with difficulty managed by the rider himself, but which no other mortal durst

approach: he rode among the enemy's ranks, and bore down all before him. Say, goddess, whom he slew first and whom he slew last! First, Gondibert advanced against him, clad in heavy armor and mounted on a staid, sober gelding, not so famed for his speed as his docility in kneeling whenever his rider would mount or alight. He had made a vow to Pallas that he would never leave the field till he had spoiled Homer of his armor: madman, who had never once seen the wearer, nor understood his strength! Him Homer overthrew, horse and man, to the ground, there to be trampled and choked in the dirt. Then with a long spear he slew Denham, a stout Modern, who from his father's side derived his lineage from Apollo, but his mother was of mortal race. He fell, and bit the earth. The celestial part Apollo took, and made it a star; but the terrestrial lay wallowing upon the ground. Then Homer slew Wesley with a kick of his horse's heel; he took Perrault by mighty force out of his saddle, then hurled him at Fontenelle, with the same blow dashing out both their brains.

On the left wing of the horse Virgil appeared, in shining armor, completely fitted to his body: he was mounted on a dapple-gray steed, the slowness of whose pace was an effect of the highest mettle and vigor. He cast his eye on the adverse wing, with a desire to find an object worthy of his valor, when, behold, upon a sorrel gelding of a monstrous size appeared a foe issuing from among the thickest of the enemy's squadrons; but his speed was less than his noise, for his horse, old and lean, spent the dregs of his strength in a high trot, which, though it made slow advances, yet caused a loud clashing of his armor, terrible to hear. The two cavaliers had now approached within the throw of a lance, when the stranger desired a parley, and, lifting up the vizor of his helmet, a face hardly appeared from within, which, after a pause, was known for that of the renowned Dryden. The brave Ancient suddenly started, as one possessed with surprise and disappointment together: for the helmet was nine times too large for the head, which appeared situate far in the hinder part, even like the lady in a lobster, or like a mouse under a canopy of state, or like a shrivelled beau from within the penthouse of a modern periwig; and the voice was suited to the visage, sounding weak and remote. Dryden, in a long harangue, soothed up the good Ancient; called him father; and by a large deduction of genealogies made it plainly appear that they were nearly related. Then he humbly proposed an exchange of armor, as a lasting mark of hospitality between them. Virgil consented (for the goddess Diffidence came unseen, and cast a mist before his eyes), though his was of gold and cost a hundred beeves, the other's but of rusty iron. However, this glittering armor became the Modern yet worse than his own. Then they agreed to exchange horses; but when it came to the trial, Dryden was afraid, and utterly unable to mount. * * * * * *

* * * * * * * *Alter hiatus*
* * * * * * * *in MS.*

Lucan appeared upon a fiery horse of admirable shape, but headstrong, bearing the rider where he list over the field: he made a mighty slaughter among the enemy's horse; which destruction to stop, Blackmore, a famous Modern (but one of the mercenaries), strenuously opposed himself, and darted his javelin with a strong hand, which, falling short of its mark, struck deep in the earth. Then Lucan threw a lance, but Æsculapius came unseen and turned off the point. "Brave Modern," said Lucan, "I perceive some god protects you, for never did my arm so deceive me before; but what mortal can contend with a god? Therefore let us fight no longer, but present gifts to each other." Lucan then bestowed the Modern a pair of spurs, and Blackmore gave Lucan a bridle. * * * * * *

Pauca desunt. * * * * * *

Creech: but the goddess Dulness took a cloud, formed into the shape of Horace, armed and mounted, and placed in a flying posture before him. Glad was the cavalier to begin a combat with a flying foe, and pursued the image, threatening aloud; till at last it led him to the peaceful bower of his father, Ogleby, by whom he was disarmed and assigned to his repose.

Then Pindar slew ——, and ——, and Oldham, and ——,

and Afra the Amazon, light of foot; never advancing in a direct line, but wheeling with incredible agility and force, he made a terrible slaughter among the enemy's light-horse. Him when Cowley observed, his generous heart burnt within him, and he advanced against the fierce Ancient, imitating his address and pace and career as well as the vigor of his horse and his own skill would allow. When the two cavaliers had approached within the length of three javelins, first Cowley threw a lance, which missed Pindar, and, passing into the enemy's ranks, fell ineffectual to the ground. Then Pindar darted a javelin so large and weighty that scarce a dozen cavaliers, as cavaliers are in our degenerate days, could raise it from the ground; yet he threw it with ease, and it went, by an unerring hand, singing through the air; nor could the Modern have avoided present death if he had not luckily opposed the shield that had been given him by Venus. And now both heroes drew their swords; but the Modern was so aghast and disordered that he knew not where he was; his shield dropped from his hands; thrice he fled, and thrice he could not escape. At last he turned, and, lifting up his hands in the posture of a suppliant, "God-like Pindar," said he, "spare my life, and possess my horse, with these arms, besides the ransom which my friends will give when they hear I am alive and your prisoner." "Dog!" said Pindar, "let your ransom stay with your friends; but your carcass shall be left for the fowls of the air and the beasts of the field." With that he raised his sword, and with a mighty stroke cleft the wretched Modern in twain, the sword pursuing the blow; and one half lay panting on the ground, to be trod in pieces by the horses' feet; the other half was borne by the frighted steed through the field. This Venus took, washed it seven times in ambrosia, then struck it thrice with a sprig of amarant; upon which the leather grew round and soft, and the leaves turned into feathers, and, being gilded before, continued gilded still; so it became a dove, and she harnessed it to her chariot. * * * * * * *

* * * * * * * *Hiatus valde de-*
* * * * * * * *flendus in MS.*

Day being far spent, and the numerous forces of the Moderns half inclining to a retreat, there issued forth from a squadron of their heavy-armed foot a captain whose name was Bentley, in person the most deformed of all the Moderns; tall, but without shape or comeliness; large, but without strength or proportion. His armor was patched up of a thousand incoherent pieces, and the sound of it, as he marched, was loud and dry, like that made by the fall of a sheet of lead which an Etesian wind blows suddenly down from the roof of some steeple. His helmet was of old rusty iron, but the vizard was brass, which, tainted by his breath, corrupted into copperas, nor wanted gall from the same fountain, so that, whenever provoked by anger or labor, an atramentous quality, of most malignant nature, was seen to distil from his lips. In his right hand he grasped a flail, and (that he might never be unprovided of an offensive weapon) a vessel full of ordure in his left. Thus completely armed, he advanced with a slow and heavy pace where the Modern chiefs were holding a consult upon the sum of things; who, as he came onwards, laughed to behold his crooked leg and humped shoulder, which his boot and armor, vainly endeavoring to hide, were forced to comply with and expose. The generals made use of him for his talent of railing, which, kept within government, proved frequently of great service to their cause, but at other times did more mischief than good, for at the least touch of offence, and often without any at all, he would, like a wounded elephant, convert it against his leaders. Such, at this juncture, was the disposition of Bentley, grieved to see the enemy prevail and dissatisfied with everybody's conduct but his own. He humbly gave the Modern generals to understand that he conceived, with great submission, they were all a pack of rogues and fools . . . and d——d cowards and confounded logger-heads and illiterate whelps and nonsensical scoundrels: that if himself had been constituted general, those presumptuous dogs, the Ancients, would long before this have been beaten out of the field. "You," said he, "sit here idle; but when I or any other valiant Modern kill an enemy, you are sure to seize the spoil. But I will not march one foot against the foe till you all swear to me that, whomsoever I take or kill, his arms I shall quietly possess." Bentley having spoke thus, Scaliger, bestowing him a sour look, "Miscreant prater!" said he, "eloquent only in thine own eyes, thou railest without wit or truth or discretion. The malignity of thy temper perverteth nature; thy learning makes thee more barbarous; thy study of humanity, more inhuman; thy converse amongst poets, more grovelling, miry, and dull. All arts of civilizing others render thee rude and untractable; courts have taught thee ill manners, and polite conversation hath finished thee a pedant. Besides, a greater coward burdeneth not the army. But never despond: I pass my word, whatever spoil thou takest shall certainly be thy own, though I hope that vile carcass will first become a prey to kites and worms."

Bentley durst not reply, but, half choked with spleen and rage, withdrew, in full resolution of performing some great achievement. With him, for his aid and companion, he took his beloved Wotton, resolving, by policy or surprise, to attempt some neglected quarter of the Ancient's army. They began their march over carcasses of their slaughtered friends; then to the right of their own forces; then wheeled northward, till they came to Aldrovandus's tomb, which they passed on the side of the declining sun. And now they arrived, with fear, toward the enemy's out-guards, looking about if haply they might spy the quarters of the wounded, or some straggling sleepers unarmed and remote from the rest. As when two mongrel curs, whom native greediness and domestic want provoke and join in partnership, though fearful, nightly to invade the folds of some rich grazier, they, with tails depressed and lolling tongues, creep soft and slow; meanwhile the conscious moon, now in her zenith, on their guilty heads darts perpendicular rays; nor dare they bark, though much provoked at her refulgent visage, whether seen in puddle by reflection or in sphere direct; but one surveys the region round, while the t'other scouts the plain, if haply to discover, at distance from the flock, some carcass half-devoured, the refuse of gorged wolves or ominous ravens. So marched this lovely, loving pair of friends, nor with less fear and circumspection; when at distance they might perceive two shining suits of armor hanging upon an oak, and the owners not far off, in a profound sleep. The two friends drew lots, and the pursuing of this adventure fell to Bentley; on he went, and, in his van, Confusion and Amaze, while Horror and Affright brought up the rear. As he came near, behold two heroes of the Ancients' army, Phalaris and Æsop, lay fast asleep. Bentley would fain have dispatched them both, and, stealing close, aimed his flail at Phalaris's breast; but then the goddess Affright, interposing, caught the Modern in her icy arms, and dragged him from the danger she foresaw; both the dormant heroes happened to turn at the same instant, though soundly sleeping, and busy in a dream. For Phalaris was just that minute dreaming how a most vile poetaster had lampooned him, and how he had got him roaring in his bull. And Æsop dreamed that, as he and the Ancient chiefs were lying on the ground, a wild ass broke loose, ran about, trampling and kicking . . . in their faces. Bentley, leaving the two heroes asleep, seized on both their armors, and withdrew in quest of his darling Wotton.

He, in the meantime, had wandered long in search of some enterprise, till at length he arrived at a small rivulet that issued from a fountain hard by, called, in the language of mortal men, Helicon. Here he stopped, and, parched with thirst, resolved to allay it in this limpid stream. Thrice with profane hands he essayed to raise the water to his lips, and thrice it slipped all through his fingers. Then he stooped prone on his breast; but ere his mouth had kissed the liquid crystal, Apollo came, and in the channel held his shield betwixt the Modern and the fountain, so that he drew up nothing but mud. For although no fountain on earth can compare with the clearness of Helicon, yet there lies at bottom a thick sediment of slime and mud; for so Apollo begged of Jupiter, as a punishment to those who durst attempt to taste it with unhallowed lips, and for a lesson to all not to draw too deep or far from the spring.

At the fountain-head Wotton discerned two heroes; the one

he could not distinguish, but the other was soon known for Temple, general of the allies to the Ancients. His back was turned, and he was employed in drinking large draughts in his helmet from the fountain, where he had withdrawn himself to rest from the toils of the war. Wotton, observing him, with quaking knees and trembling hands, spoke thus to himself: "O that I could kill this destroyer of our army! what renown should I purchase among the chiefs! But to issue out against him, man for man, shield against shield, and lance against lance, what Modern of us dare? For he fights like a god, and Pallas or Apollo are ever at his elbow. But, O mother! if what Fame reports be true, that I am the son of so great a goddess, grant me to hit Temple with this lance, that the stroke may send him to hell, and that I may return in safety and triumph, laden with his spoils." The first part of this prayer the gods granted at the intercession of his mother and of Momus; but the rest, by a perverse wind sent from Fate, was scattered in the air. Then Wotton grasped his lance, and, brandishing it thrice over his head, darted it with all his might; the goddess, his mother, at the same time adding strength to his arm. Away the lance went hizzing, and reached even to the belt of the averted Ancient, upon which lightly grazing, it fell to the ground. Temple neither felt the weapon touch him nor heard it fall, and Wotton might have escaped to his army, with the honor of having remitted his lance against so great a leader, unrevenged: but Apollo, enraged that a javelin flung by the assistance of so foul a goddess should pollute his fountain, put on the shape of ——, and softly came to young Boyle, who then accompanied Temple; he pointed first to the lance, then to the distant Modern that flung it, and commanded the young hero to take immediate revenge. Boyle, clad in a suit of armor which had been given him by all the gods, immediately advanced against the trembling foe, who now fled before him. As a young lion in the Libyan plains or Araby desert, sent by his aged sire to hunt for prey or health or exercise, he scours along, wishing to meet some tiger from the mountains or a furious boar; if chance a wild ass, with brayings importune, affronts his ear, the generous beast, though loathing to distain his claws with blood so vile, yet, much provoked at the offensive noise, which Echo, foolish nymph, like her ill-judging sex, repeats much louder and with more delight than Philomela's song, he vindicates the honor of the forest, and hunts the noisy long-eared animal. So Wotton fled, so Boyle pursued. But Wotton, heavy-armed and slow of foot, began to slack his course, when his lover Bentley appeared, returning laden with the spoils of the two sleeping Ancients. Boyle observed him well, and soon discovering the helmet and shield of Phalaris his friend, both which he had lately with his own hands new polished and gilded, rage sparkled in his eyes, and, leaving his pursuit after Wotton, he furiously rushed on against this new approacher. Fain would he be revenged on both, but both now fled different ways: and as a woman in a little house that gets a painful livelihood by spinning, if chance her geese be scattered o'er the common, she courses round the plain from side to side, compelling here and there the stragglers to the flock; they cackle loud, and flutter o'er the champaign; so Boyle pursued, so fled this pair of friends. Finding at length their flight was vain, they bravely joined, and drew themselves in phalanx. First Bentley threw a spear with all his force, hoping to pierce the enemy's breast; but Pallas came unseen, and in the air took off the point and clapped on one of lead, which, after a dead bang against the enemy's shield, fell blunted to the ground. Then Boyle, observing well his time, took a lance of wondrous length and sharpness; and as this pair of friends, compacted, stood close side to side, he wheeled him to the right, and with unusual force darted the weapon. Bentley saw his fate approach, and flanking down his arms close to his ribs, hoping to save his body, in went the point, passing through arm and side, nor stopped or spent its force till it had also pierced the valiant Wotton, who, going to sustain his dying friend, shared his fate. As when a skilful cook has trussed a brace of woodcocks, he with iron skewer pierces the tender sides of both, their legs and wings close pinioned to their ribs, so was this pair of friends transfixed, till down they fell, joined in their lives, joined in their deaths, so closely joined that Charon will mistake them both for one and waft them over Styx for half his fare. Farewell, beloved, loving pair! Few equals have you left behind; and happy and immortal shall you be, if all my wit and eloquence can make you.

And now * * * * * * * * * *Desunt cœtera.*

Sir Richard Steele.

1672–1729.

THE CLUB AT "THE TRUMPET."

(From *The Tatler*, 1709–1711.)

"Habeo senectuti magnam gratiam; quæ mihi sermonis aviditatem auxit, potionis et cibi sustulit."—Tull. *de Sen.*

Sheer Lane, February 10 [1710].

After having applied my mind with more than ordinary attention to my studies, it is my usual custom to relax and unbend it in the conversation of such as are rather easy than shining companions. This I find particularly necessary for me before I retire to rest, in order to draw my slumbers upon me by degrees and fall asleep insensibly. This is the particular use I make of a set of heavy honest men with whom I have passed many hours with much indolence though not with great pleasure. Their conversation is a kind of preparative for sleep; it takes the mind down from its abstractions, leads it into the familiar traces of thought, and lulls it into that state of tranquillity which is the condition of a thinking man when he is but half-awake. After this my reader will not be surprised to hear the account which I am about to give of a club of my own contemporaries, among whom I pass two or three hours every evening. This I look upon as taking my first nap before I go to bed. The truth of it is, I should think myself unjust to posterity, as well as to the society at "The Trumpet," of which I am a member, did not I in some part of my writings give an account of the persons among whom I have passed almost a sixth part of my time for these last forty years. Our club consisted originally of fifteen; but, partly by the severity of the law in arbitrary times, and partly by the natural effects of old age, we are at present reduced to a third part of that number: in which, however, we have this consolation, that the best company is said to consist of five persons. I must confess, besides the aforementioned benefit which I meet with in the conversation of this select society, I am not the less pleased with the company in that I find myself the greatest wit among them, and am heard as their oracle in all points of learning and difficulty.

Sir Jeoffery Notch, who is the oldest of the club, has been in possession of the right-hand chair time out of mind, and is the only man among us that has the liberty of stirring the fire. This our foreman is a gentleman of an ancient family, that came to a great estate some years before he had discretion, and run it out in hounds, horses, and cock-fighting; for which reason he looks upon himself as an honest, worthy gentleman, who has had misfortunes in the world, and calls every thriving man a pitiful upstart.

Major Matchlock is the next senior, who served in the last civil wars and has all the battles by heart. He does not think any action in Europe worth talking of since the fight of Marston Moor; and every night tells us of his having been knocked off his horse at the rising of the London apprentices, for which he is in great esteem among us.

Honest old Dick Reptile is the third of our society. He is a good-natured, indolent man, who speaks little himself but laughs at our jokes, and brings his young nephew along with him, a youth of eighteen years old, to show him good company and give him a taste of the world. This young fellow sits generally silent; but whenever he opens his mouth, or laughs at anything that passes, he is constantly told by his uncle after a jocular manner, "Ay, ay, Jack, you young men think us fools; but we old men know you are."

The greatest wit of our company, next to myself, is a bencher of the neighboring inn, who in his youth frequented the ordinaries about Charing Cross, and pretends to have been intimate with Jack Ogle. He has about ten distichs of *Hudibras* without book, and never leaves the club until he has applied them all. If any modern wit be mentioned or any town-frolic spoken of, he shakes his head at the dulness of the present age, and tells us a story of Jack Ogle.

For my own part, I am esteemed among them because they see I am something respected by others, though at the same time I understand by their behavior that I am considered by them as a man of a great deal of learning but no knowledge of the world; insomuch that the major sometimes, in the height of his military pride, calls me the Philosopher, and Sir Jeoffery no longer ago than last night, upon a dispute what day of the month it was then in Holland, pulled his pipe out of his mouth, and cried, "What does the Scholar say to it?"

Our club meets precisely at six of the clock in the evening; but I did not come last evening until half an hour after seven, by which means I escaped the battle of Naseby, which the major usually begins at about three-quarters after six. I found, also, that my good friend the bencher had already spent three of his distichs, and only waited an opportunity to hear a sermon spoken of that he might introduce the couplet where "a stick" rhymes to "ecclesiastic." At my entrance into the room they were naming a red petticoat and a cloak, by which I found that the bencher had been diverting them with a story of Jack Ogle.

I had no sooner taken my seat but Sir Jeoffery, to show his good will towards me, gave me a pipe of his own tobacco, and stirred up the fire. I look upon it as a point of morality to be obliged by those who endeavor to oblige me; and therefore, in requital for his kindness, and to set the conversation a-going, I took the best occasion I could to put him upon telling us the story of old Gantlett, which he always does with very particular concern. He traced up his descent on both sides for several generations, describing his diet and manner of life, with his several battles, and particularly that in which he fell. This Gantlett was a game cock, upon whose head the knight, in his youth, had won five hundred pounds and lost two thousand. This naturally set the major upon the account of Edge-hill fight, and ended in a duel of Jack Ogle's.

Old Reptile was extremely attentive to all that was said, though it was the same he had heard every night for these twenty years, and upon all occasions winked upon his nephew to mind what passed.

This may suffice to give the world a taste of our innocent conversation, which we spun out until about ten of the clock, when my maid came with a lantern to light me home. I could not but reflect with myself, as I was going out, upon the talkative humor of old men, and the little figure which that part of life makes in one who cannot employ his natural propensity in discourses which would make him venerable. I must own it makes me very melancholy in company when I hear a young man begin a story; and have often observed that one of a quarter of an hour long, in a man of five-and-twenty, gathers circumstances every time he tells it, until it grows into a long Canterbury tale of two hours by that time he is threescore.

The only way of avoiding such a trifling and frivolous old age is to lay up in our way to it such stores of knowledge and observation as may make us useful and agreeable in our declining years. The mind of man in a long life will become a magazine of wisdom or folly, and will consequently discharge itself in something impertinent or improving. For which reason, as there is nothing more ridiculous than an old trifling story-teller, so there is nothing more venerable than one who has turned his experience to the entertainment and advantage of mankind.

In short, we who are in the last stage of life, and are apt to indulge ourselves in talk, ought to consider if what we speak be worth being heard, and endeavor to make our discourse like that of Nestor, which Homer compares to the flowing of honey for its sweetness.

I am afraid I shall be thought guilty of this excess I am speaking of, when I cannot conclude without observing that Milton certainly thought of this passage in Homer, when, in his description of an eloquent spirit, he says,—

"His tongue dropped manna."

Joseph Addison.

1672–1719.

A VERY PRETTY POET.

(From *The Tatler*, 1709–1711.)

"Idem inficeto est inficetior rure
Simul poemata attigit; neque idem unquam
Æquè est beatus, ac poema cum scribit:
Tam gaudet in se, tamque se ipse miratur.
Nimirum idem omnes fallimur; neque est quisquam
Quem non in aliqua re videre Suffenum
Possis"——

—CATUL. *de Suffeno*, 20.14.

Will's Coffee-house, April 24 [1710].

I yesterday came hither about two hours before the company generally make their appearance, with a design to read over all the newspapers; but upon my sitting down I was accosted by Ned Softly, who saw me from a corner in the other end of the room, where I found he had been writing something. "Mr. Bickerstaff," says he, "I observe by a late paper of yours that you and I are just of a humor; for you must know, of all impertinences there is nothing which I so much hate as news. I never read a gazette in my life; and never trouble my head about our armies, whether they win or lose, or in what part of the world they lie encamped." Without giving me time to reply he drew a paper of verses out of his pocket, telling me that he had something which would entertain me more agreeably, and that he would desire my judgment upon every line, for that we had time enough before us until the company came in.

Ned Softly is a very pretty poet and a great admirer of easy lines. Waller is his favorite: and as that admirable writer has the best and worst verses of any among our great

English poets, Ned Softly has got all the bad ones without book, which he repeats upon occasion, to show his reading and garnish his conversation. Ned is indeed a true English reader, incapable of relishing the great and masterly strokes of this art, but wonderfully pleased with the little gothic ornaments of epigrammatical conceits, turns, points, and quibbles, which are so frequent in the most admired of our English poets, and practised by those who want genius and strength to represent, after the manner of the ancients, simplicity in its natural beauty and perfection.

Finding myself unavoidably engaged in such a conversation, I was resolved to turn my pain into a pleasure and to divert myself as well as I could with so very odd a fellow. "You must understand," says Ned, "that the sonnet I am going to read to you was written upon a lady, who showed me some verses of her own making, and is perhaps the best poet of our age. But you shall hear it." Upon which he begun to read as follows:

"TO MIRA, ON HER INCOMPARABLE POEMS.

1.

"When dressed in laurel wreaths you shine,
And tune your soft melodious notes,
You seem a sister of the Nine,
Or Phœbus' self in petticoats.

2.

"I fancy, when your song you sing
(Your song you sing with so much art),
Your pen was plucked from Cupid's wing;
For ah! it wounds me like his dart."

"Why," says I, "this is a little nosegay of conceits, a very lump of salt: every verse hath something in it that piques; and then the dart in the last line is certainly as pretty a sting in the tail of an epigram (for so I think your critics call it) as ever entered into the thought of a poet." "Dear Mr. Bickerstaff," says he, shaking me by the hand, "everybody knows you to be a judge of these things; and to tell you truly, I read over Roscommon's translation of Horace's

Art of Poetry three several times before I sat down to write the sonnet which I have shown you. But you shall hear it again, and pray observe every line of it, for not one of them shall pass without your approbation.

"When dressed in laurel wreaths you shine.

"That is," says he, "when you have your garland on; when you are writing verses." To which I replied, "I know your meaning: a metaphor!" "The same," said he, and went on:

"And tune your soft melodious notes.

"Pray observe the gliding of that verse; there is scarce a consonant in it: I took care to make it run upon liquids. Give me your opinion of it." "Truly," said I, "I think it as good as the former." "I am very glad to hear you say so," says he; "but mind the next:

"You seem a sister of the Nine.

"That is," says he, "you seem a sister of the Muses; for if you look into ancient authors, you will find it was their opinion that there were nine of them." "I remember it very well," said I; "but pray proceed."

"Or Phœbus' self in petticoats.

"Phœbus," says he, "was the god of poetry. These little instances, Mr. Bickerstaff, show a gentleman's reading. Then, to take off from the air of learning which Phœbus and the Muses have given to this first stanza, you may observe how it falls all of a sudden into the familiar: 'in petticoats!'

"Or Phœbus' self in petticoats."

"Let us now," says I, "enter upon the second stanza. I find the first line is still a continuation of the metaphor:

"I fancy when your song you sing."

"It is very right," says he; "but pray observe the turn of words in those two lines. I was a whole hour in adjusting of them, and have still a doubt upon me whether in the second line it should be, 'Your song you sing'; or, 'You sing your song.' You shall hear them both:

"I fancy, when your song you sing,
(Your song you sing with so much art),

"or,

"I fancy, when your song you sing,
(You sing your song with so much art).

"Truly," said I, "the turn is so natural either way that you have made me almost giddy with it." "Dear sir," said he, grasping me by the hand, "you have a great deal of patience; but pray what do you think of the next verse?

"Your pen was plucked from Cupid's wing."

"Think!" says I, "I think you have made Cupid look like a little goose." "That was my meaning," says he; "I think the ridicule is well enough hit off. But we come now to the last, which sums up the whole matter.

"For ah! it wounds me like his dart.

"Pray how do you like that 'ah'? Doth it not make a pretty figure in that place? 'Ah!'—it looks as if I felt the dart and cried out at being pricked with it.

'For ah! it wounds me like his dart.

"My friend, Dick Easy," continued he, "assured me he would rather have written that 'ah!' than to have been the author of the *Æneid.* He indeed objected that I made Mira's pen like a quill in one of the lines, and like a dart in the other. But as to that——" "Oh, as to that," says I, "it is but supposing Cupid to be like a porcupine, and his quills and darts will be the same thing." He was going to embrace me for the hint; but half a dozen critics coming into the room, whose faces he did not like, he conveyed the sonnet into his pocket, and whispered me in the ear he would show it me again as soon as his man had written it over fair.

TRUE AND FALSE HUMOR.

(From *The Spectator*, 1711–1712.)

"Risu inepto res ineptior nulla est."—MART.

Among all kinds of writing there is none in which authors are more apt to miscarry than in works of humor, as there is none in which they are more ambitious to excel. It is not an imagination that teems with monsters, an head that is filled with extravagant conceptions, which is capable of furnishing the world with diversions of this nature; and yet if we look into the productions of several writers who set up for men of humor, what wild, irregular fancies, what unnatural distortions of thought, do we meet with? If they speak nonsense, they believe they are talking humor; and when they have drawn together a scheme of absurd, inconsistent ideas, they are not able to read it over themselves without laughing. These poor gentlemen endeavor to gain themselves the reputation of wits and humorists by such monstrous conceits as almost qualify them for Bedlam; not considering that humor should always lie under the check of reason, and that it requires the direction of the nicest judgment by so much the more as it indulges itself in the most boundless freedoms. There is a kind of nature that is to be observed in this sort of compositions, as well as in all other; and a certain regularity of thought which must discover the writer to be a man of sense, at the same time that he appears altogether given up to caprice. For my part, when I read the delirious mirth of an unskilful author, I cannot be so barbarous as to divert myself with it, but am rather apt to pity the man than to laugh at anything he writes.

The deceased Mr. Shadwell, who had himself a great deal of the talent which I am treating of, represents an empty rake, in one of his plays, as very much surprised to hear one say that breaking of windows was not humor; and I question not but several English readers will be as much startled to hear me affirm that many of those raving, incoherent pieces which are often spread among us, under odd, chimerical titles, are rather the offsprings of a distempered brain than works of humor.

It is, indeed, much easier to describe what is not humor than what is; and very difficult to define it otherwise than as Cowley has done wit, by negatives. Were I to give my own notions of it, I would deliver them after Plato's manner, in a kind of allegory, and, by supposing Humor to be a person, deduce to him all his qualifications according to the following genealogy. Truth was the founder of the family, and the father of Good Sense. Good Sense was the father of Wit, who married a lady of a collateral line, called Mirth, by whom he had issue, Humor. Humor therefore being the youngest of this illustrious family, and descended from parents of such different dispositions, is very various and unequal in his temper: sometimes you see him putting on grave looks and a solemn habit, sometimes airy in his behavior and fantastic in his dress; insomuch that at different times he appears as serious as a judge and as jocular as a merry-andrew. But as he has a great deal of the mother in his constitution, whatever mood he is in he never fails to make his company laugh.

But since there is an impostor abroad, who takes upon him the name of this young gentleman and would willingly pass for him in the world, to the end that well-meaning persons may not be imposed upon by cheats I would desire my readers, when they meet with this pretender, to look into his parentage, and to examine him strictly, whether or no he be remotely allied to Truth and lineally descended from Good Sense; if not, they may conclude him a counterfeit. They may likewise distinguish him by a loud and excessive laughter, in which he seldom gets his company to join with him; for as True Humor generally looks serious while everybody laughs about him, False Humor is always laughing whilst everybody about him looks serious. I shall only add, if he has not in him a mixture of both parents, that is, if he would pass for the offspring of Wit without Mirth, or Mirth without Wit, you may conclude him to be altogether spurious and a cheat.

The impostor of whom I am speaking descends originally from Falsehood, who was the mother of Nonsense, who was brought to bed of a son called Frenzy, who married one of the daughters of Folly, commonly known by the name of Laughter, on whom he begot that monstrous infant of which I have been here speaking. I shall set down at length the genealogical table of False Humor, and at the same time place under it the genealogy of True Humor, that the reader may at one view behold their different pedigrees and relations.

Falsehood.
Nonsense.
Frenzy.———Laughter.
False Humor.

Truth.
Good Sense.
Wit.———Mirth.
Humor.

I might extend the allegory by mentioning several of the children of False Humor, who are more in number than the sands of the sea, and might in particular enumerate the many sons and daughters which he has begot in this island. But as this would be a very invidious task, I shall only observe in general that False Humor differs from the True as a monkey does from a man:—

First of all, he is exceedingly given to little apish tricks and buffooneries.

Secondly, he so much delights in mimicry that it is all one to him whether he exposes by it vice and folly, luxury and avarice, or, on the contrary, virtue and wisdom, pain and poverty.

Thirdly, he is wonderfully unlucky, insomuch that he will bite the hand that feeds him, and endeavor to ridicule both friends and foes indifferently. For, having but small talents, he must be merry where he can, not where he should.

Fourthly, being entirely void of reason, he pursues no point either of morality or instruction, but is ludicrous only for the sake of being so.

Fifthly, being incapable of anything but mock representations, his ridicule is always personal and aimed at the vicious man or the writer, not at the vice or at the writing.

I have here only pointed at the whole species of false humorists; but as one of my principal designs in this paper is to beat down that malignant spirit which discovers itself in the writings of the present age, I shall not scruple, for the future, to single out any of the small wits that infest the world with such compositions as are ill-natured, immoral, and absurd. This is the only exception which I shall make to the general rule I have prescribed myself of attacking multitudes; since every honest man ought to look upon himself as in a natural state of war with the libeller and lampooner, and to annoy them wherever they fall in his way. This is but retaliating upon them, and treating them as they treat others.

THE VISION OF MIRZAH.

(From the same.)

——— " Omnem quæ nunc obducta tuenti
Mortales hebetat visus tibi, et humida circum
Caligat, nubem eripiam"—VIRG.

When I was at Grand Cairo, I picked up several Oriental manuscripts, which I have still by me. Among others I met with one entitled *The Visions of Mirzah*, which I have read over with great pleasure. I intend to give it to the public when I have no other entertainment for them; and shall begin with the first vision, which I have translated word for word as follows:—

" On the fifth day of the moon, which, according to the custom of my forefathers, I always keep holy, after having washed myself and offered up my morning devotions, I ascended the high hills of Bagdat, in order to pass the rest of the day in meditation and prayer. As I was here airing myself on the tops of the mountains, I fell into a profound contemplation on the vanity of human life; and passing from one thought to another, 'Surely,' said I, 'man is but a shadow, and life a dream.' Whilst I was thus musing, I cast my eyes towards the summit of a rock that was not far from me, where I discovered one in the habit of a shepherd, with a little musical instrument in his hand. As I looked upon him, he applied it to his lips and began to play upon it. The sound of it was exceeding sweet, and wrought into a variety of tunes that were inexpressibly melodious and altogether different from anything I had ever heard. They put me in mind of those heavenly airs that are played to the departed souls of good men upon their first arrival in Paradise, to wear out the impressions of the last agonies and qualify them for the pleasures of that happy place. My heart melted away in secret raptures.

"I had been often told that the rock before me was the haunt of a genius, and that several had been entertained with music who had passed by it; but never heard that the musician had before made himself visible. When he had raised my thoughts, by those transporting airs which he played, to taste the pleasures of his conversation, as I looked upon him like one astonished he beckoned to me, and by the waving of his hand directed me to approach the place where he sat. I drew near with that reverence which is due to a superior nature; and as my heart was entirely subdued by the captivating strains I had heard, I fell down at his feet and wept. The genius smiled upon me with a look of compassion and affability that familiarized him to my imagination and at once dispelled all the fears and apprehensions with which I approached him. He lifted me from the ground, and, taking me by the hand, 'Mirzah,' said he, 'I have heard thee in thy soliloquies; follow me.'

"He then led me to the highest pinnacle of the rock, and, placing me on the top of it, 'Cast thy eyes eastward,' said he, 'and tell me what thou seest.' 'I see,' said I, 'a huge valley, and a prodigious tide of water rolling through it.' 'The valley that thou seest,' said he, 'is the Vale of Misery, and the tide of water that thou seest is part of the great tide of Eternity.' 'What is the reason,' said I, 'that the tide I see rises out of a thick mist at one end and again loses itself in a thick mist at the other?' 'What thou seest,' said he, 'is that portion of Eternity which is called Time, measured out by the sun, and reaching from the beginning of the world to its consummation. Examine now,' said he, 'this sea that is bounded with darkness at both ends, and tell me what thou discoverest in it.' 'I see a bridge,' said I, 'standing in the midst of the tide.' 'The bridge thou seest,' said he, 'is human life; consider it attentively.' Upon a more leisurely survey of it, I found that it consisted of threescore and ten entire arches, with several broken arches, which, added to those that were entire, made up the number about an hundred. As I was counting the arches, the genius told me that this bridge consisted at first of a thousand arches, but that a great flood swept away the rest and left the bridge in the ruinous condition I now beheld it. 'But tell me further,' said he, 'what thou discoverest on it.' 'I see multitudes of people passing over it,' said I, 'and a black cloud hanging on each end of it.' As I looked more attentively, I saw several of the passengers dropping through the bridge into the great tide that flowed underneath it; and upon farther examination perceived there were innumerable trap-doors that lay concealed in the bridge, which the passengers no sooner trod upon but they fell through them into the tide and immediately disappeared. These hidden pitfalls were set very thick at the entrance of the bridge, so that the throngs of people no sooner broke through the cloud but many of them fell into them. They grew thinner towards the middle, but multiplied and lay closer together towards the end of the arches that were entire.

"There were, indeed, some persons, but their number was very small, that continued a kind of hobbling march on the broken arches, but fell through one after another, being quite tired and spent with so long a walk.

"I passed some time in the contemplation of this wonderful structure and the great variety of objects which it presented. My heart was filled with a deep melancholy to see several dropping unexpectedly in the midst of mirth and jollity and catching at everything that stood by them to save themselves. Some were looking up towards the heavens in a thoughtful posture, and in the midst of a speculation stumbled and fell out of sight. Multitudes were very busy in the pursuit of bubbles that glittered in their eyes and danced before them; but often when they thought themselves within the reach of them, their footing failed and down they sunk. In this confusion of objects I observed some with scimitars in their hands, . . . who ran to and fro upon the bridge, thrusting several persons on trap-doors which did not seem to lie in their way, and which they might have escaped had they not been forced upon them.

"The genius, seeing me indulge myself in this melancholy prospect, told me I had dwelt long enough upon it. 'Take thine eyes off the bridge,' said he, 'and tell me if thou yet seest anything thou dost not comprehend.' Upon looking up, 'What mean,' said I, 'those great flights of birds that are perpetually hovering about the bridge and settling upon it from time to time? I see vultures, harpies, ravens, cormorants, and, among many other feathered creatures, several little winged boys that perch in great numbers upon the middle arches.' 'These,' said the genius, 'are Envy, Avarice, Superstition, Despair, Love, with the like cares and passions that infest human life.'

"I here fetched a deep sigh. 'Alas,' said I, 'man was made in vain! How is he given away to misery and mortality! tortured in life, and swallowed up in death!' The genius, being moved with compassion towards me, bid me quit so uncomfortable a prospect. 'Look no more,' said he, 'on man in the first stage of his existence, in his setting out for Eternity; but cast thine eye on that thick mist into which the tide bears the several generations of mortals that fall into it.' I directed my sight as I was ordered, and, whether or no the good genius strengthened it with any supernatural force, or dissipated part of the mist that was before too thick for the eye to penetrate, I saw the valley opening at the farther end and spreading forth into an immense ocean, that had a huge rock of adamant running through the midst of it and dividing it into two equal parts. The clouds still rested on one half of it, insomuch that I could discover nothing in it; but the other appeared to me a vast ocean planted with innumerable islands, that were covered with fruits and flowers, and interwoven with a thousand little shining seas that ran among them. I could see persons dressed in glorious habits, with garlands upon their heads, passing among the trees, lying down by the side of fountains, or resting on beds of flowers; and could hear a confused harmony of singing birds, falling waters, human voices, and musical instruments. Gladness grew in me upon the discovery of so delightful a scene. I wished for the wings of an eagle, that I might fly away to those happy seats; but the genius told me there was no passage to them except through the gates of death that I saw opening every moment upon the bridge. 'The islands,' said he, 'that lie so fresh and green before thee, and with which the whole face of the ocean appears spotted as far as thou canst see, are more in number than the sands on the sea-shore: there are myriads of islands behind those which thou here discoverest, reaching further than thine eye, or even thine imagination, can extend itself. These are the mansions of good men after death, who, according to the degree and kinds of virtue in which they excelled, are distributed among these several islands, which abound with pleasures of different kinds and degrees, suitable to the relishes and perfections of those who are settled in them: every island is a paradise accommodated to its respective inhabitants. Are not these, O Mirzah, habitations worth contending for? Does life appear miserable, that gives thee opportunties of earning such a reward? Is death to be feared, that will convey thee to so happy an existence? Think not man was made in vain, who has such an Eternity reserved for him.' I gazed with inexpressible pleasure on these happy islands. At length said I, 'Show me now, I beseech thee, the secrets that lie hid under those dark clouds which cover the ocean on the other side of the rock of adamant.' The genius making me no answer, I turned about to address myself to him a second time, but I found that he had left me. I then turned again to the vision which I had been so long contemplating; but instead of the rolling tide, the arched bridge, and the happy islands, I saw nothing but the long hollow valley of Bagdat, with oxen, sheep, and camels grazing upon the sides of it."

DISSECTION OF A COQUET'S HEART.

(From the same.)

"Pectoribus inhians spirantia consulit exta."—VIRG.

Having already given an account of the dissection of a beau's head, with the several discoveries made on that occasion, I shall here, according to my promise, enter upon the dissection of a coquet's heart, and communicate to the public such particularities as we observed in that curious piece of anatomy.

I should perhaps have waived this undertaking, had not I been put in mind of my promise by several of my unknown correspondents, who are very importunate with me to make an example of the coquet, as I have already done of the beau. It is therefore in compliance with the request of friends that I have looked over the minutes of my former dream, in order to give the public an exact relation of it, which I shall enter upon without further preface.

Our operator, before he engaged in this visionary dissection, told us that there was nothing in his art more difficult than to lay open the heart of a coquet, by reason of the many labyrinths and recesses which are to be found in it and which do not appear in the heart of any other animal.

He desired us first of all to observe the *pericardium*, or outward case of the heart, which we did very attentively; and by the help of our glasses discerned in it millions of little scars, which seemed to have been occasioned by the points of innumerable darts and arrows that from time to time had glanced upon the outward coat, though we could not discover the smallest orifice by which any of them had entered and pierced the inward substance.

Every smatterer in anatomy knows that this *pericardium*, or case of the heart, contains in it a thin reddish liquor, supposed to be bred from the vapors which exhale out of the heart, and, being stopped here, are condensed into this watery substance. Upon examining this liquor we found that it had in it all the qualities of that spirit which is made use of in the thermometer to show the change of weather.

Nor must I here omit an experiment one of the company assured us he himself had made with this liquor, which he found in great quantity about the heart of a coquet whom he had formerly dissected. He affirmed to us that he had actually inclosed it in a small tube made after the manner of a weather-glass; but that instead of acquainting him with the variations of the atmosphere, it showed him the qualities of those persons who entered the room where it stood. He affirmed also that it rose at the approach of a plume of feathers, an embroidered coat, or a pair of fringed gloves, and that it fell as soon as an ill-shaped periwig, a clumsy pair of shoes, or an unfashionable coat came into his house. Nay, he proceeded so far as to assure us that, upon his laughing aloud when he stood by it, the liquor mounted very sensibly, and immediately sunk again upon his looking serious. In short, he told us that he knew very well by this invention whenever he had a man of sense or a coxcomb in his room.

Having cleared away the *pericardium*, or the case and liquor above mentioned, we came to the heart itself. The outward surface of it was extremely slippery, and the *mucro*, or point, so very cold withal that upon endeavoring to take hold of it it glided through the fingers like a smooth piece of ice.

The fibres were turned and twisted in a more intricate and perplexed manner than they are usually found in other hearts; insomuch that the whole heart was wound up together in a Gordian knot, and must have had very irregular and unequal motions whilst it was employed in its vital function.

One thing we thought very observable, namely, that upon

examining all the vessels which came into it or issued out of it we could not discover any communication that it had with the tongue.

We could not but take notice, likewise, that several of those little nerves in the heart which are affected by the sentiments of love, hatred, and other passions, did not descend to this before us from the brain but from the muscles which lie about the eye.

Upon weighing the heart in my hand I found it to be extremely light and consequently very hollow, which I did not wonder at when, upon looking into the inside of it, I saw multitudes of cells and cavities running one within another, as our historians describe the apartments of Rosamond's Bower. Several of these little hollows were stuffed with innumerable sorts of trifles, which I shall forbear giving any particular account of, and shall therefore only take notice of what lay first and uppermost, which, upon our unfolding it and applying our microscopes to it, appeared to be a flame-colored hood.

We were informed that the lady of this heart, when living, received the addresses of several who made love to her, and did not only give each of them encouragement but made every one she conversed with believe that she regarded him with an eye of kindness; for which reason we expected to have seen the impression of multitudes of faces among the several plaits and foldings of the heart, but to our great surprise not a single print of this nature discovered itself till we came into the very core and centre of it. We there observed a little figure, which, upon applying our glasses to it, appeared dressed in a very fantastic manner. The more I looked upon it the more I thought I had seen the face before, but could not possibly recollect either the place or time; when at length one of the company, who had examined this figure more nicely than the rest, showed us plainly by the make of its face and the several turns of its features that the little idol which was thus lodged in the very middle of the heart was the deceased beau whose head I gave some account of in my last Tuesday's paper.

As soon as we had finished our dissection we resolved to make an experiment of the heart, not being able to determine among ourselves the nature of its substance, which differed in so many particulars from that of the heart in other females. Accordingly we laid it into a pan of burning coals, when we observed in it a certain salamandrine quality that made it capable of living in the midst of fire and flame without being consumed or so much as singed.

As we were admiring this strange phenomenon, and standing around the heart in a circle, it gave a most prodigious sigh, or rather crack, and dispersed all at once in smoke and vapor. This imaginary noise, which methought was louder than the burst of a cannon, produced such a violent shake in my brain that it dissipated the fumes of sleep and left me in an instant broad awake.

Daniel Defoe.

1661(?)–1731.

AN ACADEMY FOR WOMEN.

(From *An Essay upon Projects*, 1697.)

I have often thought of it as one of the most barbarous customs in the world, considering us as a civilized and a Christian country, that we deny the advantages of learning to women. We reproach the sex every day with folly and impertinence, while I am confident, had they the advantages of education equal to us, they would be guilty of less than ourselves. One would wonder, indeed, how it should happen that women are conversible at all, since they are only beholden to natural parts for all their knowledge. Their youth is spent to teach them to stitch and sew or make baubles. They are taught to read, indeed, and perhaps to write their names or so, and that is the height of a woman's education. And I would but ask any who slight the sex for their understanding, What is a man (a gentleman, I mean) good for that is taught no more? I need not give instances, or examine the character of a gentleman with a good estate and of a good family and with tolerable parts, and examine what figure he makes for want of education.

The soul is placed in the body like a rough diamond, and must be polished, or the lustre of it will never appear. And it is manifest that as the rational soul distinguishes us from brutes, so education carries on the distinction and makes some less brutish than others. This is too evident to need any demonstration. But why, then, should women be denied the benefit of instruction? If knowledge and understanding had been useless additions to the sex, God Almighty would never have given them capacities, for He made nothing needless.

Besides, I would ask such what they can see in ignorance that they should think it a necesary ornament to a woman. Or how much worse is a wise woman than a fool? Or what has the woman done to forfeit the privilege of being taught? Does she plague us with her pride and impertinence? Why did we not let her learn, that she might have had more wit? Shall we upbraid women with folly, when it is only the error of this inhuman custom that hindered them being made wiser? The capacities of women are supposed to be greater and their senses quicker than those of the men; and what they might be capable of being bred to is plain from some instances of female wit which this age is not without; which upbraids us with injustice, and looks as if we denied women the advantages of education for fear they should vie with the men in their improvements.

To remove this objection, and that women might have at least a needful opportunity of education in all sorts of useful learning, I propose the draught of an academy for that purpose.

I know it is dangerous to make public appearances of the sex. They are not either to be confined or exposed: the first will disagree with their inclinations, and the last with their reputations; and therefore it is somewhat difficult; and I doubt a method proposed by an ingenious lady, in a little book called *Advice to the Ladies,* would be found impracticable, for, saving my respect to the sex, the levity which perhaps is a little peculiar to them (at least in their youth) will not bear the restraint, and I am satisfied nothing but the height of bigotry can keep up a nunnery. . . . Wherefore the academy I propose should differ but little from public schools, wherein such ladies as were willing to study should have all the advantages of learning suitable to their genius.

But since some severities of discipline more than ordinary would be absolutely necessary to preserve the reputation of the house, that persons of quality and fortune might not be afraid to venture their children thither, I shall venture to make a small scheme by way of essay.

The house I would have built in a form by itself, as well

as in a place by itself. The building should be of three plain fronts, without any jettings or bearing-work, that the eye might at a glance see from one coin to the other; the gardens walled in the same triangular figure, with a large moat and but one entrance.

When thus every part of the situation was contrived as well as might be for discovery, and to render intriguing dangerous, I would have no guards, no eyes, no spies set over the ladies, but shall expect them to be tried by the principles of honor and strict virtue. . . .

Upon this ground I am persuaded such measures might be taken that the ladies might have all the freedom in the world within their own walls, and yet no intriguing, no indecencies, nor scandalous affairs happen; and, in order to this, the following customs and laws should be observed in the colleges, of which I would propose one at least in every county in England, and about ten for the city of London. After the regulation of the form of the building as before:—

1. All the ladies who enter into the house should set their hands to the orders of the house, to signify their consent to submit to them.

2. As no woman should be received but who declared herself willing, and that it was the act of her choice to enter herself, so no person should be confined to continue there a moment longer than the same voluntary choice inclined her.

3. The charges of the house being to be paid by the ladies, every one that entered should have only this encumbrance—that she should pay for the whole year, though her mind should change as to her continuance.

4. An act of Parliament should make it felony, without clergy, for any man to enter by force or fraud into the house, or to solicit any woman, though it were to marry, while she was in the house. And this law would by no means be severe, because any woman who was willing to receive the addresses of a man might discharge herself of the house when she pleased; and, on the contrary, any woman who had occasion might discharge herself of the impertinent addresses of any person she had an aversion to by entering into the house.

In this house the persons who enter should be taught all sorts of breeding suitable to both their genius and their quality, and, in particular, music and dancing, which it would be cruelty to bar the sex of, because they are their darlings; but, besides this, they should be taught languages, as particularly French and Italian; and I would venture the injury of giving a woman more tongues than one. They should, as a particular study, be taught all the graces of speech and all the necessary air of conversation, which our common education is so defective in that I need not expose it. They should be brought to read books, and especially history, and so to read as to make them understand the world and be able to know and judge of things when they hear of them. To such whose genius would lead them to it I would deny no sort of learning: but the chief thing in general is to cultivate the understandings of the sex, that they may be capable of all sorts of conversation; that, their parts and judgments being improved, they may be as profitable in their conversation as they are pleasant.

Women, in my observation, have little or no difference in them but as they are or are not distinguished by education. Tempers indeed may in some degree influence them, but the main distinguishing part is their breeding. The whole sex are generally quick and sharp; I believe I may be allowed to say generally so, for you rarely see them lumpish and heavy when they are children, as boys will often be. If a woman be well bred, and taught the proper management of her natural wit, she proves generally very sensible and retentive; and, without partiality, a woman of sense and manners is the finest and most delicate part of God's creation, the glory of her Maker, and the great instance of His singular regard to man (His darling creature), to whom He gave the best gift either God could bestow or man receive; and it is the sordidest piece of folly and ingratitude in the world to withhold from the sex the due lustre which the advantages of education gives to the natural beauty of their minds.

A woman well bred and well taught, furnished with the additional accomplishments of knowledge and behavior, is a creature without comparison: her society is the emblem of sublimer enjoyments; her person is angelic, and her conversation heavenly; she is all softness and sweetness, peace, love, wit, and delight; she is every way suitable to the sublimest wish, and the man that has such a one to his portion has nothing to do but to rejoice in her and be thankful.

On the other hand, suppose her to be the very same woman and rob her of the benefit of education, and it follows thus:—

If her temper be good, want of education makes her soft and easy. Her wit, for want of teaching, makes her impertinent and talkative. Her knowledge, for want of judgment and experience, makes her fanciful and whimsical. If her temper be bad, want of breeding makes her worse, and she grows haughty, insolent, and loud. If she be passionate, want of manners makes her a termagant and a scold, which is much at one with lunatic. If she be proud, want of discretion (which still is breeding) makes her conceited, fantastic, and ridiculous. And from these she degenerates to be turbulent, clamorous, noisy, nasty, and the devil.

Methinks mankind for their own sakes (since, say what we will of the women, we all think fit, one time or other, to be concerned with them) should take some care to breed them up to be suitable and serviceable, if they expected no such thing as delight from them. Bless us! what care do we take to breed up a good horse, and to break him well! and what a value do we put upon him when it is done!—and all because he should be fit for our use. And why not a woman?—since all her ornaments and beauty, without suitable behavior, is a cheat in nature, like the false tradesman who puts the best of his goods uppermost that the buyer may think the rest are of the same goodness.

Beauty of the body, which is the woman's glory, seems to be now unequally bestowed, and nature (or rather Providence) to lie under some scandal about it, as if it was given a woman for a snare to men and so make a kind of she-devil of her: because, they say, exquisite beauty is rarely given with wit, more rarely with goodness of temper, and never at all with modesty. And some, pretending to justify the equity of such a distribution, will tell us it is the effect of the justice of Providence in dividing particular excellences among all His creatures, share and share alike, as it were, that all might for something or other be acceptable to one another, else some would be despised.

I think both these notions false; and yet the last, which has the show of respect to Providence, is the worst, for it supposes Providence to be indigent and empty, as if it had not wherewith to furnish all the creatures it had made, but was fain to be parsimonious in its gifts, and distribute them by piece-meal, for fear of being exhausted. If I might venture my opinion against an almost universal notion, I would say most men mistake the proceedings of Providence in this case, and all the world at this day are mistaken in their practice about it. And because the assertion is very bold, I desire to explain myself.

That Almighty First Cause, Which made us all, is certainly the fountain of excellence, as It is of being, and by an invisible influence could have diffused equal qualities and perfections to all the creatures It has made, as the sun does its light, without the least ebb or diminution to Himself; and has given indeed to every individual sufficient to the figure His Providence had designed him in the world. I believe it might be defended if I should say that I do suppose God has given to all mankind equal gifts and capacities, in that He has given them all souls equally capable, and that the whole difference in mankind proceeds either from accidental difference in the make of their bodies or from the foolish difference of education.

1. From accidental difference in bodies.—I would avoid discoursing here of the philosophical position of the soul in the body: but if it be true, as philosophers do affirm, that the understanding and memory is dilated or contracted according to the accidental dimensions of the organ through which it is conveyed, then, though God has given a soul as capable to me as another, yet if I have any natural defect in those parts of the body by which the soul should act, I may have the same soul infused as another man, and yet he be a wise man

and I a very fool. For example, if a child naturally have a defect in the organ of hearing, so that he could never distinguish any sound, that child shall never be able to speak or read, though it have a soul capable of all the accomplishments in the world. The brain is the centre of the soul's actings, where all the distinguishing faculties of it reside; and it is observable a man who has a narrow, contracted head, in which there is not room for the due and necessary operations of nature by the brain, is never a man of very great judgment; and that proverb, "A great head and little wit," is not meant by nature, but is a reproof upon sloth, as if one should, by way of wonder, say, "Fie, fie, you that have a great head have but little wit; that 's strange! that must certainly be your own fault." From this notion I do believe there is a great matter in the breed of men and women; not that wise men shall always get wise children, but I believe strong and healthy bodies have the wisest children, and sickly, weakly bodies affect the wits as well as the bodies of their children. We are easily persuaded to believe this in the breeds of horses, cocks, dogs, and other creatures, and I believe it is as visible in men.

2. But to come closer to the business: the great distinguishing difference which is seen in the world between men and women is in their education, and this is manifested by comparing it with the difference between one man or woman and another. And herein it is that I take upon me to make such a bold assertion that all the world are mistaken in their practice about women; for I cannot think that God Almighty ever made them so delicate, so glorious creatures, and furnished them with such charms, so agreeable and so delightful to mankind, with souls capable of the same accomplishments with men, and all to be only stewards of our houses, cooks, and slaves.

Not that I am for exalting the female government in the least; but, in short, I would have men take women for companions, and educate them to be fit for it. A woman of sense and breeding will scorn as much to encroach upon the prerogative of the man as a man of sense will scorn to oppress the weakness of the woman. But if the women's souls were refined and improved by teaching, that word would be lost; to say "the weakness of the sex," as to judgment, would be nonsense, for ignorance and folly would be no more to be found among women than men. I remember a passage which I heard from a very fine woman. She had wit and capacity enough, an extraordinary shape and face, and a great fortune, but had been cloistered up all her time, and, for fear of being stolen, had not had the liberty of being taught the common necessary knowledge of women's affairs; and when she came to converse in the world, her natural wit made her so sensible of the want of education that she gave this short reflection on herself: "I am ashamed to talk with my very maids," says she, "for I don't know when they do right or wrong. I had more need go to school than be married."

I need not enlarge on the loss the defect of education is to the sex, nor argue the benefit of the contrary practice; it is a thing will be more easily granted than remedied. This chapter is but an essay at the thing; and I refer the practice to those happy days, if ever they shall be, when men shall be wise enough to mend it.

Samuel Johnson.

1709–1784.

SHAKESPEARE.

(From the *Preface to Shakespeare*, 1765.)

Shakespeare is, above all writers, at least above all modern writers, the poet of nature, the poet that holds up to his readers a faithful mirror of manners and of life. His characters are not modified by the customs of particular places, unpractised by the rest of the world, by the peculiarities of studies or professions, which can operate but upon small numbers, or by the accidents of transient fashions or temporary opinions; they are the genuine progeny of common humanity, such as the world will always supply and observation will always find. His persons act and speak by the influence of those general passions and principles by which all minds are agitated and the whole system of life is continued in motion. In the writings of other poets a character is too often an individual; in those of Shakespeare it is commonly a species.

It is from this wide extension of design that so much instruction is derived. It is this which fills the plays of Shakespeare with practical axioms and domestic wisdom. It was said of Euripides that every verse was a precept; and it may be said of Shakespeare that from his works may be collected a system of civil and economical prudence. Yet his real power is not shown in the splendor of particular passages, but by the progress of his fable and the tenor of his dialogue; and he that tries to recommend him by select quotations will succeed like the pedant in Hierocles, who, when he offered his house to sale, carried a brick in his pocket as a specimen.

It will not easily be imagined how much Shakespeare excels in accommodating his sentiments to real life but by comparing him with other authors. It was observed of the ancient schools of declamation that the more diligently they were frequented the more was the student disqualified for the world, because he found nothing there which he should ever meet in any other place. The same remark may be applied to every stage but that of Shakespeare. The theatre when it is under any other direction is peopled by such characters as were never seen, conversing in a language which was never heard, upon topics which will never arise in the commerce of mankind. But the dialogue of this author is often so evidently determined by the incident which produces it, and is pursued with so much ease and simplicity, that it seems scarcely to claim the merit of fiction but to have been gleaned by diligent selection out of common conversation and common occurrences.

Upon every other stage the universal agent is love, by whose power all good and evil is distributed and every action quickened or retarded. To bring a lover, a lady, and a rival into the fable; to entangle them in contradictory obligations, perplex them with oppositions of interest, and harass them with violence of desires inconsistent with each other; to make them meet in rapture and part in agony; to fill their mouths with hyperbolical joy and outrageous sorrow; to distress them as nothing human ever was distressed; to deliver them as nothing human ever was delivered; is the business of a modern dramatist. For this, probability is violated, life is misrepresented, and language is depraved. But love is only one of many passions; and as it has no great influence upon the sum of life, it has little operation in the dramas of a poet who caught his ideas from the living world and exhibited only what he saw before him. He knew that any other passion, as it was regular or exorbitant, was a cause of happiness or calamity.

Characters thus ample and general were not easily discriminated and preserved, yet perhaps no poet ever kept his personages more distinct from each other. I will not say, with Pope, that every speech may be assigned to the proper speaker, because many speeches there are which have nothing characteristical; but, perhaps, though some may be equally adapted to every person, it will be difficult to find that any can be properly transferred from the present possessor to another claimant. The choice is right when there is reason for choice.

Other dramatists can only gain attention by hyperbolical or aggravated characters, by fabulous and unexampled excellence or depravity, as the writers of barbarous romances invigorated the reader by a giant and a dwarf; and he that should form his expectations of human affairs from the play or from the tale would be equally deceived. Shakespeare has no heroes: his scenes are occupied only by men, who act and speak as the reader thinks that he should himself have spoken or acted on the same occasion; even where the agency is supernatural, the dialogue is level with life. Other writers disguise the most natural passions and most frequent incidents, so that he who contemplates them in the book will not know them in the world. Shakespeare approximates the remote and familiarizes the wonderful; the event which he represents will not happen, but if it were possible its effects would probably be such as he has assigned; and it may be said that he has not only shown human nature as it acts in real exigencies but as it would be found in trials to which it cannot be exposed.

This, therefore, is the praise of Shakespeare, that his drama is the mirror of life; that he who has mazed his imagination in following the phantoms which other writers raise up before him may here be cured of his delirious ecstasies by reading human sentiments in human language, by scenes from which a hermit may estimate the transactions of the world and a confessor predict the progress of the passions.

His adherence to general nature has exposed him to the censure of critics who form their judgments upon narrower principles. Dennis and Rymer think his Romans not sufficiently Roman, and Voltaire censures his kings as not completely royal. Dennis is offended that Menenius, a senator of Rome, should play the buffoon; and Voltaire perhaps thinks decency violated when the Danish usurper is represented as a drunkard. But Shakespeare always makes nature predominate over accident; and if he preserves the essential character, is not very careful of distinctions superinduced and adventitious. His story requires Romans or kings, but he thinks only on men. He knew that Rome, like every other city, had men of all dispositions; and, wanting a buffoon, he went into the senate-house for that which the senate-house would certainly have afforded him. He was inclined to show an usurper and a murderer not only odious but despicable; he therefore added drunkenness to his other qualities, knowing that kings love wine, like other men, and that wine exerts its natural powers upon kings. These are the petty cavils of petty minds. A poet overlooks the casual distinction of country and condition, as a painter, satisfied with the figure, neglects the drapery. . . .

Shakespeare, with his excellences, has likewise faults, and faults sufficient to obscure and overwhelm any other merit. I shall show them in the proportion in which they appear to me, without envious malignity or superstitious veneration. No question can be more innocently discussed than a dead poet's pretensions to renown, and little regard is due to that bigotry which sets candor higher than truth.

His first defect is that to which may be imputed most of the evil in books or in men. He sacrifices virtue to convenience, and is so much more careful to please than to instruct that he seems to write without any moral purpose. From his writings, indeed, a system of social duty may be selected, for he that thinks reasonably must think morally: but his precepts and axioms drop casually from him; he makes no just distribution of good or evil, nor is always careful to show in the virtuous a disapprobation of the wicked; he carries his persons indifferently through right and wrong, and at the close dismisses them without further care and leaves their examples to operate by chance. This fault the barbarity of his age cannot extenuate, for it is always a writer's duty to make the world better, and justice is a virtue independent on time or place.

The plots are often so loosely formed that a very slight consideration may improve them, and so carelessly pursued that he seems not always fully to comprehend his own design.

He omits opportunities of instructing or delighting, which the train of his story seems to force upon him, and apparently rejects those exhibitions which would be more affecting, for the sake of those which are more easy.

It may be observed that in many of his plays the latter part is evidently neglected. When he found himself near the end of his work and in view of his reward, he shortened the labor to snatch the profit. He therefore remits his efforts where he should most vigorously exert them, and his catastrophe is improbably produced or imperfectly represented.

He had no regard to distinction of time or place, but gives to one age or nation, without scruple, the customs, institutions, and opinions of another, at the expense not only of likelihood but of possibility. These faults Pope has endeavored, with more zeal than judgment, to transfer to his imagined interpolators. We need not wonder to find Hector quoting Aristotle, when we see the loves of Theseus and Hippolyta combined with the gothic mythology of fairies. Shakespeare, indeed, was not the only violator of chronology, for in the same age Sidney, who wanted not the advantages of learning, has, in his *Arcadia*, confounded the pastoral with the feudal times, the days of innocence, quiet, and security with those of turbulence, violence, and adventure.

In his comic scenes he is seldom very successful when he engages his characters in reciprocations of smartness and contests of sarcasm: their jests are commonly gross, and their pleasantry licentious; neither his gentlemen nor his ladies have much delicacy, nor are sufficiently distinguished from his clowns by any appearance of refined manners. Whether he represented the real conversation of his time is not easy to determine: the reign of Elizabeth is commonly supposed to have been a time of stateliness, formality, and reserve; yet perhaps the relaxations of that severity were not very elegant. There must, however, have been always some modes of gayety preferable to others, and a writer ought to choose the best.

In tragedy his performance seems constantly to be worse as his labor is more. The effusions of passion which exigence forces out are for the most part striking and energetic;

but whenever he solicits his invention or strains his faculties, the offspring of his throes is tumor, meanness, tediousness, and obscurity.

In narration he affects a disproportionate pomp of diction and a wearisome train of circumlocution, and tells the incident imperfectly in many words which might have been more plainly delivered in few. Narration in dramatic poetry is naturally tedious, as it is unanimated and inactive and obstructs the progress of the action; it should therefore always be rapid, and enlivened by frequent interruption. Shakespeare found it an incumbrance, and, instead of lightening it by brevity, endeavored to recommend it by dignity and splendor.

His declamations, or set speeches, are commonly cold and weak, for his power was the power of nature; when he endeavored, like other tragic writers, to catch opportunities of amplification, and, instead of inquiring what the occasion demanded, to show how much his stores of knowledge could supply, he seldom escapes without the pity or resentment of his reader.

It is incident to him to be now and then entangled with an unwieldy sentiment, which he cannot well express and will not reject; he struggles with it a while, and, if it continues stubborn, comprises it in words such as occur, and leaves it to be disentangled and evolved by those who have more leisure to bestow upon it. Not that always where the language is intricate the thought is subtle, or the image always great where the line is bulky; the equality of words to things is very often neglected, and trivial sentiments and vulgar ideas disappoint the attention, to which they are recommended by sonorous epithets and swelling figures.

But the admirers of this great poet have most reason to complain when he approaches nearest to his highest excellence, and seems fully resolved to sink them in dejection and mollify them with tender emotions by the fall of greatness, the danger of innocence, or the crosses of love. What he does best he soon ceases to do. He is not soft and pathetic without some idle conceit or contemptible equivocation. He no sooner begins to move than he counteracts himself; and terror and pity, as they are rising in the mind, are checked and blasted by sudden frigidity.

A quibble is to Shakespeare what luminous vapors are to the traveller: he follows it at all adventures; it is sure to lead him out of his way, and sure to engulf him in the mire. It has some malignant power over his mind, and its fascinations are irresistible. Whatever be the dignity or profundity of his disquisition, whether he be enlarging knowledge or exalting affection, whether he be amusing attention with incidents or enchaining it in suspense, let but a quibble spring up before him and he leaves his work unfinished. A quibble is the golden apple for which he will always turn aside from his career or stoop from his elevation. A quibble, poor and barren as it is, gave him such delight that he was content to purchase it by the sacrifice of reason, propriety, and truth. A quibble was to him the fatal Cleopatra for which he lost the world and was content to lose it.

It will be thought strange that in enumerating the defects of this writer I have not yet mentioned his neglect of the unities, his violation of those laws which have been instituted and established by the joint authority of poets and critics.

For his other deviations from the art of writing I resign him to critical justice without making any other demand in his favor than that which must be indulged to all human excellence—that his virtues be rated with his failings; but from the censure which this irregularity may bring upon him I shall, with due reverence to that learning which I must oppose, adventure to try how I can defend him.

His histories, being neither tragedies nor comedies, are not subject to any of their laws: nothing more is necessary to all the praise which they expect than that the changes of action be so prepared as to be understood, that the incidents be various and affecting, and the characters consistent, natural, and distinct. No other unity is intended, and therefore none is to be sought.

In his other works he has well enough preserved the unity of action. He has not, indeed, an intrigue regularly perplexed and regularly unravelled; he does not endeavor to hide his design only to discover it, for this is seldom the order of real events and Shakespeare is the poet of nature: but his plan has commonly, what Aristotle requires, a beginning, a middle, and an end; one event is concatenated with another, and the conclusion follows by easy consequence. There are perhaps some incidents that might be spared, as in other poets there is much talk that only fills up time upon the stage; but the general system makes gradual advances, and the end of the play is the end of expectation.

To the unities of time and place he has shown no regard; and perhaps a nearer view of the principles on which they stand will diminish their value and withdraw from them the veneration which, from the time of Corneille, they have very generally received, by discovering that they have given more trouble to the poet than pleasure to the auditor.

The necessity of observing the unities of time and place arises from the supposed necessity of making the drama credible. The critics hold it impossible that an action of months or years can be possibly believed to pass in three hours, or that the spectator can suppose himself to sit in the theatre while ambassadors go and return between distant kings, while armies are levied and towns besieged, while an exile wanders and returns, or till he whom they saw courting his mistress shall lament the untimely fall of his son. The mind revolts from evident falsehood, and fiction loses its force when it departs from the resemblance of reality. From the narrow limitation of time necessarily arises the contraction of place. The spectator, who knows that he saw the first act at Alexandria, cannot suppose that he sees the next at Rome, at a distance to which not the dragons of Medea could in so short a time have transported him; he knows with certainty that he has not changed his place, and he knows that place cannot change itself—that what was a house cannot become a plain, that what was Thebes can never be Persepolis.

Such is the triumphant language with which a critic exults over the misery of an irregular poet, and exults commonly without resistance or reply. It is time, therefore, to tell him, by the authority of Shakespeare, that he assumes, as an unquestionable principle, a position which, while his breath is forming it into words, his understanding pronounces to be false. It is false that any representation is mistaken for reality, that any dramatic fable in its materiality was ever credible or for a single moment was ever credited.

The objection arising from the impossibility of passing the first hour at Alexandria and the next at Rome, supposes that, when the play opens, the spectator really imagines himself at Alexandria, and believes that his walk to the theatre has been a voyage to Egypt and that he lives in the days of Antony and Cleopatra. Surely he that imagines this may imagine more. He that can take the stage at one time for the palace of the Ptolemies, may take it in half an hour for the promontory of Actium. Delusion, if delusion be admitted, has no certain limitation; if the spectator can be once persuaded that his old acquaintance are Alexander and Cæsar, that a room illuminated with candles is the plain of Pharsalia or the bank of Granicus, he is in a state of elevation above the reach of reason or of truth, and from the heights of empyrean poetry may despise the circumscriptions of terrestrial nature. There is no reason why a mind thus wandering in ecstasy should count the clock, or why an hour should not be a century in that calenture of the brain that can make the stage a field.

The truth is that the spectators are always in their senses, and know, from the first act to the last, that the stage is only a stage and that the players are only players. They came to hear a certain number of lines recited with just gesture and elegant modulation. The lines relate to some action, and an action must be in some place; but the different actions that complete a story may be in places very remote from each other; and where is the absurdity of allowing that space to represent first Athens and then Sicily, which was always known to be neither Sicily nor Athens but a modern theatre?

By supposition, as place is introduced, time may be extended; the time required by the fable elapses for the most part between the acts, for of so much of the action as is represented the real and poetical duration is the same. If in the first act preparations for war against Mithridates are represented to be made in Rome, the event of the war may without absurdity be represented, in the catastrophe, as happening in Pontus: we know that there is neither war nor preparation for war; we know that we are neither in Rome nor Pontus, that neither Mithridates nor Lucullus are before us. The drama exhibits successive imitations of successive actions; and why may not the second imitation represent an action that happened years after the first, if it be so connected with it that nothing but time can be supposed to intervene? Time is, of all modes of existence, most obsequious to the imagination; a lapse of years is as easily conceived as a passage of hours. In contemplation we easily contract the time of real actions, and therefore willingly permit it to be contracted when we only see their imitation.

It will be asked how the drama moves if it is not credited. It is credited with all the credit due to a drama. It is credited, whenever it moves, as a just picture of a real original, as representing to the auditor what he would himself feel if he were to do or suffer what is there feigned to be suffered or to be done. The reflection that strikes the heart is not that the evils before us are real evils, but that they are evils to which we ourselves may be exposed. If there be any fallacy, it is not that we fancy the players, but that we fancy ourselves, unhappy for a moment; but we rather lament the possibility than suppose the presence of misery, as a mother weeps over her babe when she remembers that death may take it from her. The delight of tragedy proceeds from our consciousness of fiction; if we thought murders and treasons real, they would please no more. . . .

Voltaire expresses his wonder that our author's extravagances are endured by a nation which has seen the tragedy of *Cato*. Let him be answered that Addison speaks the language of poets, and Shakespeare of men. We find in *Cato* innumerable beauties which enamor us of its author, but we see nothing that acquaints us with human sentiments or human actions; we place it with the fairest and the noblest progeny which judgment propagates by conjunction with learning, but *Othello* is the vigorous and vivacious offspring of observation impregnated by genius. *Cato* affords a splendid exhibition of artificial and fictitious manners, and delivers just and noble sentiments, in diction easy, elevated, and harmonious, but its hopes and fears communicate no vibration to the heart; the composition refers us only to the writer; we pronounce the name of *Cato*, but we think on Addison.

The work of a correct and regular writer is a garden accurately formed and diligently planted, varied with shades, and scented with flowers: the composition of Shakespeare is a forest, in which oaks extend their branches, and pines tower in the air, interspersed sometimes with weeds and brambles, and sometimes giving shelter to myrtles and to roses; filling the eye with awful pomp, and gratifying the mind with endless diversity. Other poets display cabinets of precious rarities, minutely finished, wrought into shape, and polished into brightness. Shakespeare opens a mine which contains gold and diamonds in unexhaustible plenty, though clouded by incrustations, debased by impurities, and mingled with a mass of meaner materials.

Oliver Goldsmith.

1728–1774.

BEAU TIBBS, A CHARACTER.

(From *Essays*, 1765.)

Though naturally pensive, yet I am fond of gay company and take every opportunity of thus dismissing the mind from duty. From this motive I am often found in the centre of a crowd, and wherever pleasure is to be sold am always a purchaser. In those places, without being remarked by any, I join in whatever goes forward, work my passions into a similitude of frivolous earnestness, shout as they shout, and condemn as they happen to disapprove. A mind thus sunk for a while below its natural standard is qualified for stronger flights, as those first retire who would spring forward with greater vigor.

Attracted by the serenity of the evening, a friend and I lately went to gaze upon the company in one of the public walks near the city. Here we sauntered together for some time, either praising the beauty of such as were handsome or the dresses of such as had nothing else to recommend them. We had gone thus deliberately forward for some time, when my friend, stopping on a sudden, caught me by the elbow and led me out of the public walk. I could perceive, by the quickness of his pace and by his frequently looking behind, that he was attempting to avoid somebody who followed. We now turned to the right, then to the left. As we went forward, he still went faster, but in vain: the person whom he attempted to escape hunted us through every doubling, and gained upon us each moment; so that at last we fairly stood still, resolving to face what we could not avoid.

Our pursuer soon came up, and joined us with all the familiarity of an old acquaintance. "My dear Charles," cries he, shaking my friend's hand, "where have you been hiding this half a century? Positively I had fancied you were gone down to cultivate matrimony and your estate in the country." During the reply I had an opportunity of surveying the appearance of our new companion. His hat was pinched up with peculiar smartness; his looks were pale, thin, and sharp; round his neck he wore a broad black ribbon, and in his bosom a buckle studded with glass; his coat was trimmed with tarnished twist; he wore by his side a sword with a black hilt; and his stockings of silk, though newly washed, were grown yellow by long service. I was so much engaged with the peculiarity of his dress that I attended only to the latter part of my friend's reply, in which he complimented Mr. Tibbs on the taste of his clothes and the bloom in his countenance. "Pshaw, pshaw, Charles!" cried the figure, "no more of that if you love me. You know I hate flattery—on my soul I do; and yet, to be sure, an intimacy with the great will improve one's appearance, and a course of venison will fatten. And yet, faith, I despise the great as much as you do; but there are a great many damned honest fellows among them, and we must not quarrel with one half because the other wants breeding. If they were all such as my Lord Mudler, one of the most good-natured creatures that ever squeezed a lemon, I should myself be among the number of their admirers. I was yesterday to dine at the Duchess of Piccadilly's. My lord was there. 'Ned,' says he to me, 'Ned,' says he, 'I 'll hold gold to silver I can tell where you were poaching last night.' 'Poaching, my lord!' says I; 'faith, you have missed already; for I stayed at home, and let the girls poach for me. That 's my way; I take a fine woman as some animals do their prey—stand still, and, swoop, they fall into my mouth.'"

"Ah, Tibbs, thou art an happy fellow," cried my companion, with looks of infinite pity. "I hope your fortune is as much improved as your understanding in such company?" "Improved!" replied the other; "you shall know—but let it go no further—a great secret—five hundred a year to begin with. My lord's word of honor for it. His lordship took me down in his own chariot yesterday, and we had a *tête-à-tête* dinner in the country, where we talked of nothing else." "I fancy you forgot, sir," cried I, "you told us but this moment of your dining yesterday in town!" "Did I say so?" replied he coolly; "to be sure, if I said so, it was so—dined in town. Egad, now I do remember, I did dine in town; but I dined in the country too; for you must know, my boys, I eat two dinners. By-the-bye, I am grown as nice as the devil in my eating. I 'll tell you a pleasant affair about that. We were a select party of us to dine at Lady Grogram's, an affected piece, but let it go no farther—a secret. 'Well,' says I, 'I 'll hold a thousand guineas, and say done first, that'—But dear Charles, you are an honest creature; lend me half a crown for a minute or two, or so, just till—But harkee, ask me for it the next time we meet, or it may be twenty to one but I forget to pay you."

When he left us, our conversation naturally turned upon so extraordinary a character. "His very dress," cries my friend, "is not less extraordinary than his conduct. If you meet him this day, you find him in rags; if the next, in embroidery. With those persons of distinction of whom he talks so familiarly he has scarce a coffee-house acquaintance. However, both for the interests of society, and perhaps for his own, Heaven has made him poor; and while all the world perceives his wants, he fancies them concealed from every eye. An agreeable companion, because he understands flattery; and all must be pleased with the first part of his conversation, though all are sure of its ending with a demand on their purse. While his youth countenances the levity of his conduct, he may thus earn a precarious subsistence; but when age comes on, the gravity of which is incompatible with buffoonery, then will he find himself forsaken by all, condemned in the decline of life to hang upon some rich family whom he once despised, there to undergo all the ingenuity of studied contempt, to be employed only as a spy upon the servants or a bugbear to frighten children into duty."

There are some acquaintances whom it is no easy matter to

shake off. My little beau yesterday overtook me again in one of the public walks, and, slapping me on the shoulder, saluted me with an air of the most perfect familiarity. His dress was the same as usual, except that he had more powder in his hair, wore a dirtier shirt, and had on a pair of temple spectacles, with his hat under his arm.

As I knew him to be an harmless, amusing little thing, I could not return his smiles with any degree of severity; so we walked forward on terms of the utmost intimacy, and in a few minutes discussed all the usual topics of a general conversation.

The oddities that marked his character, however, soon began to appear. He bowed to several well-dressed persons, who, by their manner of returning the compliment, appeared perfect strangers. At intervals he drew out a pocket-book, seeming to take memorandums before all the company, with much importance and assiduity. In this manner he led me through the length of the whole Mall, fretting at his absurdities, and fancying myself laughed at as well as he by every spectator.

When we were got to the end of our procession, "Blast me," cries he, with an air of vivacity, "I never saw the Park so thin in my life before! there 's no company at all to-day; not a single face to be seen." "No company!" interrupted I, peevishly; "no company where there is such a crowd? Why, man, there is too much. What are the thousands that have been laughing at us but company?" "Lord, my dear," returned he, with the utmost good humor, "you seem immensely chagrined; but, blast me, when the world laughs at me, I laugh at the world, and so we are even. My Lord Trip, Bill Squash the Creolian, and I sometimes make a party at being ridiculous. But I see you are grave; so if you are for a fine, grave, sentimental companion, you shall dine with my wife to-day; I must insist on't; I'll introduce you to Mrs. Tibbs, a lady of as elegant qualifications as any in nature; she was bred—but that 's between ourselves—under the inspection of the Countess of Shoreditch. A charming body of voice!—but no more of that, she shall give us a song. You shall see my little girl too, Carolina Wilhelmina Amelia Tibbs, a sweet, pretty creature. I design her for my Lord Drumstick's eldest son—but that 's in friendship; let it go no farther. She 's but six years old, and yet she walks a minuet and plays on the guitar immensely, already. I intend she shall be as perfect as possible in every accomplishment. In the first place I'll make her a scholar; I'll teach her Greek myself, and I intend to learn that language purposely to instruct her—but let that be a secret."

Thus saying, without waiting for a reply he took me by the arm and hauled me along. We passed through many dark alleys and winding ways; for, from some motives to me unknown, he seemed to have a particular aversion to every frequented street. At last, however, we got to the door of a dismal-looking house in the outlets of the town, where he informed me he chose to reside for the benefit of the air.

We entered the lower door, which seemed ever to lie most hospitably open, and I began to ascend an old and creaking staircase; when, as he mounted to show me the way, he demanded whether I delighted in prospects; to which answering in the affirmative, "Then," says he, "I shall show you one of the most charming out of my windows; we shall see the ships sailing, and the whole country for twenty miles round, tip-top, quite high. My Lord Swamp would give ten thousand guineas for such a one; but, as I sometimes pleasantly tell him, I always love to keep my prospects at home, that my friends may come to see me the oftener."

By this time we were arrived as high as the stairs would permit us to ascend, till we came to what he was facetiously pleased to call the first floor down the chimney; and knocking at the door, a voice with a Scotch accent, from within, demanded, "Wha's there?" My conductor answered that it was him. But this not satisfying the querist, the voice again repeated the demand; to which he answered louder than before, and now the door was opened by an old maid-servant with cautious reluctance.

When we were got in, he welcomed me to his house with great ceremony, and, turning to the old woman, asked where her lady was. "Good troth," replied she, in the Northern dialect, "she 's washing your twa shirts at the next door, because they have taken an oath against lending out the tub any longer." "My two shirts," cries he, in a tone that faltered with confusion; "what does the idiot mean?" "I ken what I mean well enough," replied the other; "she 's washing your twa shirts at the next door, because——" "Fire and fury! no more of thy stupid explanations!" cried he. "Go and inform her we have got company. Were that Scotch hag," continued he, turning to me, "to be forever in my family, she would never learn politeness, nor forget that absurd, poisonous accent of hers, or testify the smallest specimen of breeding or high life; and yet it is very surprising too, as I had her from a Parliament man, a friend of mine, from the Highlands, one of the politest men in the world; but that 's a secret."

We waited some time for Mrs. Tibbs's arrival, during which interval I had a full opportunity of surveying the chamber and all its furniture; which consisted of four chairs with old wrought bottoms, that he assured me were his wife's embroidery; a square table that had been once japanned; a cradle in one corner, a lumbering cabinet in the other; a broken shepherdess and a mandarin without an head were stuck over the chimney; and round the walls several paltry, unframed pictures, which he observed were all of his own drawing. "What do you think, sir, of that head in the corner, done in the manner of Grisoni? There's the true keeping in it. It 's my own face; and though there happens to be no likeness, a countess offered me an hundred for its fellow. I refused her, for, hang it, that would be mechanical, you know."

The wife at last made her appearance—at once a slattern and a coquette; much emaciated, but still carrying the remains of beauty. She made twenty apologies for being seen in such an odious dishabille, but hoped to be excused, as she had stayed out all night at Vauxhall Gardens with the countess, who was excessively fond of the horns. "And indeed, my dear," added she, turning to her husband, "his lordship drank your health in a bumper." "Poor Jack," cries he, "a dear, good-natured creature; I know he loves me. But I hope, my dear, you have given orders for dinner. You need make no great preparations, neither; there are but three of us. Something elegant and little will do: a turbot, an ortolan, or a——" "Or what do you think, my dear," interrupts the wife, "of a nice, pretty bit of ox-cheek, piping hot, and dressed with a little of my own sauce?" "The very thing," replies he; "it will eat best with some smart bottled beer; but be sure to let 's have the sauce his grace was so fond of. I hate your immense loads of meat; that is country all over—extreme disgusting to those who are in the least acquainted with high life."

By this time my curiosity began to abate and my appetite to increase; the company of fools may at first make us smile, but at last never fails of rendering us melancholy. I therefore pretended to recollect a prior engagement, and, after having shown my respects to the house by giving the old servant a piece of money at the door, I took my leave, Mr. Tibbs assuring me that dinner, if I stayed, would be ready at least in less than two hours.

Edmund Burke.

1729 (?)–1797.

ENGLAND AND THE FRENCH REVOLUTION.

(From *Reflections on the Revolution in France*, 1790.)

Dear Sir,

You are pleased to call again, and with some earnestness, for my thoughts on the late proceedings in France. I will not give you reason to imagine that I think my sentiments of such value as to wish myself to be solicited about them. They are of too little consequence to be very anxiously either communicated or withheld. It was from attention to you, and to you only, that I hesitated at the time when you first desired to receive them. In the first letter I had the honor to write to you, and which at length I send, I wrote neither for nor from any description of men; nor shall I in this. My errors, if any, are my own. My reputation alone is to answer for them.

You see, sir, by the long letter I have transmitted to you, that, though I do most heartily wish that France may be animated by a spirit of rational liberty, and that I think you bound, in all honest policy, to provide a permanent body in which that spirit may reside and an effectual organ by which it may act, it is my misfortune to entertain great doubts concerning several material points in your late transactions.

You imagined, when you wrote last, that I might possibly be reckoned among the approvers of certain proceedings in France, from the solemn public seal of sanction they have received from two clubs of gentlemen in London, called the Constitutional Society and the Revolution Society.

I certainly have the honor to belong to more clubs than one in which the Constitution of this kingdom and the principles of the glorious Revolution are held in high reverence;

and I reckon myself among the most forward in my zeal for maintaining that Constitution and those principles in their utmost purity and vigor. It is because I do so that I think it necessary for me that there should be no mistake. Those who cultivate the memory of our Revolution, and those who are attached to the Constitution of this kingdom, will take good care how they are involved with persons, who under the pretext of zeal towards the Revolution and Constitution, too frequently wander from their true principles and are ready on every occasion to depart from the firm but cautious and deliberate spirit which produced the one and which presides in the other. Before I proceed to answer the more material particulars in your letter, I shall beg leave to give you such information as I have been able to obtain of the two clubs which have thought proper, as bodies, to interfere in the concerns of France, first assuring you that I am not and that I have never been a member of either of those societies.

The first, calling itself the Constitutional Society, or Society for Constitutional Information, or by some such title, is, I believe, of seven or eight years' standing. The institution of this society appears to be of a charitable, and so far of a laudable, nature: it was intended for the circulation, at the expense of the members, of many books which few others would be at the expense of buying, and which might lie on the hands of the booksellers, to the great loss of an useful body of men. Whether the books so charitably circulated were ever as charitably read is more than I know. Possibly several of them have been exported to France, and, like goods not in request here, may with you have found a market. I have heard much talk of the lights to be drawn from books that are sent from hence. What improvements they have had in their passage (as it is said some liquors are meliorated by crossing the sea) I cannot tell: but I never heard a man of common judgment or the least degree of information speak a word in praise of the greater part of the publications circulated by that society; nor have their proceedings been accounted, except by some of themselves, as of any serious consequence.

Your National Assembly seems to entertain much the same opinion that I do of this poor charitable club. As a nation you reserved the whole stock of your eloquent acknowledgments for the Revolution Society, when their fellows in the Constitutional were in equity entitled to some share. Since you have selected the Revolution Society as the great object of your national thanks and praises, you will think me excusable in making its late conduct the subject of my observations. The National Assembly of France has given importance to these gentlemen by adopting them; and they return the favor by acting as a committee in England for extending the principles of the National Assembly. Henceforward we must consider them as a kind of privileged persons, as no inconsiderable members in the diplomatic body. This is one among the revolutions which have given splendor to obscurity, and distinction to undiscerned merit. Until very lately I do not recollect to have heard of this club. I am quite sure that it never occupied a moment of my thoughts, nor, I believe, those of any person out of their own set. I find, upon inquiry, that on the anniversary of the Revolution in 1688 a club of dissenters, but of what denomination I know not, have long had the custom of hearing a sermon in one of their churches, and that afterwards they spent the day cheerfully, as other clubs do, at the tavern. But I never heard that any public measure or political system, much less that the merits of the constitution of any foreign nation, had been the subject of a formal proceeding at their festivals, until, to my inexpressible surprise, I found them in a sort of public capacity, by a congratulatory address, giving an authoritative sanction to the proceedings of the National Assembly in France.

In the ancient principles and conduct of the club, so far at least as they were declared, I see nothing to which I could take exception. I think it very probable that, for some purpose, new members may have entered among them; and that some truly Christian politicians, who love to dispense benefits but are careful to conceal the hand which distributes the dole, may have made them the instruments of their pious designs. Whatever I may have reason to suspect concerning private management, I shall speak of nothing as of a certainty but what is public.

For one I should be sorry to be thought, directly or indirectly, concerned in their proceedings. I certainly take my full share, along with the rest of the world, in my individual and private capacity, in speculating on what has been done or is doing on the public stage, in any place ancient or modern, in the republic of Rome or the republic of Paris; but, having no general apostolical mission, being a citizen of a particular state, and being bound up, in a considerable degree, by its public will, I should think it at least improper and irregular for me to open a formal public correspondence with the actual government of a foreign nation, without the express authority of the government under which I live.

I should be still more unwilling to enter into that correspondence under anything like an equivocal description, which to many, unacquainted with our usages, might make the address in which I joined appear as the act of persons in some sort of corporate capacity, acknowledged by the laws of this kingdom and authorized to speak the sense of some part of it. On account of the ambiguity and uncertainty of unauthorized general descriptions, and of the deceit which may be practised under them, and not from mere formality, the House of Commons would reject the most sneaking petition for the most trifling object, under that mode of signature to which you have thrown open the folding-doors of your presence chamber and have ushered into your National Assembly, with as much ceremony and parade and with as great a bustle of applause as if you had been visited by the whole representative majesty of the whole English nation. If what this society has thought proper to send forth had been a piece of argument, it would have signified little whose argument it was. It would be neither the more nor the less convincing on account of the party it came from. But this is only a vote and resolution. It stands solely on authority; and in this case it is the mere authority of individuals, few of whom appear. Their signatures ought, in my opinion, to have been annexed to their instrument. The world would then have the means of knowing how many they are, who they are, and of what value their opinions may be, from their personal abilities, from their knowledge, their experience, or their lead and authority in this state. To me, who am but a plain man, the proceeding looks a little too refined and too ingenious; it has too much the air of a political stratagem, adopted for the sake of giving, under an high-sounding name, an importance to the public declarations of this club, which, when the matter came to be closely inspected, they did not altogether so well deserve. It is a policy that has very much the complexion of a fraud.

I flatter myself that I love a manly, moral, regulated liberty as well as any gentleman of that society, be he who he will; and perhaps I have given as good proofs of my attachment to that cause, in the whole course of my public conduct. I think I envy liberty as little as they do, to any other nation. But I cannot stand forward and give praise or blame to anything which relates to human actions and human concerns on a simple view of the object, as it stands stripped of every relation, in all the nakedness and solitude of metaphysical abstraction. Circumstances (which with some gentlemen pass for nothing) give in reality to every political principle its distinguishing color and discriminating effect. The circumstances are what render every civil and political scheme beneficial or noxious to mankind. Abstractedly speaking, government, as well as liberty, is good; yet could I, in common sense, ten years ago, have felicitated France on her enjoyment of a government (for she then had a government), without inquiry what the nature of that government was or how it was administered? Can I now congratulate the same nation upon its freedom? Is it because liberty in the abstract may be classed amongst the blessings of mankind that I am seriously to felicitate a madman, who has escaped from the protecting restraint and wholesome darkness of his cell, on his restoration to the enjoyment of light and liberty? Am I to congratulate an highwayman and murderer, who has broke prison, upon the recovery of his natural rights? This would be to act over again the scene of the criminals condemned to the galleys, and their heroic deliverer, the metaphysic Knight of the Sorrowful Countenance.

When I see the spirit of liberty in action, I see a strong principle at work; and this, for a while, is all I can possibly know of it. The wild gas, the fixed air, is plainly broke loose; but we ought to suspend our judgment until the first effervescence is a little subsided, till the liquor is cleared, and until we see something deeper than the agitation of a troubled and frothy surface. I must be tolerably sure, before I venture publicly to congratulate men upon a blessing, that they have really received one. Flattery corrupts both the receiver and the giver, and adulation is not of more service to the people than to kings. I should therefore suspend my congratulations on the new liberty of France until I was informed how it had been combined with government, with public force, with the discipline and obedience of armies, with the collection of an effective and well-distributed revenue, with morality and religion, with the solidity of property, with peace and order, with civil and social manners. All these (in their way) are good things too; and without them liberty is not a benefit whilst it lasts, and is not likely to continue long. The effect of liberty to individuals is that they may do what they please: we ought to see what it will please them to do, before we risk congratulations which may be soon turned into complaints. Prudence would dictate this in the case of separate, insulated, private men; but liberty when men act in bodies is power. Considerate people, before they declare themselves, will observe the use which is made of power; and particularly of so trying a thing as new power in new persons, of whose principles, tempers, and dispositions they have little or no experience, and in situations where those who appear the most stirring in the scene may possibly not be the real movers.

All these considerations, however, were below the transcendental dignity of the Revolution Society. Whilst I continued in the country, from whence I had the honor of writing to you, I had but an imperfect idea of their transactions. On my coming to town I sent for an account of their proceedings, which had been published by their authority, containing a sermon of Dr. Price, with the Duke de Rochefoucault's and the Archbishop of Aix's letter, and several other documents annexed. The whole of that publication, with the manifest design of connecting the affairs of France with those of England by drawing us into an imitation of the conduct of the National Assembly, gave me a considerable degree of uneasiness. The effect of that conduct upon the power, credit, prosperity, and tranquillity of France became every day more evident. The form of constitution to be settled, for its future polity, became more clear. We are now in a condition to discern with tolerable exactness the true nature of the object held up to our imitation. If the prudence of reserve and decorum dictates silence in some circumstances, in others prudence of an higher order may justify us in speaking our thoughts. The beginnings of confusion with us in England are at present feeble enough; but with you we have seen an infancy still more feeble growing by moments into a strength to heap mountains upon mountains and to wage war with Heaven itself. Whenever our neighbor's house is on fire, it cannot be amiss for the engines to play a little on our own. Better to be despised for too anxious apprehensions than ruined by too confident a security.

Solicitous chiefly for the peace of my own country, but by no means unconcerned for yours, I wish to communicate more largely what was at first intended only for your private satisfaction. I shall still keep your affairs in my eye, and continue to address myself to you. Indulging myself in the freedom of epistolary intercourse, I beg leave to throw out my thoughts and express my feelings just as they arise in my mind, with very little attention to formal method. I set out with the proceedings of the Revolution Society, but I shall not confine myself to them. Is it possible I should? It looks to me as if I were in a great crisis, not of the affairs of France alone, but of all Europe, perhaps of more than Europe. All circumstances taken together, the French Revolution is the most astonishing that has hitherto happened in the world. The most wonderful things are brought about, in many instances, by means the most absurd and ridiculous, in the most ridiculous modes, and apparently by the most contemptible instruments. Everything seems out of nature in this strange chaos of levity and ferocity and of all sorts of crimes jumbled together with all sorts of follies. In viewing this monstrous tragi-comic scene, the most opposite passions necessarily succeed, and sometimes mix with each other in the mind: alternate laughter and tears, alternate scorn and horror.

It cannot, however, be denied that to some this strange scene appeared in quite another point of view. Into them it inspired no other sentiments than those of exultation and rapture. They saw nothing in what has been done in France but a firm and temperate exertion of freedom; so consistent, on the whole, with morals and with piety as to make it deserving not only of the secular applause of dashing Machiavellian politicians, but to render it a fit theme for all the devout effusions of sacred eloquence.

On the forenoon of the fourth of November last, Dr. Richard Price, a non-conforming minister of eminence, preached at the dissenting meeting-house of the Old Jewry, to his club or society, a very extraordinary miscellaneous sermon, in which there are some good moral and religious sentiments, and not ill expressed, mixed up in a sort of porridge of various political opinions and reflections; but the Revolution in France is the grand ingredient in the caldron. I consider the address transmitted by the Revolution Society to the National Assembly, through Earl Stanhope, as originating in the principles of the sermon and as a corollary from them. It was moved by the preacher of that discourse. It was passed by those who came reeking from the effect of the sermon, without any censure or qualification, expressed or implied. If, however, any of the gentlemen concerned shall wish to separate the sermon from the resolution, they know how to acknowledge the one and to disavow the other. They may do it: I cannot. For my part, I looked on that sermon as the public declaration of a man much connected with literary caballers and intriguing philosophers, with political theologians and theological politicians, both at home and abroad. I know they set him up as a sort of oracle; because, with the best intentions in the world, he naturally philippizes, and chants his prophetic song in exact unison with their designs.

That sermon is in a strain which I believe has not been heard in this kingdom, in any of the pulpits which are tolerated or encouraged in it, since the year 1648, when a predecessor of Dr. Price, the Rev. Hugh Peters, made the vault of the king's own chapel at St. James's ring with the honor and privilege of the saints, who, with the "high praises of God in their mouths and a two-edged sword in their hands, were to execute judgment on the heathen and punishments upon the people, to bind their kings with chains and their nobles with fetters of iron." Few harangues from the pulpit, except in the days of your league in France or in the days of our solemn league and covenant in England, have ever breathed less of the spirit of moderation than this lecture in the Old Jewry. Supposing, however, that something like moderation were visible in this political sermon, yet politics and the pulpit are terms that have little agreement. No sound ought to be heard in the Church but the healing voice of Christian charity. The cause of civil liberty and civil government gains as little as that of religion by this confusion of duties. Those who quit their proper character, to assume what does not belong to them, are, for the greater part, ignorant both of the character they leave and of the character they assume. Wholly unacquainted with the world in which they are so fond of meddling, and inexperienced in all its affairs on which they pronounce with so much confidence, they have nothing of politics but the passions they excite. Surely the Church is a place where one day's truce ought to be allowed to the dissensions and animosities of mankind.

This pulpit style, revived after so long a discontinuance, had to me the air of novelty, and of a novelty not wholly without danger. I do not charge this danger equally to every part of the discourse. The hint given to a noble and reverend lay-divine, who is supposed high in office in one of our universities, and to other lay-divines "of rank and literature," may be proper and seasonable, though somewhat new. If the noble seekers should find nothing to satisfy their pious fancies in the old staple of the National Church or in all the rich variety to be found in the well-assorted warehouses of the dissenting congregations, Dr. Price advises them to improve upon non-conformity, and to set up, each of them, a separate meeting-house upon his own particular principles. It is somewhat remarkable that this reverend divine should be so earnest for setting up new churches, and so perfectly indifferent concerning the doctrine which may be taught in them. His zeal is of a curious character. It is not for the propagation of his own opinions, but of any opinions. It is not for the diffusion of truth, but for the spreading of contradiction. Let the noble teachers but dissent, it is no matter from whom or from what. This great point once secured, it is taken for granted their religion will be rational and manly. I doubt whether religion would reap all the benefits which the calculating divine computes from this "great company of great preachers." It would certainly be a valuable addition of nondescripts to the ample collection of known classes, genera, and species, which at present beautify the *hortus siccus* of dissent. A sermon from a noble duke or a noble marquis or a noble earl or baron bold would certainly increase and diversify the amusements of this town, which begins to grow satiated with the uniform round of its vapid dissipations. I should only stipulate that these new Mess-Johns in robes and coronets should keep some sort of bounds in the democratic and levelling principles which are expected from their titled pulpits. The new evangelists will, I dare say, disappoint the hopes that are conceived of them. They will not become, literally as well as figuratively, polemic divines, nor be disposed so to drill their congregations that they may, as in former blessed times, preach their doctrines to regiments of dragoons and corps of infantry and artillery. Such arrangements, however favorable to the cause of compulsory freedom, civil and religious, may not be equally conducive to the national tranquillity. These few restrictions I hope are no great stretches of intolerance, no very violent exertions of despotism.

But I may say of our preacher, "Utinam nugis tota illa dedisset tempora sævitiæ." All things in this his fulminating bull are not of so innoxious a tendency. His doctrines affect our Constitution in its vital parts. He tells the Revolution Society, in this political sermon, that his Majesty "is almost the only lawful king in the world, because the only one who owes his crown to the choice of his people." As to the kings of the world, all of whom (except one) this archpontiff of the rights of men, with all the plenitude and with more than the boldness of the papal deposing power in its meridian fervor of the twelfth century, puts into one sweeping clause of ban and anathema, and proclaims usurpers by circles of longitude and latitude, over the whole globe, it behooves them to consider how they admit into their territories these apostolic missionaries, who are to tell their subjects they are not lawful kings. That is their concern. It is ours, as a domestic interest of some moment, seriously to consider the solidity of the only principle upon which these gentlemen acknowledge a king of Great Britain to be entitled to their allegiance.

This doctrine, as applied to the prince now on the British throne, either is nonsense and therefore neither true nor false, or it affirms a most unfounded, dangerous, illegal, and unconstitutional position. According to this spiritual doctor of politics, if his Majesty does not owe his crown to the choice of his people he is no lawful king. Now, nothing can be more untrue than that the crown of this kingdom is so held by his Majesty. Therefore, if you follow their rule, the king of Great Britain, who most certainly does not owe his high office to any form of popular election, is in no respect better than the rest of the gang of usurpers who reign, or rather rob, all over the face of this our miserable world, without any sort of right or title to the allegiance of their people. The policy of this general doctrine, so qualified, is evident enough.

The propagators of this political gospel are in hopes their abstract principle (their principle that a popular choice is necessary to the legal existence of the sovereign magistracy) would be overlooked whilst the king of Great Britain was not affected by it. In the meantime the ears of their congregations would be gradually habituated to it as if it were a first principle admitted without dispute. For the present it would only operate as a theory, pickled in the preserving juices of pulpit eloquence and laid by for future use. "Condo et compono quæ mox depromere possim." By this policy, whilst our government is soothed with a reservation in its favor to which it has no claim, the security which it has in common with all governments, so far as opinion is security, is taken away.

Thus these politicians proceed whilst little notice is taken of their doctrines; but when they come to be examined upon the plain meaning of their words and the direct tendency of their doctrines, then equivocations and slippery constructions come into play. When they say the king owes his crown to the choice of his people and is therefore the only lawful sovereign in the world, they will perhaps tell us they mean to say no more than that some of the king's predecessors have been called to the throne by some sort of choice and therefore he owes his crown to the choice of his people. Thus by a miserable subterfuge they hope to render their proposition safe by rendering it nugatory. They are welcome to the asylum they seek for their offence, since they take refuge in their folly. For if you admit this interpretation, how does their idea of election differ from our idea of inheritance? and how does the settlement of the crown in the Brunswick line derived from James the First come to legalize our monarchy rather than that of any of the neighboring countries? At some time or other, to be sure, all the beginners of dynasties were chosen by those who called them to govern. There is ground enough for the opinion that all the kingdoms of Europe were, at a remote period, elective, with more or fewer limitations in the objects of choice: but whatever kings might have been here or elsewhere, a thousand years ago, or in whatever manner the ruling dynasties of England or France may have begun, the king of Great Britain is at this day king by a fixed rule of succession, according to the laws of his country; and whilst the legal conditions of the compact of sovereignty are performed by him (as they are performed), he holds his crown in contempt of the choice of the Revolution Society, who have not a single vote for a king amongst them, either individually or collectively, though I make no doubt they would soon erect themselves into an electoral college if things were ripe to give effect to their claim. His Majesty's heirs and successors, each in his time and order, will come to the crown with the same contempt of their choice with which his Majesty has succeeded to that he wears.

Whatever may be the success of evasion in explaining away the gross error of fact which supposes that his Majesty (though he holds it in concurrence with the wishes) owes his crown to the choice of his people, yet nothing can evade their full, explicit declaration concerning the principle of a right in the people to choose, which right is directly maintained and tenaciously adhered to. All the oblique insinuations concerning election bottom in this proposition and are referable to it. Lest the foundation of the king's exclusive legal title should pass for a mere rant of adulatory freedom, the political divine proceeds dogmatically to assert that by the principles of the Revolution the people of England have acquired three fundamental rights, all which, with him, compose one system and lie together in one short sentence, namely, that we have acquired a right (1) "to choose our own governors," (2) "to cashier them for misconduct," (3) "to frame a government for ourselves." This new and hitherto unheard-of bill of rights, though made in the name of the whole people, belongs to those gentlemen and their faction only. The body of the people of England have no share in it. They utterly disclaim it. They will resist the practical assertion of it with their lives and fortunes. They are bound to do so by the laws of their country, made at the time of that very Revolution which is appealed to in favor of the fictitious rights claimed by the society which abuses its name.

William Hazlitt.

1778-1830.

ON READING OLD BOOKS.

(From *The Plain Speaker*, 1826.)

I hate to read new books. There are twenty or thirty volumes that I have read over and over again, and these are the only ones that I have any desire ever to read at all. It was a long time before I could bring myself to sit down to the *Tales of My Landlord*, but now that author's works have made a considerable addition to my scanty library. I am told that some of Lady Morgan's are good, and have been recommended to look into *Anastasius;* but I have not yet ventured upon that task. A lady, the other day, could not refrain from expressing her surprise to a friend who said he had been reading *Delphine:* she asked if it had not been published some time back. Women judge of books as they do of fashions or complexions, which are admired only "in their newest gloss." That is not my way. I am not one of those who trouble the circulating libraries much, or pester the booksellers for mail-coach copies of standard periodical publications. I cannot say that I am greatly addicted to black-letter, but I profess myself well versed in the marble bindings of Andrew Millar, in the middle of the last century; nor does my taste revolt at Thurloe's *State Papers* in Russia leather, or an ample impression of Sir William Temple's *Essays*, with a portrait after Sir Godfrey Kneller in front. I do not think altogether the worse of a book for having survived the author a generation or two. I have more confidence in the dead than the living. Contemporary writers may generally be divided into two classes—one's friends or one's foes. Of the first we are compelled to think too well, and of the last we are disposed to think too ill, to receive much genuine pleasure from the perusal or to judge fairly of the merits of either. One candidate for literary fame, who happens to be of our acquaintance, writes finely and like a man of genius, but unfortunately has a foolish face, which spoils a delicate passage; another inspires us with the highest respect for his personal talents and character, but does not quite come up to our expectations in print. All these contradictions and petty details interrupt the calm current of our reflections. If you want to know what any of the authors were who lived before our time and are still objects of anxious inquiry, you have only to look into their works. But the dust and smoke and noise of modern literature have nothing in common with the pure, silent air of immortality.

When I take up a work that I have read before (the oftener the better), I know what I have to expect. The satisfaction is not lessened by being anticipated. When the entertainment is altogether new, I sit down to it as I should to a strange dish—turn and pick out a bit here and there, and am in doubt what to think of the composition. There is a want of confidence and security to second appetite. New-fangled books are also like made dishes in this respect, that they are generally little else than hashes and *rifaccimentos* of what has been served up entire, and in a more natural state, at other times. Besides, in thus turning to a well-known author there is not only an assurance that my time will not be thrown away, or my palate nauseated with the most insipid or vilest trash, but I shake hands with and look an old, tried, and valued friend in the face, compare notes, and chat the hours away. It is true we form dear friendships with such ideal guests—dearer, alas, and more lasting than those with our most intimate acquaintance. In reading a book which is an old favorite with me (say the first novel I ever read) I not only have the pleasure of imagination and of a critical relish of the work, but the pleasures of memory added to it. It recalls the same feelings and associations which I had in first reading it and which I can never have again in any other way. Standard productions of this kind are links in the chain of our conscious being. They bind together the different scattered divisions of our personal identity. They are landmarks and guides in our journey through life. They are pegs and loops on which we can hang up, or from which we can take down, at pleasure, the wardrobe of a moral imagination, the relics of our best affections, the tokens and records of our happiest hours. They are "for thoughts and for remembrance." They are like Fortunatus's wishing-cap—they give us the best riches, those of fancy, and transport us, not over half the globe, but (which is better) over half our lives, at a word's notice.

My father Shandy solaced himself with *Bruscambille.* Give me for this purpose a volume of *Peregrine Pickle* or *Tom Jones.* Open either of them anywhere—at the *Memoirs of Lady Vane,* or the adventures at the masquerade with Lady Bellaston, or the disputes between Thwackum and Square, or the escape of Molly Seagrim, or the incident of Sophia and her muff, or the edifying prolixity of her aunt's lecture,—and there I find the same delightful, busy, bustling scene as ever, and feel myself the same as when I was first introduced into the midst of it. Nay, sometimes the sight of an odd volume of these good old English authors on a stall, or the name lettered on the back among others on the shelves of a library, answers the purpose, revives the whole train of ideas, and sets "the puppets dallying." Twenty years are struck off the list, and I am a child again. A sage philosopher, who was not a very wise man, said that he should like very well to be young again if he could take his experience along with him. This ingenious person did not seem to be aware, by the gravity of his remark, that the great advantage of being young is to be without this weight of experience, which he would fain place upon the shoulders of youth and which never comes too late with years. O what a privilege to be able to let this hump, like Christian's burthen, drop from off one's back, and transport oneself, by the help of a little musty duodecimo, to the time when "ignorance was bliss," and when we first got a peep at the raree-show of the world through the glass of fiction, gazing at mankind, as we do at wild beasts in a menagerie, through the bars of their cages, or at curiosities in a museum, that we must not touch! For myself, not only are the old ideas of the contents of the work brought back to my mind in all their vividness, but the old associations of the faces and persons of those I then knew, as they were in their lifetime—the place where I sat to read the volume, the day when I got it, the feeling of the air, the fields, the sky—return, and all my early impressions with them. This is better to me—those places, those times, those persons, and those feelings that come across me as I retrace the story and devour the page, are to me better far than the wet sheets of the last new novel from the Ballantyne press, to say nothing of the Minerva press in Leadenhall Street. It is like visiting the scenes of early youth. I think of the time "when I was in my father's house, and my path ran down with butter and honey"—when I was a little thoughtless child, and had no other wish or care but to con my daily task and be happy. *Tom Jones*, I remember, was the first work that broke the spell. It came down in numbers once a fortnight, in Cooke's pocket-edition, embellished with cuts. I had hitherto read only in school-books and a tiresome ecclesiastical history (with the exception of Mrs. Radcliffe's *Romance of the Forest*); but this had a different relish with it—"sweet in the mouth," though not "bitter in the belly." It smacked of the world I lived in and in which I was to live, and showed me groups, "gay creatures" not "of the element" but of the earth, not "living in the clouds" but travelling the same road that I did—some that had passed on before me, and others that might soon overtake me. My heart had palpitated at the thoughts of a boarding-school ball, or gala-day at midsummer or Christmas; but the world I had found out in Cooke's edition of the *British Novelists* was to me a dance through life, a perpetual gala-day. The sixpenny numbers of this work regularly contrived to leave off just in the middle of a sentence and in the nick of a story. . . . With what eagerness I used to look forward to the next number, and open the prints! Ah, never again shall I feel the enthusiastic delight with which I gazed at the figures, and anticipated the story and adventures of Major

Bath and Commodore Trunnion, of Trim and my Uncle Toby, of Don Quixote and Sancho and Dapple, of Gil Blas and Dame Lorenza Sephora, of Laura and the fair Lucretia, whose lips open and shut like buds of roses. To what nameless ideas did they give rise, with what airy delights I filled up the outlines, as I hung in silence over the page. Let me still recall them, that they may breathe fresh life into me and that I may live that birthday of thought and romantic pleasure over again! Talk of the ideal! This is the only true ideal—the heavenly tints of fancy reflected in the bubbles that float upon the spring-tide of human life.

> " O Memory, shield me from the world's poor strife,
> And give those scenes thine everlasting life ! "

The paradox with which I set out is, I hope, less startling that it was; the reader will, by this time, have been let into my secret. Much about the same time, or I believe rather earlier, I took a particular satisfaction in reading Chubb's *Tracts*, and I often think I will get them again to wade through. There is a high gusto of polemical divinity in them; and you fancy that you hear a club of shoemakers at Salisbury debating a disputable text from one of St. Paul's epistles in a workmanlike style, with equal shrewdness and pertinacity. I cannot say much for my metaphysical studies, into which I launched shortly after with great ardor, so as to make a toil of a pleasure. I was presently entangled in the briers and thorns of subtle distinctions—of " fate, free-will, fore-knowledge absolute," though I cannot add that " in their wandering mazes I found no end," for I did arrive at some very satisfactory and potent conclusions; nor will I go so far, however ungrateful the subject might seem, as to exclaim with Marlowe's Faustus, " Would I had never seen Wittenberg, never read book "—that is, never studied such authors as Hartley, Hume, Berkeley, etc. Locke's *Essay on the Human Understanding* is, however, a work from which I never derived either pleasure or profit; and Hobbes, dry and powerful as he is, I did not read till long afterwards. I read a few poets, which did not much hit my taste—for

I would have the reader understand I am deficient in the faculty of imagination; but I fell early upon French romances and philosophy, and devoured them tooth-and-nail. Many a dainty repast have I made of the *New Eloise*—the description of the kiss; the excursion on the water; the letter of St. Preux, recalling the time of their first loves; and the account of Julia's death: these I read over and over again with unspeakable delight and wonder. Some years after, when I met with this work again, I found I had lost nearly my whole relish for it (except some few parts), and was, I remember, very much mortified with the change in my taste, which I sought to attribute to the smallness and gilt edges of the edition I had bought, and its being perfumed with rose-leaves. Nothing could exceed the gravity, the solemnity, with which I carried home and read the dedication to the *Social Contract*, with some other pieces of the same author, which I had picked up at a stall in a coarse leathern cover. Of the *Confessions* I have spoken elsewhere, and may repeat what I have said: "Sweet is the dew of their memory, and pleasant the balm of their recollection." Their beauties are not "scattered like stray gifts o'er the earth," but sown thick on the page, rich and rare. I wish I had never read the *Emilius*, or read it with less implicit faith. I had no occasion to pamper my natural aversion to affectation or pretence, by romantic and artificial means. I had better have formed myself on the model of Sir Fopling Flutter. There is a class of persons whose virtues and most shining qualities sink in, and are concealed by, an absorbent ground of modesty and reserve; and such a one I do, without vanity, profess myself. Now, these are the very persons who are likely to attach themselves to the character of Emilius, and of whom it is sure to be the bane. This dull, phlegmatic, retiring humor is not in a fair way to be corrected, but confirmed and rendered desperate, by being in that work held up as an object of imitation, as an example of simplicity and magnanimity, by coming upon us with all the recommendations of novelty, surprise, and superiority to the prejudices of the world, by being stuck upon a pedestal, made amiable, dazzling, a *leurre de dupe.* The reliance on solid worth which it inculcates, the preference of sober truth to gaudy tinsel, hangs like a millstone round the neck of the imagination—"a load to sink a navy,"—impedes our progress, and blocks up every prospect in life. A man, to get on, to be successful, conspicuous, applauded, should not retire upon the centre of his conscious resources, but be always at the circumference of appearances. He must envelope himself in a halo of mystery—he must ride in an equipage of opinion—he must walk with a train of self-conceit following him—he must not strip himself to a buff-jerkin, to the doublet and hose of his real merits, but must surround himself with a *cortége* of prejudices, like the signs of the Zodiac—he must seem anything but what he is, and then he may pass for anything he pleases. The world love to be amused by hollow professions, to be deceived by flattering appearances, to live in a state of hallucination, and can forgive everything but the plain, downright, simple, honest truth—such as we see it chalked out in the character of Emilius.—To return from this digression, which is a little out of place here.

Books have in a great measure lost their power over me, nor can I revive the same interest in them as formerly. I perceive when a thing is good, rather than feel it. It is true,

> "Marcian Colonna is a dainty book";

and the reading of Mr. Keats's *Eve of St. Agnes* lately made me regret that I was not young again. The beautiful and tender images there conjured up "come like shadows—so depart." The "tiger-moth's wings," which he has spread over his rich poetic blazonry, just flit across my fancy; the gorgeous twilight window which he has painted over again in his verse, to me "blushes" almost in vain "with blood of queens and kings." I know how I should have felt at one time in reading such passages; and that is all. The sharp, luscious flavor, the fine aroma, is fled, and nothing but the stalk, the bran, the husk of literature is left. If anyone were to ask me what I read now, I might answer with my Lord Hamlet in the play, "Words, words, words." "What is the matter?" "Nothing"—they have scarce a meaning. But it was not always so. There was a time when to my thinking every word was a flower or a pearl, like those which dropped from the mouth of the little peasant-girl in the fairy tale, or like those that fall from the great preacher in the Caledonian Chapel. I drank of the stream of knowledge that tempted but did not mock my lips, as of the river of life, freely. How eagerly I slaked my thirst of German sentiment, "as the hart that panteth for the water-springs"; how I bathed and revelled, and added my floods of tears to Goethe's *Sorrows of Werter* and to Schiller's *Robbers*.

> "Giving my stock of more to that which had too much."

I read and assented with all my soul to Coleridge's fine sonnet beginning,

> "Schiller, that hour I would have wished to die,
> If through the shuddering midnight I had sent,
> From the dark dungeon of the tow'r, time-rent,
> That fearful voice, a famish'd father's cry!"

I believe I may date my insight into the mysteries of poetry from the commencement of my acquaintance with the authors of the *Lyrical Ballads;* at least, my discrimination of the higher sorts, not my predilection for such writers as Goldsmith or Pope: nor do I imagine they will say I got my liking for the novelists or the comic writers, for the characters of Valentine, Tattle, or Miss Prue, from them. If so, I must have got from them what they never had themselves. In points where poetic diction and conception are concerned, I may be at a loss and liable to be imposed upon; but in forming an estimate of passages relating to common life and manners I cannot think I am a plagiarist from any man. I there "know my cue without a prompter." I may say of such studies, "intus et in cute." I am just able to admire those literal touches of observation and description which persons of loftier pretensions overlook and despise. I think I comprehend something of the characteristic part of Shakespeare;

and in him, indeed, all is characteristic, even the nonsense and poetry. I believe it was the celebrated Sir Humphrey Davy who used to say that Shakespeare was rather a metaphysician than a poet. At any rate, it was not ill said. I wish that I had sooner known the dramatic writers contemporary with Shakespeare, for in looking them over, about a year ago, I almost revived my old passion for reading and my old delight in books, though they were very nearly new to me. The periodical essayists I read long ago. *The Spectator* I liked extremely, but *The Tatler* took my fancy most. I read the others soon after—*The Rambler, The Adventurer, The World, The Connoisseur;* I was not sorry to get to the end of them, and have no desire to go regularly through them again. I consider myself a thorough adept in Richardson. I like the longest of his novels best, and think no part of them tedious; nor should I ask to have anything better to do than to read them from beginning to end, to take them up when I chose and lay them down when I was tired, in some old family mansion in the country, till every word and syllable relating to the bright Clarissa, the divine Clementina, the beautiful Pamela, "with every trick and line of their sweet favor," were once more "graven in my heart's table." I have a sneaking kindness for Mackenzie's *Julia de Roubigné*—for the deserted mansion, and straggling gilliflowers on the mouldering garden wall; and still more for his *Man of Feeling*—not that it is better, nor so good, but at the time I read it I sometimes thought of the heroine, Miss Walton, and of Miss —— together, and "that ligament, fine as it was, was never broken."—One of the poets that I have always read with most pleasure, and can wander about in forever with a sort of voluptuous indolence, is Spenser; and I like Chaucer even better. The only writer among the Italians I can pretend to any knowledge of is Boccaccio, and of him I cannot express half my admiration. His story of the hawk I could read and think of from day to day, just as I would look at a picture of Titian's.

I remember, as long ago as the year 1798, going to a neighboring town (Shrewsbury, where Farquhar has laid the plot of his *Recruiting Officer*) and bringing home with me, "at one proud swoop," a copy of Milton's *Paradise Lost* and another of Burke's *Reflections on the French Revolution*—both which I have still; and I still recollect, when I see the covers, the pleasure with which I dipped into them as I returned with my double prize. I was set up for one while. That time is past, "with all its giddy raptures"; but I am still anxious to preserve its memory, "embalmed with odors." With respect to the first of these works, I would be permitted to remark here, in passing, that it is a sufficient answer to the German criticism which has since been started against the character of Satan (viz., that it is not one of disgusting deformity, or pure, defecated malice) to say that Milton has there drawn, not the abstract principle of evil, not a devil incarnate, but a fallen angel. This is the Scriptural account, and the poet has followed it. We may safely retain such passages as that well-known one,

> "His form had not yet lost
> All her original brightness; nor appear'd
> Less than archangel ruin'd, and the excess
> Of glory obscur'd,"

for the theory which is opposed to them "falls flat upon the grunsel edge and shames its worshippers." Let us hear no more, then, of this monkish cant and bigoted outcry for the restoration of the horns and tail of the devil. Again, as to the other work, Burke's *Reflections*, I took a particular pride and pleasure in it, and read it to myself and others for months afterwards. I had reason for my prejudice in favor of this author. To understand an adversary is some praise; to admire him is more. I thought I did both; I knew I did one. From the first time I ever cast my eyes on anything of Burke's (which was an extract from his *Letter to a Noble Lord*, in a three-times-a-week paper, *The St. James's Chronicle*, in 1796) I said to myself, "This is true eloquence: this is a man pouring out his mind on paper." All other style seemed to me pedantic and impertinent. Dr. Johnson's was walking on stilts; and even Junius's (who was at that time a favorite with me), with all his terseness, shrunk up into little antithetic points and well-trimmed sentences. But Burke's style was forked and playful as the lightning, crested like the serpent. He delivered plain things on a plain ground; but when he rose, there was no end of his flights and circumgyrations—and in this very *Letter* "he, like an eagle in a dove-cot, fluttered *his* Volscians" (the Duke of Bedford and the Earl of Lauderdale) "in Corioli." I did not care for his doctrines. I was then, and am still, proof against their contagion; but I admired the author, and was considered as not a very staunch partisan of the opposite side, though I thought myself that an abstract proposition was one thing, a masterly transition, a brilliant metaphor, another. I conceived, too, that he might be wrong in his main argument, and yet deliver fifty truths in arriving at a false conclusion. I remember Coleridge assuring me, as a poetical and political set-off to my sceptical admiration, that Wordsworth had written an *Essay on Marriage* which, for manly thought and nervous expression, he deemed incomparably superior. As I had not, at that time, seen any specimens of Mr. Wordsworth's prose style, I could not express my doubts on the subject. If there are greater prose-writers than Burke, they either lie out of my course of study or are beyond my sphere of comprehension. I am too old to be a convert to a new mythology of genius. The niches are occupied, the tables are full. If such is still my admiration of this man's misapplied powers, what must it have been at a time when I myself was in vain trying, year after year, to write a single essay, nay, a single page or sentence; when I regarded the wonders of his pen with the longing eyes of one who was dumb and a changeling; and when to be able to convey the slightest conception of my meaning to others in words was the height of an almost hopeless ambition. But I never measured others' excellences by my own defects, though a sense of my own incapacity and of the steep, impassable ascent from me to them made me regard them with greater awe and fondness.

I have thus run through most of my early studies and

favorite authors, some of whom I have since criticised more at large. Whether those observations will survive me I neither know nor do I much care; but to the works themselves, "worthy of all acceptation," and to the feelings they have always excited in me since I could distinguish a meaning in language, nothing shall ever prevent me from looking back with gratitude and triumph. To have lived in the cultivation of an intimacy with such works, and to have familiarly relished such names, is not to have lived quite in vain.

There are other authors whom I have never read, and yet whom I have frequently had a great desire to read from some circumstance relating to them. Among these is Lord Clarendon's *History of the Grand Rebellion*, after which I have a hankering from hearing it spoken of by good judges, from my interest in the events and knowledge of the characters from other sources, and from having seen fine portraits of most of them. I like to read a well-penned character, and Clarendon is said to have been a master in this way. I should like to read Froissart's *Chronicles*, Holinshed and Stowe, and Fuller's *Worthies*. I intend, whenever I can, to read Beaumont and Fletcher all through. There are fifty-two of their plays, and I have only read a dozen or fourteen of them. *A Wife for a Month* and *Thierry and Theodoret* are, I am told, delicious, and I can believe it. I should like to read the speeches in Thucydides, and Guicciardini's *History of Florence*, and *Don Quixote* in the original. I have often thought of reading *The Loves of Persiles and Sigismunda* and the *Galatea* of the same author. But I somehow reserve them, like "another Yarrow." I should also like to read the last new novel (if I could be sure it was so) of the author of *Waverley;* no one would be more glad than I to find it the best.

Charles Lamb.

1775–1834.

NEW YEAR'S EVE.

(From *The Essays of Elia*, 1823.)

Every man hath two birthdays: two days, at least, in every year, which set him upon revolving the lapse of time as it affects his mortal duration. The one is that which in an especial manner he termeth *his*. In the gradual desuetude of old observances, this custom of solemnizing our proper birthday hath nearly passed away, or is left to children, who reflect nothing at all about the matter, nor understand anything in it beyond cake and orange. But the birth of a New Year is of an interest too wide to be pretermitted by king or cobbler. No one ever regarded the first of January with indifference. It is that from which all date their time and count upon what is left. It is the nativity of our common Adam.

Of all sounds of all bells—(bells, the music nighest bordering upon heaven)—most solemn and touching is the peal which rings out the Old Year. I never hear it without a gathering up of my mind to a concentration of all the images that have been diffused over the past twelvemonth; all I have dor or suffered, performed or neglected—in that regretted time. I begin to know its worth, as when a person dies. It takes a personal color; nor was it a poetical flight in a contemporary when he exclaimed,

"I saw the skirts of the departing Year."

It is no more than what in sober sadness every one of us seems to be conscious of in that awful leave-taking. I am sure I felt it, and all felt it with me, last night; though some of my companions affected rather to manifest an exhilaration at the birth of the coming year than any very tender regrets for the decease of its predecessor. But I am none of those who—

"Welcome the coming, speed the parting guest."

I am naturally, beforehand, shy of novelties; new books, new faces, new years—from some mental twist which makes it difficult in me to face the prospective. I have almost ceased to hope, and am sanguine only in the prospects of other (former) years. I plunge into foregone visions and conclusions. I encounter pellmell with past disappointments. I am armor-proof against old discouragements. I forgive, or overcome in fancy, old adversaries. I play over again *for love*, as the gamesters phrase it, games for which I once paid so dear. I would scarce now have any of those untoward accidents and events of my life reversed. I would no more alter them than the incidents of some well-contrived novel. Methinks it is better that I should have pined away seven of my goldenest years, when I was thrall to the fair hair and fairer eyes of Alice W——n, than that so passionate a love-adventure should be lost. It was better that our family should have missed that legacy which old Dorrell cheated us of than that I should have at this moment two thousand pounds *in banco* and be without the idea of that specious old rogue.

In a degree beneath manhood, it is my infirmity to look back upon those early days. Do I advance a paradox when I say that, skipping over the intervention of forty years, a man may have leave to love *himself* without the imputation of self-love?

If I know aught of myself, no one whose mind is introspective—and mine is painfully so—can have a less respect for his present identity than I have for the man Elia. I know him to be light and vain and humorsome; a notorious * * *; addicted to * * * *; averse from counsel, neither taking it nor offering it;— * * * besides; a stammering buffoon; what you will; lay it on, and spare not; I subscribe to it all, and much more than thou canst be willing to lay at his door——but for the child Elia—that "other me," there, in the background—I must take leave to cherish the remembrance of that young master—with as little reference, I protest, to this stupid changeling of five-and-forty as if it had been a child of some other house and not of my parents. I can cry over its patient smallpox at five, and rougher medicaments. I can lay its poor fevered head upon the sick pillow at Christ's, and wake with it in surprise at the gentle posture of maternal tenderness hanging over it, that unknown had watched its sleep. I know how it shrank from any the least color of falsehood.—God help thee, Elia, how art thou changed! Thou art sophisticated.—I know how honest, how courageous (for a weakling) it was—how religious, how imaginative, how hopeful! From what have I not fallen, if the child I remember was indeed myself—and not some dissembling guardian, presenting a false identity, to give the rule to my unpractised steps and regulate the tone of my moral being!

That I am fond of indulging, beyond a hope of sympathy, in such retrospection, may be the symptom of some sickly idiosyncrasy. Or is it owing to another cause: simply that, being without wife or family, I have not learned to project myself enough out of myself; and, having no offspring of my own to dally with, I turn back upon memory, and adopt my own early idea as my heir and favorite? If these speculations seem fantastical to thee, reader—(a busy man, perchance), if I tread out of the way of thy sympathy and am singularly conceited only, I retire, impenetrable to ridicule, under the phantom-cloud of Elia.

The elders with whom I was brought up were of a character not likely to let slip the sacred observance of any old institution; and the ringing out of the Old Year was kept by them with circumstances of peculiar ceremony.—In those days the sound of those midnight chimes, though it seemed to raise hilarity in all around me, never failed to bring a train of pensive imagery into my fancy. Yet I then scarce conceived what it meant, or thought of it as a reckoning that concerned me. Not childhood alone, but the young man till thirty, never feels practically that he is mortal. He knows it indeed, and if need were he could preach a homily on the fragility of life; but he brings it not home to himself, any more than in a hot June we can appropriate to our imagination the freezing days of December. But now,—shall I confess a truth?—I feel these audits but too powerfully. I begin to count the probabilities of my duration, and to grudge at the expenditure of moments and shortest periods, like miser's farthings. In proportion as the years both lessen and shorten, I set more count upon their periods, and would fain lay my ineffectual finger upon the spoke of the great wheel. I am not content to pass away "like a weaver's shuttle." Those metaphors solace me not, nor sweeten the unpalatable draught of mortality. I care not to be carried with the tide that smoothly bears human life to eternity; and reluct at the inevitable course of destiny. I am in love with this green earth: the face of town and country, the unspeakable rural solitudes, and the sweet security of streets. I would set up my tabernacle here. I am content to stand still at the age to which I am arrived; I, and my friends; to be no younger, no richer, no handsomer. I do not want to be weaned by age; or drop, like mellow fruit, as they say, into the grave.—Any alteration, on this earth of mine, in diet or in lodging, puzzles and discomposes me. My household-gods plant a terrible fixed foot, and are not rooted up without blood. They do not willingly seek Lavinian shores. A new state of being staggers me.

Sun, and sky, and breeze, and solitary walks, and summer holidays, and the greenness of fields, and the delicious juices of meats and fishes, and society, and the cheerful glass, and candlelight, and fireside conversations, and innocent vanities, and jests, and *irony itself*—do these things go out with life?

Can a ghost laugh, or shake his gaunt sides, when you are pleasant with him?

And you, my midnight darlings, my Folios! must I part with the intense delight of having you (huge armfuls) in my embraces? Must knowledge come to me, if it come at all, by some awkward experiment of intuition, and no longer by this familiar process of reading?

Shall I enjoy friendships there, wanting the smiling indications which point me to them here—the recognizable face—the "sweet assurance of a look"—?

In winter this intolerable disinclination to dying—to give it its mildest name—does more especially haunt and beset me. In a genial August noon, beneath a sweltering sky, death is almost problematic. At those times do such poor snakes as myself enjoy an immortality. Then we expand and bourgeon. Then are we as strong again, as valiant again, as wise again, and a great deal taller. The blast that nips and shrinks me puts me in thoughts of death. All things allied to the insubstantial wait upon that master-feeling: cold, numbness, dreams, perplexity; moonlight itself, with its shadowy and spectral appearances—that cold ghost of the sun, or Phœbus' sickly sister, like that innutritious one denounced in the *Canticles*:—I am none of her minions—I hold with the Persian.

Whatsoever thwarts or puts me out of my way brings death into my mind. All partial evils, like humors, run into that capital plague-sore.—I have heard some profess an indifference to life. Such hail the end of their existence as a port of refuge; and speak of the grave as of some soft arms, in which they may slumber as on a pillow. Some have wooed death——but out upon thee, I say, thou foul, ugly phantom! I detest, abhor, execrate, and (with Friar John) give thee to six-score thousand devils, as in no instance to be excused or tolerated, but shunned as a universal viper; to be branded, proscribed, and spoken evil of! In no way can I be brought to digest thee, thou thin, melancholy *Privation*, or more frightful and confounding *Positive!*

Those antidotes prescribed against the fear of thee are altogether frigid and insulting, like thyself. For what satisfaction hath a man, that he shall "lie down with kings and emperors in death," who in his lifetime never greatly coveted the society of such bedfellows?—or, forsooth, that "so shall the fairest face appear"?—why, to comfort me, must Alice

W——n be a goblin? More than all, I conceive disgust at those impertinent and misbecoming familiarities inscribed upon your ordinary tombstones. Every dead man must take upon himself to be lecturing me with his odious truism that "such as he now is I must shortly be." Not so shortly, friend, perhaps as thou imaginest. In the meantime I am alive. I move about. I am worth twenty of thee. Know thy betters! Thy New Years' Days are past. I survive, a jolly candidate for 1821. Another cup of wine—and while that turncoat bell, that just now mournfully chanted the obsequies of 1820 departed, with changed notes lustily rings in a successor, let us attune to its peal the song made on a like occasion, by hearty, cheerful Mr. Cotton.

"THE NEW YEAR.

"Hark, the cock crows, and yon bright star
Tells us the day himself 's not far;
And see where, breaking from the night,
He gilds the western hills with light.
With him old Janus doth appear,
Peeping into the future year,
With such a look as seems to say
The prospect is not good that way.
Thus do we rise ill sights to see,
And 'gainst ourselves to prophesy;
When the prophetic fear of things
A more tormenting mischief brings,
More full of soul-tormenting gall,
Than direst mischiefs can befall.
But stay! but stay! methinks my sight,
Better inform'd by clearer light,
Discerns sereneness in that brow
That all contracted seem'd but now.
His revers'd face may show distaste,
And frown upon the ills are past;
But that which this way looks is clear,
And smiles upon the New-born Year.
He looks too from a place so high,
The Year lies open to his eye;
And all the moments open are
To the exact discoverer.
Yet more and more he smiles upon
The happy revolution,

Why should we, then, suspect or fear
The influences of a year,
So smiles upon us the first morn,
And speaks us good so soon as born?
Plague on't! the last was ill enough,
This cannot but make better proof;
Or, at the worst, as we brush'd through
The last, why so we may this too;
And then the next in reason shou'd
Be superexcellently good:
For the worst ills (we daily see)
Have no more perpetuity
Than the best fortunes that do fall;
Which also bring us wherewithal
Longer their being to support
Than those do of the other sort:
And who has one good year in three,
And yet repines at destiny,
Appears ungrateful in the case,
And merits not the good he has.
Then let us welcome the New Guest
With lusty brimmers of the best;
Mirth always should Good Fortune meet,
And renders e'en Disaster sweet:
And though the Princess turn her back,
Let us but line ourselves with sack,
We better shall by far hold out,
Till the next Year she face about."

How say you, reader—do not these verses smack of the rough magnanimity of the old English vein? Do they not fortify like a cordial; enlarging the heart, and productive of sweet blood and generous spirits, in the concoction? Where be those puling fears of death, just now expressed or affected? —Passed like a cloud—absorbed in the purging sunlight of clear poetry—clean washed away by a wave of genuine Helicon, your only Spa for these hypochondries.—And now another cup of the generous! and a merry New Year, and many of them, to you all, my masters!

A DISSERTATION UPON ROAST PIG.

(From the same.)

Mankind, says a Chinese manuscript, which my friend M. was obliging enough to read and explain to me, for the first seventy thousand ages ate their meat raw, clawing or biting it from the living animal, just as they do in Abyssinia to this day. This period is not obscurely hinted at by their great Confucius in the second chapter of his *Mundane Mutations*, where he designates a kind of golden age by the term Cho-fang, literally the Cooks' Holiday. The manuscript goes on to say that the art of roasting, or rather broiling (which I take to be the elder brother), was accidentally discovered in the manner following. The swine-herd, Ho-ti, having gone out into the woods one morning, as his manner was, to collect mast for his hogs, left his cottage in the care of his eldest son Bo-bo, a great lubberly boy, who being fond of playing with fire, as younkers of his age commonly are, let some sparks escape into a bundle of straw, which, kindling quickly, spread the conflagration over every part of their poor mansion, till it was reduced to ashes. Together with the cottage (a sorry antediluvian make-shift of a building, you may think it), what was of much more importance, a fine litter of new-farrowed pigs, no less than nine in number, perished. China pigs have been esteemed a luxury all over the East, from the remotest periods that we read of. Bo-bo was in the utmost consternation, as you may think, not so much for the sake of the tenement, which his father and he could easily build up again with a few dry branches and the labor of an hour or two, at any time, as for the loss of the pigs. While he was thinking what he should say to his father, and wringing his hands over the smoking remnants of one of those untimely sufferers, an odor assailed his nostrils, unlike any scent which he had before experienced. What could it proceed from?—not from the burnt cottage—he had smelt that smell before—indeed, this was by no means the first accident of the kind which had occurred through the negligence of this unlucky young firebrand. Much less did it resemble that of any known herb, weed, or flower. A premonitory moistening at the same time overflowed his nether lip. He knew not what to think. He next stooped down to feel the pig, if there were any signs of life in it. He burnt his fingers, and to cool them he applied them in his booby fashion to his mouth. Some of the crumbs of the scorched skin had come away with his fingers, and for the first time in his life (in the world's life indeed, for before him no man had known it) he tasted—*crackling!* Again he felt and fumbled at the pig. It did not burn him so much now; still he licked his fingers from a sort of habit. The truth at length broke into his slow understanding, that it was the pig that smelt so and the pig that tasted so delicious; and, surrendering himself up to the new-born pleasure, he fell to tearing up whole handfuls of the scorched skin with the flesh next it, and was cramming it down his throat in his beastly fashion, when his sire entered amid the smoking rafters, armed with retributory cudgel, and, finding how affairs stood, began to rain blows upon the young rogue's shoulders as thick as hail-stones, which Bo-bo heeded not any more than if they had been flies. The tickling pleasure which he experienced in his lower regions, had rendered him quite callous to any inconveniences he might feel in those remote quarters. His father might lay on, but he could not beat him from his pig till he had fairly made an end of it, when, becoming a little more sensible of his situation, something like the following dialogue ensued:—

"You graceless whelp, what have you got there devouring? Is it not enough that you have burnt me down three houses with your dog's tricks, and be hanged to you! but you must be eating fire, and I know not what—what have you got there, I say?"

"O father, the pig, the pig! do come and taste how nice the burnt pig eats."

The ears of Ho-ti tingled with horror. He cursed his son, and he cursed himself that ever he should beget a son that should eat burnt pig.

Bo-bo, whose scent was wonderfully sharpened since morning, soon raked out another pig, and, fairly rending it asunder, thrust the lesser half by main force into the fists of Ho-ti, still shouting out, "Eat, eat, eat the burnt pig, father; only taste—O Lord!"—with such-like barbarous ejaculations, cramming all the while as if he would choke.

Ho-ti trembled every joint while he grasped the abominable thing, wavering whether he should not put his son to death for an unnatural young monster, when, the crackling scorching his fingers as it had done his son's, and applying the same remedy to them, he in his turn tasted some of its flavor, which, make what sour mouths he would for a pretence, proved not altogether displeasing to him. In conclusion (for the manuscript here is a little tedious) both father and son fairly sat down to the mess, and never left off till they had despatched all that remained of the litter.

Bo-bo was strictly enjoined not to let the secret escape, for the neighbors would certainly have stoned them for a couple of abominable wretches, who could think of improving upon the good meat which God had sent them. Nevertheless, strange stories got about. It was observed that Ho-ti's cottage was burnt down now more frequently than ever. Nothing but fires from this time forward. Some would break out in broad day, others in the night-time. As often as the sow farrowed, so sure was the house of Ho-ti to be in a blaze; and Ho-ti himself, which was the more remarkable, instead of chastising his son, seemed to grow more indulgent to him than ever. At length they were watched, the terrible mystery discovered, and father and son summoned to take their trial at Pekin, then an inconsiderable assize town. Evidence was given, the obnoxious food itself produced in court, and verdict about to be pronounced, when the foreman of the jury begged that some of the burnt pig, of which the culprits stood accused, might be handed into the box. He handled it, and they all handled it; and burning their fingers, as Bo-bo and his father had done before them, and nature prompting to each of them the same remedy, against the face of all the facts and the clearest charge which judge had ever given,—

to the surprise of the whole court, townsfolk, strangers, reporters, and all present—without leaving the box, or any manner of consultation whatever, they brought in a simultaneous verdict of Not Guilty.

The judge, who was a shrewd fellow, winked at the manifest iniquity of the decision: and when the court was dismissed, went privily and bought up all the pigs that could be had for love or money. In a few days his lordship's town-house was observed to be on fire. The thing took wing, and now there was nothing to be seen but fires in every direction. Fuel and pigs grew enormously dear all over the district. The insurance-offices one and all shut up shop. People built slighter and slighter every day, until it was feared that the very science of architecture would in no long time be lost to the world. Thus this custom of firing houses continued, till in process of time, says my manuscript, a sage arose, like our Locke, who made a discovery that the flesh of swine, or indeed of any other animal, might be cooked (*burnt* as they called it) without the necessity of consuming a whole house to dress it. Then first began the rude form of a gridiron. Roasting by the string or spit came in a century or two later, I forget in whose dynasty. By such slow degrees, concludes the manuscript, do the most useful and seemingly the most obvious arts make their way among mankind.

Without placing too implicit faith in the account above given, it must be agreed that if a worthy pretext for so dangerous an experiment as setting houses on fire (especially in these days) could be assigned in favor of any culinary object, that pretext and excuse might be found in ROAST·PIG.

Of all the delicacies in the whole *mundus edibilis*, I will maintain it to be the most delicate—*princeps obsoniorum.*

I speak not of your grown porkers—things between pig and pork—those hobbydehoys—but a young and tender suckling—under a moon old—guiltless as yet of the sty—with no original speck of the *amor immunditiæ*, the hereditary failing of the first parent, yet manifest—his voice as yet not broken, but something between a childish treble and a grumble—the mild forerunner, or *præludium*, of a grunt.

He must be roasted. I am not ignorant that our ancestors ate them seethed, or boiled—but what a sacrifice of the exterior tegument!

There is no flavor comparable, I will contend, to that of the crisp, tawny, well-watched, not over-roasted, *crackling*, as it is well called—the very teeth are invited to their share of the pleasure at this banquet in overcoming the coy, brittle resistance—with the adhesive oleaginous—oh call it not fat—but an indefinable sweetness growing up to it—the tender blossoming of fat—fat cropped in the bud—taken in the shoot—in the first innocence—the cream and quintessence of the child-pig's yet pure food——the lean, no lean, but a kind of animal manna—or, rather, fat and lean (if it must be so) so blended and running into each other that both together make but one ambrosian result, or common substance.

Behold him while he is doing—it seemeth rather a refreshing warmth, than a scorching heat, that he is so passive to. How equably he twirleth round the string!—Now he is just done. To see the extreme sensibility of that tender age! he hath wept out his pretty eyes—radiant jellies—shooting stars—

See him in the dish, his second cradle, how meek he lieth! —wouldst thou have had this innocent grow up to the grossness and indocility which too often accompany maturer swinehood? Ten to one he would have proved a glutton, a sloven, an obstinate, disagreeable animal—wallowing in all manner of filthy conversation—from these sins he is happily snatched away—

> "Ere sin could blight or sorrow fade,
> Death came with timely care"—

his memory is odoriferous—no clown curseth, while his stomach half rejecteth, the rank bacon—no coal-heaver bolteth him in reeking sausages—he hath a fair sepulchre in the grateful stomach of the judicious epicure—and for such a tomb might be content to die.

He is the best of sapors. Pine-apple is great. She is indeed almost too transcendent—a delight, if not sinful, yet so like to sinning that really a tender-conscienced person would do well to pause—too ravishing for mortal taste, she woundeth and excoriateth the lips that approach her—like lovers' kisses, she biteth—she is a pleasure bordering on pain from the fierceness and insanity of her relish—but she stoppeth at the palate—she meddleth not with the appetite—and the coarsest hunger might barter her consistently for a mutton-chop.

Pig—let me speak his praise—is no less provocative of the appetite than he is satisfactory to the criticalness of the censorious palate. The strong man may batten on him, and the weakling refuseth not his mild juices.

Unlike to mankind's mixed characters, a bundle of virtues and vices, inexplicably intertwisted, and not to be unravelled without hazard, he is—good throughout. No part of him is better or worse than another. He helpeth, as far as his little means extend, all around. He is the least envious of banquets. He is all neighbors' fare.

I am one of those who freely and ungrudgingly impart a share of the good things of this life which fall to their lot (few as mine are in this kind) to a friend. I protest I take as great an interest in my friend's pleasures, his relishes, and proper satisfactions, as in mine own. "Presents," I often say, "endear Absents." Hares, pheasants, partridges, snipes, barn-door chicken (those "tame villatic fowl"), capons, plovers, brawn, barrels of oysters, I dispense as freely as I receive them. I love to taste them, as it were, upon the tongue of my friend. But a stop must be put somewhere. One would not, like Lear, "give everything." I make my stand upon pig. Methinks it is an ingratitude to the Giver of all good flavors to extradomiciliate, or send out of the house, slightingly (under pretext of friendship, or I know not what), a blessing so particularly adapted, predestined, I may say, to my individual palate—it argues an insensibility.

I remember a touch of conscience in this kind at school. My good old aunt, who never parted from me at the end of a holiday without stuffing a sweet-meat, or some nice thing, into my pocket, had dismissed me one evening with a smoking plum-cake, fresh from the oven. In my way to school (it was over London Bridge) a grey-headed old beggar saluted me (I have no doubt at this time of day that he was a counterfeit). I had no pence to console him with, and in the vanity of self-denial and the very coxcombry of charity, schoolboy-like, I made him a present of—the whole cake! I walked on a little, buoyed up, as one is on such occasions, with a sweet soothing of self-satisfaction; but before I had got to the end of the bridge, my better feelings returned, and I burst into tears, thinking how ungrateful I had been to my good aunt to go and give her good gift away to a stranger that I had never seen before and who might be a bad man for aught I knew; and then I thought of the pleasure my aunt would be taking in thinking that I—I myself and not another—would eat her nice cake—and what should I say to her the next time I saw her—how naughty I was to part with her pretty present—and the odor of that spicy cake came back upon my recollection, and the pleasure and the curiosity I had taken in seeing her make it, and her joy when she sent it to the oven, and how disappointed she would feel that I had never had a bit of it in my mouth at last—and I blamed my impertinent spirit of almsgiving and out-of-place hypocrisy of goodness; and above all I wished never to see the face again of that insidious, good-for-nothing, old grey impostor.

Our ancestors were nice in their method of sacrificing these tender victims. We read of pigs whipt to death with something of a shock, as we hear of any other obsolete custom. The age of discipline is gone by, or it would be curious to inquire (in a philosophical light merely) what effect this process might have towards intenerating and dulcifying a substance naturally so mild and dulcet as the flesh of young pigs. It looks like refining a violet. Yet we should be cautious, while we condemn the inhumanity, how we censure the wisdom of the practice. It might impart a gusto—

I remember an hypothesis, argued upon by the young students, when I was at St. Omer's, and maintained with much learning and pleasantry on both sides, "Whether, supposing that the flavor of a pig who obtained his death by whipping (*per flagellationem extremam*) superadded a pleasure upon the palate of a man more intense than any possible suffering we can conceive in the animal, is man justified in using that method of putting the animal to death?" I forget the decision.

His sauce should be considered. Decidedly, a few bread crumbs, done up with his liver and brains, and a dash of mild sage. But banish, dear Mrs. Cook, I beseech you, the whole onion tribe. Barbecue your whole hogs to your palate, steep them in shalots, stuff them out with plantations of the rank and guilty garlic; you cannot poison them, or make them stronger than they are—but consider, he is a weakling—a flower.

POOR RELATIONS.

(From *The Last Essays of Elia*, 1833.)

A Poor Relation—is the most irrelevant thing in nature,—a piece of impertinent correspondency,—an odious approximation,—a haunting conscience,—a preposterous shadow, lengthening in the noontide of your prosperity,—an unwelcome remembrancer,—a perpetually recurring mortification,—a drain on your purse,—a more intolerable dun upon your pride,—a drawback upon success,—a rebuke to your rising,—a stain in your blood,—a blot on your scutcheon,—a rent in your garment,—a death's head at your banquet,—Agathocles' pot,—a Mordecai in your gate,—a Lazarus at your door,—a lion in your path,—a frog in your chamber,—a fly in your ointment,—a mote in your eye,—a triumph to your enemy, an apology to your friends,—the one thing not needful,—the hail in harvest,—the ounce of sour in a pound of sweet.

He is known by his knock. Your heart telleth you, "That is Mr. ——." A rap, between familiarity and respect; that demands, and at the same time seems to despair of, entertainment. He entereth smiling and—embarrassed. He holdeth out his hand to you to shake, and—draweth it back again. He casually looketh in about dinner-time—when the table is full. He offereth to go away, seeing you have company—but is induced to stay. He filleth a chair, and your visitor's two children are accommodated at a side table. He never cometh upon open days, when your wife says with some complacency, "My dear, perhaps Mr. —— will drop in to-day." He remembereth birthdays—and professeth he is fortunate to have stumbled upon one. He declareth against fish, the turbot being small—yet suffereth himself to be importuned into a slice, against his first resolution. He sticketh by the port—yet will be prevailed upon to empty the remainder glass of claret, if a stranger press it upon him. He is a puzzle to the servants, who are fearful of being too obsequious, or not civil enough, to him. The guests think "they have seen him before." Every one speculateth upon his condition; and the most part take him to be—a tide-waiter. He calleth you by your Christian name, to imply that his other is the same with your own. He is too familiar by half, yet you wish he had less diffidence. With half the familiarity, he might pass for a casual dependant; with more boldness, he would be in no danger of being taken for what he is. He is too humble for a friend; yet taketh on him more state than befits a client. He is a worse guest than a country tenant, inasmuch as he bringeth up no rent—yet 'tis odds, from his garb and demeanor, that your guests take him for one. He is asked to make one at the whist-table; refuseth on the score of poverty, and—resents being left out. When the company break up, he proffereth to go for a coach—and lets the servant go. He recollects your grandfather; and will thrust in some mean and quite unimportant anecdote of—the family. He knew it when it was not quite so flourishing as "he is blest in seeing it now." He reviveth past situations, to institute what he calleth—favorable comparisons. With a reflecting sort of congratulation, he will inquire the price of your furniture; and insults you with a special commendation of your window-curtains. He is of opinion that the urn is the more elegant shape, but, after all, there was something more comfortable about the old tea-kettle—which you must remember. He dare say you must find a great convenience in having a carriage of your own, and appealeth to your lady if it is not so. Inquireth if you have had your arms done on vellum yet; and did not know, till lately, that such-and-such had been the crest of the family. His memory is unseasonable; his compliments perverse; his talk a trouble; his stay pertinacious; and when he goeth away, you dismiss his chair into a corner, as precipitately as possible, and feel fairly rid of two nuisances.

There is a worse evil under the sun, and that is—a female Poor Relation. You may do something with the other; you may pass him off tolerably well; but your indigent she-relative is hopeless. "He is an old humorist," you may say, "and affects to go threadbare. His circumstances are better than folks would take them to be. You are fond of having a Character at your table, and truly he is one." But in the indications of female poverty there can be no disguise. No woman dresses below herself from caprice. The truth must out without shuffling. "She is plainly related to the L——s; or what does she at their house?" She is, in all probability, your wife's cousin. Nine times out of ten, at least, this is the case. Her garb is something between a gentlewoman and a beggar, yet the former evidently predominates. She is most provokingly humble, and ostentatiously sensible to her inferiority. He may require to be repressed sometimes—*aliquando sufflaminandus erat;*—but there is no raising her. You send her soup at dinner, and she begs to be helped—after the gentlemen. Mr. —— requests the honor of taking wine with her; she hesitates between port and Madeira, and chooses the former—because he does. She calls the servant "Sir"; and insists on not troubling him to hold her plate. The housekeeper patronizes her. The children's governess takes upon her to correct her when she has mistaken the piano for a harpsichord.

Richard Amlet, Esq., in the play, is a notable instance of the disadvantages to which this chimerical notion of *affinity constituting a claim to acquaintance* may subject the spirit of a gentleman. A little foolish blood is all that is betwixt him and a lady of great estate. His stars are perpetually crossed by the malignant maternity of an old woman, who persists in calling him "her son Dick." But she has wherewithal in the end to recompense his indignities, and float him again upon the brilliant surface, under which it had been her seeming business and pleasure all along to sink him. All men, besides, are not of Dick's temperament. I knew an Amlet in real life, who, wanting Dick's buoyancy, sank indeed. Poor W—— was of my own standing at Christ's, a fine classic, and a youth of promise. If he had a blemish, it was too much pride; but its quality was inoffensive; it was not of that sort which hardens the heart, and serves to keep inferiors at a distance; it only sought to ward off derogation from itself. It was the principle of self-respect carried as far as it could go without infringing upon that respect which he would have every one else equally maintain for himself. He would have you to think alike with him on this topic. Many a quarrel have I had with him, when we were rather older boys and our tallness made us more obnoxious to observation in the blue clothes, because I would not thread the alleys and blind ways of the town with him to elude notice, when we have been out together on a holiday in the streets of this sneering and prying metropolis. W—— went, sore with these notions, to Oxford, where the dignity and sweetness of a scholar's life, meeting with the alloy of a humble introduction, wrought in him a passionate devotion to the place, with a profound aversion from the society. The servitor's gown (worse than his school array) clung to him with Nessian venom. He thought himself ridiculous in a garb under which Latimer must have walked erect, and in which Hooker, in his young days, possibly flaunted in a vein of no discommendable vanity. In the depth of college shades or in his lonely chamber, the poor student shrunk from observation. He found shelter among books, which insult not; and studies, that ask no questions of a youth's finances. He was lord of his library, and seldom cared for looking out beyond his domains. The healing influence of studious pursuits was upon him, to soothe and to abstract. He was almost a healthy man; when the waywardness of his fate broke out against him with a second and worse malignity. The father of W—— had hitherto exercised the humble profession of house-painter at N——, near Oxford. A supposed interest with some of the heads of the colleges had now induced him to take up his abode in that city, with the hope of being employed upon some public works which were talked of. From that moment I read in the countenance of the young man the determination which at length tore him from academical pursuits forever. To a person unacquainted with our universities, the distance between the gownsmen and the townsmen, as they are called—the trading part of the latter especially—is carried to an excess that would appear harsh and incredible. The temperament of W——'s father was diametrically the reverse of his own. Old W—— was a little, busy, cringing tradesman, who, with his son upon his arm, would stand bowing and scraping, cap in hand, to anything that wore the semblance of a gown—insensible to the winks and opener remonstrances of the young man, to whose chamber-fellow or equal in standing, perhaps, he was thus obsequiously and gratuitously ducking. Such a state of things could not last. W—— must change the air of Oxford or be suffocated. He chose the former; and let the sturdy moralist, who strains the point of the filial duties as high as they can bear, censure the dereliction; he cannot estimate the struggle. I stood with W——, the last afternoon I ever saw him, under the eaves of his paternal dwelling. It was in the fine lane leading from the High-street to the back of ****** college, where W—— kept his rooms. He seemed thoughtful and more reconciled. I ventured to rally him —finding him in a better mood—upon a representation of the artist Evangelist, which the old man, whose affairs were beginning to flourish, had caused to be set up in a splendid sort of frame over his really handsome shop, either as a token of prosperity or badge of gratitude to his saint. W—— looked up at the Luke, and, like Satan, "knew his mounted sign—and fled." A letter on his father's table the next morning announced that he had accepted a commission in a regiment about to embark for Portugal. He was among the first who perished before the walls of St. Sebastian.

I do not know how, upon a subject which I began with treating half seriously, I should have fallen upon a recital so eminently painful; but this theme of poor relationship is replete with so much matter for tragic as well as comic associations that it is difficult to keep the account distinct without blending. The earliest impressions which I received on this matter are certainly not attended with anything painful or very humiliating in the recalling. At my father's table (no very splendid one) was to be found, every Saturday, the mysterious figure of an aged gentleman, clothed in neat black, of a sad yet comely appearance. His deportment was of the essence of gravity; his words few or none; and I was not to make a noise in his presence. I had little inclination to have done so—for my cue was to admire in silence. A particular elbow-chair was appropriated to him, which was in no case to be violated. A peculiar sort of sweet pudding, which appeared on no other occasion, distinguished the days of his coming. I used to think him a prodigiously rich man. All I could make out of him was that he and my father had been schoolfellows a world ago at Lincoln, and that he came from the Mint. The Mint I knew to be a place where all the money was coined—and I thought he was the owner of all that money. Awful ideas of the Tower twined themselves about his presence. He seemed above human infirmities and passions. A sort of melancholy grandeur invested him. From some inexplicable doom I fancied him obliged to go about in an eternal suit of mourning; a captive, a stately being, let out of the Tower on Saturdays. Often have I wondered at the temerity of my father, who, in spite of an habitual general respect which we all in common manifested towards him, would venture now and then to stand up against him in some argument touching their youthful days. The houses of the ancient city of Lincoln are divided (as most of my readers know) between the dwellers on the hill and in the valley. This marked distinction formed an obvious division between the boys who lived above (however brought together in a common school) and the boys whose paternal residence was on the plain; a sufficient cause of hostility in the code of these young Grotiuses. My father had been a leading Mountaineer; and would still maintain the general superiority, in skill and hardihood, of the *Above Boys* (his own faction) over the *Below Boys* (so were they called), of which party his contemporary had been a chieftain. Many and hot were the skirmishes on this topic—the only one upon which the old gentleman was ever brought out—and bad blood bred; even sometimes almost to the recommencement (so I expected) of actual hostilities. But my father, who scorned to insist upon advantages, generally contrived to turn the conversation upon some adroit by-commendation of the old minster; in the general preference of which before all other cathedrals in the island, the dweller on the hill and the plain-born could meet on a conciliating level, and lay down their less important differences. Once only I saw the old gentleman really ruffled, and I remembered with anguish the thought that came over me: "Perhaps he will never come here again." He had been pressed to take another plate of the viand which I have already mentioned as the indispensable concomitant of his visits. He had refused with a resistance amounting to rigor, when my aunt—an old Lincolnian, but who had something of this, in common with my cousin Bridget, that she would sometimes press civility out of season—uttered the following memorable application: "Do take another slice, Mr. Billet, for you do not get pudding every day." The old gentleman said nothing at the time; but he took occasion in the course of the evening, when some argument had intervened between them, to utter with an emphasis which chilled the company, and which chills me now as I write it—"Woman, you are superannuated!" John Billet did not survive long after the digesting of this affront, but he survived long enough to assure me that peace was actually restored; and if I remember aright, another pudding was discreetly substituted in the place of that which had occasioned the offence. He died at the Mint (*anno* 1781), where he had long held what he accounted a comfortable independence;

and with five pounds, fourteen shillings, and a penny, which were found in his *escritoire* after his decease, left the world, blessing God that he had enough to bury him and that he had never been obliged to any man for a sixpence. This was —a Poor Relation.

Walter Savage Landor.

1775–1864.

PETRARCH ATTENDS THE PARISH CHURCH.

(From *The Pentameron*, 1837.)

It being now the Lord's Day, Messer Francesco thought it meet that he should rise early in the morning and bestir himself, to hear mass in the parish church at Certaldo. Whereupon he went on tiptoe, if so weighty a man could indeed go in such a fashion, and lifted softly the latch of Ser Giovanni's chamber-door, that he might salute him ere he departed, and occasion no wonder at the step he was about to take. He found Ser Giovanni fast asleep, with the missal wide open across his nose, and a pleasant smile on his genial, joyous mouth. Ser Francesco leaned over the couch, closed his hands together, and, looking with even more than his usual benignity, said in a low voice, "God bless thee, gentle soul! the Mother of purity and innocence protect thee!"

He then went into the kitchen, where he found the girl Assunta, and mentioned his resolution. She informed him that the horse had eaten his two beans, and was as strong as a lion and as ready as a lover. Ser Francesco patted her on the cheek, and called her "semplicetta!" She was overjoyed at this honor from so great a man, the bosom-friend of her good master, whom she had always thought the greatest man in the world, not excepting Monsignore, until he told her he was only a dog confronted with Ser Francesco. She tripped alertly across the paved court into the stable, and took down the saddle and bridle from the farther end of the rack. But Ser Francesco, with his natural politeness, would not allow her to equip his palfrey. "This is not the work for maidens," said he; "return to the house, good girl!"

She lingered a moment, then went away; but, mistrusting

the dexterity of Ser Francesco, she stopped and turned back again, and peeped through the half-closed door, and heard sundry sobs and wheezes round about the girth. Ser Francesco's wind ill seconded his intention; and although he had thrown the saddle valiantly and stoutly in its station, yet the girths brought him into extremity. She entered again, and, dissembling the reason, asked him whether he would not take a small beaker of the sweet white wine before he set out, and offered to girdle the horse while his Reverence bitted and bridled him. Before any answer could be returned, she had begun. And having now satisfactorily executed her undertaking, she felt irrepressible delight and glee at being able to do what Ser Francesco had failed in. He was scarcely more successful with his allotment of the labor; found unlooked-for intricacies and complications in the machinery, wondered that human wit could not simplify it, and declared that the animal had never exhibited such restiveness before. In fact he never had experienced the same grooming. At this conjuncture a green cap made its appearance, bound with straw-colored ribbon and surmounted with two bushy sprigs of hawthorn, of which the globular buds were swelling, and some bursting, but fewer yet open. It was young Simplizio Nardi, who sometimes came on the Sunday morning to sweep the court-yard for Assunta.

"O! this time you are come just when you were wanted," said the girl. "Bridle directly Ser Francesco's horse, and then go away about your business."

The youth blushed, and kissed Ser Francesco's hand, begging his permission. It was soon done. He then held the stirrup; and Ser Francesco, with scarcely three efforts, was seated and erect on the saddle. The horse, however, had somewhat more inclination for the stable than for the expedition; and as Assunta was handing to the rider his long ebony staff, bearing an ivory caduceus, the quadruped turned suddenly round. Simplizio called him "bestiaccia!" and then, softening it, "poco garbato!" and proposed to Ser Francesco that he should leave the *bastone* behind, and take the crab-switch he presented to him, giving at the same time a sample of its efficacy, which covered the long grizzle hair of the worthy quadruped with a profusion of pink blossoms, like embroidery. The offer was declined; but Assunta told Simplizio to carry it himself, and to walk by the side of Ser Canonico quite up to the church-porch, having seen what a sad dangerous beast his Reverence had under him. With perfect good will, partly in the pride of obedience to Assunta, and partly to enjoy the renown of accompanying a canon of holy church, Simplizio did as she enjoined.

And now the sound of village bells, in many hamlets and convents and churches out of sight, was indistinctly heard and lost again; and at last the five of Certaldo seemed to crow over the faintness of them all. The freshness of the morning was enough of itself to excite the spirits of youth; a portion of which never fails to descend on years that are far removed from it, if the mind has partaken in innocent mirth while it was its season and its duty to enjoy it. Parties of young and old passed the *canonico* and his attendant with mute respect, bowing and bare-headed; for that ebony staff threw its spell over the tongue, which the frank and hearty salutation of the bearer was inadequate to break. Simplizio, once or twice, attempted to call back an intimate of the same age with himself; but the utmost he could obtain was a "Riveritissimo" and a genuflexion to the rider. It is reported that a heart-burning rose up from it in the breast of a cousin, some days after, too distinctly apparent in the long-drawn appellation of "Gnor Simplizio."

Ser Francesco moved gradually forward, his steed picking his way along the lane and looking fixedly on the stones with all the sobriety of a mineralogist. He himself was well satisfied with the pace, and told Simplizio to be sparing of the switch unless in case of a hornet or a gadfly. Simplizio smiled toward the hedge, and wondered at the condescension of so great a theologian and astrologer in joking with him about the gadflies and hornets in the beginning of April. "Ah! there are men in the world who can make wit out of anything!" said he to himself. As they approached the walls of the town, the whole country was pervaded by a stirring and diversified air of gladness. Laughter and songs and flutes and viols, inviting voices and complying responses, mingled with merry bells and with processional hymns, along the woodland paths and along the yellow meadows. It was really the Lord's Day, for he made his creatures happy in it, and their hearts were thankful. Even the cruel had ceased from cruelty, and the rich man alone exacted from the animal his daily labor. Ser Francesco made this remark, and told his youthful guide that he had never been before where he could not walk to church on a Sunday; and that nothing should persuade him to urge the speed of his beast, on the Seventh Day, beyond his natural and willing foot's pace.

He reached the gates of Certaldo more than half an houı before the time of service, and he found laurels suspended over them and being suspended; and many pleasant and beautiful faces were protruded between the ranks of gentry and clergy who awaited him. Little did he expect such an attendance; but Fra Biagio of San Vivaldo, who himself had offered no obsequiousness or respect, had scattered the secret of his visit throughout the whole country. A young poet, the most celebrated in the town, approached the *canonico* with a long scroll of verses, which fell below the knee, beginning,

"How shall we welcome our illustrious guest ?"

To which Ser Francesco immediately replied, "Take your favorite maiden, lead the dance with her, and bid all your friends follow; you have a good half hour for it."

Universal applauses succeeded, the music struck up, couples were instantly formed. The gentry on this occasion led out the *cittadinanza*, as they usually do in the *villeggiatura*, rarely in the carnival, and never at other times. The elder of the priests stood round in their sacred vestments, and looked with cordiality and approbation on the youths, whose hands and arms could indeed do much and did it, but whose active eyes could rarely move upward the modester of their partners. While the elder of the clergy were thus gathering the fruits of their liberal cares and paternal exhortations, some of the younger looked on with a tenderer sentiment, not unmingled with regret. Suddenly the bells ceased; the figure of the dance was broken; all hastened into the church; and many hands that joined on the green met together at the font and touched the brow reciprocally with its lustral waters, in soul-devotion.

After the service, and after a sermon a good church-hour in length to gratify him, enriched with compliments from all authors, Christian and pagan, informing him at the conclusion that, although he had been crowned in the Capitol, he must die, being born mortal, Ser Francesco rode homeward. The sermon seemed to have sunk deeply into him, and even into the horse under him, for both of them nodded, both snorted, and one stumbled. Simplizio was twice fain to cry, "Ser Canonico! Riverenza! in this country if we sleep before dinner it does us harm. There are stones in the road, Ser Canonico, loose as eggs in a nest, and pretty nigh as thick together, huge as mountains."

"Good lad!" said Ser Francesco, rubbing his eyes, "toss the biggest of them out of the way, and never mind the rest."

The horse, although he walked, shuffled almost into an amble as he approached the stable, and his master looked up at it with nearly the same contentment. Assunta had been ordered to wait for his return, and cried, "O Ser Francesco! you are looking at our long apricot, that runs the whole length of the stable and barn, covered with blossoms as the old white hen is with feathers. You must come in the summer, and eat this fine fruit with Signor Padrone. You cannot think how ruddy and golden and sweet and mellow it is. There are peaches in all the fields, and plums and pears and apples, but there is not another apricot for miles and miles. Ser Giovanni brought the stone from Naples before I was born; a lady gave it to him when she had eaten only half the fruit off it: but perhaps you may have seen her, for you have ridden as far as Rome, or beyond. Padrone looks often at the fruit, and eats it willingly; and I have seen him turn over the stones in his plate, and choose one out from the rest, and put it into his pocket, but never plant it."

"Where is the youth?" inquired Ser Francesco.

"Gone away," answered the maiden.

"I wanted to thank him," said the Canonico.

"May I tell him so?" asked she.

"And give him," continued he, holding a piece of silver——

"I will give him something of my own, if he goes on and behaves well," said she; "but Signor Padrone would drive him away forever, I am sure, if he were tempted in an evil hour to accept a *quattrino* for any service he could render the friends of the house."

Ser Francesco was delighted with the graceful animation of this ingenuous girl, and asked her, with a little curiosity, how she could afford to make him a present."

"I do not intend to make him a present," she replied; "but it is better he should be rewarded by me," she blushed and hesitated, "or by Signor Padrone," she added, "than by your Reverence. He has not done half his duty yet; not half. I will teach him: he is quite a child; four months younger than me."

Ser Francesco went into the house, saying to himself at the doorway, "Truth, innocence, and gentle manners have not yet left the earth. There are sermons that never make the ears weary. I have heard but few of them, and come from church for this."

Whether Simplizio had obeyed some private signal from Assunta, or whether his own delicacy had prompted him to disappear, he was now again in the stable, and the manger was replenished with hay. A bucket was soon after heard ascending from the well; and then two words:—

"Thanks, Simplizio."

Thomas De Quincey.

1785–1859.

LEVANA AND OUR LADIES OF SORROW.

(From *Suspiria de Profundis,* 1845.)

Oftentimes at Oxford I saw Levana in my dreams. I knew her by her Roman symbols. Who is Levana? Reader, that do not pretend to have leisure for very much scholarship, you will not be angry with me for telling you. Levana was the Roman goddess that performed for the new-born infant the earliest office of ennobling kindness,—typical, by its mode, of that grandeur which belongs to man everywhere, and of that benignity in powers invisible which even in pagan worlds sometimes descends to sustain it. At the very moment of birth, just as the infant tasted for the first time the atmosphere of our troubled planet, it was laid on the ground. *That* might bear different interpretations. But immediately, lest so grand a creature should grovel there for more than one instant, either the paternal hand, as proxy for the goddess Levana, or some near kinsman, as proxy for the father, raised it upright, bade it look erect as the king of all this world, and presented its forehead to the stars, saying, perhaps, in his heart, "Behold what is greater than yourselves!" This symbolic act represented the function of Levana. And that mysterious lady, who never revealed her face (except to me in dreams), but always acted by delegation, had her name from the Latin verb (as still it is the Italian verb) *levare,* "to raise aloft."

This is the explanation of Levana. And hence it has arisen that some people have understood by Levana the tutelary power that controls the education of the nursery. She, that would not suffer at his birth even a prefigurative or mimic degradation for her awful ward, far less could be supposed to suffer the real degradation attaching to the non-development of his powers. She therefore watches over human education. Now, the word *edŭco,* with the penultimate short, was derived (by a process often exemplified in the crystallization of languages) from the word *edūco,* with the penultimate long. Whatsoever *educes,* or develops, *educates.* By the education of Levana, therefore, is meant, not the poor machinery that moves by spelling-books and grammars, but by that mighty system of central forces hidden in thc deep bosom of human life, which by passion, by strife, by temptation, by the energies of resistance, works forever upon children, resting not day or night, any more than the mighty wheel of day and night themselves, whose moments, like restless spokes, are glimmering forever as they revolve.

If, then, *these* are the ministries by which Levana works, how profoundly must she reverence the agencies of grief! But you, reader, think that children generally are not liable to grief such as mine. There are two senses in the word "generally,"—the sense of Euclid, where it means "universally" (or in the whole extent of the *genus*), and a foolish sense of this world, where it means "usually." Now, I am far from saying that children universally are capable of grief like mine. But there are more than you ever heard of who die of grief in this island of ours. I will tell you a common case. The rules of Eton require that a boy on the "foundation" should be there twelve years: he is superannuated at eighteen, consequently he must come at six. Children torn away from mothers and sisters at that age not unfrequently die. I speak of what I know. The complaint is not entered by the registrar as grief; but *that* it is. Grief of that sort, and at that age, has killed more than ever have been counted amongst its martyrs.

Therefore it is that Levana often communes with the powers that shake man's heart; therefore it is that she dotes upon grief. "These ladies," said I softly to myself, on seeing the ministers with whom Levana was conversing, "these are the Sorrows; and they are three in number: as the Graces are three, who dress man's life with beauty; the *Parcæ* are three, who weave the dark arras of man's life in their mysterious loom, always with colors sad in part, sometimes angry with tragic crimson and black; the Furies are three, who visit with retributions, called from the other side of the grave, offences that walk upon this; and once even the Muses were but three, who fit the harp, the trumpet, or the lute to the great burdens of man's impassioned creations. These are the Sorrows, all three of whom I know." The last words I say *now;* but in Oxford I said, "one of whom I know, and the others too surely I *shall* know." For already, in my fervent youth, I saw (dimly relieved upon the dark background of my dreams) the imperfect lineaments of the awful Sisters.

These Sisters—by what name shall we call them? If I say simply "The Sorrows," there will be a chance of mistaking the term: it might be understood of individual sorrow, separate cases of sorrow, whereas I want a term expressing the mighty abstractions that incarnate themselves in all individual sufferings of man's heart; and I wish to have these abstractions presented as impersonations, that is, as clothed with human attributes of life, and with functions pointing to flesh. Let us call them, therefore, *Our Ladies of Sorrow.*

I know them thoroughly, and have walked in all their kingdoms. Three sisters they are, of one mysterious household; and their paths are wide apart; but of their dominion there is no end. Them I saw often conversing with Levana, and sometimes about myself. Do they talk, then? Oh, no! Mighty phantoms like these disdain the infirmities of language. They may utter voices through the organs of man when they dwell in human hearts, but amongst themselves is no voice nor sound; eternal silence reigns in their kingdoms. They spoke not as they talked with Levana; they whispered not; they sang not; though oftentimes methought they might have sung: for I upon earth had heard their mysteries oftentimes deciphered by harp and timbrel, by dulcimer and organ. Like God, whose servants they are, they utter their pleasure, not by sounds that perish or by words that go astray, but by signs in heaven, by changes on earth, by pulses in secret rivers, heraldries painted on darkness, and hieroglyphics written on the tablets of the brain. *They* wheeled in mazes; *I* spelled the steps. *They* telegraphed from afar; *I* read the signals. *They* conspired together; and on the mirrors of darkness *my* eye traced the plots. *Theirs* were the symbols; *mine* are the words.

What is it the Sisters are? What is it that they do? Let me describe their form and their presence; if form it were that still fluctuated in its outline, or presence it were that forever advanced to the front or forever receded amongst shades.

The eldest of the three is named *Mater Lachrymarum*, Our Lady of Tears. She it is that night and day raves and moans, calling for vanished faces. She stood in Rama, where a voice was heard of lamentation—Rachel weeping for her children, and refusing to be comforted. She it was that stood in Bethlehem on the night when Herod's sword swept its nurseries of Innocents, and the little feet were stiffened forever, which, heard at times as they trotted along floors overhead, woke pulses of love in household hearts that were not unmarked in heaven. Her eyes are sweet and subtle, wild and sleepy, by turns; oftentimes rising to the clouds, oftentimes challenging the heavens. She wears a diadem round her head. And I knew by childish memories that she could go abroad upon the winds, when she heard the sobbing of litanies or the thundering of organs, and when she beheld the mustering of summer clouds. This Sister, the elder, it is that carries keys more than papal at her girdle, which open every cottage and every palace. She, to my knowledge, sat all last summer by the bedside of the blind beggar, him that so often and so gladly I talked with, whose pious daughter, eight years old, with the sunny countenance, resisted the temptations of play and village mirth, to travel all day long on dusty roads with her afflicted father. For this did God send her a great reward. In the springtime of the year, and whilst yet her own spring was budding, he recalled her to himself. But her blind father mourns forever over her; still he dreams at midnight that the little guiding hand is locked within his own; and still he wakens to a darkness that is *now* within a second and a deeper darkness. This *Mater Lachrymarum* also has been sitting all this winter of 1844-5 within the bedchamber of the Czar, bringing before his eyes a daughter (not less pious) that vanished to God not less suddenly, and left behind her a darkness not less profound. By the power of the keys it is that Our Lady of Tears glides, a ghostly intruder, into the chambers of sleepless men, sleepless women, sleepless children, from Ganges to the Nile, from Nile to Mississippi. And her, because she is the first-born of her house and has the widest empire, let us honor with the title of "Madonna."

The second Sister is called *Mater Suspiriorum*, Our Lady of Sighs. She never scales the clouds, nor walks abroad upon the winds. She wears no diadem. And her eyes, if they were ever seen, would be neither sweet nor subtle; no man could read their story; they would be found filled with perishing dreams and with wrecks of forgotten delirium. But she raises not her eyes; her head, on which sits a dilapidated turban, droops forever, forever fastens on the dust. She weeps not. She groans not. But she sighs inaudibly at intervals. Her sister Madonna is oftentimes stormy and frantic, raging in the highest against heaven, and demanding back her darlings. But Our Lady of Sighs never clamors, never defies, dreams not of rebellious aspirations. She is humble to abjectness. Hers is the meekness that belongs to the hopeless. Murmur she may, but it is in her sleep. Whisper she may, but it is to herself in the twilight. Mutter she does at times, but it is in solitary places that are desolate as she is desolate, in ruined cities, and when the sun has gone down to his rest. This Sister is the visitor of the Pariah, of the Jew, of the bondsman to the oar in the Mediterranean galleys; of the English criminal in Norfolk Island, blotted out from the books of remembrance in sweet far-off England; of the baffled penitent reverting his eyes forever upon a solitary grave, which to him seems the altar overthrown of some past and bloody sacrifice, on which altar no oblations can now be availing, whether towards pardon that he might implore, or towards reparation that he might attempt. Every slave that at noonday looks up to the tropical sun with timid reproach, as he points with one hand to the earth, our general mother, but for *him* a step-mother, as he points with the other hand to the Bible, our general teacher, but against *him* sealed and sequestered; every woman sitting in darkness, without love to shelter her head, or hope to illumine her solitude, because the heaven-born instincts kindling in her nature germs of holy affections, which God implanted in her womanly bosom, having been stifled by social necessities, now burn sullenly to waste, like sepulchral lamps amongst the ancients; every nun defrauded of her unreturning May-time by wicked kinsman, whom God will judge; every captive in every dungeon; all that are betrayed, and all that are rejected; outcasts by traditionary law, and children of hereditary disgrace,—all these walk with Our Lady of Sighs. She also carries a key; but she needs it little. For her kingdom is chiefly amongst the tents of Shem, and the houseless vagrant of every clime. Yet in the very highest ranks of man she finds chapels of her own; and even in glorious England there are some that, to the world, carry their heads as proudly as the reindeer, yet who secretly have received her mark upon their foreheads.

But the third Sister, who is also the youngest—! Hush! whisper whilst we talk of *her!* Her kingdom is not large, or else no flesh should live; but within that kingdom all power is hers. Her head, turreted like that of Cybele, rises almost beyond the reach of sight. She droops not; and her eyes, rising so high, *might* be hidden by distance. But, being what they are, they cannot be hidden; through the treble veil of crape which she wears, the fierce light of a blazing misery, that rests not for matins or for vespers, for noon of day or noon of night, for ebbing or for flowing tide, may be read from the very ground. She is the defier of God. She also is the mother of lunacies, and the suggestress of suicides. Deep lie the roots of her power; but narrow is the nation that she rules. For she can approach only those in whom a profound nature has been upheaved by central convulsions; in whom the heart trembles and the brain rocks under conspiracies of tempest from without and tempest from within. Madonna moves with uncertain steps, fast or slow, but still with tragic grace. Our Lady of Sighs creeps timidly and stealthily. But this youngest Sister moves with incalculable motions, bounding, and with tiger's leaps. She carries no key; for, though coming rarely amongst men, she storms all doors at which she is permitted to enter at all. And *her* name is *Mater Tenebrarum,* Our Lady of Darkness.

These were the *Semnai Theai,* or Sublime Goddesses, these were the *Eumenides,* or Gracious Ladies (so called by antiquity in shuddering propitiation), of my Oxford dreams. Madonna spoke. She spoke by her mysterious hand. Touching my head, she beckoned to Our Lady of Sighs; and what she spoke, translated out of the signs which (except in dreams) no man reads, was this:—

"Lo! here is he whom in childhood I dedicated to my altars. This is he that once I made my darling. Him I led astray, him I beguiled, and from heaven I stole away his young heart to mine. Through me did he become idolatrous; and through me it was, by languishing desires, that he worshipped the worm and prayed to the wormy grave. Holy was the grave to him; lovely was its darkness; saintly its corruption. Him, this young idolator, I have seasoned for thee, dear gentle Sister of Sighs! Do thou take him now to *thy* heart, and season him for our dreadful Sister. And thou,"—turning to the *Mater Tenebrarum,* she said,—"wicked Sister, that temptest and hatest, do thou take him from *her.* See that thy sceptre lie heavy on his head. Suffer not woman and her tenderness to sit near him in his darkness. Banish the frailties of hope; wither the relenting of love; scorch the fountains of tears; curse him as only thou canst curse. So shall he be accomplished in the furnace; so shall he see the things that ought not to be seen, sights that are abominable, and secrets that are unutterable. So shall he read elder truths, sad truth, grand truths, fearful truths. So shall he rise again *before* he dies. And so shall our commission be accomplished which from God we had—to plague his heart until we had unfolded the capacities of his spirit."

LITERATURE OF KNOWLEDGE AND LITERATURE OF POWER.

(From *The Poetry of Pope*, 1848.)

What is it that we mean by literature? Popularly, and amongst the thoughtless, it is held to include everything that is printed in a book. Little logic is required to disturb that definition. The most thoughtless person is easily made aware that in the idea of literature one essential element is some relation to a general and common interest of man, so that what applies only to a local or professional or merely personal interest, even though presenting itself in the shape of a book, will not belong to literature. So far the definition is easily narrowed; and it is as easily expanded. For not only is much that takes a station in books not literature, but, inversely, much that really is literature never reaches a station in books. The weekly sermons of Christendom, that vast pulpit literature which acts so extensively upon the popular mind—to warn, to uphold, to renew, to comfort, to alarm—does not attain the sanctuary of libraries in the ten-thousandth part of its extent. The drama, again, as for instance the finest of Shakespeare's plays in England and all leading Athenian plays in the noontide of the Attic stage, operated as a literature on the public mind, and were (according to the strictest letter of that term) published through the audiences that witnessed their representation, some time before they were published as things to be read; and they were published in this scenical mode of publication with much more effect than they could have had as books during ages of costly copying or of costly printing.

Books, therefore, do not suggest an idea co-extensive and interchangeable with the idea of literature, since much literature, scenic, forensic, or didactic (as from lecturers and public orators), may never come into books, and much that does come into books may connect itself with no literary interest. But a far more important correction, applicable to the common vague idea of literature, is to be sought, not so much in a better definition of literature, as in a sharper distinction of the two functions which it fulfils. In that great social organ which, collectively, we call literature, there may be distinguished two separate offices, that may blend and often do so, but capable, severally, of a severe insulation, and naturally fitted for reciprocal repulsion. There is, first, the literature of knowledge, and, secondly, the literature of power. The function of the first is to teach; the function of the second is to move: the first is a rudder; the second, an oar or a sail. The first speaks to the mere discursive understanding; the second speaks ultimately, it may happen, to the higher understanding, or reason, but always through affections of pleasure and sympathy. Remotely it may travel towards an object seated in what Lord Bacon calls dry light; but proximately it does and must operate—else it ceases to be a literature of power—on and through that humid light which clothes itself in the mists and glittering iris of human passions, desires, and genial emotions. Men have so little reflected on the higher functions of literature as to find it a paradox if one should describe it as a mean or subordinate purpose of books to give information. But this is a paradox only in the sense which makes it honorable to be paradoxical. Whenever we talk in ordinary language of seeking information or gaining knowledge, we understand the words as connected with something of absolute novelty. But it is the grandeur of all truth which can occupy a very high place in human interests that it is never absolutely novel to the meanest of minds: it exists eternally, by way of germ or latent principle, in the lowest as in the highest, needing to be developed but never to be planted. To be capable of transplantation is the immediate criterion of a truth that ranges on a lower scale. Besides which, there is a rarer thing than truth, namely, power, or deep sympathy with truth. What is the effect, for instance, upon society, of children? By the pity, by the tenderness, and by the peculiar modes of admiration, which connect themselves with the helplessness, with the innocence, and with the simplicity of children, not only are the primal affections strengthened and continually renewed, but the qualities which are dearest in the sight of heaven—the frailty, for instance, which appeals to forbearance, the innocence which symbolizes the heavenly, and the simplicity which is most alien from the worldly—are kept up in perpetual remembrance, and their ideals are continually refreshed. A purpose of the same nature is answered by the higher literature, viz., the literature of power. What do you learn from *Paradise Lost?* Nothing at all. What do you learn from a cookery-book? Something new, something that you did not know before, in every paragraph. But would you therefore put the wretched cookery-book on a higher level of estimation than the divine poem? What you owe to Milton is not any knowledge, of which a million separate items are still but a million of advancing steps on the same earthly level; what you owe is power, that is, exercise and expansion to your own latent capacity of sympathy with the infinite, where every pulse and each separate influx is a step upwards, a step ascending as upon a Jacob's ladder from earth to mysterious altitudes above the earth. All the steps of knowledge, from first to last, carry you further on the same plane, but could never raise you one foot above your ancient level of earth; whereas the very first step in power is a flight, is an ascending movement into another element where earth is forgotten.

Were it not that human sensibilities are ventilated and continually called out into exercise by the great phenomena of infancy, or of real life as it moves through chance and change, or of literature as it recombines these elements in the mimicries of poetry, romance, etc., it is certain that, like any animal power or muscular energy falling into disuse, all such sensibilities would gradually droop and dwindle. It is in relation to these great moral capacities of man that the literature of power, as contra-distinguished from that of knowledge, lives and has its field of action. It is concerned with what is highest in man; for the Scriptures themselves never condescended to deal by suggestion or co-operation with the mere discursive understanding: when speaking of man in his intellectual capacity, the Scriptures speak, not of the understanding, but of "the understanding heart," making the heart, *i. e.*, the great intuitive (or non-discursive) organ, to be the interchangeable formula for man in his highest state of capacity for the infinite. Tragedy, romance, fairy tale, or epopee, all alike restore to man's mind the ideals of justice, of hope, of truth, of mercy, of retribution, which else (left to the support of daily life in its realities) would languish for want of sufficient illustration. What is meant, for instance, by poetic justice? It does not mean a justice that differs by its object from the ordinary justice of human jurisprudence, for then it must be confessedly a very bad kind of justice; but it means a justice that differs from common forensic justice by the degree in which it *attains* its object, a justice that is more omnipotent over its own ends, as dealing, not with the refractory elements of earthly life, but with the elements of its own creation and with materials flexible to its own purest preconceptions. It is certain that, were it not for the literature of power, these ideals would often remain amongst us as mere arid notional forms; whereas, by the creative forces of man put forth in literature, they gain a vernal life of restoration and germinate into vital activities. The commonest novel, by moving in alliance with human fears and hopes, with human instincts of wrong and right, sustains and quickens those affections. Calling them into action, it rescues them from torpor. And hence the pre-eminency, over all authors that merely teach, of the meanest that moves, or that teaches, if at all, indirectly *by* moving. The very highest work that has ever existed in the literature of knowledge is but a provisional work, a book upon trial and sufferance, and *quamdiu bene se gesserit*. Let its teaching be even partially revised, let it be but expanded, nay, even let its teaching be but placed in a better order, and instantly it is superseded. Whereas the feeblest works in the literature of power, surviving at all, survive as finished and unalterable among men. For instance, the *Principia* of Sir Isaac Newton was a book militant on earth from the first. In all stages of its progress it would have to fight for its existence: first, as regards absolute truth; secondly, when that combat was over, as regards its form, or mode of presenting the truth. And as soon as a La Place, or anybody else, builds higher upon the foundations laid by this book, effectually he throws it out of the sunshine into decay and darkness; by weapons won from this book he superannuates and destroys this book, so that soon the name of Newton remains as a mere *nominis umbra*, but his book, as a living power, has transmigrated into other forms. Now, on the contrary, the *Iliad*, the *Prometheus* of Æschylus, the *Othello* or *King Lear*, the *Hamlet* or *Macbeth*, and the *Paradise Lost* are not militant but triumphant forever, as long as the languages exist in which they speak or can be taught to speak. They never can transmigrate into new incarnations. To reproduce these in new forms or variations, even if in some things they should be improved, would be to plagiarize. A good steam-engine is properly superseded by a better. But one lovely pastoral valley is not superseded by another, nor a statue of Praxiteles by a statue of Michael Angelo. These things are separated, not by imparity, but by disparity. They are not thought of as unequal under the same standard, but as different in kind, and, if otherwise equal, as equal under a different standard. Human works of immortal beauty and works of nature in one respect stand on the same footing: they never absolutely repeat each other, never approach so near as not to differ; and they differ not as better and worse, or simply by more and less; they differ by undecipherable and incommunicable differences, that cannot be caught by mimicries, that cannot be reflected in the mirror of copies, that cannot become ponderable in the scales of vulgar comparison.

Thomas Carlyle.

1795–1881.

BIOGRAPHY.

(1832.)

Man's sociality of nature evinces itself, in spite of all that can be said, with abundant evidence by this one fact, were there no other: the unspeakable delight he takes in Biography. It is written, "The proper study of mankind is man"; to which study, let us candidly admit, he, by true or by false methods, applies himself, nothing loath. "Man is perennially interesting to man; nay, if we look strictly to it, there is nothing else interesting." How inexpressibly comfortable to know our fellow-creature; to see into him, understand his goings-forth, decipher the whole heart of his mystery: nay, not only to see into him, but even to see out of him, to view the world altogether as he views it; so that we can theoretically construe him, and could almost practically personate him; and do now thoroughly discern both what manner of man he is, and what manner of thing he has got to work on and live on!

A scientific interest and a poetic one alike inspire us in this matter. A scientific: because every mortal has a Problem of Existence set before him, which, were it only, what for the most it is, the Problem of keeping soul and body together, must be to a certain extent original, unlike every other; and yet, at the same time, so *like* every other; like our own, therefore: instructive, moreover, since we also are indentured to *live*. A poetic interest still more: for precisely this same struggle of human Free-will against material Necessity, which every man's Life, by the mere circumstance that the man continues alive, will more or less victoriously exhibit, is that which above all else, or rather inclusive of all else, calls the Sympathy of mortal hearts into action; and whether as acted, or as represented and written of, not only is Poetry, but is the sole Poetry possible. Borne onwards by which two all-embracing interests, may the earnest Lover of Biography expand himself on all sides, and indefinitely enrich himself. Looking with the eyes of every new neighbor, he can discern a new world different for each: feeling with the heart of every neighbor, he lives with every neighbor's life, even as with his own. Of these millions of living men each individual is a mirror to us; a mirror both scientific and poetic; or, if you will, both natural and magical;—from which one would so gladly draw aside the gauze veil; and, peering therein, discern the image of his own natural face, and the supernatural secrets that prophetically lie under the same!

Observe, accordingly, to what extent, in the actual course of things, this business of Biography is practised and relished. Define to thyself, judicious Reader, the real significance of these phenomena named Gossip, Egoism, Personal Narrative (miraculous or not), Scandal, Raillery, Slander, and suchlike; the sum-total of which (with some fractional addition of a better ingredient, generally too small to be noticeable) constitutes that other grand phenomenon still called "Conversation." Do they not mean wholly: *Biography* and *Autobiography?* Not only in the common Speech of men, but in all Art, too, which is or should be the concentrated and conserved essence of what men can speak and show, Biography is almost the one thing needful.

Even in the highest works of Art our interest, as the critics complain, is too apt to be strongly or even mainly of a Biographic sort. In the Art we can nowise forget the Artist: while looking on the *Transfiguration*, while studying the *Iliad*, we ever strive to figure to ourselves what spirit dwelt in Raphael; what a head was that of Homer, wherein, woven of Elysian light and Tartarean gloom, that old world fashioned itself together, of which these written Greek characters are but a feeble though perennial copy. The Painter and the Singer are present to us; we partially and for the time become the very Painter and the very Singer while we enjoy the Picture and the Song. Perhaps, too, let the critic say what he will, this is the highest enjoyment the clearest recognition, we can have of these. Art indeed is Art; yet Man also is Man. Had the *Transfiguration* been painted without human hand, had it grown merely on the canvas, say by atmospheric influences, as lichen-pictures do on rocks, it were a grand picture doubtless; yet nothing like so grand as *the* Picture which, on opening our eyes, we everywhere in Heaven and in Earth see painted; and everywhere pass over with indifference,—because the painter was not a Man. Think of this; much lies in it. The Vatican is great; yet poor to Chimborazo or the Peak of Teneriffe: its dome is but a foolish Big-endian or Little-endian chip of an egg-shell, compared with that star-fretted Dome where Arcturus and Orion glance forever; which latter, notwithstanding, who looks at, save perhaps some necessitous star-gazer bent to make Almanacs, some thick-quilted watchman to see what weather it will prove? The Biographic interest is wanting: no Michael Angelo was He who built that "Temple of Immensity"; therefore do we, pitiful Littlenesses as we are, turn rather to wonder and to worship in the little toy-box of a Temple built by our like.

Still more decisively, still more exclusively, does the Biographic interest manifest itself as we descend into lower regions of spiritual communication; through the whole range of what is called Literature. Of History, for example, the most honored if not honorable species of composition, is not the whole purport Biographic? "History," it has been said, "is the essence of innumerable biographies." Such, at least, it should be: whether it is, might admit of question. But, in any case, what hope have we in turning over those old interminable Chronicles, with their garrulities and insipidities; or, still worse, in patiently examining those modern Narrations, of the Philosophic kind, where "Philosophy, teaching by Experience," has to sit like owl on housetop, *seeing* nothing, *understanding* nothing, uttering only, with such solemnity, her perpetual most wearisome *hoo-hoo*:—what hope have we, except the for most part fallacious one of gaining some acquaintance with our fellow-creatures, though dead and vanished, yet dear to us; how they got along in those old days, suffering and doing; to what extent, and under what circumstances, they resisted the Devil and triumphed over him, or struck their colors to him and were trodden under foot by him; how, in short, the perennial Battle went, which men name Life, which we also in these new days, with indifferent fortune, have to fight, and must bequeath to our sons and grandsons to go on fighting,—till the Enemy one day be quite vanquished and abolished, or else the great Night sink and part the combatants; and thus, either by some Millennium or some new Noah's Deluge, the Volume of Universal History wind itself up! Other hope, in studying such Books, we have none: and that it is a deceitful hope, who that has tried knows not? A feast of widest Biographic insight is spread for us; we enter full of hungry anticipations: alas, like so many other feasts which Life invites us to, a mere Ossian's "feast of *shells*,"—the food and liquor being all emptied out and clean gone, and only the vacant dishes and deceitful emblems thereof left! Your modern Historical Restaurateurs are indeed little better than high-priests of Famine, that keep choicest china dinner-sets, only no dinner to serve therein. Yet such is our Biographic appetite, we run trying from shop to shop, with ever new hope; and, unless we could eat the wind, with ever new disappointment.

Again, consider the whole class of Fictitious Narratives, from the highest category of epic or dramatic Poetry, in Shakespeare and Homer, down to the lowest of froth Prose in the Fashionable Novel. What are all these but so many mimic Biographies? Attempts, here by an inspired Speaker, there by an uninspired Babbler, to deliver himself, more or less ineffectually, of the grand secret wherewith all hearts labor oppressed: the significance of Man's Life;—which deliverance, even as traced in the unfurnished head, and printed at the Minerva Press, finds readers. For, observe, though there is *a* greatest Fool, as a superlative in every kind; and *the* most Foolish man in the Earth is now indubitably living and breathing, and did this morning or lately eat breakfast, and is even now digesting the same; and looks out on the world with his dim horn-eyes, and inwardly forms some unspeakable theory thereof: yet where shall the authentically Existing be personally met with! Can one of us, otherwise than by guess, know that we have got sight of him, have orally communed with him? To take even the narrower sphere of this our English Metropolis, can any one confidently say to himself that he has conversed with the identical, individual Stupidest man now extant in London? No one. Deep as we dive in the Profound, there is ever a new depth opens: where the ultimate bottom may lie, through what new scenes of being we must pass before reaching it (except that we know it does lie somewhere, and might by human faculty and opportunity be reached), is altogether a mystery to us. Strange, tantalizing pursuit! We have the fullest assurance, not only that there is a Stupidest of London men actually resident, with bed and board of some kind, in London, but that several persons have been or perhaps are now speaking face to face with him: while for us, chase it as we may, such scientific blessedness will too probably be for ever denied!—But the thing we meant to enforce was this comfortable fact, that no known Head was so wooden but there might be other heads to which it were a genius and Friar Bacon's Oracle. Of no given Book, not even of a Fashionable Novel, can you predicate with certainty that its vacuity is absolute; that there are not other vacuities which shall partially replenish themselves therefrom, and esteem it a *plenum*. How knowest thou, may the distressed Novelwright exclaim, that I, here where I sit, am the Foolishest of existing mortals; that this my Long-ear of a Fictitious Biography shall not find one and the other, into whose still longer ears it may be the means, under Providence, of instilling somewhat? We answer, None knows, none can certainly know: therefore, write on, worthy Brother, even as thou canst, even as it has been given thee.

Here, however, in regard to "Fictitious Biographies," and much other matter of like sort, which the greener mind in these days inditeth, we may as well insert some singular sentences on the importance and significance of *Reality*, as they stand written for us in Professor Gottfried Sauerteig's *Aesthetische Springwurzeln;* a Work, perhaps, as yet new to most English readers. The Professor and Doctor is not a man whom we can praise without reservation; neither shall we say that his *Springwurzeln* (a sort of magical pick-locks, as he affectedly names them) are adequate to "start" every *bolt* that locks-up an æsthetic mystery: nevertheless, in his crabbed, one-sided way, he sometimes hits masses of the truth. We endeavor to translate faithfully, and trust the reader will find it worth serious perusal:

"The significance, even for poetic purposes," says Sauerteig, "that lies in REALITY is too apt to escape us; is perhaps only now beginning to be discerned. When we named Rousseau's *Confessions* an elegiaco-didactic Poem, we meant more than an empty figure of speech; we meant a historical, scientific fact.

"Fiction, while the feigner of it knows that he is feigning, partakes, more than we suspect, of the nature of *lying*, and has ever an, in some degree, unsatisfactory character. All Mythologies were once Philosophies; were *believed:* the Epic Poems of old time, so long as they continued *epic* and had any complete impressiveness, were Histories, and understood to be narratives of *facts*. In so far as Homer employed his gods as mere ornamental fringes, and had not himself, or at least did not expect his hearers to have, a belief that they were real agents in those antique doings, so far did he fail to be *genuine;* so far was he a partially *hollow* and false singer; and sang to please only a portion of man's mind, not the whole thereof.

"Imagination is, after all, but a poor matter when it has to part company with Understanding, and even front it hostilely in flat contradiction. Our mind is divided in twain: there is contest; wherein that which is weaker must needs come to the worse. Now, of all feelings, states, principles, call it what you will, in man's mind, is not Belief the clearest, strongest; against which all others contend in vain? Belief is, indeed, the beginning and first condition of all spiritual

Force whatsoever: only in so far as Imagination, were it but momentarily, is *believed,* can there be any use or meaning in it, any enjoyment of it. And what is momentary Belief? The enjoyment of a moment. Whereas a perennial Belief were enjoyment perennially, and with the whole united soul.

"It is thus that I judge of the Supernatural in an Epic Poem; and would say, the instant it has ceased to be authentically supernatural, and become what you call 'Machinery,' sweep it out of sight (*schaff' es mir vom Halse*)! Of a truth, that same 'Machinery,' about which the critics make such hubbub, was well named *Machinery;* for it is in very deed mechanical, nowise inspired or poetical. Neither for us is there the smallest æsthetic enjoyment in it, save only in this way: that we believe it *to have been believed,*—by the Singer or his hearers; into whose case we now laboriously struggle to transport ourselves; and so, with stinted enough result, catch some reflex of the Reality, which for them was wholly real, and visible face to face. Whenever it has come so far that your 'Machinery' is avowedly mechanical and unbelieved, what is it else, if we dare tell ourselves the truth, but a miserable, meaningless Deception kept-up by old use and wont alone? If the gods of an *Iliad* are to us no longer authentic Shapes of Terror, heart-stirring, heart-appalling, but only vague-glittering Shadows, what must the dead Pagan gods of an *Epigoniad* be, the dead-living Pagan-Christian gods of a *Lusiad,* the concrete-abstract, evangelical-metaphysical gods of a *Paradise Lost?* Superannuated lumber! Cast raiment, at best; in which some poor mime, strutting and swaggering, may or may not set forth new, noble, Human Feelings (again a Reality), and so secure or not secure our pardon of such hoydenish masking; for which, in any case, he has a pardon to *ask.*

"True enough, none but the earliest Epic Poems can claim this distinction of entire credibility, of Reality: after an *Iliad,* a *Shaster,* a *Koran,* and other the like primitive performances, the rest seem, by this rule of mine, to be altogether excluded from the list. Accordingly, what *are* all the rest, from Virgil's *Æneid* downwards, in comparison? Frosty, artificial, heterogeneous things; more of gumflowers than of roses; at the best, of the two mixed incoherently together: to some of which, indeed, it were hard to deny the title of Poems; yet to no one of which can that title belong in any sense even resembling the old high one it, in those old days, conveyed,—when the epithet 'divine' or 'sacred,' as applied to the uttered Word of man, was not a vain metaphor, a vain sound, but a real name with meaning. Thus, too, the farther we recede from those early days, when Poetry, as true Poetry is always, was still sacred or divine, and inspired (what ours, in great part, only pretends to be), the more impossible becomes it to produce any, we say not true Poetry, but tolerable semblance of such; the hollower, in particular, grow all manner of Epics; till at length, as in this generation, the very name of Epic sets men a-yawning, the announcement of a new Epic is received as a public calamity.

"But what if, the *impossible* being once for all quite discarded, the *probable* be well adhered to: how stands it with fiction *then!* Why, then, I would say, the evil is much mended, but nowise completely cured. We have then, in place of the wholly dead modern Epic, the partially living modern Novel; to which latter it is much easier to lend that above-mentioned, so essential 'momentary credence' than to the former: indeed, infinitely easier; for the former being flatly incredible, no mortal *can* for a moment credit it, for a moment enjoy it. Thus, here and there, a *Tom Jones*, a *Meister*, a *Crusoe* will yield no little solacement to the minds of men; though still immeasurably less than a *Reality* would, were the significance thereof as impressively unfolded, were the genius that could so unfold it once given us by the kind Heavens. Neither say thou that proper Realities are wanting: for Man's Life, now, as of old, is the genuine work of God; wherever there is a Man, a God also is revealed and all that is God-like: a whole epitome of the Infinite, with its meanings, lies enfolded in the Life of every Man. Only, alas, that the Seer to discern this same God-like, and with fit utterance *un*fold it for us, is wanting, and may long be wanting!

"Nay, a question arises on us here, wherein the whole German reading-world will eagerly join: Whether man *can* any longer be so interested by the spoken Word as he often was in those primeval days, when, rapt away by its inscrutable power, he pronounced it, in such dialect as he had, to be *transcendental* (to *transcend* all measure), to be sacred, prophetic, and the inspiration of a god? For myself, I (*ich meines Ortes*), by faith or by insight, do heartily understand that the answer to such question will be, Yea! For never, that I could in searching find out, has Man been, by Time which devours so much, deprivated of any faculty whatsoever that he in any era was possessed of. To my seeming, the babe born yesterday has all the organs of Body, Soul, and Spirit, and in exactly the same combination and entireness, that the oldest Pelasgic Greek, or Mesopotamian Patriarch, or Father Adam himself could boast of. Ten fingers, one heart with venous and arterial blood therein, still belong to man that is born of woman: when did he lose any of his spiritual Endowments either; above all, his highest spiritual Endowment, that of revealing Poetic Beauty, and of adequately receiving the same? Not the material, not the susceptibility is wanting; only the Poet, or long series of Poets, to work on these. True, alas too true, the Poet *is* still utterly wanting, or all but utterly: nevertheless have we not centuries enough before us to produce him in? Him and much else.—I, for the present, will but predict that chiefly by working more and more on REALITY, and evolving more and more wisely *its* inexhaustible meanings and, in brief, speaking forth in fit utterance whatsoever our whole soul *believes*, and ceasing to speak forth what thing soever our whole soul does not believe, will this high emprise be accomplished, or approximated to."

These notable and not unfounded, though partial and *deep*-seeing rather than *wide*-seeing, observations on the great import of REALITY, considered even as a poetic material, we have inserted the more willingly, because a transient feeling to the same purpose may often have suggested itself to many readers; and, on the whole, it is good that every reader and every writer understand, with all intensity of conviction, what quite infinite worth lies in *Truth;* how all-pervading, omnipotent, in man's mind, is the thing we name *Belief.* For the rest, Herr Sauerteig, though one-sided, on this matter of Reality, seems heartily persuaded, and is not perhaps so ignorant as he looks. It cannot be unknown to him, for example, what noise is made about "Invention"; what a supreme rank this faculty is reckoned to hold in the poetic endowment. Great truly is Invention; nevertheless, that is but a poor exercise of it with which Belief is not concerned. "An Irishman with whisky in his head," as poor Byron said, will invent you, in this kind, till there is enough and to spare. Nay, perhaps, if we consider well, the highest exercise of Invention has, in very deed, nothing to do with Fiction, but is an invention of new Truth, what we can call a Revelation; which last does undoubtedly transcend all other poetic efforts, nor can Herr Sauerteig be too loud in its praises. But, on the other hand, whether such effort is still possible for man, Herr Sauerteig and the bulk of the world are probably at issue;—and will probably continue so till that same "Revelation," or new "Invention of Reality," of the sort he desiderates, shall itself make its appearance.

Meanwhile, quitting these airy regions, let any one bethink him how impressive the smallest historical *fact* may become, as contrasted with the grandest *fictitious event;* what an incalculable force lies for us in this consideration: The Thing which I here hold imaged in my mind did actually occur; was, in very truth, an element in the system of the All, whereof I too form part; had, therefore, and has, through all time, an authentic being; is not a dream, but a reality! We ourselves can remember reading, in Lord Clarendon, with feelings perhaps somehow accidentally opened to it,—certainly with a depth of impression strange to us then and now,—that insignificant-looking passage, where Charles, after the battle of Worcester, glides down, with Squire Careless, from the Royal Oak, at nightfall, being hungry: how, "making a shift to get over hedges and ditches, after walking at least eight or nine miles, which were the more grievous to the King by the weight of his boots (for he could not put *them* off when he cut off his hair, for want of shoes), before morning they came to *a poor cottage, the owner whereof, being a Roman Catholic, was known to Careless."* How this poor drudge, being knocked-up from his snoring, "carried them into a little barn full of hay, which was a better lodging than he had for himself"; and by and by, not without difficulty, brought his Majesty "a piece of bread and a great pot of buttermilk," saying candidly that "he himself lived by his daily labor, and that what he had brought him was the fare he and his wife had": on which nourishing diet his Majesty, "staying upon the haymow," feeds thankfully for two days; and then departs, under new guidance, having first changed clothes, down to the very shirt and "old pair of shoes," with his landlord; and so, as worthy Bunyan has it, "goes on his way, and sees him no more." Singular enough, if we will think of it! This, then, was a genuine, flesh-and-blood Rustic of the year 1651: he did actually swallow bread and buttermilk (not having ale and bacon), and do field-labor; with these hob-nailed "shoes" has sprawled through mud-roads in winter, and, jocund or not, driven his team a-field in summer; he made bargains; had chafferings and higglings, now a sore heart, now a glad one; was born; was a son, was a father; toiled in many ways, being forced to it, till the strength was all worn out of him; and then—lay down "to rest his galled back," and sleep there till the long-distant morning.—How comes it that he alone of all the British rustics who tilled and lived along with him, on whom the blessed sun on that same "fifth day of September" was shining, should have chanced to rise on us; that this poor pair of clouted Shoes, out of the million million hides that have been tanned and cut and worn, should still subsist and hang visibly together? We see him but for a moment; for one moment the blanket of the Night is rent asunder, so that we behold and see, and then closes over him—forever.

So too, in some *Boswell's Life of Johnson*, how indelible and magically bright does many a little *Reality* dwell in our remembrance! There is no need that the personages on the scene be a King and Clown; that the scene be the Forest of the Royal Oak, "on the borders of Staffordshire": need only that the scene lie on this old firm Earth of ours, where we also have so surprisingly arrived; that the personages be *men*, and *seen* with the eyes of a man. Foolish enough, how some slight, perhaps mean and even ugly, incident, if *real* and well presented, will fix itself in a susceptive memory and lie ennobled there, silvered over with the pale cast of thought, with the pathos which belongs only to the Dead. For the Past is all holy to us; the Dead are all holy, even they that were base and wicked while alive. Their baseness and wickedness was not *They,* was but the heavy and unmanageable Environment that lay round them, with which they fought unprevailing: *they* (the ethereal god-given Force that dwelt in them, and was their *Self*) have now shuffled-off that heavy Environment, and are free and pure: their life-long Battle, go how it might, is all ended, with many wounds or with fewer; they have been recalled from it, and the once harsh-jarring battle-field has become a silent awe-inspiring Golgotha and *Gottes-acker* (Field of God)!—Boswell relates this in itself smallest and poorest of occurrences: "As we walked along the Strand to-night, arm-in-arm, a woman of the town accosted us in the usual enticing manner. 'No, no, my girl,' said Johnson; 'it won't do.' He, however, did not treat her with harshness; and we talked of the wretched life of such women." Strange power of *Reality!* Not even this poorest of occurrences, but now, after seventy years are come and gone, has a meaning for us. Do but consider that it is *true;* that it did in very deed occur! That unhappy Outcast, with all her sins and woes, her lawless desires, too complex mischances, her wailings and her riotings, has departed utterly; alas! her siren finery has got all besmutched, ground, generations since, into dust and smoke; of her degraded body, and whole miserable earthly existence, all is away: *she* is no longer here, but far from us, in the bosom of Eternity,—whence we too came, whither we too are bound! Johnson said, "No, no, my girl; it won't do"; and then "we talked";—and herewith the wretched one, seen but for the twinkling of an eye, passes on into the utter Darkness. No high Calista, that ever issued from Story-teller's brain, will impress us more deeply than this meanest of the mean; and for a good reason: That *she* issued from the Maker of Men.

It is well worth the Artist's while to examine for himself what it is that gives such pitiable incidents their memorableness; his aim likewise is, above all things, to be *memorable.* Half the effect, we already perceive, depends on the object; on its being *real,* on its being really *seen.* The other half will depend on the observer; and the question now is: How are real objects to be *so* seen; on what quality of observing, or of style in describing, does this so intense pictorial power depend? Often a slight circumstance contributes curiously to the result: some little, and perhaps to appearance accidental, feature is presented; a light-gleam, which instantaneously *excites* the mind, and urges it to complete the picture, and evolve the meaning thereof for itself. By critics, such light-gleams and their almost magical influence have frequently been noted: but the power to produce such, to select such features as will produce them, is generally treated as a knack, or trick of the trade, a secret for being "graphic"; whereas these magical feats are, in truth, rather inspirations; and the gift of performing them, which acts unconsciously, without forethought, and as if by nature alone, is properly a *genius* for description.

One grand, invaluable secret there is, however, which includes all the rest, and, what is comfortable, lies clearly in every man's power: *To have an open, loving heart, and what follows from the possession of such.* Truly it has been said, emphatically in these days ought it to be repeated: A loving Heart is the beginning of all Knowledge. This it is that opens the whole mind, quickens every faculty of the intellect to do its fit work, that of *knowing;* and therefrom, by sure consequence, of *vividly uttering-forth.* Other secret for being "graphic" is there none, worth having; but this is an all-sufficient one. See, for example, what a small Boswell can do! Hereby, indeed, is the whole man made a living mirror, wherein the wonders of this ever-wonderful Universe are, in their true light (which is ever a magical, miraculous one), represented, and reflected back on us. It has been said, "The heart sees farther than the head": but, indeed, without the seeing heart there is no true seeing for the head so much as possible; all is mere *oversight*, hallucination, and vain, superficial phantasmagoria, which can permanently profit no one.

Here, too, may we not pause for an instant, and make a practical reflection? Considering the multitude of mortals that handle the Pen in these days, and can mostly spell, and write without glaring violations of grammar, the question naturally arises: How is it, then, that no Work proceeds from them bearing any stamp of authenticity and permanence; of worth for more than one day? Shiploads of Fashionable Novels, Sentimental Rhymes, Tragedies, Farces, Diaries of Travel, Tales by flood and field, are swallowed monthly into the bottomless Pool; still does the Press toil; innumerable Paper-makers, Compositors, Printers' Devils, Book-binders, and Hawkers grown hoarse with loud proclaiming, rest not from their labor; and still, in torrents, rushes on the great array of Publications, unpausing, to their final home; and still Oblivion, like the Grave, cries, Give! Give! How is it that of all these countless multitudes no one can attain to the smallest mark of excellence, or produce aught that shall endure longer than "snow-flake on the river" or the foam of penny-beer? We answer: Because they *are* foam; because there is no *Reality* in them. These Three Thousand men, women, and children, that make up the army of British Authors, do not, if we will well consider it, *see* anything whatever; consequently *have* nothing that they can record and utter, only more or fewer things that they can plausibly pretend to record. The Universe, of Man and Nature, is still quite shut-up from them; the "open secret" still utterly a secret: because no sympathy with Man or Nature, no love and free simplicity of heart has yet unfolded the same. Nothing but a pitiful Image of their own pitiful Self, with its vanities, and grudgings, and ravenous hunger of all kinds, hangs forever painted in the retina of these unfortunate persons: so that the starry ALL, with whatsoever it embraces, does but appear as some expanded magic-lantern shadow of that same Image,—and naturally looks pitiful enough.

It is vain for these persons to allege that they are naturally without gift, naturally stupid and sightless, and so *can* attain to no knowledge of anything; therefore, in writing of anything, must needs write falsehoods of it, there being in it no truth for them. Not so, good Friends. The stupidest of you has a certain faculty, were it but that of articulate speech (say in the Scottish, the Irish, the Cockney dialect, or even in "Governess-English"), and of physically discerning what lies under your nose. The stupidest of you would perhaps grudge to be compared in faculty with James Boswell; yet see what he has produced! You do not use your faculty honestly; your heart is shut up; full of greediness, malice, discontent; so your intellectual sense cannot be open. It is vain also to urge that James Boswell had opportunities; saw great men and great things, such as you can never hope to look on. What make ye of Parson White in Selborne? He had not only no great men to look on, but not even men; merely sparrows and cock-chafers: yet has he left us a *Biography* of these; which, under its title *Natural History of Selborne,* still remains valuable to us; which has copied a little sentence or two *faithfully* from the Inspired Volume of Nature, and so is itself not without inspiration. Go ye and do likewise. Sweep away utterly all frothiness and falsehood from your heart; struggle unweariedly to acquire, what is possible for every god-created Man, a free, open, humble soul: *speak not at all, in any wise, till you have somewhat to speak;* care not for the *reward* of your speaking, but simply and with undivided mind for the *truth* of your speaking: then be placed in what section of Space and of Time soever, do but open your eyes, and they shall actually *see,* and bring you real *knowledge,* wondrous, worthy of *belief;* and instead of one Boswell and one White, the world will rejoice in a thousand,—stationed on their thousand several watch-towers, to instruct us by indubitable documents, of whatsoever in our so stupendous World comes to light and *is!* O, had the Editor of this Magazine but a magic rod to turn all that not inconsiderable Intellect, which now deluges us with artificial, fictitious soap-lather and mere Lying, into the faithful study of Reality, what knowledge of great, everlasting Nature, and of Man's ways and doings therein, would not every year bring us in! Can we but change one single soap-latherer and mountebank Juggler into a true Thinker and Doer, who even *tries* honestly to think and do, great will be our reward.

But to return; or rather from this point to begin our journey! If now, what with Herr Sauerteig's *Springwurzeln,* what with so much lucubration of our own, it have become apparent how deep, immeasurable is the "worth that lies in *Reality,*" and, farther, how exclusive the interest which man takes in Histories of Man, may it not seem lamentable that so few genuinely good *Biographies* have yet been accumulated in Literature; that in the whole world one cannot find, going strictly to work, above some dozen, or baker's dozen, and those chiefly of very ancient date? Lamentable; yet, after what we have just seen, accountable. Another question might be asked: How comes it that in England we have simply one good Biography, this *Boswell's Johnson;* and of good, indifferent, or even bad attempts at Biography, fewer than any civilised people? Consider the French and Germans, with their Moreris, Bayles, Jördenses, Jöchers, their innumerable *Mémoires* and *Schilderungen* and *Biographies Universelles;* not to speak of Rousseaus, Goethes, Schubarts, Jung-Stillings: and then contrast with these our poor Birches and Kippises and Pecks, the whole breed of whom, moreover, is now extinct!

With this question, as the answer might lead us far, and come out unflattering to patriotic sentiment, we shall not intermeddle; but turn rather, with great pleasure, to the fact, that one excellent Biography *is* actually English; and even now lies, in Five new Volumes, at our hand, soliciting a new consideration from us; such as, age after age (the Perennial showing ever new phases as *our* position alters), it may long be profitable to bestow on it;—to which task we here, in this position, in this age, gladly address ourselves.

First, however, let the foolish April-fool Day pass by; and our Reader, during these twenty-nine days of uncertain weather that will follow, keep pondering, according to convenience, the purport of Biography in general: then, with the blessed dew of May-day, and in unlimited convenience of space, shall all that we have written on *Johnson*, and *Boswell's Johnson*, and *Croker's Boswell's Johnson*, be faithfully laid before him.

HEROES AND HERO-WORSHIP.

(From *Heroes and Hero-Worship*, Lecture I., 1841.)

We have undertaken to discourse here for a little on Great Men, their manner of appearance in our world's business, how they have shaped themselves in the world's history, what ideas men formed of them, what work they did;—on Heroes, namely, and on their reception and performance; what I call Hero-worship and the Heroic in human affairs. Too evidently this is a large topic; deserving quite other treatment than we can expect to give it at present. A large topic; indeed, an illimitable one; wide as Universal History itself. For, as I take it, Universal History, the history of what man has accomplished in this world, is at bottom the History of the Great Men who have worked here. They were the leaders of men, these great ones; the modellers, patterns, and in a wide sense creators, of whatsoever the general mass of men contrived to do or to attain; all things that we see standing accomplished in the world are properly the outer material result, the practical realization and embodiment, of Thoughts that dwelt in the Great Men sent into the world: the soul of the whole world's history, it may justly be considered, were the history of these. Too clearly it is a topic we shall do no justice to in this place!

One comfort is, that Great Men, taken up in any way, are profitable company. We cannot look, however imperfectly, upon a great man, without gaining something by him. He is the living light-fountain, which it is good and pleasant to be near. The light which enlightens, which has enlightened, the darkness of the world; and this not as a kindled lamp only, but rather as a natural luminary shining by the gift of Heaven; a flowing light-fountain, as I say, of native original insight, of manhood and heroic nobleness;—in whose radiance all souls feel that it is well with them. On any terms whatsoever, you will not grudge to wander in such neighborhood for a while. These Six classes of Heroes, chosen out of widely-distant countries and epochs, and in mere external figure differing altogether, ought, if we look faithfully at them, to illustrate several things for us. Could we see *them* well, we should get some glimpses into the very marrow of the world's history. How happy, could I but, in any measure, in such times as these, make manifest to you the meanings of Heroism; the divine relation (for I may well call it such) which in all times unites a Great Man to other men; and thus, as it were, not exhaust my subject, but so much as break ground on it! At all events, I must make the attempt.

It is well said, in every sense, that a man's religion is the chief fact with regard to him. A man's, or a nation of men's. By religion I do not mean here the church-creed which he professes, the articles of faith which he will sign and, in words or otherwise, assert; not this wholly, in many cases not this at all. We see men of all kinds of professed creeds attain to almost all degrees of worth or worthlessness under each or any of them. This is not what I call religion, this profession and assertion; which is often only a profession and assertion from the outworks of the man, from the mere argumentative region of him, if even so deep as that. But the thing a man does practically believe (and this is often enough *without* asserting it even to himself, much less to others); the thing a man does practically lay to heart, and know for certain, concerning his vital relations to this mysterious Universe, and his duty and destiny there, that is in all cases the primary thing for him, and creatively determines all the rest.

That is his *religion;* or, it may be, his mere scepticism and *no-religion:* the manner it is in which he feels himself to be spiritually related to the Unseen World or No-World; and I say, if you tell me what that is, you tell me to a very great extent what the man is, what the kind of things he will do is. Of a man or of a nation we inquire, therefore, first of all, What religion they had? Was it Heathenism,—plurality of gods, mere sensuous representation of this Mystery of Life, and for chief recognized element therein Physical Force? Was it Christianism; faith in an Invisible, not as real only, but as the only reality; Time, through every meanest moment of it, resting on Eternity; Pagan empire of Force displaced by a nobler supremacy, that of Holiness? Was it Scepticism, uncertainty, and inquiry whether there was an Unseen World, any Mystery of Life except a mad one;—doubt as to all this, or perhaps unbelief and flat denial? Answering of this question is giving us the soul of the history of the man or nation. The thoughts they had were the parents of the actions they did; their feelings were parents of their thoughts: it was the unseen and spiritual in them that determined the outward and actual;—their religion, as I say, was the great fact about them. In these Discourses, limited as we are, it will be good to direct our survey chiefly to that religious phasis of the matter. That once known well, all is known. We have chosen as the first Hero in our series, Odin the central figure of Scandinavian Paganism; an emblem to us of a most extensive province of things. Let us look for a little at the Hero as Divinity, the oldest primary form of Heroism.

Surely it seems a very strange-looking thing, this Paganism; almost inconceivable to us in these days. A bewildering, inextricable jungle of delusions, confusions, falsehoods, and absurdities, covering the whole field of Life! A thing that fills us with astonishment; almost, if it were possible, with incredulity,—for truly it is not easy to understand that sane men could ever calmly, with their eyes open, believe and live by such a set of doctrines. That men should have worshipped their poor fellow-man as a God, and not him only, but stocks and stones and all manner of animate and inanimate objects;

and fashioned for themselves such a distracted chaos of hallucinations by way of Theory of the Universe: all this looks like an incredible fable. Nevertheless it is a clear fact that they did it. Such hideous, inextricable jungle of misworships, misbeliefs, men, made as we are, did actually hold by and live at home in. This is strange. Yes, we may pause in sorrow and silence over the depths of darkness that are in man; if we rejoice in the heights of purer vision he has attained to. Such things were and are in man; in all men; in us too.

Some speculators have a short way of accounting for the Pagan religion: mere quackery, priestcraft, and dupery, say they; no sane man ever did believe it,—merely contrived to persuade other men, not worthy of the name of sane, to believe it! It will be often our duty to protest against this sort of hypothesis about men's doings and history; and I here, on the very threshold, protest against it in reference to Paganism, and to all other *isms* by which man has ever for a length of time striven to walk in this world. They have all had a truth in them, or men would not have taken them up. Quackery and dupery do abound; in religions, above all in the more advanced decaying stages of religions, they have fearfully abounded: but quackery was never the originating influence in such things; it was not the health and life of such things, but their disease, the sure precursor of their being about to die! Let us never forget this. It seems to me a most mournful hypothesis, that of quackery giving birth to any faith even in savage men. Quackery gives birth to nothing; gives death to all things. We shall not see into the true heart of anything, if we look merely at the quackeries of it; if we do not reject the quackeries altogether; as mere diseases, corruptions, with which our and all men's sole duty is to have done with them, to sweep them out of our thoughts as out of our practice. Man everywhere is the born enemy of lies. I find Grand Lamaism itself to have a kind of truth in it. Read the candid, clear-sighted, rather sceptical Mr. Turner's *Account of his Embassy* to that country, and see. They have their belief, these poor Thibet people, that Providence sends down always an Incarnation of Himself into every generation. At bottom some belief in a kind of Pope! At bottom still better, belief that there is a *Greatest* Man; that *he* is discoverable; that, once discovered, we ought to treat him with an obedience which knows no bounds! This is the truth of Grand Lamaism; the "discoverability" is the only error here. The Thibet priests have methods of their own of discovering what Man is Greatest, fit to be supreme over them. Bad methods: but are they so much worse than our methods,—of understanding him to be always the eldest-born of a certain genealogy? Alas, it is a difficult thing to find good methods for!——We shall begin to have a chance of understanding Paganism, when we first admit that to its followers it was, at one time, earnestly true. Let us consider it very certain that men did believe in Paganism; men with open eyes, sound senses, men made altogether like ourselves; that we, had we been there, should have believed in it. Ask now, What Paganism could have been?

Another theory, somewhat more respectable, attributes such things to Allegory. It was a play of poetic minds, say these theorists; a shadowing-forth, in allegorical fable, in personification and visual form, of what such poetic minds had known and felt of this Universe. Which agrees, add they, with a primary law of human nature, still everywhere observably at work, though in less important things, That what a man feels intensely, he struggles to speak-out of him, to see represented before him in visual shape, and as if with a kind of life and historical reality in it. Now, doubtless there is such a law, and it is one of the deepest in human nature; neither need we doubt that it did operate fundamentally in this business. The hypothesis which ascribes Paganism wholly or mostly to this agency, I call a little more respectable; but I cannot yet call it the true hypothesis. Think, would *we* believe, and take with us as our life-guidance, an allegory, a poetic sport? Not sport but earnest is what we should require. It is a most earnest thing to be alive in this world; to die is not sport for a man. Man's life never was a sport to him; it was a stern reality, altogether a serious matter to be alive!

I find, therefore, that though these Allegory theorists are on the way towards truth in this matter, they have not reached it either. Pagan Religion is indeed an Allegory, a Symbol of what men felt and knew about the Universe; and all Religions are symbols of that, altering always as that alters: but it seems to me a radical perversion, and even *in*version, of the business, to put that forward as the origin and moving cause, when it was rather the result and termination. To get beautiful allegories, a perfect poetic symbol, was not the want of men; but to know what they were to believe about this Universe, what course they were to steer in it; what, in this mysterious Life of theirs, they had to hope and to fear, to do and to forbear doing. The *Pilgrim's Progress* is an Allegory, and a beautiful, just, and serious one: but consider whether Bunyan's Allegory could have *preceded* the Faith it symbolises! The Faith had to be already there, standing believed by everybody;—of which the Allegory could *then* become a shadow; and, with all its seriousness, we may say a *sportful* shadow, a mere play of the Fancy, in comparison with that awful Fact and scientific certainty which it poetically strives to emblem. The Allegory is the product of the certainty, not the producer of it; not in Bunyan's, nor in any other case. For Paganism, therefore, we have still to inquire, Whence came that scientific certainty, the parent of such a bewildered heap of allegories, errors, and confusions? How was it, what was it?

Surely it were a foolish attempt to pretend "explaining," in this place, or in any place, such a phenomenon as that far-distant, distracted, cloudy imbroglio of Paganism,—more like a cloudfield than a distant continent of firm land and facts! It is no longer a reality, yet it was one. We ought to understand that this seeming cloudfield was once a reality; that not poetic allegory, least of all that dupery and deception, was the origin of it. Men, I say, never did believe idle songs, never risked their soul's life on allegories; men in all times, especially in early earnest times, have had an instinct for detecting quacks, for detesting quacks. Let us try if, leaving out both the quack theory and the allegory one, and listening with affectionate attention to that far-off, confused rumor of the Pagan ages, we cannot ascertain so much as this at least, That there was a kind of fact at the heart of them; that they too were not mendacious and distracted, but in their own poor way true and sane!

You remember that fancy of Plato's, of a man who had grown to maturity in some dark distance, and was brought on a sudden into the upper air to see the sun rise. What would his wonder be, his rapt astonishment, at the sight we daily witness with indifference! With the free, open sense of a child, yet with the ripe faculty of a man, his whole heart would be kindled by that sight, he would discern it well to be Godlike, his soul would fall down in worship before it. Now, just such a childlike greatness was in the primitive nations. The first Pagan Thinker among rude men, the first man that began to think, was precisely this child-man of Plato's. Simple, open as a child, yet with the depth and strength of a man. Nature had as yet no name to him; he had not yet united under a name the infinite variety of sights, sounds, shapes, and motions, which we now collectively name Universe, Nature, or the like,—and so with a name dismiss it from us. To the wild, deep-hearted man all was yet new, not veiled under names or formulas; it stood naked, flashing-in on him there, beautiful, awful, unspeakable. Nature was to this man, what to the Thinker and Prophet it forever is, *preter*natural. This green, flowery, rock-built earth, the trees, the mountains, rivers, many-sounding seas;—that great, deep sea of azure that swims overhead; the winds sweeping through it; the black cloud fashioning itself together, now pouring out fire, now hail and rain; what *is* it? Ay, what? At bottom we do not yet know; we can never know at all. It is not by our superior insight that we escape the difficulty; it is by our superior levity, our inattention, our *want* of insight. It is by *not* thinking that we cease to wonder at it. Hardened round us, encasing wholly every notion we form, is a wrappage of traditions, hearsays, mere *words*. We call that fire of the black thunder-cloud "electricity," and lecture learnedly about it, and grind the like of it out of glass and silk: but *what* is it? What made it? Whence comes it? Whither goes it? Science has done much for us; but it is a poor science that would hide from us the great, deep, sacred infinitude of Nescience, whither we can never penetrate, on which all science swims as a mere superficial film. This world, after all our science and sciences, is still a miracle; wonderful, inscrutable, *magical,* and more, to whosoever will *think* of it.

That great mystery of TIME, were there no other; the illimitable, silent, never-resting thing called Time, rolling, rushing on, swift, silent, like an all-embracing ocean-tide, on which we and all the Universe swim like exhalations, like apparitions which *are*, and then *are not:* this is forever very literally a miracle; a thing to strike us dumb,—for we have no word to speak about it. This Universe, ah me—what could the wild man know of it; what can we yet know? That it is a Force, and thousandfold Complexity of Forces; a Force which is *not we*. That is all; it is not we, it is altogether different from *us*. Force, Force, everywhere Force; we ourselves a mysterious Force in the centre of that. "There is not a leaf rotting on the highway but has Force in it: how else could it rot?" Nay surely, to the Atheistic Thinker, if such a one were possible, it must be a miracle too, this huge, illimitable whirlwind of Force, which envelops us here; never-resting whirlwind, high as Immensity, old as Eternity. What is it? God's creation, the religious people answer; it is the Almighty God's! Atheistic science babbles poorly of it, with scientific nomenclatures, experiments, and what-not, as if it were a poor dead thing, to be bottled up in Leyden jars and sold over counters; but the natural sense of man, in all times, if he will honestly apply his sense, proclaims it to be a living thing,—ah, an unspeakable, godlike thing; towards which the best attitude for us, after never so much science, is awe, devout prostration, and humility of soul; worship, if not in words, then in silence.

But now I remark farther: What in such a time as ours it requires a Prophet or Poet to teach us, namely, the stripping-off of those poor undevout wrappages, nomenclatures, and scientific hearsays,—this, the ancient, earnest soul, as yet unencumbered with these things, did for itself. The world, which is now divine only to the gifted, was then divine to whosoever would turn his eye upon it. He stood bare before it face to face. "All was Godlike or God:"—Jean Paul still finds it so; the giant Jean Paul, who has power to escape out of hearsays: but there then were no hearsays. Canopus shining-down over the desert, with its blue, diamond brightness (that wild, blue, spirit-like brightness, far brighter than we ever witness here), would pierce into the heart of the wild Ishmaelitish man, whom it was guiding through the solitary waste there. To his wild heart, with all feelings in it, with no *speech* for any feeling, it might seem a little eye, that Canopus, glancing-out on him from the great, deep Eternity; revealing the inner Splendor to him. Cannot we understand how these men *worshipped* Canopus; became what we call Sabeans, worshipping the stars? Such is to me the secret of all forms of Paganism. Worship is transcendent wonder; wonder for which there is now no limit or measure; that is worship. To these primeval men, all things and everything they saw exist beside them were an emblem of the Godlike, of some God.

And look what perennial fibre of truth was in that. To us also, through every star, through every blade of grass, is not a God made visible, if we will open our minds and eyes? We do not worship in that way now: but is it not reckoned still a merit, proof of what we call a "poetic nature," that we recognise how every object has a divine beauty in it; how every object still verily is "a window through which we may look into Infinitude itself"? He that can discern the loveliness of things, we call him Poet, Painter, Man of Genius, gifted, lovable. These poor Sabeans did even what he does, in their own fashion. That they did it, in what fashion soever, was a merit; better than what the entirely stupid man did, what the horse and camel did,—namely, nothing!

But, now, if all things whatsoever that we look upon are emblems to us of the Highest God, I add that more so than any of them is man such an emblem. You have heard of St. Chrysostom's celebrated saying in reference to the Shekinah, or Ark of Testimony, visible Revelation of God, among the Hebrews: "The true Shekinah is Man!" Yes, it is even so: this is no vain phrase; it is veritably so. The essence of our being, the mystery in us that calls itself "I,"—ah, what words have we for such things?—is a breath of Heaven; the Highest Being reveals himself in man. This body, these faculties, this life of ours, is it not all as a vesture for that Unnamed? "There is but one Temple in the Universe," says the devout Novalis, "and that is the Body of Man. Nothing is holier than that high form. Bending before men is a reverence done to this Revelation in the Flesh. We touch Heaven when we lay our hand on a human body!" This sounds much like a mere flourish of rhetoric; but it is not so. If well meditated, it will turn out to be a scientific fact; the expression, in such words as can be had, of the actual truth of the thing. *We* are the miracle of miracles,—the great, inscrutable mystery of God. We cannot understand it, we know not how to speak of it; but we may feel and know, if we like, that it is verily so.

Well, these truths were once more readily felt than now. The young generations of the world, who had in them the freshness of young children, and yet the depth of earnest men, who did not think that they had finished-off all things in Heaven and Earth by merely giving them scientific names, but had to gaze direct at them there, with awe and wonder: they felt better what of divinity is in man and Nature;—they, without being mad, could *worship* Nature, and man more than anything else in Nature. Worship, that is, as I said above, admire without limit: this, in the full use of their faculties, with all sincerity of heart, they could do. I consider Hero-worship to be the grand modifying element in that ancient system of thought. What I called the perplexed jungle of Paganism sprang, we may say, out of many roots: every admiration, adoration of a star or natural object, was a root or fibre of a root; but Hero-worship is the deepest root of all; the tap-root, from which in a great degree all the rest were nourished and grown.

And now, if worship even of a star had some meaning in

it, how much more might that of a Hero! Worship of a Hero is transcendent admiration of a Great Man. I say great men are still admirable; I say there is, at bottom, nothing else admirable! No nobler feeling than this of admiration for one higher than himself dwells in the breast of man. It is to this hour, and at all hours, the vivifying influence in man's life. Religion I find stand upon it; not Paganism only, but far higher and truer religions,—all religion hitherto known. Hero-worship, heartfelt, prostrate admiration, submission, burning, boundless, for a noblest, godlike Form of Man,—is not that the germ of Christianity itself? The greatest of all Heroes is One—whom we do not name here! Let sacred silence meditate that sacred matter; you will find it the ultimate perfection of a principle extant throughout man's whole history on earth.

Or coming into lower, less *un*speakable provinces, is not all Loyalty akin to religious Faith also? Faith is loyalty to some inspired Teacher, some spiritual Hero. And what therefore is loyalty proper, the life-breath of all society, but an effluence of Hero-worship, submissive admiration for the truly great? Society is founded on Hero-worship. All dignities of rank, on which human association rests, are what we may call a *Hero*archy (Government of Heroes),—or a Hierarchy, for it is "sacred" enough withal! The Duke means *Dux*, Leader; King is *Kön-ning*, *Kan-ning*, Man that *knows* or *cans*. Society everywhere is some representation, not *in*supportably inaccurate, of a graduated Worship of Heroes;—reverence and obedience done to men really great and wise. Not *in*supportably inaccurate, I say! They are all as bank-notes, these social dignitaries, all representing gold:—and several of them, alas, always are *forged* notes. We can do with some forged, false notes; with a good many even; but not with all, or the most of them, forged! No: there have to come revolutions then; cries of Democracy, Liberty, and Equality, and I know not what:—the notes being all false, and no gold to be had for *them*, people take to crying in their despair that there is no gold, that there never was any!—"Gold," Hero-worship, *is* nevertheless, as it was always and everywhere, and cannot cease till man himself ceases.

I am well aware that in these days Hero-worship, the thing I call Hero-worship, professes to have gone out, and finally ceased. This, for reasons which it will be worth while some time to inquire into, is an age that as it were denies the existence of great men; denies the desirableness of great men. Show our critics a great man, a Luther for example, they begin to what they call "account" for him; not to worship him, but take the dimensions of him,—and bring him out to be a little kind of man! He was the "creature of the Time," they say; the Time called him forth, the Time did everything, he nothing—but what we the little critic could have done too! This seems to me but melancholy work. The Time call forth? Alas, we have known Times *call* loudly enough for their great man; but not find him when they called! He was not there; Providence had not sent him; the Time, *calling* its loudest, had to go down to confusion and wreck because he would not come when called.

For, if we will think of it, no Time need have gone to ruin, could it have *found* a man great enough, a man wise and good enough: wisdom to discern truly what the Time wanted, valor to lead it on the right road thither; these are the salvation of any Time. But I liken common, languid Times, with their unbelief, distress, perplexity, with their languid, doubting characters and embarrassed circumstances, impotently crumbling-down into ever worse distress towards final ruin;—all this I liken to dry, dead fuel, waiting for the lightning out of Heaven that shall kindle it. The great man, with his free force direct out of God's own hand, is the lightning. His word is the wise, healing word which all can believe in. All blazes round him now, when he has once struck on it, into fire like his own. The dry, mouldering sticks are thought to have called him forth. They did want him greatly; but as to calling him forth—!—Those are critics of small vision, I think, who cry: "See, is it not the sticks that made the fire?" No sadder proof can be given by a man of his own littleness than disbelief in great men. There is no sadder symptom of a generation than such general blindness to the spiritual lightning, with faith only in the heap of barren, dead fuel. It is the last consummation of unbelief. In all epochs of the world's history, we shall find the Great Man to have been the indispensable savior of his epoch;—the lightning, without which the fuel never would have burnt. The History of the World, I said already, was the Biography of Great Men.

Such small critics do what they can to promote unbelief and universal spiritual paralysis: but happily they cannot always completely succeed. In all times it is possible for a man to arise great enough to feel that they and their doctrines are chimeras and cobwebs. And what is notable, in no time whatever can they entirely eradicate out of living men's hearts a certain altogether peculiar reverence for Great Men; genuine admiration, loyalty, adoration, however dim and perverted it may be. Hero-worship endures forever while man endures. Boswell venerates his Johnson, right truly even in the Eighteenth century. The unbelieving French believe in their Voltaire; and burst-out round him into very curious Hero-worship, in that last act of his life when they "stifle him under roses." It has always seemed to me extremely curious, this of Voltaire. Truly, if Christianity be the highest instance of Hero-worship, then we may find here in Voltaireism one of the lowest! He whose life was that of a kind of Antichrist, does again on this side exhibit a curious contrast. No people ever were so little prone to admire at all as those French of Voltaire. *Persiflage* was the character of their whole mind; adoration had nowhere a place in it. Yet see! The old man of Ferney comes up to Paris; an old, tottering, infirm man of eighty-four years. They feel that he too is a kind of Hero; that he has spent his life in opposing error and injustice, delivering Calases, unmasking hypocrites in high places;—in short that *he* too, though in a strange way, has fought like a valiant man. They feel withal that, if *persiflage* be the great thing, there never was such a *persifleur*. He is the realised ideal of every one of them; the thing they are all wanting to be; of all Frenchmen the most French. *He* is properly their god,—such god as they are fit for. Accordingly all persons, from the Queen Antoinette to the Douanier at the Porte St. Denis, do they not worship him? People of quality disguise themselves as tavern-waiters. The Maître de Poste, with a broad oath, orders his Postillion, "*Va bon train;* thou art driving M. de Voltaire." At Paris his carriage is "the nucleus of a comet, whose train fills whole streets." The ladies pluck a hair or two from his fur, to keep it as a sacred relic. There was nothing highest, beautifulest, noblest in all France, that did not feel this man to be higher, beautifuler, nobler.

Yes, from Norse Odin to English Samuel Johnson, from the divine Founder of Christianity to the withered Pontiff of Encyclopedism, in all times and places, the Hero has been worshipped. It will ever be so. We all love great men; love, venerate, and bow down submissive before great men: nay, can we honestly bow down to anything else? Ah, does not every true man feel that he is himself made higher by doing reverence to what is really above him? No nobler or more blessed feeling dwells in man's heart. And to me it is very cheering to consider that no sceptical logic, or general triviality, insincerity, and aridity of any Time and its influences can destroy this noble inborn loyalty and worship that is in man. In times of unbelief, which soon have to become times of revolution, much down-rushing, sorrowful decay and ruin is visible to everybody. For myself in these days, I seem to see in this indestructibility of Hero-worship the everlasting adamant lower than which the confused wreck of revolutionary things cannot fall. The confused wreck of things crumbling and even crashing and tumbling all round us, in these revolutionary ages, will get down so far; *no* farther. It is an eternal corner-stone, from which they can begin to build themselves up again. That man, in some sense or other, worships Heroes; that we all of us reverence and must ever reverence Great Men: this is, to me, the living rock amid all rushings-down whatsoever;—the one fixed point in modern revolutionary history, otherwise as if bottomless and shoreless.

Thomas Babington Macaulay.

1800–1859.

OLIVER GOLDSMITH.

(1856.)

Oliver Goldsmith, one of the most pleasing English writers of the eighteenth century. He was of a Protestant and Saxon family which had been long settled in Ireland, and which had, like most other Protestant and Saxon families, been, in troubled times, harassed and put in fear by the native population. His father, Charles Goldsmith, studied in the reign of Queen Anne at the diocesan school of Elphin, became attached to the daughter of the schoolmaster, married her, took orders, and settled at a place called Pallas in the county of Longford. There he with difficulty supported his wife and children on what he could earn, partly as a curate and partly as a farmer.

At Pallas, Oliver Goldsmith was born in November, 1728. The spot was then, for all practical purposes, almost as remote from the busy and splendid capital in which his later years were passed, as any clearing in Upper Canada or any sheep-walk in Australasia now is. Even at this day those enthusiasts who venture to make a pilgrimage to the birthplace of the poet are forced to perform the latter part of their journey on foot. The hamlet lies far from any highroad, on a dreary plain which, in wet weather, is often a lake. The lanes would break any jaunting-car to pieces; and there are ruts and sloughs through which the most strongly-built wheels cannot be dragged.

While Oliver was still a child, his father was presented to a living worth about £200 a year, in the county of Westmeath. The family accordingly quitted their cottage in the wilderness for a spacious house on a frequented road, near the village of Lissoy. Here the boy was taught his letters by a maid-servant, and was sent in his seventh year to a village school kept by an old quartermaster on half-pay, who professed to teach nothing but reading, writing, and arithmetic, but who had an inexhaustible fund of stories about ghosts, banshees, and fairies, about the great Rapparee chiefs, Baldearg O'Donnell and galloping Hogan, and about the exploits of Peterborough and Stanhope, the surprise of Monjuich, and the glorious disaster of Brihuega. This man must have been of the Protestant religion; but he was of the aboriginal race, and not only spoke the Irish language but could pour forth unpremeditated Irish verses. Oliver early became, and through life continued to be, a passionate admirer of the Irish music, and especially of the compositions of Carolan, some of the last notes of whose harp he heard. It ought to be added that Oliver, though by birth one of the Englishry, and though connected by numerous ties with the Established Church, never showed the least sign of that contemptuous antipathy with which, in his days, the ruling minority in Ireland too generally regarded the subject majority. So far indeed was he from sharing in the opinions and feelings of the caste to which he belonged, that he conceived an aversion to the Glorious and Immortal Memory, and, even when George the Third was on the throne, maintained that nothing but the restoration of the banished dynasty could save the country.

From the humble academy kept by the old soldier Goldsmith was removed in his ninth year. He went to several grammar schools, and acquired some knowledge of the ancient languages. His life at this time seems to have been far from happy. He had, as appears from the admirable portrait of him at Knowle, features harsh even to ugliness. The small-pox had set its mark on him with more than usual severity. His stature was small, and his limbs ill put together. Among boys little tenderness is shown to personal defects; and the ridicule excited by poor Oliver's appearance was heightened by a peculiar simplicity and a disposition to blunder which he retained to the last. He became the common butt of boys and masters, was pointed at as a fright in the playground, and flogged as a dunce in the schoolroom. When he had risen to eminence, those who had once derided him ransacked their memory for the events of his early years, and recited repartees and couplets which had dropped from him, and which, though little noticed at the time, were supposed, a quarter of a century later, to indicate the powers which produced *The Vicar of Wakefield* and *The Deserted Village*.

In his seventeenth year Oliver went up to Trinity College, Dublin, as a sizar. The sizars paid nothing for food and tuition, and very little for lodging; but they had to perform some menial services from which they have long been relieved. They swept the court; they carried up the dinner to the fellows' table, and changed the plates and poured out the ale of the rulers of the society. Goldsmith was quartered, not alone, in a garret, on the window of which his name, scrawled by himself, is still read with interest. From such garrets many men of less parts than his have made their way to the woolsack or to the episcopal bench. But Goldsmith, while he suffered all the humiliations, threw away all the advantages, of his situation. He neglected the studies of the place, stood low at the examinations, was turned down to the bottom of his class for playing the buffoon in the lecture-room, was severely reprimanded for pumping on a constable, and was caned by a brutal tutor for giving a ball in the attic story of the college to some gay youths and damsels from the city.

While Oliver was leading at Dublin a life divided between squalid distress and squalid dissipation, his father died, leaving a mere pittance. The youth obtained his bachelor's degree, and left the university. During some time the humble dwelling to which his widowed mother had retired was his home. He was now in his twenty-first year; it was necessary that he should do something; and his education seemed to have fitted him to do nothing but to dress himself in gaudy colors, of which he was as fond as a magpie, to take a hand at cards, to sing Irish airs, to play the flute, to angle in summer, and to tell ghost-stories by the fire in winter. He tried five or six professions in turn without success. He applied for ordination; but as he applied in scarlet clothes, he was speedily turned out of the episcopal palace. He then became tutor in an opulent family, but soon quitted his situation in consequence of a dispute about play. Then he determined to emigrate to America. His relations, with much satisfaction, saw him set out for Cork on a good horse, with thirty pounds in his pocket. But in six weeks he came back on a miserable hack, without a penny, and informed his mother that the ship in which he had taken his passage, having got a fair wind while he was at a party of pleasure, had sailed without him. Then he resolved to study the law. A generous kinsman advanced fifty pounds. With this sum Goldsmith went to Dublin, was enticed into a gaming-house, and lost every shilling. He then thought of medicine. A small purse was made up; and in his twenty-fourth year he was sent to Edinburgh. At Edinburgh he passed eighteen months in nominal attendance on lectures, and picked up some superficial information about chemistry and natural history. Thence he went to Leyden, still pretending to study physic. He left that celebrated university, the third university at which he had resided, in his twenty-seventh year, without a degree, with the merest smattering of medical knowledge, and with no property but his clothes and his flute. His flute, however, proved a useful friend. He rambled on foot through Flanders, France, and Switzerland, playing tunes which everywhere set the peasantry dancing, and which often procured for him a supper and a bed. He wandered as far as Italy. His musical performances, indeed, were not to the taste of the Italians; but he contrived to live on the alms which he obtained at the gates of convents. It should, however, be observed that the stories which he told about this part of his life ought to be received with great caution; for strict veracity was never one of his virtues; and a man who is ordinarily inaccurate in narration is likely to be more than ordinarily inaccurate when he talks about his own travels. Goldsmith, indeed, was so regardless of truth as to assert in print that he was present at a most interesting conversation between Voltaire and Fontenelle, and that this conversation took place at Paris. Now, it is certain that Voltaire never was within a hundred leagues of Paris during the whole time which Goldsmith passed on the Continent.

In 1756 the wanderer landed at Dover, without a shilling, without a friend, and without a calling. He had, indeed, if his own unsupported evidence may be trusted, obtained from the university of Padua a doctor's degree; but this dignity proved utterly useless to him. In England his flute was not in request; there were no convents; and he was forced to have recourse to a series of desperate expedients. He turned strolling player; but his face and figure were ill suited to the boards even of the humblest theatre. He pounded drugs and ran about London with phials for charitable chemists. He joined a swarm of beggars, which made its nest in Axe Yard. He was for a time usher of a school, and felt the miseries and humiliations of this situation so keenly that he thought it a promotion to be permitted to earn his bread as a bookseller's hack; but he soon found the new yoke more galling than the old one, and was glad to become an usher again. He obtained a medical appointment in the service of the East India Company; but the appointment was speedily revoked. Why it was revoked we are not told. The subject was one on which he never liked to talk. It is probable that he was incompetent to perform the duties of the place. Then he presented himself at Surgeons' Hall for examination as mate to a naval hospital. Even to so humble a post he was found unequal. By this time the schoolmaster whom he had served for a morsel of food and the third part of a bed was no more. Nothing remained but to return to the lowest drudgery of literature. Goldsmith took a garret in a miserable court, to which he had to climb from the brink of Fleet Ditch by a dizzy ladder of flagstones called Breakneck Steps. The court and the ascent have long disappeared; but old Londoners will remember both. Here, at thirty, the unlucky adventurer sat down to toil like a galley-slave.

In the succeeding six years he sent to the press some things which have survived and many which have perished. He produced articles for reviews, magazines, and newspapers; children's books, which, bound in gilt paper and adorned with hideous woodcuts, appeared in the window of the once far-famed shop at the corner of St. Paul's Churchyard; *An Inquiry into the State of Polite Learning in Europe*, which, though of little or no value, is still reprinted among his works; a *Life of Beau Nash*, which is not reprinted, though it well deserves to be so; a superficial and incorrect, but very readable, *History of England*, in a series of letters purporting to be addressed by a nobleman to his son; and some very lively and amusing *Sketches of London Society*, in a series of letters purporting to be addressed by a Chinese traveller to his friends. All these works were anonymous; but some of them were well known to be Goldsmith's; and he gradually rose in the estimation of the booksellers for whom he drudged. He was, indeed, emphatically a popular writer. For accurate research or grave disquisition he was not well qualified by nature or by education. He knew nothing accurately: his reading had been desultory; nor had he meditated deeply on what he had read. He had seen much of the world; but he had noticed and retained little more of what he had seen than some grotesque incidents and characters which had happened to strike his fancy. But though his mind was very scantily stored with materials, he used what materials he had in such a way as to produce a wonderful effect. There have been many greater writers, but perhaps no writer was ever more uniformly agreeable. His style was always pure and easy, and, on proper occasions, pointed and energetic. His narratives were always amusing, his descriptions always picturesque, his humor rich and joyous yet not without an occasional tinge of amiable sadness. About everything that he wrote, serious or sportive, there was a certain natural grace and decorum, hardly to be expected from a man a great part of whose life had been passed among thieves and beggars, street-walkers and merry-andrews, in those squalid dens which are the reproach of great capitals.

As his name gradually became known, the circle of his acquaintance widened. He was introduced to Johnson, who was then considered as the first of living English writers; to

Reynolds, the first of English painters; and to Burke, who had not yet entered Parliament, but had distinguished himself greatly by his writings and by the eloquence of his conversation. With these eminent men Goldsmith became intimate. In 1763 he was one of the nine original members of that celebrated fraternity which has sometimes been called "The Literary Club," but which has always disclaimed that epithet, and still glories in the simple name of "The Club."

By this time Goldsmith had quitted his miserable dwelling at the top of Breakneck Steps, and had taken chambers in the more civilised region of the Inns of Court. But he was still often reduced to pitiable shifts. Towards the close of 1764 his rent was so long in arrear that his landlady one morning called in the help of a sheriff's officer. The debtor, in great perplexity, despatched a messenger to Johnson; and Johnson, always friendly though often surly, sent back the messenger with a guinea, and promised to follow speedily. He came, and found that Goldsmith had changed the guinea and was railing at the landlady over a bottle of Madeira. Johnson put the cork into the bottle, and entreated his friend to consider calmly how money was to be procured. Goldsmith said that he had a novel ready for the press. Johnson glanced at the manuscript, saw that there were good things in it, took it to a bookseller, sold it for £60, and soon returned with the money. The rent was paid, and the sheriff's officer withdrew. According to one story, Goldsmith gave his landlady a sharp reprimand for her treatment of him; according to another, he insisted on her joining him in a bowl of punch. Both stories are probably true. The novel which was thus ushered into the world was *The Vicar of Wakefield.*

But before *The Vicar of Wakefield* appeared in print, came the great crisis of Goldsmith's literary life. In Christmas week, 1764, he published a poem, entitled *The Traveller.* It was the first work to which he had put his name, and it at once raised him to the rank of a legitimate English classic. The opinion of the most skilful critics was that nothing finer had appeared in verse since the fourth book of *The Dunciad.* In one respect *The Traveller* differs from all Goldsmith's other writings. In general his designs were bad, and his execution good. In *The Traveller* the execution, though deserving of much praise, is far inferior to the design. No philosophical poem, ancient or modern, has a plan so noble and at the same time so simple. An English wanderer, seated on a crag among the Alps, near the point where three great countries meet, looks down on the boundless prospect, reviews his long pilgrimage, recalls the varieties of scenery, of climate, of government, of religion, of national character, which he has observed, and comes to the conclusion, just or unjust, that our happiness depends little on political institutions and much on the temper and regulation of our own minds.

While the fourth edition of *The Traveller* was on the counters of the booksellers, *The Vicar of Wakefield* appeared. and rapidly obtained a popularity which has lasted down to our own time and which is likely to last as long as our language. The fable is, indeed, one of the worst that ever was constructed. It wants, not merely that probability which ought to be found in a tale of common English life, but that consistency which ought to be found even in the wildest fiction about witches, giants, and fairies. But the earlier chapters have all the sweetness of pastoral poetry, together with all the vivacity of comedy. Moses and his spectacles, the vicar and his monogamy, the sharper and his cosmogony, the squire proving from Aristotle that relatives are related, Olivia preparing herself for the arduous task of converting a rakish lover by studying the controversy between Robinson Crusoe and Friday, the great ladies with their scandal about Sir Tomkyn's amours and Dr. Burdock's verses, and Mr. Burchell with his "Fudge," have caused as much harmless mirth as has ever been caused by matter packed into so small a number of pages. The latter part of the tale is unworthy of the beginning. As we approach the catastrophe the absurdities lie thicker and thicker, and the gleams of pleasantry become rarer and rarer.

The success which had attended Goldsmith as a novelist emboldened him to try his fortune as a dramatist. He wrote

The Good-Natured Man, a piece which had a worse fate than it deserved. Garrick refused to produce it at Drury Lane. It was acted at Covent Garden in 1768, but was coldly received. The author, however, cleared by his benefit nights, and by the sale of the copyright, no less than £500, five times as much as he had made by *The Traveller* and *The Vicar of Wakefield* together. The plot of *The Good-Natured Man* is, like almost all Goldsmith's plots, very ill constructed. But some passages are exquisitely ludicrous, much more ludicrous, indeed, than suited the taste of the town at that time. A canting, mawkish play, entitled *False Delicacy,* had just had an immense run. Sentimentality was all the mode. During some years, more tears were shed at comedies than at tragedies, and a pleasantry which moved the audience to anything more than a grave smile was reprobated as low. It is not strange, therefore, that the very best scene in *The Good-Natured Man,* that in which Miss Richland finds her lover attended by the bailiff and the bailiff's follower in full court-dresses, should have been mercilessly hissed, and should have been omitted after the first night.

In 1770 appeared *The Deserted Village.* In mere diction and versification this celebrated poem is fully equal, perhaps superior, to *The Traveller;* and it is generally preferred to *The Traveller* by that large class of readers who think, with Bayes in *The Rehearsal,* that the only use of a plan is to bring in fine things. More discerning judges, however, while they admire the beauty of the details, are shocked by one unpardonable fault which pervades the whole. The fault we mean is not that theory about wealth and luxury which has so often been censured by political economists. The theory is indeed false; but the poem, considered merely as a poem, is not necessarily the worse on that account. The finest poem in the Latin language, indeed the finest didactic poem in any language, was written in defence of the silliest and meanest of all systems of natural and moral philosophy. A poet may easily be pardoned for reasoning ill; but he cannot be pardoned for describing ill, for observing the world in which he lives so carelessly that his portraits bear no resemblance to the originals, for exhibiting as copies from real life monstrous combinations of things which never were and never could be found together. What would be thought of a painter who should mix August and January in one landscape, who should introduce a frozen river into a harvest scene? Would it be a sufficient defence of such a picture to say that every part was exquisitely colored, that the green hedges, the apple-trees loaded with fruit, the wagons reeling under the yellow sheaves, and the sunburned reapers wiping their foreheads were very fine, and that the ice and the boys sliding were also very fine? To such a picture *The Deserted Village* bears a great resemblance. It is made up of incongruous parts. The village in its happy days is a true English village. The village in its decay is an Irish village. The felicity and the misery which Goldsmith has brought close together belong to two different countries and to two different stages in the progress of society. He had assuredly never seen in his native island such a rural paradise, such a seat of plenty, content, and tranquillity, as his "Auburn." He had assuredly never seen in England all the inhabitants of such a paradise turned out of their homes in one day and forced to emigrate in a body to America. The hamlet he had probably seen in Kent; the ejectment he had probably seen in Munster: but, by joining the two, he has produced something which never was and never will be seen in any part of the world.

In 1773 Goldsmith tried his chance at Covent Garden with a second play, *She Stoops to Conquer.* The manager was not without great difficulty induced to bring this piece out. The sentimental comedy still reigned; and Goldsmith's comedies were not sentimental. *The Good-Natured Man* had been too funny to succeed; yet the mirth of *The Good-Natured Man* was sober when compared with the rich drollery of *She Stoops to Conquer*, which is, in truth, an incomparable farce in five acts. On this occasion, however, genius triumphed. Pit, boxes, and galleries were in a constant roar of laughter. If any bigoted admirer of Kelly and Cumberland ventured to hiss or groan, he was speedily silenced by a general cry of "Turn him out," or "Throw him over." Two generations have since confirmed the verdict which was pronounced on that night.

While Goldsmith was writing *The Deserted Village* and *She Stoops to Conquer*, he was employed on works of a very different kind, works from which he derived little reputation but much profit. He compiled for the use of schools a *History of Rome*, by which he made £300, a *History of England*, by which he made £600, a *History of Greece*, for which he received £250, a *Natural History*, for which the booksellers covenanted to pay him 800 guineas. These works he produced without any elaborate research, by merely selecting, abridging, and translating into his own clear, pure, and flowing language what he found in books well known to the world but too bulky or too dry for boys and girls. He committed some strange blunders, for he knew nothing with accuracy. Thus in his *History of England* he tells us that Naseby is in Yorkshire; nor did he correct this mistake when the book was reprinted. He was very nearly hoaxed into putting into the *History of Greece* an account of a battle between Alexander the Great and Montezuma. In his *Animated Nature* he relates, with faith and with perfect gravity, all the most absurd lies which he could find in books of travels about gigantic Patagonians, monkeys that preach sermons, nightingales that repeat long conversations. "If he can tell a horse from a cow," said Johnson, "that is the extent of his knowledge of zoölogy." How little Goldsmith was qualified to write about the physical sciences is sufficiently proved by two anecdotes. He on one occasion denied that the sun is longer in the northern than in the southern signs. It was vain to cite the authority of Maupertuis. "Maupertuis!" he cried, "I understand those matters better than Maupertuis." On another occasion he, in defiance of the evidence of his own senses, maintained obstinately, and even angrily, that he chewed his dinner by moving his upper jaw.

Yet, ignorant as Goldsmith was, few writers have done more to make the first steps in the laborious road to knowledge easy and pleasant. His compilations are widely distinguished from the compilations of ordinary book-makers. He was a great, perhaps an unequalled, master of the arts of selection and condensation. In these respects his histories of Rome and of England, and still more his own abridgments of these histories, well deserve to be studied. In general, nothing is less attractive than an epitome; but the epitomes of Goldsmith, even when most concise, are always amusing, and to read them is considered by intelligent children, not as a task, but as a pleasure.

Goldsmith might now be considered as a prosperous man. He had the means of living in comfort, and even in what to one who had so often slept in barns and on bulks must have been luxury. His fame was great and was constantly rising. He lived in what was intellectually far the best society of the kingdom, in a society in which no talent or accomplishment was wanting and in which the art of conversation was cultivated with splendid success. There probably were never four talkers more admirable in four different ways than Johnson, Burke, Beauclerk, and Garrick; and Goldsmith was on terms of intimacy with all the four. He aspired to share in their colloquial renown; but never was ambition more unfortunate. It may seem strange that a man who wrote with so much perspicuity, vivacity, and grace should have been, whenever he took a part in conversation, an empty, noisy, blundering rattle. But on this point the evidence is overwhelming. So extraordinary was the contrast between Goldsmith's published works and the silly things which he said, that Horace Walpole described him as an inspired idiot. "Noll," said Garrick, "wrote like an angel, and talked like poor Poll." Chamier declared that it was a hard exercise of faith to believe that so foolish a chatterer could have really written *The Traveller*. Even Boswell could say, with contemptuous compassion, that he liked very well to hear honest Goldsmith run on. "Yes, sir," said Johnson; "but he should not like to hear himself." Minds differ as rivers differ. There are transparent and sparkling rivers from which it is delightful to drink as they flow; to such rivers the minds of such men as Burke and Johnson may be compared. But there are rivers of which the water when first drawn is turbid and noisome, but becomes pellucid as crystal and delicious to the taste if it be suffered to stand till it has deposited a sediment; and such a river is a type of the mind of Goldsmith. His first thoughts on every subject were confused even to absurdity, but they required only a little time to work themselves clear. When he wrote they had that time, and therefore his readers pronounced him a man of genius; but when he talked he talked nonsense, and made himself the laughing-stock of his hearers. He was painfully sensible of his inferiority in conversation; he felt every failure keenly; yet he had not sufficient judgment and self-command to hold his tongue. His animal spirits and vanity were always impelling him to try to do the one thing which he could not do. After every attempt he felt that he had exposed himself, and writhed with shame and vexation; yet the next moment he began again.

His associates seem to have regarded him with kindness, which, in spite of their admiration of his writings, was not unmixed with contempt. In truth, there was in his character much to love but very little to respect. His heart was soft even to weakness: he was so generous that he quite forgot to be just; he forgave injuries so readily that he might be said to invite them; and was so liberal to beggars that he had nothing left for his tailor and his butcher. He was vain, sensual, frivolous, profuse, improvident. One vice of a darker shade was imputed to him, envy. But there is not the least reason to believe that this bad passion, though it sometimes made him wince and utter fretful exclamations, ever impelled him to injure by wicked arts the reputation of any of his rivals. The truth probably is that he was not more envious, but merely less prudent, than his neighbors. His heart was on his lips. All those small jealousies, which are but too common among men of letters, but which a man of letters who is also a man of the world does his best to conceal, Goldsmith avowed with the simplicity of a child. When he was envious, instead of affecting indifference, instead of damning with faint praise, instead of doing injuries slily and in the dark, he told everybody that he was envious. "Do not, pray, do not talk of Johnson in such terms," he said to Boswell; "you harrow up my very soul." George Steevens and Cumberland were men far too cunning to say such a thing. They would have echoed the praises of the man whom they envied, and then have sent to the newspapers anonymous libels upon him. Both what was good and what was bad in Goldsmith's character was to his associates a perfect security that he would never commit such villainy. He was neither ill-natured enough, nor long-headed enough, to be guilty of any malicious act which required contrivance and disguise.

Goldsmith has sometimes been represented as a man of genius, cruelly treated by the world, and doomed to struggle with difficulties which at last broke his heart. But no representation can be more remote from the truth. He did, indeed, go through much sharp misery before he had done anything considerable in literature. But after his name had appeared on the title-page of *The Traveller* he had none but himself to blame for his distresses. His average income, during the last seven years of his life, certainly exceeded £400 a year; and £400 a year ranked, among the incomes of that day, at least as high as £800 a year would rank at present. A single man living in the Temple with £400 a year might then be called opulent. Not one in ten of the young gentlemen of good families who were studying the law there had so much. But all the wealth which Lord Clive had brought from Bengal, and Sir Lawrence Dundas from Germany, joined together, would not have sufficed for Goldsmith. He spent twice as much as he had. He wore fine clothes, gave dinners of several courses, paid court to venal beauties. He had also, it should be remembered, to the honor of his heart though not of his head, a guinea, or five, or ten, according to the state of his purse, ready for any tale of distress, true or false. But it was not in dress or feasting, in promiscuous amours or promiscuous charities, that his chief expense lay. He had been from boyhood a gambler, and at once the most sanguine and the most unskilful of gamblers. For a time he put off the day of inevitable ruin by temporary expedients. He obtained advances from booksellers, by promising to execute works which he never began. But at length this source of supply failed. He owed more than £2000, and he saw no hope of extrication from his embarrassments. His spirits and health gave way. He was attacked by a nervous fever, which he thought himself competent to treat. It would have been happy for him if his medical skill had been appreciated as justly by himself as by others. Notwithstanding the degree which he pretended to have received at Padua, he could procure no patients. "I do not practise," he once said; "I make it a rule to prescribe only for my friends." "Pray, dear Doctor," said Beauclerk, "alter your rule, and prescribe only for your enemies." Goldsmith now, in spite of this excellent advice, prescribed for himself. The remedy aggravated the malady. The sick man was induced to call in real physicians, and they at one time imagined that they had cured the disease. Still his weakness and restlessness continued. He could get no sleep. He could take no food. "You are worse," said one of his medical attendants, "than you should be from the degree of fever which you have. Is your mind at ease?" "No, it is not," were the last recorded words of Oliver Goldsmith. He died on the third of April, 1774, in his forty-sixth year. He was laid in the churchyard of the Temple; but the spot was not marked by any inscription, and is now forgotten. The coffin was followed by Burke and Reynolds. Both these great men were sincere mourners. Burke, when he heard of Goldsmith's death, had burst into a flood of tears. Reynolds had been so much moved by the news that he had flung aside his brush and palette for the day.

A short time after Goldsmith's death, a little poem appeared, which will, as long as our language lasts, associate the names of his two illustrious friends with his own. It has already been mentioned that he sometimes felt keenly the sarcasm which his wild blundering talk brought upon him. He was, not long before his last illness, provoked into retaliating. He wisely betook himself to his pen; and at that weapon he proved himself a match for all his assailants together. Within a small compass he drew with a singularly easy and vigorous pencil the characters of nine or ten of his intimate associates. Though this little work did not receive his last touches, it must always be regarded as a masterpiece. It is impossible, however, not to wish that four or five likenesses which have no interest for posterity were wanting to that noble gallery, and that their places were supplied by sketches of Johnson and Gibbon as happy and vivid as the sketches of Burke and Garrick.

Some of Goldsmith's friends and admirers honored him with a cenotaph in Westminster Abbey. Nollekens was the sculptor, and Johnson wrote the inscription. It is much to be lamented that Johnson did not leave to posterity a more durable and a more valuable memorial of his friend. A life of Goldsmith would have been an inestimable addition to *The Lives of the Poets.* No man appreciated Goldsmith's writings more justly than Johnson; no man was better acquainted with Goldsmith's character and habits; and no man was more competent to delineate with truth and spirit the peculiarities of a mind in which great powers were found in company with great weaknesses. But the list of poets to whose works Johnson was requested by the booksellers to furnish prefaces ended with Lyttleton, who died in 1773. The line seems to have been drawn expressly for the purpose of excluding the person whose portrait would have most fitly closed the series. Goldsmith, however, has been fortunate in his biographers. Within a few years his life has been written by Mr. Prior, by Mr. Washington Irving, and by Mr. Forster. The diligence of Mr. Prior deserves great praise; the style of Mr. Washington Irving is always pleasing; but the highest place must, in justice, be assigned to the eminently interesting work of Mr. Forster.

William Makepeace Thackeray.

1811–1863.

OLIVER GOLDSMITH.

(From *The English Humorists of the Eighteenth Century*, 1853.)

"Jeté sur cette boule,
Laid, chétif et souffrant ;
Etouffé dans la foule,
Faute d'être assez grand :

Une plainte touchante
De ma bouche sortit.
Le bon Dieu me dit : Chante,
Chante, pauvre petit !

Chanter ou je m'abuse,
Est ma tâche ici-bas.
Tous ceux qu'ainsi j'amuse
Ne m'aimeront-ils pas ?"

In those charming lines of Béranger one may fancy described the career, the sufferings, the genius, the gentle nature of Goldsmith, and the esteem in which we hold him. Who, of the millions whom he has amused, doesn't love him? To be the most beloved of English writers, what a title that is for a man! A wild youth, wayward but full of tenderness and affection, quits the country village where his boyhood has been passed in happy musing, in idle shelter, in fond longing to see the great world out of doors, and achieve name and fortune: and after years of dire struggle and neglect and poverty, his heart turning back as fondly to his native place as it had longed eagerly for change when sheltered there, he writes a book and a poem, full of the recollections and feelings of home; he paints the friends and scenes of his youth, and peoples Auburn and Wakefield with remembrances of Lissoy. Wander he must, but he carries away a home-relic with him and dies with it on his breast. His nature is truant;

in repose it longs for change, as on the journey it looks back for friends and quiet. He passes to-day in building an air-castle for to-morrow or in writing yesterday's elegy; and he would fly away this hour but that a cage and necessity keep him. What is the charm of his verse, of his style, and humor? His sweet regrets, his delicate compassion, his soft smile, his tremulous sympathy, the weakness which he owns? Your love for him is half pity. You come hot and tired from the day's battle, and this sweet minstrel sings to you. Who could harm the kind vagrant harper? Whom did he ever hurt? He carries no weapon—save the harp on which he plays to you, and with which he delights great and humble, young and old, the captains in the tents, or the soldiers round the fire, or the women and children in the villages, at whose porches he stops and sings his simple songs of love and beauty. With that sweet story of *The Vicar of Wakefield* he has found entry into every castle and every hamlet in Europe. Not one of us, however busy or hard, but once or twice in our lives has passed an evening with him and undergone the charm of his delightful music.

Goldsmith's father was no doubt the good Doctor Primrose, whom we all of us know. Swift was yet alive when the little Oliver was born at Pallas, or Pallasmore, in the county of Longford, in Ireland. In 1730, two years after the child's birth, Charles Goldsmith removed his family to Lissoy, in the county Westmeath, that sweet "Auburn" which every person who hears me has seen in fancy. Here the kind parson brought up his eight children; and loving all the world, as his son says, fancied all the world loved him. He had a crowd of poor dependents besides those hungry children. He kept an open table, round which sat flatterers and poor friends, who laughed at the honest rector's many jokes and ate the produce of his seventy acres of farm. Those who have seen an Irish house in the present day can fancy that one of Lissoy. The old beggar still has his allotted corner by the kitchen turf; the maimed old soldier still gets his potatoes and buttermilk; the poor cottier still asks his Honor's charity, and prays God bless his Reverence for the sixpence; the ragged pensioner still takes his place by right and sufferance. There 's still a crowd in the kitchen, and a crowd round the parlor table; profusion, confusion, kindness, poverty. If an Irishman comes to London to make his fortune, he has a half-dozen of Irish dependents who take a percentage of his earnings. The good Charles Goldsmith left but little provision for his hungry race when death summoned him; and one of his daughters being engaged to a squire of rather superior dignity, Charles Goldsmith impoverished the rest of his family to provide the girl with a dowry.

The small-pox, which scourged all Europe at that time, and ravaged the roses off the cheeks of half the world, fell foul of poor little Oliver's face, when the child was eight years old, and left him scarred and disfigured for his life. An old woman in his father's village taught him his letters, and pronounced him a dunce: Paddy Byrne, the hedge-schoolmaster, took him in hand: and from Paddy Byrne he was transmitted to a clergyman at Elphin. When a child was sent to school in those days the classic phrase was that he was placed under Mr. So-and-So's *ferule*. Poor little ancestors! It is hard to think how ruthlessly you were birched, and how much of needless whipping and tears our small forefathers had to undergo! A relative, kind Uncle Contarine, took the main charge of little Noll, who went through his school-days righteously doing as little work as he could, robbing orchards, playing at ball, and making his pocket-money fly about whenever fortune sent it to him. Everybody knows the story of that famous "Mistake of a Night," when the young schoolboy, provided with a guinea and a nag, rode up to the "best house" in Ardagh, called for the landlord's company over a bottle of wine at supper, and for a hot cake for breakfast in the morning; and found, when he asked for the bill, that the best house was Squire Featherstone's, and not the inn for which he mistook it. Who does not know every story about Goldsmith? That is a delightful and fantastic picture of the child dancing and capering about in the kitchen at home, when the old fiddler gibed at him for his ugliness and called him Æsop; and little Noll made his repartee of "Heralds proclaim aloud this saying—See Æsop dancing and his monkey playing." One can fancy a queer, pitiful look of humor and appeal upon that little scarred face—the funny little dancing figure, the funny little brogue. In his life, and his writings, which are the honest expression of it, he is constantly bewailing that homely face and person; anon he surveys them in the glass ruefully; and presently assumes the most comical dignity. He likes to deck out his little person in splendor and fine colors. He presented himself to be examined for ordination in a pair of scarlet breeches; and said honestly that he did not like to go into the Church, because he was fond of colored clothes. When he tried to practise as a doctor, he got by hook or by crook a black velvet suit, and looked as big and grand as he could, and kept his hat over a patch on the old coat: in better days he bloomed out in plum-color, in blue silk, and in new velvet. For some of those splendors the heirs and assignees of Mr. Filby, the tailor, have never been paid to this day: perhaps the kind tailor and his creditor have met and settled their little account in Hades.

They showed until lately a window at Trinity College, Dublin, on which the name of "O. Goldsmith" was engraved with a diamond. Whose diamond was it? Not the young sizar's, who made but a poor figure in that place of learning. He was idle, penniless, and fond of pleasure: he learned his way early to the pawnbroker's shop. He wrote ballads, they say, for the street-singers, who paid him a crown for a poem; and his pleasure was to steal out at night and hear his verses sung. He was chastised by his tutor for giving a dance in his rooms, and took the box on the ear so much to heart that he packed up his all, pawned his books and little property, and disappeared from college and family. He said he intended to go to America; but when his money was spent, the young prodigal came home ruefully, and the good folks there killed their calf—it was but a lean one—and welcomed him back.

After college, he hung about his mother's house, and lived

for some years the life of a buckeen—passed a month with this relation and that, a year with one patron, a great deal of time at the public-house. Tired of this life, it was resolved that he should go to London and study at the Temple; but he got no farther on the road to London and the woolsack than Dublin, where he gambled away the fifty pounds given to him for his outfit, and whence he returned to the indefatigable forgiveness of home. Then he determined to be a doctor, and Uncle Contarine helped him to a couple of years at Edinburgh. Then from Edinburgh he felt that he ought to hear the famous professors of Leyden and Paris, and wrote most amusing pompous letters to his uncle about the great Farheim, Du Petit, and Duhamel du Monceau, whose lectures he proposed to follow. If Uncle Contarine believed those letters; if Oliver's mother believed that story which the youth related of his going to Cork, with the purpose of embarking for America, of his having paid his passage-money and having sent his kit on board; of the anonymous captain sailing away with Oliver's valuable luggage in a nameless ship, never to return—if Uncle Contarine and the mother at Ballymahon believed his stories, they must have been a very simple pair, as it was a very simple rogue indeed who cheated them. When the lad, after failing in his clerical examination, after failing in his plan for studying the law, took leave of these projects and of his parents, and set out for Edinburgh, he saw mother and uncle and lazy Ballymahon and green native turf and sparkling river for the last time. He was never to look on old Ireland more, and only in fancy revisit her.

> "But me, not destined such delights to share,
> My prime of life in wandering spent and care;
> Impelled, with steps unceasing, to pursue
> Some fleeting good that mocks me with the view;
> That, like the circle bounding earth and skies,
> Allures from far, yet, as I follow, flies;
> My fortune leads to traverse realms alone,
> And find no spot of all the world my own."

I spoke in a former lecture of that high courage which enabled Fielding, in spite of disease, remorse, and poverty, always to retain a cheerful spirit, and to keep his manly benevolence and love of truth intact, as if these treasures had been confided to him for the public benefit, and he was accountable to posterity for their honorable employ; and a constancy equally happy and admirable, I think, was shown by Goldsmith, whose sweet and friendly nature bloomed kindly always in the midst of a life's storm and rain and bitter weather. The poor fellow was never so friendless but he could befriend some one, never so pinched and wretched but he could give of his crust and speak his word of compassion. If he had but his flute left, he could give that, and make the children happy in the dreary London court. He could give the coals in that queer coal-scuttle we read of to his poor neighbor; he could give away his blankets in college to the poor widow, and warm himself as he best might in the feathers; he could pawn his coat to save his landlord from jail; when he was a school-usher, he spent his earnings in treats for the boys, and the good-natured schoolmaster's wife said justly that she ought to keep Mr. Goldsmith's money as well as the young gentlemen's. When he met his pupils in later life, nothing would satisfy the Doctor but he must treat them still. "Have you seen the print of me after Sir Joshua Reynolds?" he asked of one of his old pupils. "Not seen it? not bought it? Sure, Jack, if your picture had been published, I'd not have been without it half-an-hour." His purse and his heart were everybody's, and his friends' as much as his own. When he was at the height of his reputation, and the Earl of Northumberland, going as Lord Lieutenant to Ireland, asked if he could be of any service to Doctor Goldsmith, Goldsmith recommended his brother, and not himself, to the great man. "My patrons," he gallantly said, "are the booksellers, and I want no others." Hard patrons they were, and hard work he did; but he did not complain much: if in his early writings some bitter words escaped him, some allusions to neglect and poverty, he withdrew these expressions when his works were republished and better days seemed to open for him; and he did not care to complain that printer or publisher had overlooked his merit or left him poor. The

Court face was turned from honest Oliver—the Court patronised Beattie. The fashion did not shine on him—fashion adored Sterne. Fashion pronounced Kelly to be the great writer of comedy of his day. A little—not ill-humor, but plaintiveness, a little betrayal of wounded pride which he showed, render him not the less amiable. The author of *The Vicar of Wakefield* had a right to protest when Newbery kept back the manuscript for two years; had a right to be a little peevish with Sterne; a little angry when Coleman's actors declined their parts in his delightful comedy, when the manager refused to have a scene painted for it, and pronounced its damnation before hearing. He had not the great public with him; but he had the noble Johnson and the admirable Reynolds and the great Gibbon and the great Burke and the great Fox—friends and admirers illustrious indeed; as famous as those who, fifty years before, sat round Pope's table.

Nobody knows, and I dare say Goldsmith's buoyant temper kept no account of, all the pains which he endured during the early period of his literary career. Should any man of letters in our day have to bear up against such, Heaven grant he may come out of the period of misfortune with such a pure, kind heart as that which Goldsmith obstinately bore in his breast. The insults to which he had to submit are shocking to read of—slander, contumely, vulgar satire, brutal malignity perverting his commonest motives and actions; he had his share of these, and one's anger is roused at reading of them, as it is at seeing a woman insulted or a child assaulted, at the notion that a creature so very gentle and weak and full of love should have had to suffer so. And he had worse than insult to undergo—to own to fault and deprecate the anger of ruffians. There is a letter of his extant to one Griffiths, a bookseller, in which poor Goldsmith is forced to confess that certain books sent by Griffiths are in the hands of a friend from whom Goldsmith had been forced to borrow money. "He was wild, sir," Johnson said, speaking of Goldsmith to Boswell with his great, wise benevolence and noble mercifulness of heart, "Dr. Goldsmith was wild, sir; but he is so no more." Ah! if we pity the good and weak man who suffers undeservedly, let us deal very gently with him from whom misery extorts not only tears but shame; let us think humbly and charitably of the human nature that suffers so sadly and falls so low. Whose turn may it be to-morrow? What weak heart, confident before trial, may not succumb under temptation invincible? Cover the good man who has been vanquished—cover his face and pass on.

For the last half-dozen years of his life, Goldsmith was far removed from the pressure of any ignoble necessity, and in the receipt, indeed, of a pretty large income from the booksellers, his patrons. Had he lived but a few years more, his public fame would have been as great as his private reputation, and he might have enjoyed alive a part of that esteem which his country has ever since paid to the vivid and versatile genius who has touched on almost every subject of literature, and touched nothing that he did not adorn. Except in rare instances, a man is known in our profession and esteemed as a skilful workman, years before the lucky hit which trebles his usual gains and stamps him a popular author. In the strength of his age and the dawn of his reputation, having for backers and friends the most illustrious literary men of his time, fame and prosperity might have been in store for Goldsmith, had fate so willed it, and, at forty-six, had not sudden disease carried him off. I say prosperity rather than competence, for it is probable that no sum could have put order into his affairs or sufficed for his irreclaimable habits of dissipation. It must be remembered that he owed £2000 when he died. "Was ever poet," Johnson asked, "so trusted before?" As has been the case with many another good fellow of his nation, his life was tracked and his substance wasted by crowds of hungry beggars and lazy dependents. If they came at a lucky time (and be sure they knew his affairs better than he did himself, and watched his pay-day), he gave them of his money: if they begged on empty-purse days, he gave them his promissory bills; or he treated them to a tavern where he had credit; or he obliged them with an order upon honest Mr. Filby for coats, for which he paid as long as he could earn and until the shears of Filby were to cut for him no more. Staggering under a load of debt and labor; tracked by bailiffs and reproachful creditors; running from a hundred poor dependents, whose appealing looks were perhaps the hardest of all pains for him to bear; devising fevered plans for the morrow, new histories, new comedies, all sorts of new literary schemes; flying from all these into seclusion, and out of seclusion into pleasure—at last, at five-and-forty, death seized him and closed his career. I have been many time in the chambers in the Temple which were his, and passed up the staircase which Johnson and Burke and Reynolds trod to see their friend, their poet, their kind Goldsmith—the stair on which the poor women sat weeping bitterly when they heard that the greatest and most generous of all men was dead within the black oak door. Ah, it was a different lot from that for which the poor fellow sighed when he wrote, with heart yearning for home, those most charming of all fond verses, in which he fancies he revisits Auburn:—

"Here as I take my solitary rounds,
Amidst thy tangling walks and ruined grounds,
And, many a year elapsed, return to view
Where once the cottage stood, the hawthorn grew,
Remembrance wakes, with all her busy train,
Swells at my breast, and turns the past to pain.
In all my wanderings round this world of care,
In all my griefs—and God has given my share—
I still had hopes, my latest hours to crown,
Amidst these humble bowers to lay me down;
To husband out life's taper at the close,
And keep the flame from wasting by repose:
I still had hopes—for pride attends us still—
Amidst the swains to show my book-learned skill,
Around my fire an evening group to draw,
And tell of all I felt and all I saw;
And as a hare whom hounds and horns pursue
Pants to the place from whence at first he flew—
I still had hopes, my long vexations past,
Here to return, and die at home at last.
O blest retirement, friend to life's decline,
Retreats from care that never must be mine,

How blest is he who crowns, in shades like these,
A youth of labor with an age of ease;
Who quits a world where strong temptations try,
And, since 'tis hard to combat, learns to fly!
For him no wretches born to work and weep
Explore the mine or tempt the dangerous deep;
Nor surly porter stands in guilty state
To spurn imploring famine from the gate:
But on he moves to meet his latter end,
Angels around befriending virtue's friend;
Sinks to the grave with unperceived decay,
Whilst resignation gently slopes the way;
And, all his prospects brightening to the last,
His heaven commences ere the world be past."

In these verses, I need not say with what melody, with what touching truth, with what exquisite beauty of comparison—as indeed in hundreds more pages of the writings of this honest soul—the whole character of the man is told—his humble confession of faults and weakness; his pleasant little vanity, and desire that his village should admire him; his simple scheme of good in which everybody was to be happy—no beggar was to be refused his dinner—nobody in fact was to work much, and he to be the harmless chief of the Utopia, and the monarch of the Irish Yvetot. He would have told again, and without fear of their failing, those famous jokes which had hung fire in London; he would have talked of his great friends of the Club—of my Lord Clare and my Lord Bishop, my Lord Nugent—sure he knew them intimately, and was hand and glove with some of the best men in town—and he would have spoken of Johnson and of Burke, and of Sir Joshua, who had painted him—and he would have told wonderful sly stories of Ranelagh and the Pantheon, and the masquerades at Madame Cornelys; and he would have toasted, with a sigh, the Jessamy Bride—the lovely Mary Horneck.

The figure of that charming young lady forms one of the prettiest recollections of Goldsmith's life. She and her beautiful sister, who married Bunbury, the graceful and humorous amateur artist of those days, when Gilray had but just begun to try his powers, were among the kindest and dearest of

Goldsmith's many friends; cheered and pitied him, travelled abroad with him, made him welcome at their home, and gave him many a pleasant holiday. He bought his finest clothes to figure at their country-house at Barton—he wrote them droll verses. They loved him, laughed at him, played him tricks, and made him happy. He asked for a loan from Garrick, and Garrick kindly supplied him, to enable him to go to Barton: but there were to be no more holidays and only one brief struggle more for poor Goldsmith. A lock of his hair was taken from the coffin and given to the Jessamy Bride. She lived quite into our time. Hazlitt saw her, an old lady but beautiful still, in Northcote's painting-room, who told the eager critic how proud she always was that Goldsmith had admired her.

The younger Coleman has left a touching reminiscence of him: "I was only five years old," he says, "when Goldsmith took me on his knee one evening whilst he was drinking coffee with my father, and began to play with me, which amiable act I returned, with the ingratitude of a peevish brat, by giving him a very smart slap on the face: it must have been a tingler, for it left the marks of my spiteful paw on his cheek. This infantile outrage was followed by summary justice, and I was locked up by my indignant father in an adjoining room to undergo solitary imprisonment in the dark. Here I began to howl and scream most abominably, which was no bad step towards my liberation, since those who were not inclined to pity me might be likely to set me free for the purpose of abating a nuisance. At length a generous friend appeared to extricate me from jeopardy, and that generous friend was no other than the man I had so wantonly molested by assault and battery—it was the tender-hearted Doctor himself, with a lighted candle in his hand, and a smile upon his countenance, which was still partially red from the effects of my petulance. I sulked and sobbed as he fondled and soothed, till I began to brighten. Goldsmith seized the propitious moment of returning good-humor, when he put down the candle and began to conjure. He placed three hats, which happened to be in the room, and a shilling under each. The shillings he told me were England, France, and Spain. 'Hey presto cockalorum!' cried the Doctor, and lo, on uncovering the shillings, which had been dispersed each beneath a separate hat, they were all found congregated under one. I was no politician at five years old, and therefore might not have wondered at the sudden revolution which brought England, France, and Spain all under one crown; but as also I was no conjuror, it amazed me beyond measure. . . . From that time, whenever the Doctor came to visit my father, 'I plucked his gown to share the good man's smile'; a game at romps constantly ensued, and we were always cordial friends and merry playfellows. Our unequal companionship varied somewhat as to sports as I grew older; but it did not last long: my senior playmate died in his forty-fifth year, when I had attained my eleventh. . . . In all the numerous accounts of his virtues and foibles, his genius and absurdities, his knowledge of nature and ignorance of the world, his 'compassion for another's woe' was always predominant; and my trivial story of his humoring a froward child weighs but as a feather in the recorded scale of his benevolence."

Think of him reckless, thriftless, vain, if you like—but merciful, gentle, generous, full of love and pity. He passes out of our life, and goes to render his account beyond it. Think of the poor pensioners weeping at his grave; think of the noble spirits that admired and deplored him; think of the righteous pen that wrote his epitaph—and of the wonderful and unanimous response of affection with which the world has paid back the love he gave it. His humor delighting us still, his song fresh and beautiful as when first he charmed with it, his words in all our mouths, his very weaknesses beloved and familiar—his benevolent spirit seems still to smile upon us, to do gentle kindnesses, to succor with sweet charity, to soothe, caress, and forgive, to plead with the fortunate for the unhappy and the poor.

John Ruskin.

1819–1900.

SELECTIONS FROM MODERN PAINTERS.

THE SKY.

(From *Modern Painters*, Vol. I., 1843.)

It is a strange thing how little in general people know about the sky. It is the part of creation in which nature has done more for the sake of pleasing man, more for the sole and evident purpose of talking to him and teaching him, than in any other of her works, and it is just the part in which we least attend to her. There are not many of her other works in which some more material or essential purpose than the mere pleasing of man is not answered by every part of their organisation; but every essential purpose of the sky might, so far as we know, be answered if once in three days, or thereabouts, a great, ugly, black rain-cloud were brought up over the blue, and everything well watered, and so all left blue again till next time, with perhaps a film of morning and evening mist for dew. And instead of this there is not a moment of any day of our lives when nature is not producing scene after scene, picture after picture, glory after glory, and working still upon such exquisite and constant principles of the most perfect beauty that it is quite certain it is all done for us and intended for our perpetual pleasure. And every man, wherever placed, however far from other sources of interest or of beauty, has this doing for him constantly. The noblest scenes of the earth can be seen and known but by few; it is not intended that man should live always in the midst of them; he injures them by his presence, he ceases to feel them if he be always with them: but the sky is for all; bright as it is, it is not

> "Too bright or good
> For human nature's daily food;"

it is fitted in all its functions for the perpetual comfort and exalting of the heart, for soothing it and purifying it from its dross and dust. Sometimes gentle, sometimes capricious, sometimes awful, never the same for two moments together, almost human in its passions, almost spiritual in its tenderness, almost divine in its infinity, its appeal to what is immortal in us is as distinct as its ministry of chastisement or of blessing to what is mortal is essential. And yet we never attend to it, we never make it a subject of thought, but as it has to do with our animal sensations: we look upon all by which it speaks to us more clearly than to brutes, upon all which bears witness to the intention of the Supreme that we are to receive more from the covering vault than the light and the dew which we share with the weed and the worm, only as a succession of meaningless and monotonous accident, too common and too vain to be worthy of a moment of watchfulness or a glance of admiration. If in our moments of utter idleness and insipidity we turn to the sky as a last resource, which of its phenomena do we speak of? One says it has been wet; and another, it has been windy; and another, it has been warm. Who, among the whole chattering crowd, can tell me of the forms and the precipices of the chain of tall white mountains that girded the horizon at noon yesterday? Who saw the narrow sunbeam that came out of the south and smote upon their summits until they melted and mouldered away in a dust of blue rain? Who saw the dance of the dead clouds when the sunlight left them last night and the west wind blew them before it like withered leaves? All has passed, unregretted as unseen; or if the apathy be ever shaken off, even for an instant, it is only by what is gross or what is extraordinary; and yet it is not in the broad and fierce manifestations of the elemental energies, not in the clash of the hail nor the drift of the whirlwind, that the highest characters of the sublime are developed. God is not in the earthquake nor in the fire, but in the still, small voice. They are but the blunt and the low faculties of our nature which can only be addressed through lamp-black and lightning. It is in quiet and subdued passages of unobtrusive majesty, the deep and the calm and the perpetual; that which must be sought ere it is seen, and loved ere it is understood; things which the angels work out for us daily and yet vary eternally, which are never wanting and never repeated, which are to be found always yet each found but once; it is through these that the lesson of devotion is chiefly taught, and the blessing of beauty given. These are what the artist of highest aim must study; it is these, by the combination of which his ideal is to be created; these, of which so little notice is ordinarily taken by common observers that I fully believe, little as people in general are concerned with art, more of their ideas of sky are derived from pictures than from reality, and that if we could examine the conception formed in the minds of most educated persons when we talk of clouds, it would frequently be found composed of fragments of blue and white reminiscences of the old masters.

RUNNING WATER.

(From the same.)

When water, not in very great body, runs in a rocky bed much interrupted by hollows, so that it can rest every now and then in a pool as it goes along, it does not acquire a continuous velocity of motion. It pauses after every leap, and curdles about, and rests a little, and then goes on again; and if in this comparatively tranquil and rational state of mind it meets with any obstacle, as a rock or stone, it parts on each side of it with a little bubbling foam, and goes round; if it comes to a step in its bed, it leaps it lightly, and then, after a little splashing at the bottom, stops again to take breath. But if its bed be on a continuous slope, not much interrupted by hollows, so that it cannot rest, or if its own mass be so increased by flood that its usual resting-places are not sufficient for it but that it is perpetually pushed out of them by the following current before it has had time to tranquilize itself, it of course gains velocity with every yard that it runs; the impetus got at one leap is carried to the credit of the next, until the whole stream becomes one mass of unchecked, accelerating motion. Now, when water in this state comes to an obstacle, it does not part at it, but clears it like a race-horse; and when it comes to a hollow, it does not fill it up and run out leisurely at the other side, but it rushes down into it and comes up again on the other side, as a ship into the hollow of the sea. Hence the whole appearance of the bed of the stream is changed, and all the lines of the water altered in their nature. The quiet stream is a succession of leaps and pools; the leaps are light and springy and parabolic, and make a great deal of splashing when they tumble into the pools; then we have a space of quiet curdling water and another similar leap below. But the stream when it has gained an impetus *takes the shape* of its bed, goes down into every hollow, not with a leap, but with a swing, not foaming nor splashing, but in the bending line of a strong sea-wave, and comes up again on the other side, over rock and ridge, with the ease of a bounding leopard; if it meet a rock three or four feet above the level of its bed, it will often neither part nor foam, nor express any concern about the matter, but clear it in a smooth dome of water, without apparent exertion, the whole surface of the surge being drawn into parallel lines by its extreme velocity; so that the whole river has the appearance of a deep and raging sea, with this only difference, that the torrent-waves always break backwards, and sea-waves forwards. Thus, then, in the water which has gained an impetus, we have the most exquisite arrangements of curved lines, perpetually changing from convex to concave, and *vice versa,* following every swell and hollow of the bed with their modulating grace, and all in unison of motion, presenting perhaps the most beautiful series of inorganic forms which nature can possibly produce; for the sea runs too much into similar and concave curves with sharp edges, but every motion of the torrent is united, and all its curves are modifications of beautiful line.

THE SEA.

(From the same.)

Few people, comparatively, have ever seen the effect on the sea of a powerful gale continued without intermission for three or four days and nights; and to those who have not, I believe it must be unimaginable, not from the mere force or size of surge, but from the complete annihilation of the limit between sea and air. The water, from its prolonged agitation, is beaten, not into mere creaming foam, but into masses of accumulated yeast, which hang in ropes and wreaths from wave to wave, and, where one curls over to break, form a festoon like a drapery, from its edge; these are taken up by the wind, not in dissipating dust, but bodily, in writhing, hanging, coiling masses, which make the air white and thick as with snow, only the flakes are a foot or two long each; the surges themselves are full of foam in their very bodies, underneath, making them white all through, as the water is under a great cataract; and their masses, being thus half water and half air, are torn to pieces by the wind whenever they rise, and carried away in roaring smoke, which chokes and strangles like actual water. Add to this that when the air has been exhausted of its moisture by long rain, the spray of the sea is caught by it as described above (Section III., Chapter IV., § 13), and covers its surface, not merely with the smoke of finely divided water, but with boiling mist; imagine also the low rain-clouds brought down to the very level of the sea, as I have often seen them, whirling and flying in rags and fragments from wave to wave; and finally, conceive the surges themselves in their utmost pitch of power, velocity, vastness, and madness, lifting themselves in precipices and peaks, furrowed with their whirl of ascent, through all this chaos; and you will understand that there is indeed no distinction left between the sea and air; that no object, nor horizon, nor any landmark or natural evidence of position is left; that the heaven is all spray, and the ocean all cloud, and that you can see no farther in any direction than you could see through a cataract. Suppose the effect of the first sunbeam sent from above to show this annihilation to itself, and you have the sea picture of the Academy, 1842—*The Snow-storm,* one of the very grandest statements of sea-motion, mist, and light that has ever been put on canvas, even by Turner. Of course it was not understood; his finest works never are; but there was some apology for the public's not comprehending this, for few people have had the opportunity of seeing the sea at such a time, and, when they have, cannot face it. To hold by a mast or a rock, and watch it, is a prolonged endurance of drowning which few people have courage to go through. To those who have it is one of the noblest lessons of nature.

But I think the noblest sea that Turner has ever painted, and, if so, the noblest certainly ever painted by man, is that of *The Slave Ship,* the chief Academy picture of the exhibition of 1840. It is a sunset on the Atlantic after prolonged storm; but the storm is partially lulled, and the torn and streaming rain-clouds are moving in scarlet lines to lose themselves in the hollow of the night. The whole surface of sea included in the picture is divided into two ridges of enormous swell, not high nor local, but a low, broad heaving of the whole ocean, like the lifting of its bosom by deep-drawn breath after the torture of the storm. Between these two ridges the fire of the sunset falls along the trough of the sea, dyeing it with an awful but glorious light, the intense and lurid splendor which burns like gold and bathes like blood. Along this fiery path and valley the tossing waves by which the swell of the sea is restlessly divided lift themselves in dark, indefinite, fantastic forms, each casting a faint and ghastly shadow behind it along the illumined foam. They do not rise everywhere, but three or four together in wild groups, fitfully and furiously, as the under-strength of the swell compels or permits them; leaving between them treacherous spaces of level and whirling water, now lighted with green and lamp-like fire, now flashing back the gold of the declining sun, now fearfully dyed from above with the undistinguishable images of the burning clouds, which fall upon them in flakes of crimson and scarlet and give to the reckless waves the added motion of their own fiery flying. Purple and blue, the lurid shadows of the hollow breakers are cast upon the mist of night, which gathers cold and low, advancing like the shadow of death upon the guilty ship as it labors amidst the lightning of the sea, its thin masts written upon the sky in lines of blood, girded with condemnation in that fearful hue which signs the sky with horror, and mixes its flaming flood with the sunlight, and, cast far along the desolate heave of the sepulchral waves, incarnadines the multitudinous sea.

MOUNTAINS.

(From *Modern Painters*, Vol. IV., 1856.)

Inferior hills ordinarily interrupt, in some degree, the richness of the valleys at their feet; the grey downs of southern England, and treeless coteaux of central France, and grey swells of Scottish moor, whatever peculiar charm they may possess in themselves, are at least destitute of those which belong to the woods and fields of the lowlands. But the great mountains *lift* the lowlands *on their sides.* Let the reader imagine, first, the appearance of the most varied plain of some richly cultivated country; let him imagine it dark with graceful woods and soft with deepest pastures; let him fill the space of it, to the utmost horizon, with innumerable and changeful incidents of scenery and life, leading pleasant streamlets through its meadows, strewing clusters of cottages beside their banks, tracing sweet footpaths through its avenues, and animating its fields with happy flocks and slow wandering spots of cattle: and when he has wearied himself with endless imagining, and left no space without some loveliness of its own, let him conceive all this great plain, with its infinite treasures of natural beauty and happy human life, gathered up in God's hands from one edge of the horizon to the other, like a woven garment; and shaken into deep, falling folds, as the robes droop from a king's shoulders; all its bright rivers leaping into cataracts along the hollows of its fall; and all its forests rearing themselves aslant against its slopes, as a rider rears himself back when his horse plunges; and all its villages nestling themselves into the new windings of its glens; and all its pastures thrown into steep waves of greensward, dashed with dew along the edges of their folds, and sweeping down into endless slopes, with a cloud here and there lying quietly, half on the grass, half in the air; and he will have as yet, in all this lifted world, only the foundation of one of the great Alps. And whatever is lovely in the lowland scenery becomes lovelier in this change: the trees which grew heavily and stiffly from the level line of plain assume strange curves of strength and grace as they bend themselves against the mountain side; they breathe more freely and toss their branches more carelessly, as each climbs higher, looking to the clear light above the topmost leaves of its brother tree; the flowers which on the arable plain fell before the plough now find out for themselves unapproachable places, where year by year they gather into happier fellowship and fear no evil; and the streams which in the level land crept in dark eddies by unwholesome banks now move in showers of silver, and are clothed with rainbows, and bring health and life wherever the glance of their waves can reach.

LEAVES MOTIONLESS.

(From *Modern Painters*, Vol. V., 1860.)

Leaves motionless. The strong pines wave above them, and the weak grasses tremble beside them; but the blue stars rest upon the earth with a peace as of heaven; and far along the ridges of iron rock, moveless as they, the rubied crests of Alpine rose flush in the low rays of morning. Nor these yet the stillest leaves. Others there are, subdued to a deeper quietness, the mute slaves of the earth, to whom we owe, perhaps, thanks and tenderness the most profound of all we have to render for the leaf-ministries.

It is strange to think of the gradually diminished power and withdrawn freedom among the orders of leaves—from the sweep of the chestnut and gadding of the vine, down to the close-shrinking trefoil and contented daisy, pressed on earth; and, at last, to the leaves that are not merely close to earth but themselves a part of it, fastened down to it by their sides, here and there only a wrinkled edge rising from the granite crystals. We have found beauty in the tree yielding fruit and in the herb yielding seed. How of the herb yielding *no* seed, the fruitless, flowerless lichen of the rock?

Lichen and mosses (though these last in their luxuriance are deep and rich as herbage, yet both for the most part humblest of the green things that live), how of these? Meek creatures! the first mercy of the earth, veiling with hushed softness its dintless rocks; creatures full of pity, covering with strange and tender honor the scarred disgrace of ruin, laying quiet finger on the trembling stones to teach them rest. No words that I know of will say what these mosses are. None are delicate enough, none perfect enough, none rich enough. How is one to tell of the rounded bosses of furred and beaming green; the starred divisions of rubied bloom, fine-filmed as if the Rock Spirits could spin porphyry as we do glass; the traceries of intricate silver, and fringes of amber, lustrous, arborescent, burnished through every fibre into fitful brightness and glossy traverses of silken change, yet all subdued and pensive, and framed for simplest, sweetest offices of grace. They will not be gathered, like the flowers, for chaplet or love-token; but of these the wild bird will make its nest, and the wearied child his pillow.

And, as the earth's first mercy, so they are its last gift to us. When all other service is vain, from plant and tree, the soft mosses and gray lichen take up their watch by the headstone. The woods, the blossoms, the gift-bearing grasses have done their parts for a time, but these do service forever.

Trees for the builder's yard, flowers for the bride's chamber, corn for the granary, moss for the grave.

Yet, as in one sense the humblest, in another they are the most honored, of the earth-children. Unfading as motionless, the worm frets them not, and the autumn wastes not. Strong in lowliness, they neither blanch in heat nor pine in frost. To them, slow-fingered, constant-hearted, is entrusted the weaving of the dark, eternal tapestries of the hills; to them, slow-pencilled, iris-dyed, the tender framing of their endless imagery. Sharing the stillness of the unimpassioned rock, they share also its endurance; and while the winds of departing spring scatter the white hawthorn blossom like drifted snow, and summer dims on the parched meadow the drooping of its cowslip-gold, far above, among the mountains, the silver lichen-spots rest, star-like, on the stone, and the gathering orange stain upon the edge of yonder western peak reflects the sunsets of a thousand years.

AN IDEALIST'S ARRAIGNMENT OF THE AGE.

(*Fors Clavigera*, Letter V., 1871.)

"For lo, the winter is past,
The rain is over and gone,
The flowers appear on the earth,
The time of the singing of birds is come,
Arise, oh my fair one, my dove,
And come."

DENMARK HILL,
1st May, 1871.

MY FRIENDS,

It has been asked of me, very justly, why I have hitherto written to you of things you were little likely to care for, in words which it was difficult for you to understand. I have no fear but that you will one day understand all my poor words—the saddest of them perhaps too well. But I have great fear that you may never come to understand these written above, which are part of a king's love-song, in one sweet May, of many long since gone. I fear that for you the wild winter's rain may never pass, the flowers never appear on the earth; that for you no bird may ever sing; for you no perfect Love arise and fulfil your life in peace. "And why not for us as for others?" Will you answer me so, and take my fear for you as an insult? Nay, it is no insult; nor am I happier than you. For me the birds do not sing, nor ever will. But they would for you, if you cared to have it so. When I told you that you would never understand that love-song, I meant only that you would not desire to understand it.

Are you again indignant with me? Do you think, though you should labor and grieve and be trodden down in dishonor, all your days, at least you can keep that one joy of Love and that one honor of Home? Had you, indeed, kept that, you had kept all. But no men yet, in the history of the race, have lost it so piteously. In many a country and many an age, women have been compelled to labor for their husbands' wealth or bread; but never until now were they so homeless as to say, like the poor Samaritan, "I have no husband." Women of every country and people have sustained without complaint the labor of fellowship; for the women of the latter days in England it has been reserved to claim the privilege of isolation.

This, then, is the end of your universal education and civilization, and contempt of the ignorance of the Middle Ages and of their chivalry. Not only do you declare yourselves too indolent to labor for daughters and wives, and too poor to support them, but you have made the neglected and distracted creatures hold it for an honor to be independent of you and shriek for some hold of the mattock for themselves. Believe it or not, as you may, there has not been so low a level of thought reached by any race since they grew to be male and female out of star-fish or chickweed or whatever else they have been made from by natural selection—according to modern science.

That modern science, also, economic and of other kinds, has reached its climax at last. For it seems to be the appointed function of the nineteenth century to exhibit in all things the elect pattern of perfect Folly, for a warning to the farthest future. Thus the statement of principle which I quoted to you in my last letter, from the circular of the Emigration Society, that it is overproduction which is the cause of distress, is accurately the most Foolish thing, not only hitherto ever said by men, but which it is possible for men ever to say, respecting their own business. It is a kind of opposite pole (or negative acme of mortal stupidity) to Newton's discovery of gravitation as an acme of mortal wisdom: as no wise being on earth will ever be able to make such another wise discovery, so no foolish being on earth will ever be capable of saying such another foolish thing, through all the ages.

And the same crisis has been exactly reached by our natural science and by our art. It has several times chanced to me, since I began these papers, to have the exact thing shown or brought to me that I wanted for illustration, just in time; and it happened that, on the very day on which I published my last letter, I had to go to the Kensington Museum, and there I saw the most perfectly and roundly ill-done thing which, as yet, in my whole life, I ever saw produced by art. It had a tablet in front of it, bearing this inscription:—

"Statue in black and white marble, a Newfoundland Dog standing on a Serpent, which rests on a marble cushion, the pedestal ornamented with *pietra dura* fruits in relief.—*English. Present Century.* No. I."

It was so very right for me, the Kensington people having been good enough to number it "I.," the thing itself being almost incredible in its one-ness; and, indeed, such a punctual accent over the iota of Miscreation, so absolutely and exquisitely miscreant, that I am not myself capable of conceiving a Number Two or Three, or any rivalship or association with it whatsoever. The extremity of its unvirtue consisted, observe, mainly in the quantity of instruction which was abused in it. It showed that the persons who produced it had seen everything, and practised everything; and misunderstood everything they saw, and misapplied everything they did.

They had seen Roman work and Florentine work and Byzantine work and Gothic work; and misunderstanding of everything had passed through them as the mud does through earthworms, and here at last was their worm-cast of a Production.

But the second chance that came to me that day was more significant still. From the Kensington Museum I went to an afternoon tea, at a house where I was sure to meet some nice people. And among the first I met was an old friend who had been hearing some lectures on botany at the Kensington Museum, and been delighted by them. She is the kind of person who gets good out of everything, and she was quite right in being delighted; besides that, as I found by her account of them, the lectures were really interesting and pleasantly given. She had expected botany to be dull, and had not found it so, and "had learned so much." On hearing this I proceeded naturally to inquire what; for my idea of her was that before she went to the lectures at all she had known more botany than she was likely to learn by them. So she told me that she had learned first of all that there "were seven sorts of leaves." Now, I have always a great suspicion of the number Seven; because when I wrote *The Seven Lamps of Architecture*, it required all the ingenuity I was master of to prevent them from becoming Eight, or even Nine, on my hands. So I thought to myself that it would be very charming if there were only seven sorts of leaves; but that, perhaps, if one looked the woods and forests of the world carefully through, it was just possible that one might discover as many as eight sorts; and then where would my friend's new knowledge of botany be? So I said, "That was very pretty; but what more?" Then my friend told me that she had no idea, before, that petals were leaves. On which I thought to myself that it would not have been any great harm to her if she had remained under her old impression that petals were petals. But I said, "That was very pretty, too; and what more?" So then my friend told me that the lecturer said "the object of his lectures would be entirely accomplished if he could convince his hearers that there was no such thing as a flower." Now, in that sentence you have the most perfect and admirable summary given you of the general temper and purposes of modern science. It gives lectures on Botany, of which the object is to show that there is no such thing as a Flower; on Humanity, to show that there is no such thing as a Man; and on Theology, to show there is no such thing as a God. No such thing as a Man, but only a Mechanism; no such thing as a God, but only a series of Forces. The two faiths are essentially one: if you feel yourself to be only a machine, constructed to be a regulator of minor machinery, you will put your statue of such science on your Holborn Viaduct, and necessarily recognize only major machinery as regulating *you.*

I must explain the real meaning to you, however, of that saying of the botanical lecturer, for it has a wide bearing. Some fifty years ago the poet Goethe discovered that all the parts of plants had a kind of common nature and would change into each other. Now, this was a true discovery and a notable one; and you will find that, in fact, all plants are composed of essentially two parts—the leaf and root; one loving the light, the other darkness; one liking to be clean, the other to be dirty; one liking to grow for the most part up, the other for the most part down; and each having faculties and purposes of its own. But the pure one, which loves the light, has, above all things, the purpose of being married to another leaf, and having child-leaves and children's children of leaves, to make the earth fair forever. And when the leaves marry, they put on wedding-robes and are more glorious than Solomon in all his glory, and they have feasts of honey; and we call them "Flowers."

In a certain sense, therefore, you see the botanical lecturer was quite right. There are no such things as Flowers—there are only Leaves. Nay, farther than this, there may be a dignity in the less happy but unwithering leaf, which is, in some sort, better than the brief lily of its bloom;—which the great poets always knew well, Chaucer before Goethe, and the writer of the *First Psalm* before Chaucer. The botanical lecturer was, in a deeper sense than he knew, right.

But in the deepest sense of all, the botanical lecturer was, to the extremity of wrongness, wrong; for leaf and root and fruit exist, all of them, only that there may be flowers. He disregarded the life and passion of the creature, which were its essence. Had he looked for these, he would have recognized that in the thought of Nature herself there is in a plant nothing else but its flowers.

Now, in exactly the sense that modern science declares there is no such thing as a Flower, it has declared there is no such thing as a Man but only a transitional form of Ascidians and apes. It may or may not be true—it is not of the smallest consequence whether it be or not. The real fact is that, seen with human eyes, there is nothing else but Man; that all animals and beings beside him are only made that they may change into him; that the world truly exists only in the presence of Man, acts only in the passion of Man. The essence of Light is in his eyes, the centre of Force in his soul, the pertinence of Action in his deeds. And all true science—which my Savoyard guide rightly scorned me when he thought I had not—all true science is *savoir vivre.* But all your modern science is the contrary of that. It is *savoir mourir.* And of its very discoveries, such as they are, it cannot make use.

That telegraphic signalling was a discovery; and conceivably, some day, may be a useful one. And there was some excuse for your being a little proud when, about last sixth of April (Cœur de Lion's death-day, and Albert Dürer's), you knotted a copper wire all the way to Bombay, and flashed a message along it and back. But what was the message, and what the answer? Is India the better for what you said to her? Are you the better for what she replied? If not, you have only wasted an all-round-the-world's length of copper wire—which is, indeed, about the sum of your doing. If you had had, perchance, two words of common sense to say, though you had taken wearisome time and trouble to send them—though you had written them slowly in gold, and sealed them with a hundred seals, and sent a squadron of ships of the line to carry the scroll, and the squadron had fought its way round the Cape of Good Hope, through a year of storms, with loss of all its ships but one,—the two words of common sense would have been worth the carriage, and more. But you have not anything like so much as that to say, either to India or to any other place.

You think it a great triumph to make the sun draw brown landscapes for you. That was also a discovery, and some day may be useful. But the sun had drawn landscapes before for you, not in brown, but in green and blue and all imaginable colors, here in England. Not one of you ever looked at them then; not one of you cares for the loss of them now, when you have shut the sun out with smoke, so that he can draw nothing more except brown blots through a hole in a box. There was a rocky valley between Buxton and Bakewell, once upon a time, divine as the Vale of Tempe; you might have seen the Gods there morning and evening—Apollo and all the sweet Muses of the Light—walking in fair procession on the lawns of it and to and fro among the pinnacles of its crags. You cared neither for Gods nor grass, but for cash (which you did not know the way to get); you thought you could get it by what the *Times* calls "Railroad Enterprise." You Enterprised a Railroad through the valley—you blasted its rocks away, heaped thousands of tons of shale into its lovely stream. The valley is gone, and the Gods with it; and now every fool in Buxton can be at Bakewell in half an hour, and every fool in Bakewell at Buxton; which you think a lucrative process of exchange—you Fools Everywhere.

To talk at a distance, when you have nothing to say though you were ever so near; to go fast from this place to that, with nothing to do either at one or the other—these are powers certainly. Much more, power of increased Production, if you indeed had got it, would be something to boast of. But are you so entirely sure that you *have* got it—that the mortal disease of plenty, and afflictive affluence of good things, are all you have to dread?

Observe. A man and a woman, with their children, properly trained, are able easily to cultivate as much ground as will feed them, to build as much wall and roof as will lodge them, and to spin and weave as much cloth as will clothe them. They can all be perfectly happy and healthy in doing this. Supposing that they invent machinery which will build, plough, thresh, cook, and weave, and that they have none of these things any more to do, but may read, or play croquet or cricket, all day long, I believe myself that they will neither be so good nor so happy as without the machines. But I waive my belief in this matter for the time. I will assume that they become more refined and moral persons, and that idleness is in future to be the mother of all good. But observe, I repeat, the power of your machine is only in enabling them to be idle. It will not enable them to live better than they did before, nor to live in greater numbers. Get your heads quite clear on this matter. Out of so much ground only so much living is to be got, with or without machinery. You may set a million of steam-ploughs to work on an acre, if you like—out of that acre only a given number of grains of corn will grow, scratch or scorch it as you will. So that the question is not at all whether, by having more machines, more of you can live. No machines will increase the possibilities of life. They only increase the possibilities of idleness. Suppose, for instance, you could get the oxen in your plough driven by a goblin, who would ask for no pay, not even a cream bowl (you have nearly managed to get it driven by an iron goblin, as it is), well, your furrow will take no more seeds than if you had held the stilts yourself. But instead of holding them you sit, I presume, on a bank beside the field, under an eglantine—watch the goblin at his work, and read poetry. Meantime, your wife in the house has also got a goblin to weave and wash for her. And she is lying on the sofa, reading poetry.

Now, as I said, I don't believe you would be happier so, but I am willing to believe it; only, since you are already such brave mechanists, show me at least one or two places where you *are* happier. Let me see one small example of approach to this seraphic condition. *I* can show *you* examples, millions of them, of happy people made happy by their own industry. Farm after farm I can show you in Bavaria, Switzerland, the Tyrol, and such other places, where men and women are perfectly happy and good, without any iron servants. Show me, therefore, some English family, with its fiery familiar, happier than these. Or bring me—for I am not inconvinceable by any kind of evidence—bring me the testimony of an English family or two to their increased felicity. Or if you cannot do so much as that, can you convince even themselves of it? They *are* perhaps happy, if only they knew how happy they were. Virgil thought so, long ago, of simple rustics; but you hear at present your steam-propelled rustics are crying out that they are anything else than happy, and that they regard their boasted progress "in the light of a monstrous Sham." I must tell you one little thing, however, which greatly perplexes my imagination of the relieved ploughman sitting under his rose-bower, reading poetry. I have told it you before, indeed, but I forget where. There was really a great festivity, and expression of satisfaction in the new order of things, down in Cumberland, a little while ago; some first of May, I think it was, a country festival, such as the old heathens, who had no iron servants, used to keep with piping and dancing. So I thought, from the liberated country people—their work all done for them by goblins—we should have some extraordinary piping and dancing. But there was no dancing at all, and they could not even provide their own piping. They had their goblin to pipe for them. They walked in procession after their steam-plough, and their steam-plough whistled to them occasionally in the most melodious manner it could. Which seemed to me, indeed, a return to more than Arcadian simplicity; for in old Arcadia ploughboys truly whistled as they went, for want of thought, whereas here was verily a large company walking without thought but not having any more even the capacity of doing their own whistling.

But next, as to the inside of the house. Before you got your power-looms a woman could always make herself a chemise and petticoat of bright and pretty appearance. I have seen a Bavarian peasant-woman at church in Munich, looking a much grander creature, and more beautifully dressed, than any of the crossed and embroidered angels in Hesse's high-art frescoes (which happened to be just above her, so that I could look from one to the other). Well, here you are, in England, served by household demons, with five hundred fingers at least, weaving, for one that used to weave in the days of Minerva. You ought to be able to show me five hundred dresses for one that used to be; tidiness ought to have become five-hundred-fold tidier; tapestry should be increased into *cinque-cento*-fold iridescence of tapestry. Not only your peasant-girl ought to be lying on the sofa, reading poetry, but she ought to have in her wardrobe five hundred petticoats instead of one. Is that, indeed, your issue? or are you only on a curiously crooked way to it?

It is just possible, indeed, that you may not have been allowed to get the use of the goblin's work—that other people may have got the use of it, and you none; because, perhaps, you have not been able to evoke goblins wholly for your own personal service, but have been borrowing goblins from the capitalist and paying interest, in the "position of William," on ghostly self-going planes. But suppose you had laid by capital enough, yourselves, to hire all the demons in the world—nay, all that are inside of it,—are you quite sure you know what you might best set them to work at, and what "useful things" you should command them to make for you? I told you, last month, that no economist going (whether by steam or ghost) knew what are useful things and what are not. Very few of you know, yourselves, except by bitter experience of the want of them. And no demons, either of iron or spirit, can ever make them.

There are three Material things, not only useful, but essential to Life. No one "knows how to live" till he has got them.

These are Pure Air, Water, and Earth.

There are three Immaterial things, not only useful, but essential to Life. No one knows how to live till he has got them also.

These are Admiration, Hope, and Love.

Admiration—the power of discerning and taking delight in what is beautiful in visible Form and lovely in human Character; and, necessarily, striving to produce what is beautiful in form and to become what is lovely in character.

Hope—the recognition, by true Foresight, of better things to be reached hereafter, whether by ourselves or others; necessarily issuing in the straightforward and undisappointable effort to advance, according to our proper power, the gaining of them.

Love—both of family and neighbor, faithful and satisfied.

These are the six chiefly useful things to be got by Political Economy, when it *has* become a science. I will briefly tell you what modern Political Economy—the great *savoir mourir*—is doing with them.

The first three, I said, are Pure Air, Water, and Earth.

Heaven gives you the main elements of these. You can destroy them at your pleasure, or increase, almost without limit, the available quantities of them.

You can vitiate the air by your manner of life and of death, to any extent. You might easily vitiate it so as to bring such a pestilence on the globe as would end all of you. You or your fellows, German and French, are at present vitiating it to the best of your power in every direction—chiefly at this moment with corpses and animal and vegetable ruin in war, changing men, horses, and garden-stuff into noxious gas. But everywhere, and all day long, you are vitiating it with foul chemical exhalations; and the horrible nests, which you call towns, are little more than laboratories for the distillation into heaven of venomous smokes and smells, mixed with effluvia from decaying animal matter and infectious miasmata from purulent disease. On the other hand, your power of purifying the air, by dealing properly and swiftly with all substances in corruption, by absolutely forbidding noxious manufactures, and by planting in all soils the trees which cleanse and invigorate earth and atmosphere, is literally infinite. You might make every breath of air you draw, food.

Secondly, your power over the rain and river-waters of the

earth is infinite. You can bring rain where you will, by planting wisely and tending carefully; drought where you will, by ravage of woods and neglect of the soil. You might have the rivers of England as pure as the crystal of the rock; beautiful in falls, in lakes, in living pools; so full of fish that you might take them out with your hands instead of nets. Or you may do always as you have done now—turn every river of England into a common sewer, so that you cannot so much as baptize an English baby but with filth, unless you hold its face out in the rain; and even *that* falls dirty.

Then for the third, earth, meant to be nourishing for you and blossoming. You have learned about it that there is no such thing as a flower; and as far as your scientific hands and scientific brains, inventive of explosive and deathful instead of blossoming and life-giving dust, can contrive, you have turned the Mother-Earth, Demeter, into the Avenger-Earth, Tisiphone—with the voice of your brother's blood crying out of it in one wild harmony round all its murderous sphere.

That is what you have done for the Three Material Useful Things.

Then for the Three Immaterial Useful Things. For Admiration, you have learned contempt and conceit. There is no lovely thing ever yet done by man that you care for or can understand; but you are persuaded you are able to do much finer things yourselves. You gather and exhibit together, as if equally instructive, what is infinitely bad with what is infinitely good. You do not know which is which; you instinctively prefer the Bad, and do more of it. You instinctively hate the Good, and destroy it.

Then, secondly, for Hope. You have not so much spirit of it in you as to begin any plan which will not pay for ten years; nor so much intelligence of it in you (either politicians or workmen) as to be able to form one clear idea of what you would like your country to become.

Then, thirdly, for Love. You were ordered by the Founder of your religion to love your neighbor as yourselves. You have founded an entire science of Political Economy on what you have stated to be the constant instinct of man--the desire to defraud his neighbor. And you have driven your women mad, so that they ask no more for Love nor for fellowship with you; but stand against you, and ask for "Justice."

Are there any of you who are tired of all this? Any of you, Landlords or Tenants? Employers or Workmen? Are there any landlords, any masters, who would like better to be served by men than by iron devils? Any tenants, any workmen, who can be true to their leaders and to each other? who can vow to work and to live faithfully, for the sake of the joy of their homes?

Will any such give the tenth of what they have and of what they earn, not to emigrate with, but to stay in England with, and do what is in their hands and hearts to make her a happy England?

I am not rich (as people now estimate riches), and great part of what I have is already engaged in maintaining art-workmen, or for other objects more or less of public utility. The tenth of whatever is left to me, estimated as accurately as I can (you shall see the accounts), I will make over to you in perpetuity, with the best security that English law can give, on Christmas Day of this year, with engagement to add the tithe of whatever I earn afterwards. Who else will help, with little or much? the object of such fund being to begin, and gradually—no matter how slowly—to increase, the buying and securing of land in England, which shall not be built upon, but cultivated by Englishmen with their own hands and such help of force as they can find in wind and wave. I do not care with how many or how few this thing is begun, nor on what inconsiderable scale—if it be but in two or three poor men's gardens. So much, at least, I can buy, myself, and give them. If no help come, I have done and said what I could, and there will be an end. If any help come to me, it is to be on the following conditions:—

We will try to make some small piece of English ground beautiful, peaceful, and fruitful. We will have no steam-engines upon it, and no railroads; we will have no untended or unthought-of creatures on it; none wretched but the sick;

none idle but the dead. We will have no liberty upon it, but instant obedience to known law and appointed persons; no equality upon it, but recognition of every betterness that we can find, and reprobation of every worseness. When we want to go anywhere, we will go there quietly and safely, not at forty miles an hour in the risk of our lives; when we want to carry anything anywhere, we will carry it either on the backs of beasts or on our own, or in carts or boats. We will have plenty of flowers and vegetables in our gardens, plenty of corn and grass in our fields,—and few bricks. We will have some music and poetry; the children shall learn to dance to it and sing it; perhaps some of the old people, in time, may also. We will have some art, moreover; we will at least try if, like the Greeks, we can't make some pots. The Greeks used to paint pictures of gods on their pots. We, probably, cannot do as much; but we may put some pictures of insects on them, and reptiles—butterflies and frogs, if nothing better. There was an excellent old potter in France who used to put frogs and vipers into his dishes, to the admiration of mankind; we can surely put something nicer than that. Little by little, some higher art and imagination may manifest themselves among us, and feeble rays of science may dawn for us:—botany, though too dull to dispute the existence of flowers; and history, though too simple to question the nativity of men; nay, even perhaps an uncalculating and uncovetous wisdom, as of rude Magi, presenting, at such nativity, gifts of gold and frankincense.

Faithfully yours,

JOHN RUSKIN.

John Henry Newman.

1801–1890.

THE ROMAN CATHOLIC CHURCH.

(From *Apologia pro Vita Sua*, 1864.)

From the time that I became a Catholic, of course I have no further history of my religious opinions to narrate. In saying this I do not mean to say that my mind has been idle, or that I have given up thinking on theological subjects; but that I have had no variations to record, and have had no anxiety of heart whatever. I have been in perfect peace and contentment; I never have had one doubt. I was not conscious to myself, on my conversion, of any change, intellectual or moral, wrought in my mind. I was not conscious of firmer faith in the fundamental truths of Revelation, or of more self-command; I had not more fervor; but it was like coming into port after a rough sea; and my happiness on that score remains to this day without interruption.

Nor had I any trouble about receiving those additional articles, which are not found in the Anglican creed. Some of them I believed already, but not any one of them was a trial to me. I made a profession of them, upon my reception, with the greatest ease, and I have the same ease in believing them now. I am far of course from denying that every article of the Christian creed, whether as held by Catholics or by Protestants, is beset with intellectual difficulties; and it is simple fact that, for myself, I cannot answer those difficulties. Many persons are very sensitive of the difficulties of religion; I am as sensitive of them as any one; but I have never been able to see a connection between apprehending those difficulties, however keenly, and multiplying them to any extent, and on the other hand doubting the doctrines to which they are attached. Ten thousand difficulties do not make one doubt, as I understand the subject; difficulty and doubt are incommensurate. There of course may be difficulties in the evidence; but I am speaking of difficulties intrinsic to the doctrines themselves or to their relations with each other. A man may be annoyed that he cannot work out a mathematical problem, of which the answer is or is not given to him, without doubting that it admits of an answer or that a certain particular answer is the true one. Of all points of faith the being of a God is, to my own apprehension, encompassed with most difficulty, and yet borne in upon our minds with most power.

People say that the doctrine of Transubstantiation is difficult to believe; I did not believe the doctrine till I was a Catholic. I had no difficulty in believing it as soon as I believed that the Catholic Roman Church was the oracle of God, and that she had declared this doctrine to be part of the original revelation. It is difficult, impossible, to imagine, I grant; but how is it difficult to believe? Yet Macaulay thought it so difficult to believe that he had need of a believer in it of talents as eminent as Sir Thomas More before he could bring himself to conceive that the Catholics of an enlightened age could resist "the overwhelming force of the argument against it." "Sir Thomas More," he says, "is one of the choice specimens of wisdom and virtue; and the doctrine of transubstantiation is a kind of proof charge. A faith which stands that test will stand any test." But for myself, I cannot indeed prove it, I cannot tell how it is; but I say, "Why should it not be? What 's to hinder it? What do I know of substance or matter? just as much as the greatest philosophers, and that is nothing at all"—so much is this the case that there is a rising school of philosophy now which considers phenomena to constitute the whole of our knowledge in physics. The Catholic doctrine leaves phenomena alone. It does not say that the phenomena go; on the contrary, it says that they remain; nor does it say that the same phenomena are in several places at once. It deals with what no one on earth knows anything about, the material substances themselves. And, in like manner, of that majestic article of the

Anglican as well as of the Catholic creed, the doctrine of the Trinity in Unity. What do I know of the Essence of the Divine Being? I know that my abstract idea of three is simply incompatible with my idea of one; but when I come to the question of concrete fact, I have no means of proving that there is not a sense in which one and three can equally be predicated of the Incommunicable God.

But I am going to take upon myself the responsibility of more than the mere creed of the Church—as the parties accusing me are determined I shall do. They say that now, in that I am a Catholic, though I may not have offences of my own against honesty to answer for, yet at least I am answerable for the offences of others, of my co-religionists, of my brother priests, of the Church herself. I am quite willing to accept the responsibility; and as I have been able, as I trust, by means of a few words, to dissipate, in the minds of all those who do not begin with disbelieving me, the suspicion with which so many Protestants start, in forming their judgment of Catholics, *viz.*, that our creed is actually set up in inevitable superstition and hypocrisy, as the original sin of Catholicism, so now I will proceed as before, identifying myself with the Church and vindicating it,—not of course denying the enormous mass of sin and error which exists of necessity in that world-wide, multiform Communion, but going to the proof of this one point, that its system is in no sense dishonest, and that therefore the upholders and teachers of that system, as such, have a claim to be acquitted in their own persons of that odious imputation.

Starting, then, with the being of a God (which, as I have said, is as certain to me as the certainty of my own existence, though when I try to put the grounds of that certainty into logical shape I find a difficulty in doing so in mood and figure to my satisfaction), I look out of myself into the world of men, and there I see a sight which fills me with unspeakable distress. The world seems simply to give the lie to that great truth, of which my whole being is so full; and the effect upon me is, in consequence, as a matter of necessity, as confusing as if it denied that I am in existence myself. If I looked into a mirror and did not see my face, I should have the sort of feeling which actually comes upon me when I look into this living, busy world and see no reflection of its Creator. This is, to me, one of those great difficulties of this absolute primary truth, to which I referred just now. Were it not for this voice, speaking so clearly in my conscience and my heart, I should be an atheist or a pantheist or a polytheist when I looked into the world. I am speaking for myself only, and I am far from denying the real force of the arguments in proof of a God, drawn from the general facts of human society and the course of history; but these do not warm me or enlighten me; they do not take away the winter of my desolation, or make the buds unfold and the leaves grow within me, and my moral being rejoice. The sight of the world is nothing else than the prophet's scroll, full of "lamentations and mourning and woe."

To consider the world in its length and breadth, its various history, the many races of man, their starts, their fortunes, their mutual alienation, their conflicts; and then their ways, habits, governments, forms of worship; their enterprises, their aimless courses, their random achievements and acquirements; the impotent conclusion of long-standing facts, the tokens so faint and broken of a superintending design, the blind evolution of what turn out to be great powers or truths, the progress of things as if from unreasoning elements, not towards final causes; the greatness and littleness of man, his far-reaching aims, his short duration, the curtain hung over his futurity; the disappointments of life, the defeat of good, the success of evil, physical pain, mental anguish; the prevalence and intensity of sin, the pervading idolatries, the corruptions, the dreary, hopeless irreligion, that condition of the whole race so fearfully yet exactly described in the apostle's words, "having no hope and without God in the world,"—all this is a vision to dizzy and appal, and inflicts upon the mind the sense of a profound mystery which is absolutely beyond human solution.

What shall be said to this heart-piercing, reason-bewildering fact? I can only answer that either there is no Creator, or this living society of men is in a true sense discarded from His presence. Did I see a boy of good make and mind, with the tokens on him of a refined nature, cast upon the world without provision, unable to say whence he came, his birthplace or his family connections, I should conclude that there was some mystery connected with his history and that he was one of whom, from one cause or other, his parents were ashamed. Thus only should I be able to account for the contrast between the promise and the condition of his being. And so I argue about the world. *If* there be a God, *since* there is a God, the human race is implicated in some terrible aboriginal calamity. It is out of joint with the purposes of its Creator. This is a fact, a fact as true as the fact of its existence; and thus the doctrine of what is theologically called original sin becomes to me almost as certain as that the world exists and as the existence of God.

And now, supposing it were the blessed and loving will of the Creator to interfere in this anarchical condition of things, what are we to suppose would be the methods which might be necessarily or naturally involved in His purpose of mercy? Since the world is in so abnormal a state, surely it would be no surprise to me if the interposition were of necessity equally extraordinary—or what is called miraculous. But that subject does not directly come into the scope of my present remarks. Miracles as evidence involve a process of reason, or an argument; and of course I am thinking of some mode of interference which does not immediately run into argument. I am rather asking what must be the face-to-face antagonist by which to withstand and baffle the fierce energy of passion and the all-corroding, all-dissolving scepticism of the intellect in religious inquiries? I have no intention at all of denying that truth is the real object of our reason, and that if it does not attain to truth either the premise or the process is in fault; but I am not speaking here of right reason, but of reason as it acts in fact and concretely in fallen man. I know that even the unaided reason, when correctly exercised, leads to a belief in God, in the immortality of the soul, and in a future retribution; but I am considering the faculty of reason actually and historically, and in this point of view I do not think I am wrong in saying that its tendency is towards a simple unbelief in matters of religion. No truth, however sacred, can stand against it in the long run; and hence it is that in the pagan world, when our Lord came, the last traces of the religious knowledge of former times were all but disappearing from those portions of the world in which the intellect had been active and had had a career.

And in these latter days, in like manner, outside the Catholic Church things are tending—with far greater rapidity than in that old time, from the circumstance of the age—to atheism in one shape or other. What a scene, what a prospect, does the whole of Europe present at this day! and not only Europe, but every government and every civilization through the world, which is under the influence of the European mind! Especially (for it most concerns us) how sorrowful, in the view of religion even taken in its most elementary, most attenuated form, is the spectacle presented to us by the educated intellect of England, France, and Germany! Lovers of their country and of their race, religious men, external to the Catholic Church, have attempted various expedients to arrest fierce, wilful human nature in its onward course and to bring it into subjection. The necessity of some form of religion for the interests of humanity has been generally acknowledged; but where was the concrete representative of things invisible, which would have the force and the toughness necessary to be a breakwater against the deluge? Three centuries ago the establishment of religion, material, legal, and social, was generally adopted as the best expedient for the purpose, in those countries which separated from the Catholic Church, and for a long time it was successful; but now the crevices of those establishments are admitting the enemy. Thirty years ago education was relied upon; ten years ago there was a hope that wars would cease forever, under the influence of commercial enterprise and the reign of the useful and fine arts; but will any one venture to say that there is anything anywhere on this earth which will afford a fulcrum for us whereby to keep the earth from moving onwards?

The judgment which experience passes, whether on establishments or on education, as a means of maintaining religious truth in this anarchical world, must be extended even to Scripture, though Scripture be divine. Experience proves, surely, that the Bible does not answer a purpose for which it was never intended. It may be accidentally the means of the conversion of individuals; but a book, after all, cannot make a stand against the wild, living intellect of man, and in this day it begins to testify, as regards its own structure and contents, to the power of that universal solvent which is so successfully acting upon religious establishments.

Supposing, then, it to be the will of the Creator to interfere in human affairs, and to make provisions for retaining in the world a knowledge of Himself so definite and distinct as to be proof against the energy of human scepticism, in such a case,—I am far from saying that there was no other way,—but there is nothing to surprise the mind if He should think fit to introduce a power into the world, invested with the prerogative of infallibility in religious matters. Such a provision would be a direct, immediate, active, and prompt means of withstanding the difficulty; it would be an instrument suited to the need; and when I find that this is the very claim of the Catholic Church, not only do I feel no difficulty in admitting the idea, but there is a fitness in it which recommends it to my mind. And thus I am brought to speak of the Church's infallibility as a provision adapted by the mercy of the Creator to preserve religion in the world, and to restrain that freedom of thought which of course in itself is one of the greatest of our natural gifts, and to rescue it from its own suicidal excesses. And let it be observed that, neither here nor in what follows, shall I have occasion to speak directly of Revelation in its subject-matter, but in reference to the sanction which it gives to truths which may be known independently of it—as it bears upon the defence of natural religion. I say that a power possessed of infallibility in religious teaching is happily adapted to be a working instrument, in the course of human affairs, for smiting hard and throwing back the immense energy of the aggressive, capricious, untrustworthy intellect:—and in saying this, as in the other things that I have to say, it must still be recollected that I am all along bearing in mind my main purpose, which is a defence of myself.

I am defending myself here from a plausible charge brought against Catholics, as will be seen better as I proceed. The charge is this:—that I, as a Catholic, not only make profession to hold doctrines which I cannot possibly believe in my heart, but that I also believe in the existence of a power on earth which at its own will imposes upon men any new set of *credenda*, when it pleases, by a claim to infallibility; in consequence, that my own thoughts are not my own property; that I cannot tell that to-morrow I may not have to give up what I hold to-day; and that the necessary effect of such a condition of mind must be a degrading bondage, or a bitter inward rebellion relieving itself in secret infidelity, or the necessity of ignoring the whole subject of religion in a sort of disgust, and of mechanically saying everything that the Church says, and leaving to others the defence of it. As, then, I have above spoken of the relation of my mind towards the Catholic creed, so now I shall speak of the attitude which it takes up in the view of the Church's infallibility.

And, first, the initial doctrine of the infallible teacher must be an emphatic protest against the existing state of mankind. Man had rebelled against his Maker. It was this that caused the divine interposition, and to proclaim it must be the first act of the divinely-accredited messenger. The Church must denounce rebellion as of all possible evils the greatest. She must have no terms with it; if she would be true to her Master, she must ban and anathematize it. This is the meaning of a statement of mine which has furnished matter for one of those special accusations to which I am at present replying: I have, however, no fault at all to confess in regard to it; I have nothing to withdraw, and in consequence I here deliberately repeat it. I said, "The Catholic

Church holds it better for the sun and moon to drop from heaven, for the earth to fail, and for all the many millions on it to die of starvation in extremest agony, as far as temporal affliction goes, than that one soul, I will not say should be lost, but should commit one single venial sin, should tell one wilful untruth, or should steal one poor farthing without excuse." I think the principle here enunciated to be the mere preamble in the formal credentials of the Catholic Church, as an act of Parliament might begin with a "Whereas." It is because of the intensity of the evil which has possession of mankind that a suitable antagonist has been provided against it; and the initial act of that divinely-commissioned power is of course to deliver her challenge and to defy the enemy. Such a preamble, then, gives a meaning to her position in the world and an interpretation to her whole course of teaching and action.

In like manner she has ever put forth, with most energetic distinctness, those other great elementary truths which either are an explanation of her mission or give a character to her work. She does not teach that human nature is irreclaimable, else wherefore should she be sent? not that it is to be shattered and reversed, but to be extricated, purified, and restored; not that it is a mere mass of hopeless evil, but that it has the promise upon it of great things, and even now, in its present state of disorder and excess, has a virtue and a praise proper to itself. But in the next place, she knows and she preaches that such a restoration as she aims at effecting in it must be brought about, not simply through certain outward provisions of preaching and teaching, even though they be her own, but from an inward spiritual power or grace imparted directly from above, and of which she is the channel. She has it in charge to rescue human nature from its misery, but not simply by restoring it on its own level, but by lifting it up to a higher level than its own. She recognizes in it real moral excellence though degraded, but she cannot set it free from earth except by exalting it towards heaven. It was for this end that a renovating grace was put into her hands; and therefore, from the nature of the gift, as well as from the reasonableness of the case, she goes on, as a further point, to insist that all true conversion must begin with the first springs of thought, and to teach that each individual man must be in his own person one whole and perfect temple of God, while he is also one of the living stones which build up a visible religious community. And thus the distinctions between nature and grace, and between outward and inward religion, become two further articles in what I have called the preamble of her divine commission. . . .

Passing now from what I have called the preamble of that grant of power which is made to the Church, to that power itself, Infallibility, I premise two brief remarks:—1. On the one hand I am not here determining anything about the essential seat of that power, because that is a question doctrinal, not historical and practical; 2. Nor, on the other hand, am I extending the direct subject-matter, over which that power of Infallibility has jurisdiction, beyond religious opinion. And now as to the power itself.

This power, viewed in its fulness, is as tremendous as the giant evil which has called for it. It claims, when brought into exercise but in the legitimate manner, for otherwise of course it is but quiescent, to know for certain the very meaning of every portion of that Divine Message in detail, which was committed by our Lord to His apostles. It claims to know its own limits, and to decide what it can determine absolutely and what it cannot. It claims, moreover, to have a hold upon statements not directly religious, so far as this—to determine whether they indirectly relate to religion, and, according to its own definitive judgment, to pronounce whether or not, in a particular case, they are simply consistent with revealed truth. It claims to decide magisterially, whether as within its own province or not, that such and such statements are or are not prejudicial to the *depositum* of faith, in their spirit or in their consequences, and to allow them, or condemn and forbid them, accordingly. It claims to impose silence at will on any matters or controversies of doctrine, which on its own *ipse dixit* it pronounces to be dangerous or inexpedient or inopportune. It claims that, whatever may be the judgment of Catholics upon such acts, these acts should be received by them with those outward marks of reverence, submission, and loyalty which Englishmen, for instance, pay to the presence of their sovereign, without expressing any criticism on them on the ground that in their matter they are inexpedient or in their manner violent or harsh. And lastly, it claims to have the right of inflicting spiritual punishment, of cutting off from the ordinary channels of the divine life, and of simply excommunicating, those who refuse to submit themselves to its formal declarations. Such is the infallibility lodged in the Catholic Church, viewed in the concrete, as clothed and surrounded by the appendages of its high sovereignty: it is, to repeat what I said above, a super-eminent, prodigious power sent upon earth to encounter and master a giant evil.

And now, having thus described it, I profess my own absolute submission to its claim. I believe the whole revealed dogma as taught by the apostles, as committed by the apostles to the Church, and as declared by the Church to me. I receive it, as it is infallibly interpreted by the authority to whom it is thus committed, and (implicitly) as it shall be, in like manner, further interpreted by that same authority till the end of time. I submit, moreover, to the universally received traditions of the Church, in which lies the matter of those new dogmatic definitions which are from time to time made, and which in all times are the clothing and the illustration of the Catholic dogma as already defined. And I submit myself to those other decisions of the Holy See, theological or not, through the organs which it has itself appointed, which, waiving the question of their infallibility, on the lowest ground come to me with a claim to be accepted and obeyed. Also I consider that, gradually and in the course of ages, Catholic inquiry has taken certain definite shapes, and has thrown itself into the form of a science, with a method and a phraseology of its own, under the intellectual handling of great minds, such as St. Athanasius, St. Augustine, and St. Thomas; and I feel no temptation at all to break in pieces the great legacy of thought thus committed to us for these latter days.

All this being considered as the profession which I make *ex animo*, as for myself, so also on the part of the Catholic body as far as I know it, it will at first sight be said that the restless intellect of our common humanity is utterly weighed down, to the repression of all independent effort and action whatever, so that, if this is to be the mode of bringing it into order, it is brought into order only to be destroyed. But this is far from the result, far from what I conceive to be the intention of that high Providence Who has provided a great remedy for a great evil; far from borne out by the history of the conflict between Infallibility and Reason in the past, and the prospect of it in the future. The energy of the human intellect "does from opposition grow"; it thrives and is joyous, with a tough, elastic strength, under the terrible blows of the divinely-fashioned weapon, and is never so much itself as when it has lately been overthrown. It is the custom with Protestant writers to consider that, whereas there are two great principles in action in the history of religion, Authority and Private Judgment, they have all the Private Judgment to themselves, and we have the full inheritance and the superincumbent oppression of Authority. But this is not so; it is the vast Catholic body itself, and it only, which affords an arena for both combatants in that awful, never-dying duel. It is necessary for the very life of religion, viewed in its large operations and its history, that the warfare should be incessantly carried on. Every exercise of Infallibility is brought out into act by an intense and varied operation of the Reason, both as its ally and as its opponent, and provokes again, when it has done its work, a reaction of Reason against it; and, as in a civil polity the State exists and endures by means of the rivalry and collision, the encroachments and defeats, of its constituent parts, so in like manner Catholic Christendom is no simple exhibition of religious absolutism, but presents a continuous picture of Authority and Private Judgment alternately advancing and retreating as the ebb and flow of the tide: it is a vast assemblage of human beings with wilful intellects and wild passions, brought together into one by the beauty and the majesty of a Superhuman Power—into what may be called a large reformatory or training-school, not as if into a hospital or into a prison, not in order to be sent to bed, not to be buried alive, but (if I may change my metaphor) brought together as if into some moral factory, for the melting, refining, and moulding, by an incessant, noisy process, of the raw material of human nature, so excellent, so dangerous, so capable of divine purposes.

Matthew Arnold.

1822-1888.

HEBRAISM AND HELLENISM.

(*Culture and Anarchy*, Chapter IV., 1869.)

This fundamental ground is our preference of doing to thinking.* Now, this preference is a main element in our nature, and as we study it we find ourselves opening up a number of large questions on every side.

Let me go back for a moment to Bishop Wilson, who says, "First, never go against the best light you have; secondly, take care that your light be not darkness." We show, as a nation, laudable energy and persistence in walking according to the best light we have, but are not quite careful enough, perhaps, to see that our light be not darkness. This is only another version of the old story that energy is our strong point and favorable characteristic, rather than intelligence. But we may give to this idea a more general form still, in which it will have a yet larger range of application. We may regard this energy driving at practice, this paramount sense of the obligation of duty, self-control, and work, this earnestness in going manfully with the best light we have, as one force. And we may regard the intelligence driving at those ideas which are, after all, the basis of right practice, the ardent sense for all the new and changing combinations of them which man's development brings with it, the indomitable im-

* The reference is to the concluding paragraph of the preceding chapter. "We see, then, how indispensable to that human perfection which we seek is, in the opinion of good judges, some public recognition and establishment of our best self, or right reason. We see how our habits and practice oppose themselves to such a recognition, and the many inconveniences which we therefore suffer. But now let us try to go a little deeper, and to find, beneath our actual habits and practice, the very ground and cause out of which they spring."

pulse to know and adjust them perfectly, as another force. And these two forces we may regard as in some sense rivals—rivals, not by the necessity of their own nature, but as exhibited in man and his history; and rivals dividing the empire of the world between them. And to give these forces names from the two races of men who have supplied the most signal and splendid manifestations of them, we may call them respectively the forces of Hebraism and Hellenism. Hebraism and Hellenism—between these two points of influence moves our world. At one time it feels more powerfully the attraction of one of them, at another time of the other; and it ought to be, though it never is, evenly and happily balanced between them.

The final aim of both Hellenism and Hebraism, as of all great spiritual disciplines, is no doubt the same: man's perfection, or salvation. The very language which they both of them use in schooling us to reach this aim is often identical. Even when their language indicates by variation—sometimes a broad variation, often a but slight and subtle variation—the different courses of thought which are uppermost in each discipline, even then the unity of the final end and aim is still apparent. To employ the actual words of that discipline with which we ourselves are all of us most familiar, and the words of which, therefore, come most home to us, that final end and aim is "that we might be partakers of the divine nature." These are the words of a Hebrew apostle; but of Hellenism and Hebraism alike this is, I say, the aim. When the two are confronted, as they very often are confronted, it is nearly always with what I may call a rhetorical purpose: the speaker's whole design is to exalt and enthrone one of the two, and he uses the other only as a foil and to enable him the better to give effect to his purpose. Obviously, with us, it is usually Hellenism which is thus reduced to minister to the triumph of Hebraism. There is a sermon on Greece and the Greek spirit by a man never to be mentioned without interest and respect, Frederick Robertson, in which this rhetorical use of Greece and the Greek spirit, and the inadequate exhibition of them necessarily consequent upon this, is almost ludicrous, and would be censurable if it were not to be explained by the exigencies of a sermon. On the other hand, Heinrich Heine and other writers of his sort give us the spectacle of the tables completely turned, and of Hebraism brought in just as a foil and contrast to Hellenism and to make the superiority of Hellenism more manifest. In both these cases there is injustice and misrepresentation. The aim and end of both Hebraism and Hellenism is, as I have said, one and the same, and this aim and end is august and admirable.

Still, they pursue this aim by very different courses. The uppermost idea with Hellenism is to see things as they really are; the uppermost idea with Hebraism is conduct and obedience. Nothing can do away with this ineffaceable difference. The Greek quarrel with the body and its desires is that they hinder right thinking; the Hebrew quarrel with them is that they hinder right acting. "He that keepeth the law, happy is he;" "Blessed is the man that feareth the Eternal, that delighteth greatly in His commandments;"—that is the Hebrew notion of felicity; and, pursued with passion and tenacity, this notion would not let the Hebrew rest till, as is well known, he had at last got out of the law a network of prescriptions to enwrap his whole life, to govern every moment of it, every impulse, every action. The Greek notion of felicity, on the other hand, is perfectly conveyed in these words of a great French moralist: "C'est le bonheur des hommes,"—when? when they abhor that which is evil? no;—when they exercise themselves in the law of the Lord day and night? no;—when they die daily? no;—when they walk about the New Jerusalem with palms in their hands? no;—but when they think aright, when their thought hits: "quand ils pensent juste." At the bottom of both the Greek and the Hebrew notion is the desire, native in man, for reason and the will of God, the feeling after the universal order,—in a word, the love of God. But while Hebraism seizes upon certain plain, capital intimations of the universal order, and rivets itself, one may say, with unequalled grandeur of earnestness and intensity on the study and observance of them, the bent of Hellenism is to follow, with flexible activity, the whole play of the universal order, to be apprehensive of missing any part of it, of sacrificing one part to another, to slip away from resting in this or that intimation of it, however capital. An unclouded clearness of mind, an unimpeded play of thought, is what this bent drives at. The governing idea of Hellenism is *spontaneity of consciousness;* that of Hebraism, *strictness of conscience.*

Christianity changed nothing in this essential bent of Hebraism to set doing above knowing. Self-conquest, self-devotion, the following not our own individual will but the will of God, *obedience*, is the fundamental idea of this form, also, of the discipline to which we have attached the general name of Hebraism. Only, as the old law and the network of prescriptions with which it enveloped human life were evidently a motive-power not driving and searching enough to produce the result aimed at—patient continuance in well-doing, self-conquest,—Christianity substituted for them boundless devotion to that inspiring and affecting pattern of self-conquest offered by Jesus Christ; and by the new motive-power, of which the essence was this, though the love and admiration of Christian churches have for centuries been employed in varying, amplifying, and adorning the plain description of it, Christianity, as St. Paul truly says, "establishes the law," and, in the strength of the ampler power which she has thus supplied to fulfil it, has accomplished the miracles, which we all see, of her history.

So long as we do not forget that both Hellenism and Hebraism are profound and admirable manifestations of man's life, tendencies, and powers, and that both of them aim at a like final result, we can hardly insist too strongly on the divergence of line and of operation with which they proceed. It is a divergence so great that it most truly, as the prophet Zechariah says, "has raised up thy sons, O Zion, against thy sons, O Greece!" The difference whether it is by doing or by knowing that we set most store, and the practical consequences which follow from this difference, leave their mark on all the history of our race and of its development. Language may be abundantly quoted from both Hellenism and Hebraism to make it seem that one follows the same current as the other towards the same goal. They are, truly, borne towards the same goal; but the currents which bear them are infinitely different. It is true, Solomon will praise knowing: "Understanding is a well-spring of life unto him that hath it." And in the New Testament, again, Jesus Christ is a "light," and "truth makes us free." It is true, Aristotle will undervalue knowing: "In what concerns virtue," says he, "three things are necessary—knowledge, deliberate will, and perseverance; but whereas the two last are all-important, the first is a matter of little importance." It is true that with the same impatience with which St. James enjoins a man to be not a forgetful hearer but a *doer of the word,* Epictetus exhorts us to *do* what we have demonstrated to ourselves we ought to do; or he taunts us with futility, for being armed at all points to prove that lying is wrong, yet all the time continuing to lie. It is true, Plato, in words which are almost the words of the New Testament or the *Imitation,* calls life a learning to die. But underneath the superficial agreement the fundamental divergence still subsists. The "understanding" of Solomon is "the walking in the way of the commandments"; this is "the way of peace," and it is of this that blessedness comes. In the New Testament, the truth which gives us the peace of God and makes us free is the love of Christ constraining us to crucify, as he did, and with a like purpose of moral regeneration, the flesh with its affections and lusts, and thus establishing, as we have seen, the law. The moral virtues, on the other hand, are with Aristotle but the porch and access to the intellectual, and with these last is blessedness. That partaking of the divine life, which both Hellenism and Hebraism, as we have said, fix as their crowning aim, Plato expressly denies to the man of practical virtue merely, of self-conquest with any other motive than that of perfect intellectual vision. He reserves it for the lover of pure knowledge, of seeing things as they really are,—the φιλομαθής.

Both Hellenism and Hebraism arise out of the wants of

human nature, and address themselves to satisfying those wants. But their methods are so different, they lay stress on such different points, and call into being by their respective disciplines such different activities, that the face which human nature presents when it passes from the hands of one of them to those of the other is no longer the same. To get rid of one's ignorance, to see things as they are, and by seeing them as they are to see them in their beauty, is the simple and attractive ideal which Hellenism holds out before human nature; and from the simplicity and charm of this ideal, Hellenism, and human life in the hands of Hellenism, is invested with a kind of aërial ease, clearness, and radiancy; they are full of what we call sweetness and light. Difficulties are kept out of view, and the beauty and rationalness of the ideal have all our thoughts. "The best man is he who most tries to perfect himself, and the happiest man is he who most feels that he *is* perfecting himself,"—this account of the matter by Socrates, the true Socrates of the *Memorabilia*, has something so simple, spontaneous, and unsophisticated about it that it seems to fill us with clearness and hope when we hear it. But there is a saying which I have heard attributed to Mr. Carlyle about Socrates—a very happy saying, whether it is really Mr. Carlyle's or not—which excellently marks the essential point in which Hebraism differs from Hellenism. "Socrates," this saying goes, "is terribly *at ease in Zion.*" Hebraism—and here is the source of its wonderful strength—has always been severely pre-occupied with an awful sense of the impossibility of being at ease in Zion; of the difficulties which oppose themselves to man's pursuit or attainment of that perfection of which Socrates talks so hopefully, and, as from this point of view one might almost say, so glibly. It is all very well to talk of getting rid of one's ignorance, of seeing things in their reality, seeing them in their beauty; but how is this to be done when there is something which thwarts and spoils all our efforts?

This something is *sin;* and the space which sin fills in Hebraism, as compared with Hellenism, is indeed prodigious. This obstacle to perfection fills the whole scene, and perfection appears remote and rising away from earth, in the background. Under the name of sin, the difficulties of knowing oneself and conquering oneself which impede man's passage to perfection become, for Hebraism, a positive, active entity hostile to man, a mysterious power which I heard Dr. Pusey the other day, in one of his impressive sermons, compare to a hideous hunchback seated on our shoulders, and which it is the main business of our lives to hate and oppose. The discipline of the Old Testament may be summed up as a discipline teaching us to abhor and flee from sin; the discipline of the New Testament, as a discipline teaching us to die to it. As Hellenism speaks of thinking clearly, seeing things in their essence and beauty, as a grand and precious feat for man to achieve, so Hebraism speaks of becoming conscious of sin, of awakening to a sense of sin, as a feat of this kind. It is obvious to what wide divergence these differing tendencies, actively followed, must lead. As one passes and repasses from Hellenism to Hebraism, from Plato to St. Paul, one feels inclined to rub one's eyes and ask oneself whether man is indeed a gentle and simple being, showing the traces of a noble and divine nature, or an unhappy chained captive, laboring with groanings that cannot be uttered to free himself from the body of this death.

Apparently it was the Hellenic conception of human nature which was unsound, for the world could not live by it. Absolutely to call it unsound, however, is to fall into the common error of its Hebraising enemies; but it was unsound at that particular moment of man's development, it was premature. The indispensable basis of conduct and self-control, the platform upon which alone the perfection aimed at by Greece can come into bloom, was not to be reached by our race so easily; centuries of probation and discipline were needed to bring us to it. Therefore the bright promise of Hellenism faded, and Hebraism ruled the world. Then was seen that astonishing spectacle, so well marked by the often-quoted words of the prophet Zechariah, when men of all languages and nations took hold of the skirt of him that was a Jew, saying, "We will go with you, for we have heard that God is with you."

And the Hebraism which thus received and ruled a world all gone out of the way, and altogether become unprofitable, was and could not but be the later, the more spiritual, the more attractive development of Hebraism. It was Christianity; that is to say, Hebraism aiming at self-conquest and rescue from the thrall of vile affections, not by obedience to the letter of a law, but by conformity to the image of a self-sacrificing example. To a world stricken with moral enervation Christianity offered its spectacle of an inspired self-sacrifice; to men who refused themselves nothing, it showed one who refused himself everything;—"my Saviour banished joy!" says George Herbert. When the *alma Venus*, the life-giving and joy-giving power of nature, so fondly cherished by the pagan world, could not save her followers from self-dissatisfaction and *ennui*, the severe words of the apostle came bracingly and refreshingly: "Let no man deceive you with vain words, for because of these things cometh the wrath of God upon the children of disobedience." Through age after age and generation after generation, our race, or all that part of our race which was most living and progressive, was *baptized into a death;* and endeavored, by suffering in the flesh, to cease from sin. Of this endeavor, the animating labors and afflictions of early Christianity, the touching asceticism of mediæval Christianity, are the great historical manifestations. Literary monuments of it, each in its own way incomparable, remain in the *Epistles* of St. Paul, in St. Augustine's *Confessions*, and in the two original and simplest books of the *Imitation*.

Of two disciplines laying their main stress, the one on clear intelligence, the other on firm obedience; the one on comprehensively knowing the grounds of one's duty, the other on diligently practising it; the one on taking all possible care (to use Bishop Wilson's words again) that the light we have be not darkness, the other that according to the best light we have we diligently walk,—the priority naturally belongs to that discipline which braces all man's moral powers and founds for him an indispensable basis of character. And, therefore, it is justly said of the Jewish people, who were charged with setting powerfully forth that side of the divine order to which the words "conscience" and "self-conquest" point, that they were "entrusted with the oracles of God"; as it is justly said of Christianity, which followed Judaism and which set forth this side with a much deeper effectiveness and a much wider influence, that the wisdom of the old pagan world was foolishness compared to it. No words of devotion and admiration can be too strong to render thanks to these beneficent forces which have so borne forward humanity in its appointed work of coming to the knowledge and possession of itself; above all, in those great moments when their action was the wholesomest and the most necessary.

But the evolution of these forces, separately and in themselves, is not the whole evolution of humanity, their single history is not the whole history of man; whereas their admirers are always apt to make it stand for the whole history. Hebraism and Hellenism are, neither of them, the *law* of human development, as their admirers are prone to make them; they are, each of them, *contributions* to human development,—august contributions, invaluable contributions, and each showing itself to us more august, more invaluable, more preponderant over the other, according to the moment in which we take them and the relation in which we stand to them. The nations of our modern world, children of that immense and salutary movement which broke up the pagan world, inevitably stand to Hellenism in a relation which dwarfs it and to Hebraism in a relation which magnifies it. They are inevitably prone to take Hebraism as the law of human development, and not as simply a contribution to it, however precious. And yet the lesson must perforce be learned, that the human spirit is wider than the most priceless of the forces which bear it onward, and that to the whole development of man Hebraism itself is, like Hellenism, but a contribution.

Perhaps we may help ourselves to see this clearer by an illustration drawn from the treatment of a single great idea which has profoundly engaged the human spirit, and has given it eminent opportunities for showing its nobleness and energy. It surely must be perceived that the idea of immortality, as this idea rises in its generality before the human spirit, is something grander, truer, and more satisfying than it is in the particular forms by which St. Paul, in the famous fifteenth chapter of the *Epistle to the Corinthians,* and Plato, in the *Phædo,* endeavor to develop and establish it. Surely we cannot but feel that the argumentation with which the Hebrew apostle goes about to expound this great idea is, after all, confused and inconclusive; and that the reasoning, drawn from analogies of likeness and equality, which is employed upon it by the Greek philosopher, is over-subtle and sterile. Above and beyond the inadequate solutions which Hebraism and Hellenism here attempt, extends the immense and august problem itself, and the human spirit which gave birth to it. And this single illustration may suggest to us how the same thing happens in other cases also.

But meanwhile, by alternations of Hebraism and Hellenism, of a man's intellectual and moral impulses, of the effort to see things as they really are and the effort to win peace by self-conquest, the human spirit proceeds; and each of these two forces has its appointed hours of culmination and seasons of rule. As the great movement of Christianity was a triumph of Hebraism and man's moral impulses, so the great movement which goes by the name of the Renascence was an uprising and re-instatement of man's intellectual impulses and of Hellenism. We in England, the devoted children of Protestantism, chiefly know the Renascence by its subordinate and secondary side of the Reformation. The Reformation has been often called a Hebraising revival, a return to the ardor and sincereness of primitive Christianity. No one, however, can study the development of Protestantism and of Protestant churches without feeling that into the Reformation too—Hebraising child of the Renascence, and offspring of its fervor rather than its intelligence, as it undoubtedly was—the subtle Hellenic leaven of the Renascence found its way, and that the exact respective parts, in the Reformation, of Hebraism and of Hellenism are not easy to separate. But what we may with truth say is that all which

Protestantism was to itself clearly conscious of, all which it succeeded in clearly setting forth in words, had the characters of Hebraism rather than of Hellenism. The Reformation was strong in that it was an earnest return to the Bible and to doing from the heart the will of God as there written. It was weak in that it never consciously grasped or applied the central idea of the Renascence—the Hellenic idea of pursuing, in all lines of activity, the law and science, to use Plato's words, of things as they really are. Whatever direct superiority, therefore, Protestantism had over Catholicism was a moral superiority, a superiority arising out of its greater sincerity and earnestness—at the moment of its apparition, at any rate—in dealing with the heart and conscience. Its pretensions to an intellectual superiority are in general quite illusory. For Hellenism, for the thinking side in man as distinguished from the acting side, the attitude of mind of Protestantism towards the Bible in no respect differs from the attitude of mind of Catholicism towards the Church. The mental habit of him who imagines that Balaam's ass spoke, in no respect differs from the mental habit of him who imagines that a Madonna of wood or stone winked; and the one, who says that God's Church makes him believe what he believes, and the other, who says that God's Word makes him believe what he believes, are for the philosopher perfectly alike in not really and truly knowing, when they say "God's Church" and "God's Word," what it is they say or whereof they affirm.

In the sixteenth century, therefore, Hellenism re-entered the world, and again stood in presence of Hebraism—a Hebraism renewed and purged. Now, it has not been enough observed, how, in the seventeenth century, a fate befell Hellenism is some respects analogous to that which befell it at the commencement of our era. The Renascence, that great re-awakening of Hellenism, that irresistible return of humanity to nature and to seeing things as they are, which in art, in literature, and in physics produced such splendid fruits, had, like the anterior Hellenism of the pagan world, a side of moral weakness and of relaxation or insensibility of the moral fibre, which in Italy showed itself with the most startling plainness, but which in France, England, and other countries was very apparent too. Again this loss of spiritual balance, this exclusive preponderance given to man's perceiving and knowing side, this unnatural defect of his feeling and acting side, provoked a reaction. Let us trace that reaction where it most nearly concerns us.

Science has now made visible to everybody the great and pregnant elements of difference which lie in race, and in how signal a manner they make the genius and history of an Indo-European people vary from those of a Semitic people. Hellenism is of Indo-European growth, Hebraism is of Semitic growth; and we English, a nation of Indo-European stock, seem to belong naturally to the movement of Hellenism. But nothing more strongly marks the essential unity of man than the affinities we can perceive, in this point or that, between members of one family of peoples and members of another. And no affinity of this kind is more strongly marked than that likeness in the strength and prominence of the moral fibre, which, notwithstanding immense elements of difference, knits in some special sort the genius and history of us English, and our American descendants across the Atlantic, to the genius and history of the Hebrew people. Puritanism, which has been so great a power in the English nation, and in the strongest part of the English nation, was originally the reaction in the seventeenth century of the conscience and moral sense of our race against the moral indifference and lax rule of conduct which in the sixteenth century came in with the Renascence. It was a reaction of Hebraism against Hellenism; and it powerfully manifested itself, as was natural, in a people with much of what we call a Hebraising turn, with a signal affinity for the bent which was the master-bent of Hebrew life. Eminently Indo-European by its *humor*, by the power it shows, through this gift, of imaginatively acknowledging the multiform aspects of the problem of life and of thus getting itself unfixed from its own over-certainty, of smiling at its own over-tenacity, our race has yet (and a great part of its strength lies here), in matters of practical life and moral conduct, a strong share of the assuredness, the tenacity, the intensity of the Hebrews. This turn manifested itself in Puritanism, and has had a great part in shaping our history for the last two hundred years. Undoubtedly it checked and changed amongst us that movement of the Renascence which we see producing in the reign of Elizabeth such wonderful fruits. Undoubtedly it stopped the prominent rule and direct development of that order of ideas which we call by the name of Hellenism, and gave the first rank to a different order of ideas. Apparently, too, as we said of the former defeat of Hellenism, if Hellenism was defeated this shows that Hellenism was imperfect and that its ascendency at that moment would not have been for the world's good.

Yet there is a very important difference between the defeat inflicted on Hellenism by Christianity eighteen hundred years ago, and the check given to the Renascence by Puritanism. The greatness of the difference is well measured by the difference in force, beauty, significance, and usefulness between primitive Christianity and Protestantism. Eighteen hundred years ago it was altogether the hour of Hebraism. Primitive Christianity was legitimately and truly the ascendant force in the world at that time, and the way of mankind's progress lay through its full development. Another hour in man's development began in the fifteenth century, and the main road of his progress then lay for a time through Hellenism. Puritanism was no longer the central current of the world's progress; it was a side stream crossing the central current and checking it. The cross and the check may have been necessary and salutary, but that does not do away with the essential difference between the main stream of man's advance and a cross or side stream. For more than two hundred years the main stream of man's advance has moved towards knowing himself and the world, seeing things as they are, spontaneity of consciousness; the main impulse of a great part, and that the strongest part, of our nation has been towards strictness of conscience. They have made the secondary the principal at the wrong moment, and the principal they have at the wrong moment treated as secondary. This contravention of the natural order has produced, as such contravention always must produce, a certain confusion and false movement, of which we are now beginning to feel, in almost every direction, the inconvenience. In all directions our habitual causes of action seem to be losing efficaciousness, credit, and control, both with others and even with ourselves. Everywhere we see the beginnings of confusion, and we want a clue to some sound order and authority. This we can only get by going back upon the actual instincts and forces which rule our life, seeing them as they really are, connecting them with other instincts and forces, and enlarging our whole view and rule of life.

Thomas Henry Huxley.

1825–1895.

ON A PIECE OF CHALK.

(1868.)

If a well were to be sunk at our feet in the midst of the city of Norwich, the diggers would very soon find themselves at work in that white substance, almost too soft to be called rock, with which we are all familiar as "chalk."

Not only here, but over the whole county of Norfolk, the well-sinker might carry his shaft down many hundred feet without coming to the end of the chalk; and on the sea-coast, where the waves have pared away the face of the land which breasts them, the scarped faces of the high cliffs are often wholly formed of the same material. Northward the chalk may be followed as far as Yorkshire; on the south coast it appears abruptly in the picturesque western bays of Dorset, and breaks into the Needles of the Isle of Wight; while on the shores of Kent it supplies that long line of white cliffs to which England owes her name of Albion. Were the thin soil which covers it all washed away, a curved band of white chalk, here broader and there narrower, might be followed diagonally across England from Lulworth in Dorset to Flamborough Head in Yorkshire—a distance of over 280 miles as the crow flies. From this band to the North Sea on the east, and the Channel on the south, the chalk is largely hidden by other deposits; but except in the Weald of Kent and Sussex it enters into the very foundation of all the south-eastern counties.

Attaining, as it does in some places, a thickness of more than a thousand feet, the English chalk must be admitted to be a mass of considerable magnitude. Nevertheless it covers but an insignificant portion of the whole area occupied by the chalk formation of the globe, which has precisely the same general characters as ours, and is found in detached patches, some less and others more extensive than the English. Chalk occurs in northwest Ireland; it stretches over a large part of France, the chalk which underlies Paris being, in fact, a continuation of that of the London basin; runs through Denmark and Central Europe, and extends southward to North Africa; while eastward it appears in the Crimea and in Syria, and may be traced as far as the shores of the Sea of Aral, in Central Asia. If all the points at which true chalk occurs were circumscribed, they would lie within an irregular oval about 3,000 miles in long diameter—the area of which would be as great as that of Europe, and would many times exceed that of the largest existing inland sea, the Mediterranean.

Thus the chalk is no unimportant element in the masonry of the earth's crust, and it impresses a peculiar stamp, varying with the conditions to which it is exposed, on the scenery of the districts in which it occurs. The undulating downs and rounded coombs, covered with sweet-grassed turf, of our inland chalk country, have a peacefully domestic and mutton-suggesting prettiness, but can hardly be called either grand or beautiful. But on our southern coasts the wall-sided cliffs, many hundred feet high, with vast needles and pinnacles standing out in the sea, sharp and solitary enough to serve as perches for the wary cormorant, confer a wonderful beauty and grandeur upon the chalk headlands. And in the East chalk has its share in the formation of some of the most venerable of mountain ranges, such as the Lebanon.

What is this wide-spread component of the surface of the earth? and whence did it come?

You may think this no very hopeful inquiry. You may not unnaturally suppose that the attempt to solve such problems as these can lead to no result save that of entangling the inquirer in vague speculations, incapable of refutation and of verification. If such were really the case, I should have selected some other subject than "a piece of chalk" for my discourse. But in truth, after much deliberation, I have been unable to think of any topic which would so well enable me to lead you to see how solid is the foundation upon which some of the most startling conclusions of physical science rest.

A great chapter of the history of the world is written in the chalk. Few passages in the history of man can be supported by such an overwhelming mass of direct and indirect evidence as that which testifies to the truth of the fragment of the history of the globe which I hope to enable you to read with your own eyes to-night. Let me add that few chapters of human history have a more profound significance for ourselves. I weigh my words well when I assert that the man who should know the true history of the bit of chalk which every carpenter carries about in his breeches-pocket, though ignorant of all other history, is likely, if he will think his knowledge out to its ultimate results, to have a truer and therefore a better conception of this wonderful universe, and of man's relation to it, than the most learned student who is deep-read in the records of humanity and ignorant of those of Nature.

The language of the chalk is not hard to learn, not nearly so hard as Latin, if you only want to get at the broad features of the story it has to tell; and I propose that we now set to work to spell that story out together.

We all know that if we "burn" chalk the result is quicklime. Chalk, in fact, is a compound of carbonic-acid gas and lime, and when you make it very hot the carbonic acid flies away and the lime is left. By this method of procedure we see the lime, but we do not see the carbonic acid. If, on the other hand, you were to powder a little chalk and drop it into a good deal of strong vinegar, there would be a great bubbling and fizzing, and, finally, a clear liquid, in which no sign of chalk would appear. Here you see the carbonic acid in the bubbles; the lime, dissolved in the vinegar, vanishes from sight. There are a great many other ways of showing that chalk is essentially nothing but carbonic acid and quicklime. Chemists enunciate the result of all the experiments which prove this by stating that chalk is almost wholly composed of "carbonate of lime."

It is desirable for us to start from the knowledge of this fact, though it may not seem to help us very far towards what we seek. For carbonate of lime is a widely-spread substance and is met with under very various conditions. All sorts of limestones are composed of more or less pure carbonate of lime. The crust which is often deposited by waters which have drained through limestone rocks, in the form of what are called stalagmites and stalactites, is carbonate of lime. Or to take a more familiar example, the fur on the inside of a tea-kettle is carbonate of lime; and for anything chemistry tells us to the contrary, the chalk might be a kind of gigantic fur upon the bottom of the earth-kettle, which is kept pretty hot below.

Let us try another method of making the chalk tell us its own history. To the unassisted eye chalk looks simply like a very loose and open kind of stone. But it is possible to grind a slice of chalk down so thin that you can see through it—until it is thin enough, in fact, to be examined with any magnifying power that may be thought desirable. A thin slice of the fur of a kettle might be made in the same way. If it were examined microscopically, it would show itself to be a more or less distinctly laminated mineral substance, and nothing more. But the slice of chalk presents a totally different appearance when placed under the microscope. The general mass of it is made up of very minute granules; but imbedded in this matrix are innumerable bodies, some smaller and some larger, but on a rough average not more than a hundredth of an inch in diameter, having a well-defined shape and structure. A cubic inch of some specimens of chalk may contain hundreds of thousands of these bodies, compacted together with incalculable millions of the granules.

The examination of a transparent slice gives a good notion of the manner in which the components of the chalk are arranged, and of their relative proportions. But by rubbing up some chalk with a brush in water and then pouring off the milky fluid, so as to obtain sediments of different degrees of fineness, the granules and the minute rounded bodies may be pretty well separated from one another, and submitted to microscopic examination, either as opaque or as transparent objects. By combining the views obtained in these various methods, each of the rounded bodies may be proved to be a beautifully-constructed calcareous fabric, made up of a number of chambers communicating freely with one another. The chambered bodies are of various forms. One of the commonest is something like a badly-grown raspberry, being formed of a number of nearly globular chambers of different sizes congregated together. It is called *Globigerina,* and some specimens of chalk consist of little else than *Globigerinæ* and granules. Let us fix our attention upon the *Globigerina.* It is the spoor of the game we are tracking. If we can learn what it is and what are the conditions of its existence, we shall see our way to the origin and past history of the chalk.

A suggestion which may naturally enough present itself is that these curious bodies are the result of some process of aggregation which has taken place in the carbonate of lime; that, just as in winter the rime on our windows simulates the most delicate and elegantly arborescent foliage—proving that the mere mineral, water, may under certain conditions assume the outward form of organic bodies,—so this mineral substance, carbonate of lime, hidden away in the bowels of the earth, has taken the shape of these chambered bodies. I am not raising a merely fanciful and unreal objection. Very learned men, in former days, have even entertained the notion that all the formed things found in rocks are of this nature; and if no such conception is at present held to be admissible, it is because long and varied experience has now shown that mineral matter never does assume the form and structure we find in fossils. If anyone were to try to persuade you that an oyster-shell (which is also chiefly composed of carbonate of lime) had crystallized out of sea-water, I suppose you would laugh at the absurdity. Your laughter would be justified by the fact that all experience tends to show that oyster-shells are formed by the agency of oysters, and in no other way. And if there were no better reasons, should be justified, on like grounds, in believing that *Globigerina* is not the product of anything but vital activity.

Happily, however, better evidence in proof of the organic nature of the *Globigerinæ* than that of analogy is forthcoming. It so happens that calcareous skeletons, exactly similar to the *Globigerinæ* of the chalk, are being formed at the present moment by minute living creatures, which flourish in multitudes literally more numerous than the sands of the sea-shore, over a large extent of that part of the earth's surface which is covered by the ocean.

The history of the discovery of these living *Globigerinæ*, and of the part which they play in rock-building, is singular enough. It is a discovery which, like others of no less scientific importance, has arisen incidentally, out of work devoted to very different and exceedingly practical interests. When men first took to the sea, they speedily learned to look out for shoals and rocks; and the more the burthen of their ships increased, the more imperatively necessary it became for sailors to ascertain with precision the depth of the waters they traversed. Out of this necessity grew the use of the lead and sounding-line, and, ultimately, marine surveying, which is the recording of the form of coasts and of the depth of the sea, as ascertained by the sounding-lead, upon charts. At the same time it became desirable to ascertain and to indicate the nature of the sea-bottom, since this circumstance greatly affects its goodness as holding-ground for anchors. Some ingenious tar, whose name deserves a better fate than the oblivion into which it has fallen, attained this object by "arming" the bottom of the lead with a lump of grease, to which more or less of the sand or mud or broken shells, as the case might be, adhered, and was brought to the surface. But however well adapted such an apparatus might be for rough nautical purposes, scientific accuracy could not be expected from the armed lead; and to remedy its defects (especially when applied to sounding in great depths) Lieut. Brooke, of the American Navy, some years ago invented a most ingenious machine, by which a considerable portion of the superficial layer of the sea-bottom can be scooped out and brought up from any depth to which the lead descends. In 1853, Lieut. Brooke obtained mud from the bottom of the North Atlantic, between Newfoundland and the Azores, at a depth of more than 10,000 feet, or two miles, by the help of this sounding apparatus. The specimens were sent for examination to Ehrenberg of Berlin, and to Bailey of West Point, and those able microscopists found that this deep-sea mud was almost entirely composed of the skeletons of living organisms—the greater proportion of these being just like the *Globigerinæ* already known to occur in the chalk.

Thus far the work had been carried on simply in the interests of science, but Lieut. Brooke's method of sounding acquired a high commercial value when the enterprise of laying down the telegraph-cable between this country and the United States was undertaken; for it became a matter of immense importance to know, not only the depth of the sea over the whole line along which the cable was to be laid, but the exact nature of the bottom, so as to guard against chances of cutting or fraying the strands of that costly rope. The Admiralty consequently ordered Captain Dayman, an old friend and shipmate of mine, to ascertain the depth over the whole line of the cable and to bring back specimens of the bottom. In former days such a command as this might have sounded very much like one of the impossible things which the young prince in the fairy tales is ordered to do before he can obtain the hand of the princess. However, in the months of June and July, 1857, my friend performed the task assigned to him, with great expedition and precision, without, so far as I know, having met with any reward of that kind. The specimens of Atlantic mud which he procured were sent to me to be examined and reported upon.

The result of all these operations is that we know the contours and nature of the surface-soil covered by the North Atlantic for a distance of 1,700 miles from east to west, as well as we know that of any part of the dry land. It is a prodigious plain—one of the widest and most even plains in the world. If the sea were drained off, you might drive a wagon all the way from Valentia, on the west coast of Ireland, to Trinity Bay, in Newfoundland. And, except upon one sharp incline about 200 miles from Valentia, I am not quite sure that it would even be necessary to put the skid on, so gentle are the ascents and descents upon that long route. From Valentia the road would lie down-hill for about 200 miles to the point at which the bottom is now covered by 1,700 fathoms of sea-water. Then would come the central plain, more than a thousand miles wide, the inequalities of the surface of which would be hardly perceptible, though the depth of water upon it now varies from 10,000 to 15,000 feet, and there are places in which Mont Blanc might be sunk without showing its peak above water. Beyond this the ascent on the American side commences, and gradually leads, for about 300 miles, to the Newfoundland shore.

Almost the whole of the bottom of this central plain (which extends for many hundred miles in a north and south direction) is covered by a fine mud, which, when brought to the surface, dries into a grayish-white friable substance. You can write with this on a blackboard, if you are so inclined; and to the eye it is quite like very soft grayish chalk. Examined chemically, it proves to be composed almost wholly of carbonate of lime; and if you make a section of it, in the same way as that of the piece of chalk was made, and view it with the microscope, it presents innumerable *Globigerinæ* embedded in a granular matrix. Thus this deep-sea mud is substantially chalk. I say, substantially, because there are a good many minor differences; but as these have no bearing on the question immediately before us—which is the nature of the *Globigerinæ* of the chalk,—it is unnecessary to speak of them.

Globigerinæ of every size, from the smallest to the largest, are associated together in the Atlantic mud, and the chambers of many are filled by a soft animal matter. This soft substance is, in fact, the remains of the creature to which the *Globigerina* shell, or rather skeleton, owes its existence—and which is an animal of the simplest imaginable description. It is, in fact, a mere particle of living jelly, without defined parts of any kind—without a mouth, nerves, muscles, or distinct organs, and only manifesting its vitality to ordinary observation by thrusting out and retracting from all parts of its surface long filamentous processes, which serve for arms and legs. Yet this amorphous particle, devoid of everything which, in the higher animals we call organs, is capable of feeding, growing, and multiplying, of separating from the ocean the small proportion of carbonate of lime which is dissolved in sea-water; and of building up that substance into a skeleton for itself, according to a pattern which can be imitated by no other known agency.

The notion that animals can live and flourish in the sea, at the vast depths from which apparently living *Globigerinæ* have been brought up, does not agree very well with our usual conceptions respecting the conditions of animal life; and it is not so absolutely impossible as it might at first sight appear to be that the *Globigerinæ* of the Atlantic sea-bottom do not live and die where they are found.

As I have mentioned, the soundings from the great Atlantic plain are almost entirely made up of *Globigerinæ*, with the granules which have been mentioned, and some few other calcareous shells; but a small percentage of the chalky mud—perhaps at most some five per cent. of it—is of a different nature, and consists of shells and skeletons composed of silex, or pure flint. These silicious bodies belong partly to those lowly vegetable organisms which are called *Diatomaceæ*, and partly to those minute and extremely simple animals termed *Radiolariæ*. It is quite certain that these creatures do not live at the bottom of the ocean, but at its surface—where they may be obtained in prodigious numbers by the use of a properly constructed net. Hence it follows that these silicious organisms, though they are not heavier than the lightest dust, must have fallen, in some cases, through fifteen thousand feet of water, before they reached their final resting-place on the ocean floor. And considering how large a surface these bodies expose in proportion to their weight, it is probable that they occupy a great length of time in making their burial journey from the surface of the Atlantic to the bottom.

But if the *Radiolariæ* and Diatoms are thus rained upon the bottom of the sea, from the superficial layer of its waters in which they pass their lives, it is obviously possible that the *Globigerinæ* may be similarly derived; and if they were so, it would be much more easy to understand how they obtain their supply of food than it is at present. Nevertheless the positive and negative evidence all points the other way. The skeletons of the full-grown, deep-sea *Globigerinæ* are so remarkably solid and heavy in proportion to their surface as to seem little fitted for floating; and as a matter of fact they are not to be found along with the Diatoms and *Radiolariæ* in the uppermost stratum of the open ocean. It has been observed, again, that the abundance of *Globigerinæ*, in proportion to other organisms of like kind, increases with the depth of the sea, and that deep-water *Globigerinæ* are larger than those which live in shallower parts of the sea; and such facts negative the supposition that these organisms have been swept by currents from the shallows into the deeps of the Atlantic. It therefore seems to be hardly doubtful that these wonderful creatures live and die at the depths in which they are found.

However, the important points for us are that the living *Globigerinæ* are exclusively marine animals, the skeletons of which abound at the bottom of deep seas, and that there is not a shadow of reason for believing that the habits of the *Globigerinæ* of the chalk differed from those of the existing species. But if this be true, there is no escaping the conclusion that the chalk itself is the dried mud of an ancient deep sea.

In working over the soundings collected by Captain Dayman, I was surprised to find that many of what I have called the "granules" of that mud were not, as one might have been tempted to think at first, the mere powder and waste of *Globigerinæ*, but that they had a definite form and size. I termed these bodies "coccoliths," and doubted their organic nature. Dr. Wallich verified my observation, and added the interesting discovery that not unfrequently bodies similar to these coccoliths were aggregated together into spheroids, which he termed "coccospheres." So far as we knew, these bodies, the nature of which is extremely puzzling and problematical, were peculiar to the Atlantic soundings. But a few years ago Mr. Sorby, in making a careful examination of the chalk by means of thin sections and otherwise, observed, as Ehrenberg had done before him, that much of its granular basis possesses a definite form. Comparing these formed particles with those in the Atlantic soundings, he found the two to be identical, and thus proved that the chalk, like the soundings, contains these mysterious coccoliths and coccospheres. Here was a further and a most interesting confirmation, from internal evidence, of the essential identity of the chalk with modern deep-sea mud. *Globigerinæ*, coccoliths, and coccospheres are found as the chief constituents of both and testify to the general similarity of the conditions under which both have been formed.

The evidence furnished by the hewing, facing, and superposition of the stones of the Pyramids that these structures were built by men has no greater weight than the evidence that the chalk was built by *Globigerinæ;* and the belief that those ancient pyramid-builders were terrestrial and air-breathing creatures like ourselves is not better based than the conviction that the chalk-makers lived in the sea. But as our belief in the building of the Pyramids by men is not only grounded on the internal evidence afforded by these structures, but gathers strength from multitudinous collateral proofs and is clinched by the total absence of any reason for a contrary belief, so the evidence drawn from the *Globigerinæ* that the chalk is an ancient sea-bottom is fortified by innumerable independent lines of evidence; and our belief in the truth of the conclusion to which all positive testimony tends receives the like negative justification from the fact that no other hypothesis has a shadow of foundation.

It may be worth while briefly to consider a few of these collateral proofs that the chalk was deposited at the bottom of the sea. The great mass of the chalk is composed, as we have seen, of the skeletons of *Globigerinæ* and other simple organisms, imbedded in granular matter. Here and there, however, this hardened mud of the ancient sea reveals the remains of higher animals which have lived and died and left their hard parts in the mud, just as the oysters die and leave their shells behind them in the mud of the present seas.

There are certain groups of animals at the present day which are never found in fresh waters, being unable to live anywhere but in the sea. Such are the corals; those corallines which are called *Polyzoa;* those creatures which fabricate the lampshells, and are called *Brachiopoda;* the pearly *Nautilus,* and all animals allied to it; and all the forms of sea-urchins and star-fishes. Not only are all these creatures confined to salt water at the present day, but, so far as our records of the past go, the conditions of their existence have been the same; hence their occurrence in any deposit is as strong evidence as can be obtained that that deposit was formed in the sea. Now, the remains of animals of all the kinds which have been enumerated occur in the chalk, in greater or less abundance, while not one of those forms of shell-fish which are characteristic of fresh water has yet been observed in it.

When we consider that the remains of more than three thousand distinct species of aquatic animals have been discovered among the fossils of the chalk, that the great majority of them are of such forms as are now met with only in the sea, and that there is no reason to believe that any one of them inhabited fresh water, the collateral evidence that the chalk represents an ancient sea-bottom acquires as great force as the proof derived from the nature of the chalk itself. I think you will now allow that I did not overstate my case when I asserted that we have as strong grounds for believing that all the vast area of dry land at present occupied by the chalk was once at the bottom of the sea as we have for any matter of history whatever; while there is no justification for any other belief.

No less certain is it that the time during which the countries we now call southeast England, France, Germany, Poland, Russia, Egypt, Arabia, Syria were more or less completely covered by a deep sea was of considerable duration. We have already seen that the chalk is in places more than a thousand feet thick. I think you will agree with me that it must have taken some time for the skeletons of animalculæ of an hundredth of an inch in diameter to heap up such a mass as that. I have said that throughout the thickness of the chalk the remains of other animals are scattered. These remains are often in the most exquisite state of preservation. The valves of the shell-fishes are commonly adherent; the long spines of some of the sea-urchins, which would be detached by the smallest jar, often remain in their places. In a word, it is certain that these animals have lived and died when the place which they now occupy was the surface of as much of the chalk as had then been deposited, and that each has been covered up by the layer of *Globigerina* mud, upon which the creatures imbedded a little higher up have in like manner lived and died. But some of these remains prove the existence of reptiles of vast size in the chalk sea. These lived their time, and had their ancestors and descendants, which assuredly implies time, reptiles being of slow growth.

There is more curious evidence, again, that the process of covering up, or in other words the deposit of *Globigerina* skeletons, did not go on very fast. It is demonstrable that an animal of the cretaceous sea might die, that its skeleton might lie uncovered upon the sea-bottom long enough to lose all its outward coverings and appendages by putrefaction; and that, after this had happened, another animal might attach itself to the dead and naked skeleton, might grow to maturity, and might itself die before the calcareous mud had buried the whole.

Cases of this kind are admirably described by Sir Charles Lyell. He speaks of the frequency with which geologists find in the chalk a fossilized sea-urchin, to which is attached the lower valve of a *Crania*. This is a kind of shell-fish, with a shell composed of two pieces, of which, as in the oyster, one is fixed and the other free. "The upper valve is almost invariably wanting, though occasionally found in a perfect state of preservation in the white chalk at some distance. In this case we see clearly that the sea-urchin first lived from youth to age, then died and lost its spines, which were carried away. Then the young *Crania* adhered to the bared shell, grew and perished in its turn; after which the upper valve was separated from the lower before the *Echinus* became enveloped in chalky mud."

A specimen in the Museum of Practical Geology, in London, still further prolongs the period which must have elapsed between the death of the sea-urchin and its burial by the *Globigerinæ*. For the outward face of the valve of a *Crania,* which is attached to a sea-urchin (*Micraster*), is itself overrun by an incrusting coralline, which spreads thence over more or less of the surface of the sea-urchin. It follows that, after the upper valve of the *Crania* fell off, the surface of the attached valve must have remained exposed long enough to allow of the growth of the whole coralline, since corallines do not live imbedded in mud.

The progress of knowledge may one day enable us to deduce from such facts as these the maximum rate at which the chalk can have accumulated, and thus to arrive at the minimum duration of the chalk period. Suppose that the valve of the *Crania* upon which a coralline has fixed itself, in the way just described, is so attached to the sea-urchin that no part of it is more than an inch above the face upon which the sea-urchin rests. Then, as the coralline could not have fixed itself if the *Crania* had been covered up with chalk mud, and could not have lived had itself been so covered, it follows that an inch of chalk mud could not have accumulated within the time between the death and decay of the soft parts of the sea-urchin and the growth of the coralline to the full size which it has attained. If the decay of the soft parts of the sea-urchin, the attachment, growth to maturity, and decay of the *Crania,* and the subsequent attachment and growth of the coralline took a year (which is a low estimate enough), the accumulation of the inch of chalk must have taken more than a year; and the deposit of a thousand feet of chalk must consequently have taken more than twelve thousand years. The foundation of all this calculation is of course a knowledge of the length of time the *Crania* and the coralline needed to attain their full size; and on this head precise knowledge is at present wanting. But there are circumstances which tend to show that nothing like an inch of chalk has accumulated during the life of a *Crania;* and on any probable estimate of the length of that life the chalk period must have had a much longer duration than that thus roughly assigned to it.

Thus not only is it certain that the chalk is the mud of an ancient sea-bottom, but it is no less certain that the chalk sea existed during an extremely long period, though we may not be prepared to give a precise estimate of the length of that period in years. The relative duration is clear, though the absolute duration may not be definable. The attempt to affix any precise date to the period at which the chalk sea began or ended its existence is baffled by difficulties of the same kind. But the relative age of the cretaceous epoch may be determined with as great ease and certainty as the long duration of that epoch.

You will have heard of the interesting discoveries, recently made in various parts of Western Europe, of flint implements obviously worked into shape by human hands, under circumstances which show conclusively that man is a very ancient denizen of these regions. It has been proved that the old populations of Europe whose existence has been revealed to us in this way, consisted of savages, such as the Esquimaux are now; that in the country which is now France they hunted the reindeer, and were familiar with the ways of the mammoth and the bison. The physical geography of France was in those days different from what it is now—the river Somme, for instance, having cut its bed a hundred feet deeper between that time and this; and it is probable that the climate was more like that of Canada or Siberia than that of Western Europe.

The existence of these people is forgotten even in the traditions of the oldest historical nations. The name and fame of them had utterly vanished until a few years back; and the amount of physical change which has been effected since their day renders it more than probable that, venerable as are some of the historical nations, the workers of the chipped flints of Hoxne or of Amiens are to them as they are to us in point of antiquity. But if we assign to these hoar relics of long vanished generations of men the greatest age that can possibly be claimed for them, they are not older than the drift, or boulder clay, which in comparison with the chalk is but a very juvenile deposit. You need go no further than your own seaboard for evidence of this fact. At one of the most charming spots on the coast of Norfolk, Cromer, you will see the boulder clay forming a vast mass, which lies upon the chalk and must consequently have come into existence after it. Huge boulders of chalk are in fact included in the clay, and have evidently been brought to the position they now occupy by the same agency as that which has planted blocks of syenite from Norway side by side with them.

The chalk, then, is certainly older than the boulder clay. If you ask how much, I will again take you no further than the same spot upon your own coasts for evidence. I have spoken of the boulder clay and drift as resting upon the chalk. That is not strictly true. Interposed between the chalk and the drift is a comparatively insignificant layer, containing vegetable matter. But that layer tells a wonderful history. It is full of stumps of trees standing as they grew. Fir-trees are there with their cones, and hazel-bushes with their nuts; there stand the stools of oak and yew trees, beeches and alders. Hence this stratum is appropriately called the "forest-bed."

It is obvious that the chalk must have been upheaved and converted into dry land before the timber trees could grow upon it. As the boles of some of these trees are from two to three feet in diameter, it is no less clear that the dry land thus formed remained in the same conditions for long ages. And not only do the remains of stately oaks and well-grown firs testify to the duration of this condition of things, but additional evidence to the same effect is afforded by the abundant remains of elephants, rhinoceroses, hippopotamuses, and other great wild beasts, which it has yielded to the zealous search of such men as the Rev. Mr. Gunn. When you look at such a cellection as he has formed, and bethink you that these elephantine bones did veritably carry their owners about, and these great grinders crunch, in the dark woods of which the forest-bed is now the only trace, it is impossible not to feel that they are as good evidence of the lapse of time as the annual rings of the tree stumps.

Thus there is a writing upon the wall of cliffs at Cromer, and whoso runs may read it. It tells us, with an authority which cannot be impeached, that the ancient sea-bed of the chalk-sea was raised up, and remained dry land until it was covered with forest stocked with the great game, the spoils of which have rejoiced your geologists. How long it remained in that condition cannot be said; but "the whirligig of time brought its revenges" in those days as in these. That dry land, with the bones and teeth of generations of long-lived elephants, hidden away among the gnarled roots and dried leaves of its ancient trees, sank gradually to the bottom of the icy sea, which covered it with huge masses of drift and boulder clay. Sea-beasts, such as the walrus, now restricted to the extreme north, paddled about where birds had twittered among the topmost twigs of the fir-trees. How long this state of things endured we know not, but at length it came to an end. The upheaved glacial mud hardened into the soil of modern Norfolk. Forests grew once more, the wolf and the beaver replaced the reindeer and the elephant; and at length what we call the history of England dawned.

Thus you have, within the limits of your own county, proof that the chalk can justly claim a very much greater antiquity than even the oldest physical traces of mankind. But we may go further and demonstrate, by evidence of the same authority as that which testifies to the existence of the father of men, that the chalk is vastly older than Adam himself. The *Book of Genesis* informs us that Adam, immediately upon his creation and before the appearance of Eve, was placed in the Garden of Eden. The problem of the geographical position of Eden has greatly vexed the spirits of the learned in such matters; but there is one point respecting which, so far as I know, no commentator has ever raised a doubt. This is that of the four rivers which are said to run out of it Euphrates and Hiddekel are identical with the rivers now known by the names of Euphrates and Tigris. But the whole country in which these mighty rivers take their origin, and through which they run, is composed of rocks which are either of the same age as the chalk or of later date. So that the chalk must not only have been formed, but after its formation the time required for the deposit of these later rocks and for their upheaval into dry land must have elapsed, before the smallest brook which feeds the swift stream of "the great river, the river of Babylon," began to flow.

Thus evidence which cannot be rebutted and which need not be strengthened, though if time permitted I might indefinitely increase its quantity, compels you to believe that the earth, from the time of the chalk to the present day, has been the theatre of a series of changes as vast in their amount as they were slow in their progress. The area on which we stand has been first sea and then land, for at least four alternations, and has remained in each of these conditions for a period of great length. Nor have these wonderful metamorphoses of sea into land and of land into sea been confined to one corner of England. During the chalk period, or "cretaceous epoch," not one of the present great physical features of the globe was in existence. Our great mountain ranges, Pyrenees, Alps, Himalayas, Andes, have all been upheaved since the chalk was deposited and the cretaceous sea flowed over the sites of Sinai and Ararat. All this is certain, because rocks of cretaceous or still later date have shared in the elevatory movements which gave rise to these mountain chains, and may be found perched up, in some cases, many thousand feet high upon their flanks. And evidence of equal cogency demonstrates that, though in Norfolk the forest-bed rests directly upon the chalk, yet it does so, not because the period at which the forest grew immediately followed that at which the chalk was formed, but because an immense lapse of time, represented elsewhere by thousands of feet of rock, is not indicated at Cromer.

I must ask you to believe that there is no less conclusive proof that a still more prolonged succession of similar changes occurred before the chalk was deposited. Nor have we any reason to think that the first term in the series of these changes is known. The oldest sea-beds preserved to us are sands and mud and pebbles, the wear and tear of rocks which were formed in still older oceans.

But great as is the magnitude of these physical changes of the world, they have been accompanied by a no less striking series of modifications in its living inhabitants. All the great classes of animals, beasts of the field, fowls of the air, creeping things, and things which dwell in the waters, flourished upon the globe long ages before the chalk was deposited. Very few, however, if any, of these ancient forms of animal life were identical with those which now live. Certainly not one of the higher animals was of the same species as any of those now in existence. The beasts of the field, in the days before the chalk, were not our beasts of the field, nor the fowls of the air such as those which the eye of man has seen flying, unless his antiquity dates infinitely further back than we at present surmise. If we could be carried back into those times, we should be as one suddenly set down in Australia before it was colonized. We should see mammals, birds, reptiles, fishes, insects, snails, and the like, clearly recognizable as such, and yet not one of them would be just the same as those with which we are familiar, and many would be extremely different.

From that time to the present the population of the world has undergone slow and gradual but incessant changes. There has been no grand catastrophe—no destroyer has swept away the forms of life of one period and replaced them by a totally new creation: but one species has vanished, and another has taken its place; creatures of one type of structure have diminished, those of another have increased, as time has passed on. And thus, while the differences between the living creatures of the time before the chalk, and those of the present day, appear startling if placed side by side, we are led from one to the other by the most gradual progress, if we follow the course of Nature through the whole series of those relics of her operations which she has left behind. And it is by the population of the chalk sea that the ancient and the modern inhabitants of the world are most completely connected. The groups which are dying out flourish side by side with the groups which are now the dominant forms of life. Thus the chalk contains remains of those strange flying and swimming reptiles, the pterodactyl, the *ichthyosaurus,* and the *plesiosaurus,* which are found in no later deposits but abounded in preceding ages. The chambered shells called ammonites and belemnites, which are so characteristic of the period preceding the cretaceous, in like manner die with it.

But amongst these fading remainders of a previous state of things are some very modern forms of life, looking like Yankee pedlars among a tribe of Red Indians. Crocodiles of modern type appear; bony fishes, many of them very similar to existing species, almost supplant the forms of fish which predominate in more ancient seas; and many kinds of living shell-fish first became known to us in the chalk. The vegetation acquires a modern aspect. A few living animals are not even distinguishable, as species, from those which existed at that remote epoch. The *Globigerina* of the present day, for example, is not different specifically from that of the chalk; and the same may be said of many other *Foraminiferæ.* I think it probable that critical and unprejudiced examination will show that more than one species of much higher animals have had a similar longevity; but the only example which I can at present give confidently is the snake's-head lamp-shell (*Terebratulina caput serpentis*), which lives in our English seas, and abounded (as *Terebratulina striata* of authors) in the chalk. The longest line of human ancestry must hide its diminished head before the pedigree of this insignificant shell-fish. We Englishmen are proud to have an ancestor who was present at the Battle of Hastings. The ancestors of *Terebratulina caput serpentis* may have been present at a battle of *Ichthyosauriæ* in that part of the sea which, when the chalk was forming, flowed over the site of Hastings. While all around has changed, this *Terebratulina* has peacefully propagated its species from generation to generation, and stands to this day as a living testimony to the continuity of the present with the past history of the globe.

Up to this moment I have stated, so far as I know, nothing but well-authenticated facts and the immediate conclusions which they force upon the mind. But the mind is so constituted that it does not willingly rest in facts and immediate causes, but seeks always after a knowledge of the remoter links in the chain of causation. Taking the many changes of any given spot of the earth's surface, from sea to land and from land to sea, as an established fact, we cannot refrain from asking ourselves how these changes have occurred. And when we have explained them—as they must be explained—by the alternate slow movements of elevation and depression which have affected the crust of the earth, we go still further back and ask, Why these movements?

I am not certain that any one can give you a satisfactory answer to that question. Assuredly I cannot. All that can be said, for certain, is that such movements are part of the ordinary course of nature, inasmuch as they are going on at the present time. Direct proof may be given that some parts of the land of the northern hemisphere are at this moment insensibly rising and others insensibly sinking; and there is indirect but perfectly satisfactory proof that an enormous area now covered by the Pacific has been deepened thousands of feet since the present inhabitants of that sea came into existence. Thus there is not a shadow of a reason for believing that the physical changes of the globe in past times have been effected by other than natural causes. Is there any more reason for believing that the concomitant modifications in the forms of the living inhabitants of the globe have been brought about in other ways?

Before attempting to answer this question let us try to form a distinct mental picture of what has happened in some special case. The crocodiles are animals which, as a group, have a very vast antiquity. They abounded ages before the chalk was deposited; they throng the rivers in warm climates at the present day. There is a difference in the form of the joints of the backbone, and in some minor particulars, between the crocodile of the present epoch and those which lived before the chalk; but in the cretaceous epoch, as I have already mentioned, the crocodiles had assumed the modern type of structure. Notwithstanding this the crocodiles of the chalk are not identically the same as those which lived in the times called "older tertiary," which succeeded the cretaceous epoch; and the crocodiles of the older tertiaries are not identical with those of the newer tertiaries, nor are these identical with existing forms. (I leave open the question whether particular species may have lived on from epoch to epoch.) Thus each epoch has had its peculiar crocodiles, though all, since the chalk, have belonged to the modern type, and differ simply in their proportions and in such structural particulars as are discernible only to trained eyes.

How is the existence of this long succession of different species of crocodiles to be accounted for? Only two suppositions seem to be open to us—either each species of crocodile has been specially created, or it has arisen out of some pre-existing form by the operation of natural causes. Choose your hypothesis; I have chosen mine. I can find no warranty for believing in the distinct creation of a score of successive species of crocodiles in the course of countless ages of time. Science gives no countenance to such a wild fancy; nor can even the perverse ingenuity of a commentator pretend to discover this sense in the simple words in which the writer of *Genesis* records the proceedings of the fifth and sixth days of the Creation. On the other hand I see no good reason for doubting the necessary alternative that all these varied species have been evolved from pre-existing crocodilian forms by the operation of causes as completely a part of the common order of nature as those which have effected the changes of the inorganic world. Few will venture to affirm that the reasoning which applies to crocodiles loses its force among other animals or among plants. If one series of species has come into existence by the operation of natural causes, it seems folly to deny that all may have arisen in the same way.

A small beginning has led us to a great ending. If I were to put the bit of chalk with which we started, into the hot but obscure flame of burning hydrogen, it would presently shine like the sun. It seems to me that this physical metamorphosis is no false image of what has been the result of our subjecting it to a jet of fervent though nowise brilliant thought to-night. It has become luminous; and its clear rays, penetrating the abyss of the remote past, have brought within our ken some stages of the evolution of the earth; and in the shifting, "without haste but without rest," of the land and sea, as in the endless variation of the forms assumed by living beings, we have observed nothing but the natural product of the forces originally possessed by the substance of the universe.

Walter Pater.

1839–1894.

DIONYSUS.

(From *A Study of Dionysus*, 1876.)

Writers on mythology speak habitually of the *religion* of the Greeks. In thus speaking they are really using a misleading expression, and should speak rather of *religions*, each race and class of Greeks—the Dorians, the people of the coast, the fishers—having had a religion of its own, conceived, independently, of the objects that came nearest to it and were most in its thoughts, and the resulting usages and ideas never having come to have a precisely harmonized system, after the analogy of some other religions. The religion of Dionysus is the religion of people who pass their lives among the vines. As the religion of Demeter carries us back to the cornfields and farmsteads of Greece, and places us, in fancy, among a primitive race, in the furrow and beside the granary, so the religion of Dionysus carries us back to its vineyards, and is a monument of the ways and thoughts of people whose days go by beside the wine-press and under the green and purple shadows, and whose material happiness depends on the crop of grapes. For them the thought of Dionysus and his circle, a little Olympus outside the greater, covered the whole of life and was a complete religion, a sacred representation or interpretation of the general human experience, modified by the special limitations, the special privileges of insight or suggestion, incident to their peculiar mode of existence.

Now, if the reader wishes to understand what the scope of the religion of Dionysus was to the Greeks who lived in it, all it represented to them by way of one clearly conceived yet complex symbol, let him reflect what the loss would be if all the effect and expression drawn from the imagery of the vine and the cup fell out of the whole body of existing poetry; how many fascinating trains of reflection, what color and substance, would therewith have been deducted from it, filled as it is, apart from the more awful associations of the Christian ritual, apart from Galahad's cup, with all the various symbolism of the fruit of the vine. That supposed loss is but an imperfect measure of all that the name of Dionysus recalled to the Greek mind, under a single imaginable form, an outward body of flesh compacted together, closing in, as its animating soul, a whole world of thoughts, surmises, greater and less experiences.

The student of the comparative science of religions finds in the religion of Dionysus one of those many modes of primitive tree-worship which, growing out of some universal instinctive belief that trees and flowers are indeed habitations of living spirits, is found almost everywhere in the earlier stages of civilization, enshrined in legend or custom, often graceful enough, as if the delicate beauty of the object of worship had effectually taken hold on the fancy of the worshipper. Shelley's *Sensitive Plant* shows in what mists of poetical reverie such feeling may still float about a mind full of modern culture, the feeling we too have of a life in the green world, always ready to assert its claim over our sympathetic fancies. Who has not at moments felt the scruple, which is with us always regarding animal life, following the signs of animation further still, till one almost hesitates to pluck out the little soul of flower or leaf?

And in so graceful a faith the Greeks had their share, what was crude and inane in it becoming, in the atmosphere of their energetic, imaginative intelligence, refined and humanized. The oak-grove of Dodona, the seat of their most venerable oracle, did but perpetuate the suspicion that the sounds of the wind in the trees may be, for certain prepared and chosen ears, intelligible voices; they could believe in the transmigration of souls into mulberry and laurel, mint and hyacinth; and the dainty *Metamorphoses* of Ovid are but a fossilized form of one morsel here and there, from a whole world of transformation, with which their nimble fancy was perpetually playing. "Together with them," says the Homeric hymn to Aphrodite, of the Hamadryads, the nymphs which animate the forest trees, "with them, at the moment of their birth, grew up out of the soil, oak-tree or pine, fair, flourishing among the mountains. And when at last the appointed hour of their death has come, first of all, those fair trees are dried up; the bark perishes from around them, and the branches fall away; and therewith the soul of them deserts the light of the sun."

These, then, are the nurses of the vine, bracing it with interchange of sun and shade. They bathe, dance, sing songs of enchantment, so that those who seem oddly in love with nature and strange among their fellows are still said to be *nympholepti;* above all, they are weavers or spinsters, spinning or weaving, with airiest fingers and subtlest, many-colored threads, the foliage of the trees, the petals of flowers, the skins of the fruit, the long thin stalks on which the poplar leaves are set so lightly that Homer compares to them, in their constant motion, the maids who sit spinning in the house of Alcinous. The nymphs of Naxos, where the grape-skin is darkest, weave for him a purple robe. Only, the ivy is never transformed, is visible as natural ivy to the last, pressing the dark outline of its leaves close upon the firm, white, quite human flesh of the god's forehead.

In its earliest form, then, the religion of Dionysus presents us with the most graceful phase of this graceful worship, occupying a place between the ruder fancies of half-civilized people concerning life in flower or tree, and the dreamy after-fancies of the poet of *The Sensitive Plant.* He is the soul of the individual vine, first; the young vine at the house-door of the newly married, for instance, as the vine-grower stoops over it, coaxing and nursing it, like a pet animal or a little child: afterwards, the soul of the whole species, the spirit of fire and dew, alive and leaping in a thousand vines, as the higher intelligence, brooding more deeply over things, pursues in thought the generation of sweetness and strength in the veins of the tree, the transformation of water into wine, little gush by gush; noting all the influences upon it of the heaven above and the earth beneath; and shadowing forth, in each pause of the process, an intervening person—what is to us but the secret chemistry of nature being to them the mediation of living spirits. So they passed on to think of Dionysus (naming him at last from the brightness of the sky and the moisture of the earth), not merely as the soul of the vine, but of all that life in flowing things of which the vine is the symbol because its most emphatic example. At Delos he bears a son, from whom in turn spring the three mysterious sisters Œno, Spermo, and Elais, who, dwelling in the island, exercise respectively the gifts of turning all things at will into oil and corn and wine. In the *Bacchæ* of Euripides he gives his followers, by miracle, honey and milk, and the water gushes for them from the smitten rock. He comes at last to have a scope equal to that of Demeter, a realm as wide and mysterious as hers; the whole productive power of the earth is in him, and the explanation of its annual change. As some embody their intuitions of that power in corn, so others in wine. He is the dispenser of the earth's hidden wealth, giver of riches through the vine, as Demeter through the grain. And as Demeter sends the airy, dainty-wheeled, and dainty-winged spirit of Triptolemus to bear her gifts abroad on all winds, so Dionysus goes on his eastern journey, with its many intricate adventures, in which he carries his gifts to every people.

"A little Olympus outside the greater," I said of Dionysus and his companions: he is the centre of a cycle, the hierarchy of the creatures of water and sunlight in many degrees; and that fantastic system of tree-worship places round him, not the fondly whispering spirits of the more graceful inhabitants of woodland only, the nymphs of the poplar and the pine, but the whole satyr circle, intervening between the headship of the vine and the mere earth, the grosser, less human spirits, incorporate and made visible, of the more coarse and sluggish sorts of vegetable strength—the fig, the reed, the ineradicable weed-things which will attach themselves, climbing about the vine-poles or seeking the sun between the hot stones.

For as Dionysus, the *spiritual form* of the vine, is of the highest human type, so the fig-tree and the reed have animal souls, mistakable in the thoughts of a later, imperfectly remembering age for mere embodiments of animal nature—Snubnose, and Sweetwine, and Silenus the oldest of them all, so old that he has come to have the gift of prophecy.

Quite different from them in origin and intent, but confused with them in form, are those other companions of Dionysus, Pan and his children. Homespun dream of simple people, and like them in the uneventful tenor of his existence, he has almost no story; he is but a presence: the *spiritual form* of Arcadia and the ways of human life there; the reflection, in sacred image or ideal, of its flocks and orchards and wild honey; the dangers of its hunters; its weariness in noonday heat; its children, nimble as the goats they tend, who run, in their picturesque rags, across the solitary wanderer's path, to startle him in the unfamiliar upper places; its one adornment and solace, the dance to the homely shepherd's pipe, cut by Pan first from the sedges of the brook Molpeia.

Breathing of remote nature, the sense of which is so profound in the Homeric hymn to Pan—the pines, the foldings of the hills, the leaping streams, the strange echoings and dying of sound on the heights, "the bird, which among the petals of many-flowered spring, pouring out a dirge, sends forth her honey-voiced song," "the crocus and the hyacinth disorderly mixed in the deep grass," things which the religion of Dionysus loves,—he joins the company of the satyrs. Amongst them, they give their names to insolence and mockery and the finer sorts of malice, to unmeaning and ridiculous fear. But the best spirits have found in them also a certain human pathos, as in displaced beings, coming even nearer to most men, in their very roughness, than the noble and delicate person of the vine; dubious creatures, half way between the animal and human kinds, speculating wistfully on their being because not wholly understanding themselves and their place in nature; as the animals seem always to have this expression to some noticeable degree in the presence of man. In the later school of Attic sculpture they are treated with more and more of refinement, till in some happiest moments Praxiteles conceived a model, often repeated, which concentrates this sentiment of true humor concerning them; a model of dainty natural ease in posture, but with the legs slightly crossed, as only lowly-bred gods are used to carry them, and with some puzzled trouble of youth, you might wish for a moment to smooth away, puckering the forehead a little, between the pointed ears, on which the goodly hair of his animal strength grows low. Little by little the signs of brute nature are subordinated or disappear; and at last Robetta, a humble Italian engraver of the fifteenth century, entering into the Greek fancy because it belongs to all ages, has expressed it in its most exquisite form, in a design of Ceres and her children, of whom their mother is no longer afraid as in the Homeric hymn. The puck-noses have grown delicate, so that, with Plato's infatuated lover, you may call them winsome if you please; and no one would wish those hairy little shanks away, with which one of the small Pans walks at her side, grasping her skirt stoutly; while the other, the sick or weary one, rides in the arms of Ceres herself, who in graceful Italian dress, and decked airily with fruit and corn, steps across a country of cut sheaves, pressing it closely to her, with a child's peevish trouble in its face, and its small goat-legs and tiny hoofs folded over together, precisely after the manner of a little child.

There is one element in the conception of Dionysus which his connection with the satyrs, Marsyas being one of them, and with Pan, from whom the flute passed to all the shepherds of Theocritus, alike illustrates, his interest, namely, in one of the great species of music. One form of that wilder vegetation, of which the satyr race is the soul made visible, is the reed, which the creature plucks and trims into musical pipes. And as Apollo inspires and rules over all the music of strings, so Dionysus inspires and rules over all the music of the reed, the water-plant, in which the ideas of water and of vegetable life are brought close together, natural property, therefore, of the spirit of life in the green sap. I said that the religion of Dionysus was, for those who lived in it, a complete religion, a complete sacred representation and interpretation of the whole of life; and as, in his relation to the vine, he fills for them the place of Demeter, is the life of the earth through the grape as she through the grain, so, in this other phase of his being, in his relation to the reed, he fills for them the place of Apollo; he is the inherent cause of music and poetry; he inspires: he explains the phenomena of enthusiasm, as distinguished by Plato in the *Phædrus*, the secrets of possession by a higher and more energetic spirit than one's own, the gift of self-revelation, of passing out of oneself through words, tones, gestures. A winged Dionysus, venerated at Amyclæ, was perhaps meant to represent him thus, as the god of enthusiasm, of the rising up on those spiritual wings of which also we hear something in the *Phædrus* of Plato.

The artists of the Renaissance occupied themselves much with the person and the story of Dionysus; and Michelangelo, in a work still remaining in Florence, and in which he essayed with success to produce a thing which should pass with the critics for a piece of ancient sculpture, has represented him in the fulness, as it seems, of this enthusiasm, an image of delighted, entire surrender to transporting dreams. And this is no subtle after-thought of a later age, but true to certain finer movements of old Greek sentiment, though it may seem to have waited for the hand of Michelangelo before it attained complete realization. The head of Ion leans, as they recline at the banquet, on the shoulder of Charmides; he mutters in his sleep of things seen therein, but awakes as the flute-players enter, whom Charmides has hired for his birthday supper. The soul of Callias, who sits on the other side of Charmides, flashes out; he counterfeits, with life-like gesture, the personal tricks of friend or foe; or the things he could never utter before he finds words for now; the secrets of life are on his lips. It is in this loosening of the lips and heart, strictly, that Dionysus is the Deliverer, and of such enthusiasm, or ecstasy, is in a certain sense an older patron than Apollo himself. Even at Delphi, the centre of Greek inspiration and of the religion of Apollo, his claim always maintained itself, and signs are not wanting that Apollo was but a later comer there. The pediment of the great temple was divided between them—Apollo, with the nine Muses, on that side; Dionysus, with perhaps three times three Graces, on this. A third of the whole year was held sacred to him—the four winter months were the months of Dionysus; and in the shrine of Apollo itself he was worshipped with almost equal devotion.

The religion of Dionysus takes us back into that old Greek life of the vineyards, as we see it on many painted vases, with much there as we should find it now, as we see it in Bennozzo Gozzoli's mediæval fresco of the *Invention of Wine* in the Campo Santo at Pisa—the family of Noah, presented among all the circumstances of a Tuscan vineyard, around the press from which the first wine is flowing; a painted idyll, with its vintage colors still opulent in decay, and not without its solemn touch of biblical symbolism. For differences, we detect in that primitive life and under that Greek sky a nimbler play of fancy, lightly and unsuspiciously investing all things with personal aspect and incident, and a certain mystical apprehension of unseen powers beyond the material veil of things, now almost departed, corresponding to the exceptional vigor and variety of the Greek organization. This peasant life lies, in unhistoric time, behind the definite forms with which poetry and a refined priesthood afterwards clothed the religion of Dionysus; and the mere scenery and circumstances of the vineyard have determined many things in its development. The noise of the vineyard still sounds in some of his epithets, perhaps in his best-known name—*Iacchus, Bacchus.* The masks suspended on base or cornice, so familiar an ornament in later Greek architecture, are the little faces hanging from the vines and moving in the wind, to scare the birds. That garland of ivy, the æsthetic value of which is so great in the later imagery of Dionysus and his descendants, the leaves of which, floating from his hair, become so noble in the hands of Titian and Tintoret, was actually worn on the head for coolness; his earliest and most sacred images were wrought in the wood of the vine. The people of the vineyard had their feast, the "little" or "country" *Dionysia*, which still lived on, side by side with the greater ceremonies of a later time, celebrated in December, the time of the storing of the new wine. It was then that the potters' fair came, *calpis* and *amphora*, together with lamps against the winter, laid out in order for the choice of buyers; for Keramus, the Greek Vase, is a son of Dionysus, of wine and of Athene, who teaches men all serviceable and decorative art. Then the goat was killed and its blood poured out at the root of the vines; and Dionysus literally drank the blood of goats: and being Greeks, with quick and mobile sympathies, "superstitious," or, rather, "susceptible of religious impressions," some among them, remembering those departed since last year, add yet a little more, and a little wine and water, for the dead also; brooding how the sense of these things might pass below the roots, to spirits hungry and thirsty, perhaps, in their shadowy homes. But the gaiety, that gaiety which Aristophanes in the *Acharnians* has depicted, with so many vivid touches, as a thing of which civil war had deprived the villages of Attica, preponderates over the grave. The travelling country show comes round with its puppets; even the slaves have their holiday; the mirth becomes excessive; they hide their faces under grotesque masks of bark, or stain them with wine-lees or potters' crimson, even, like the old rude idols painted red; and carry in midnight procession such rough symbols of the productive force of nature as the women and children had best not look upon; which will be frowned upon and refine themselves or disappear, in the feasts of cultivated Athens.

Of the whole story of Dionysus it was the episode of his marriage with Ariadne about which ancient art concerned itself oftenest and with most effect. Here, although the antiquarian may still detect circumstances which link the persons and incidents of the legend with the mystical life of the earth, as symbols of its annual change, yet the merely human interest of the story has prevailed over its earlier significance; the spiritual form of fire and dew has become a romantic lover. And as a story of romantic love, fullest perhaps of all the motives of classic legend of the pride of life, it survived with undiminished interest to a later world, two of the greatest masters of Italian painting having poured their whole power into it—Titian, with greater space of ingathered shore and mountain and solemn foliage and fiery animal life; Tintoret, with profounder luxury of delight in the nearness to each other, and imminent embrace, of glorious bodily presences; though both alike with consummate beauty of physical form. Hardly less humanized is the Theban legend of Dionysus, the legend of his birth from Semele, which, out of the entire body of tradition concerning him, was accepted as central by the Athenian imagination. For the people of Attica he comes from Bœotia, a country of northern marsh and mist, but from whose sombre, black-marble towns came also the vine, the musical reed cut from its sedges, and the worship of the Graces, always so closely connected with the religion of Dionysus. "At Thebes alone," says Sophocles, "mortal women bear immortal gods." His mother is the daughter of Cadmus, himself marked out by many curious circumstances as the close kinsman of the earth, to which he all but returns at last, as the serpent, in his old age, attesting some closer sense lingering there of the affinity of man with the dust from whence he came. Semele (an old Greek word, as it seems, for the surface of the earth), the daughter of Cadmus, beloved by Zeus, desires to see her lover in the glory with which he is seen by the immortal Hera. He appears to her in lightning. But the mortal may not behold him and live. Semele gives premature birth to the child Dionysus; whom, to preserve it from the jealousy of Hera, Zeus hides in a part of his thigh, the child returning into the loins of its father, whence in due time it is born again. Yet in this fantastic story, hardly less than in the legend of Ariadne, the story of Dionysus has become a story of human persons, with human fortunes and even more intimately human appeal to sympathy; so that Euripides, pre-eminent as a poet of pathos, finds in it a subject altogether to his mind. All the interest now turns on the development of its points of moral or sentimental significance—the love of the immortal for the mortal; the presumption of the daughter of man who desires to see the divine form as it is; on the fact that not without loss of sight or life itself can man look upon it. The travail of nature has been transformed into the pangs of the human mother; and the poet dwells much on the pathetic incident of death in child-birth, making Dionysus, as Calimachus calls him, a seven months' child, cast out among its enemies, motherless. And as a consequence of this human interest the legend attaches itself, as in an actual history, to definite sacred objects and places—the venerable relic of the wooden image which fell into the chamber of Semele with the lightning-flash, and which the piety of a later age covered with plates of brass; the Ivy Fountain near Thebes, the water of which was so wonderfully bright and sweet to drink, where the nymphs bathed the new-born child; the grave of Semele, in a sacred inclosure grown with ancient vines, where some volcanic heat or flame was perhaps actually traceable, near the lightning-struck ruins of her supposed abode.

Yet, though the mystical body of the earth is forgotten in the human anguish of the mother of Dionysus, the sense of his essence of fire and dew still lingers in his most sacred name, as the son of Semele—*Dithyrambus.* We speak of a certain wild music, in words or rhythm, as dithyrambic; like the dithyrambus, that is, the wild choral-singing of the worshippers of Dionysus. But "Dithyrambus" seems to have been, in the first instance, the name, not of the hymn, but of the god to whom the hymn is sung; and, through a tangle of curious etymological speculations as to the precise derivation of this name, one thing seems clearly visible, that it commemorates, namely, the double birth of the vine-god—that he is born once and again; his birth, first of fire, and afterwards of dew; the two dangers that beset him; his victory over two enemies, the capricious and excessive heats and colds of spring.

He is πυριγενής, then, "fire-born," the son of lightning; lightning being to light, as regards concentration, what wine is to the other strengths of the earth. And who that has rested a hand on the glittering silex of a vineyard slope in August, where the pale globes of sweetness lie, does not feel this? It is out of the bitter salts of a smitten, volcanic soil that it comes up with the most curious virtues. The mother faints and is parched up by the heat which brings the child to the birth; and it pierces through a wonder of freshness, drawing its everlasting green and typical coolness out of the midst of the ashes, its own stem becoming at last like a tangled mass of tortured metal. In thinking of Dionysus, then, as fire-born, the Greeks apprehend and embody the sentiment, the poetry, of all tender things which grow out of a hard soil, or in any sense blossom before the leaf, like the little mezereon-plant of English gardens, with its pale-purple, wine-scented flowers upon the leafless twigs in February, or like the almond-trees of Tuscany, or Aaron's rod that budded, or the staff in the hand of the Pope when Tannhäuser is saved.

And his second birth is of the dew. The fire of which he was born would destroy him in his turn as it withered up his mother; a second danger comes: from this the plant is protected by the influence of the cooling cloud, the lower part of his father the sky, in which it is wrapped and hidden, and of which it is born again, its second mother being, in some versions of the legend, Hyé, the Dew. The nursery where Zeus places it to be brought up is a cave in Mount Nysa, sought by a misdirected ingenuity in many lands, but really, like the place of the carrying away of Persephone, a place of fantasy, the oozy place of springs in the hollow of the hillside, nowhere and everywhere, where the vine was "invented." The nymphs of the trees overshadow it from above; the nymphs of the springs sustain it from below—the Hyades, those first leaping mænads, who, as the springs become rain-clouds, go up to heaven among the stars, and descend again, as dew or shower, upon it; so that the religion of Dionysus connects itself, not with tree-worship only, but also with ancient water-worship, the worship of the spiritual forms of springs and streams. To escape from his enemies Dionysus leaps into the sea, the original of all rain and springs, whence, in early spring, the women of Elis and Argos were wont to call him, with the singing of a hymn. And again, in thus commemorating Dionysus as born of the dew, the Greeks apprehend and embody the sentiment, the poetry, of water. For not the heat only, but the solace of it—the freshness of the cup—this too was felt by those people of the vineyard, whom the prophet Melampus had taught to mix always their wine with water, and with whom the watering of the vines became a religious ceremony, the very dead, as they thought, drinking of and refreshed by the stream. And who that has ever felt the heat of a southern country does not know this poetry, the motive of the loveliest of all the works attributed to Giorgione, the *Fête Champêtre* in the Louvre—the intense sensations, the subtle, far-reaching symbolisms, which, in these places, cling about the touch and sound and sight of it? Think of the darkness of the well in the breathless court, with the delicate ring of ferns kept alive just within the opening of it; of the sound of the fresh water flowing through the wooden pipes into the houses of Venice, on summer mornings; of the cry, "*Acqua frésca!*" at Padua or Verona, when the people run to buy what they prize, in its rare purity, more than wine, bringing pleasures so full of exquisite appeal to the imagination that in these streets the very beggars, one thinks, might exhaust all the philosophy of the epicurean.

Out of all these fancies comes the vine-growers' god, the spiritual form of fire and dew. Beyond the famous representations of Dionysus in later art and poetry—the *Bacchæ* of Euripides, the statuary of the school of Praxiteles,—a multitude of literary allusions, epithets, local customs carry us back to this world of vision unchecked by positive knowledge, in which the myth is begotten among a primitive people, as they wondered over the life of the thing their hands helped forward, till it became a kind of spirit and their culture of it a kind of worship. Dionysus, as we see him in art and poetry, is the projected expression of the ways and dreams of this primitive people, brooded over and harmonized by the energetic Greek imagination; the religious imagination of the Greeks being, precisely, a unifying, or identifying, power, bringing together things naturally asunder, making, for instance, for human body a soul of waters, for human soul flesh of flowers; welding into something like the identity of a human personality the whole range of man's experiences of a given object or series of objects—all their outward qualities, and the visible facts regarding them; all the hidden ordinances by which those facts and qualities hold of unseen forces, and have their roots in purely visionary places.

Robert Louis Stevenson.

1850–1894.

ÆS TRIPLEX.

(From *Virginibus Puerisque*, 1881.)

The changes wrought by death are in themselves so sharp and final, and so terrible and melancholy in their consequences, that the thing stands alone in man's experience and has no parallel upon earth. It outdoes all other accidents because it is the last of them. Sometimes it leaps suddenly upon its victims, like a Thug; sometimes it lays a regular siege, and creeps upon their citadel during a score of years. And when the business is done, there is sore havoc made in other people's lives, and a pin knocked out by which many subsidiary friendships hung together. There are empty chairs, solitary walks, and single beds at night. Again, in taking away our friends, death does not take them away utterly, but leaves behind a mocking, tragical, and soon intolerable residue, which must be hurriedly concealed. Hence a whole chapter of sights and customs striking to the mind, from the pyramids of Egypt to the gibbets and dule trees of mediæval Europe. The poorest persons have a bit of pageant going towards the tomb; memorial stones are set up over the least memorable; and, in order to preserve some show of respect for what remains of our old loves and friendships, we must accompany it with much grimly ludicrous ceremonial, and the hired undertaker parades before the door. All this and much more of the same sort, accompanied by the eloquence of poets, has gone a great way to put humanity in error; nay, in many philosophies the error has been embodied and laid down with every circumstance of logic; although in real life the bustle and swiftness, in leaving people little time to think, have not left them time enough to go dangerously wrong in practice.

As a matter of fact, although few things are spoken of with more fearful whisperings than this prospect of death, few have less influence on conduct under healthy circumstances. We have all heard of cities in South America built upon the side of fiery mountains, and how, even in this tremendous neighborhood, the inhabitants are not a jot more impressed by the solemnity of mortal conditions than if they were delving gardens in the greenest corner of England. There are serenades and suppers and much gallantry among the myrtles overhead; and meanwhile the foundation shudders underfoot, the bowels of the mountain growl, and at any moment living ruin may leap sky-high into the moonlight, and tumble man and his merry-making in the dust. In the eyes of very young people and very dull old ones, there is something indescribably reckless and desperate in such a picture. It seems not credible that respectable married people, with umbrellas, should find appetite for a bit of supper within quite a long distance of a fiery mountain; ordinary life begins to smell of high-handed debauch when it is carried on so close to a catastrophe; and even cheese and salad, it seems, could hardly be relished in such circumstances without something like a defiance of the Creator. It should be a place for nobody but hermits dwelling in prayer and maceration, or mere born-devils drowning care in a perpetual carouse.

And yet, when one comes to think upon it calmly, the situation of these South American citizens forms only a very pale figure for the state of ordinary mankind. This world itself, travelling blindly and swiftly in overcrowded space, among a million other worlds travelling blindly and swiftly in contrary directions, may very well come by a knock that would set it into explosion like a penny squib. And what, pathologically looked at, is the human body, with all its organs, but a mere bagful of petards? The least of these is as dangerous to the whole economy as the ship's powder-magazine to the ship; and with every breath we breathe and every meal we eat we are putting one or more of them in peril. If we clung as devotedly as some philosophers pretend we do to the abstract idea of life, or were half as frightened as they make out we are for the subversive accident that ends it all, the trumpets might sound by the hour and no one would follow them into battle—the blue-peter might fly at the truck, but who would climb into a sea-going ship? Think (if these philosophers were right) with what a preparation of spirit we should affront the daily peril of the dinner-table—a deadlier spot than any battle-field in history, where the far greater proportion of our ancestors have miserably left their bones! What woman would ever be lured into marriage, so much more dangerous than the wildest sea? And what would it be to grow old? For, after a certain distance, every step we take in life we find the ice growing thinner below our feet, and all around us and behind us we see our contemporaries going through. By the time a man gets well into the seventies his continued existence is a mere miracle; and when he lays his old bones in bed for the night, there is an overwhelming probability that he will never see the day. Do the old men mind it, as a matter of fact? Why, no. They were never merrier; they have their grog at night, and tell the raciest stories; they hear of the death of people about their own age, or even younger, not as if it was a grisly warning, but with a simple, child-like pleasure at having outlived some one else; and when a draught might puff them out like a guttering candle, or a bit of a stumble shatter them like so much glass, their old hearts keep sound and unaffrighted, and they go on, bubbling with laughter, through years of man's age compared to which the valley at Balaklava was as safe and peaceful as a village cricket-green on Sunday. It may fairly be questioned (if we look to the peril only) whether it was a much more daring feat for Curtius to plunge into the gulf than for any old gentleman of ninety to doff his clothes and clamber into bed.

Indeed, it is a memorable subject for consideration, with what unconcern and gaiety mankind pricks on along the Valley of the Shadow of Death. The whole way is one wilderness of snares; and the end of it, for those who fear the last pinch, is irrevocable ruin. And yet we go spinning through it all, like a party for the Derby. Perhaps the reader remembers one of the humorous devices of the deified Caligula: how he encouraged a vast concourse of holiday-makers on to his bridge over Baiæ bay; and when they were in the height of their enjoyment, turned loose the Prætorian guards among the company and had them tossed into the sea. This is no bad miniature of the dealings of nature with the transitory race of man. Only, what a checquered picnic we have of it, even while it lasts! and into what great waters, not to be crossed by any swimmer, God's pale Prætorian throws us over in the end!

We live the time that a match flickers; we pop the cork of a ginger-beer bottle, and the earthquake swallows us on the instant. Is it not odd, is it not incongruous, is it not, in the highest sense of human speech, incredible, that we should think so highly of the ginger-beer and regard so little the devouring earthquake? "The love of Life" and "the fear of Death" are two famous phrases that grow harder to understand the more we think about them. It is a well-known fact that an immense proportion of boat accidents would never happen if people held the sheet in their hands instead of making it fast; and yet, unless it be some martinet of a professional mariner or some landsman with shattered nerves, every one of God's creatures makes it fast. A strange instance of man's unconcern and brazen boldness in the face of death!

We confound ourselves with metaphysical phrases, which we import into daily talk with noble inappropriateness. We have no idea of what death is, apart from its circumstances and some of its consequences to others; and although we have some experience of living, there is not a man on earth who has flown so high into abstraction as to have any practical guess at the meaning of the word "life." All literature, from Job and Omar Khayyam to Thomas Carlyle or Walt Whitman, is but an attempt to look upon the human state with such largeness of view as shall enable us to rise from the consideration of living to the Definition of Life. And our sages give us about the best satisfaction in their power when they say that it is a vapor, or a show, or made out of the same stuff with dreams. Philosophy, in its more rigid sense, has been at the same work for ages; and after a myriad bald heads have wagged over the problem, and piles of words have been heaped one upon another into dry and cloudy volumes without end, philosophy has the honor of laying before us, with modest pride, her contribution towards the subject: that life is a Permanent Possibility of Sensation. Truly a fine result! A man may very well love beef, or hunting, or a woman; but surely, surely, not a Permanent Possibility of Sensation! He may be afraid of a precipice, or a dentist, or a large enemy with a club, or even an undertaker's man; but not, certainly, of abstract death. We may trick with the word "life" in its dozen senses until we are weary of tricking; we may argue in terms of all the philosophies on earth; but one fact remains true throughout—that we do not love life in the sense that we are greatly preoccupied about its conservation; that we do not, properly speaking, love life at all, but living. Into the views of the least careful there will enter some degree of providence; no man's eyes are fixed entirely on the passing hour; but although we have some anticipation of good health, good weather, wine, active employment, love, and self-approval, the sum of these anticipations does not amount to anything like a general view of life's possibilities and issues; nor are those who cherish them most vividly at all the most scrupulous of their personal safety. To be deeply interested in the accidents of our existence, to enjoy keenly the mixed texture of human experience, rather leads a man to disregard precautions and risk his neck against a straw. For surely the love of living is stronger in an Alpine climber roping over a peril, or a hunter riding merrily at a stiff fence, than in a creature who lives upon a diet and walks a measured distance in the interest of his constitution.

There is a great deal of very vile nonsense talked upon both sides of the matter: tearing divines reducing life to the dimensions of a mere funeral procession, so short as to be hardly decent; and melancholy unbelievers yearning for the tomb as if it were a world too far away. Both sides must feel a little ashamed of their performances now and again, when they draw in their chairs to dinner. Indeed, a good meal and a bottle of wine is an answer to most standard works upon the question. When a man's heart warms to his viands, he forgets a great deal of sophistry and soars into a rosy zone of contemplation. Death may be knocking at the door, like the Commander's statue; we have something else in hand, thank God, and let him knock. Passing bells are ringing all the world over. All the world over, and every hour, some one is parting company with all his aches and ecstasies. For us also the trap is laid. But we are so fond of life that we have no leisure to entertain the terror of death. It is a honeymoon with us all through, and none of the longest. Small blame to us if we give our whole hearts to this glowing bride of ours—to the appetites, to honor, to the hungry curiosity of the mind, to the pleasure of the eyes in nature, and the pride of our own nimble bodies.

We all of us appreciate the sensations; but as for caring about the Permanence of the Possibility, a man's head is generally very bald and his senses very dull, before he comes to that. Whether we regard life as a lane leading to a dead wall—a mere bag's end, as the French say,—or whether we think of it as a vestible or gymnasium, where we wait our turn and prepare our faculties for some more noble destiny; whether we thunder in a pulpit, or pule in little atheistic poetry-books, about its vanity and brevity; whether we look justly for years of health and vigor, or are about to mount into a bath-chair as a step towards the hearse; in each and all of these views and situations there is but one conclusion possible—that a man should stop his ears against paralyzing terror, and run the race that is set before him with a single mind. No one surely could have recoiled with more heart-ache and terror from the thought of death than our respected lexicographer; and yet we know how little it affected his conduct, how wisely and boldly he walked, and in what a fresh and lively vein he spoke of life. Already an old man, he ventured on his Highland tour; and his heart, bound with triple brass, did not recoil before twenty-seven individual cups of tea. As courage and intelligence are the two qualities best worth a good man's cultivation, so it is the first part of intelligence to recognize our precarious estate in life, and the first part of courage to be not at all abashed before the fact. A frank and somewhat headlong carriage, not looking too anxiously before, not dallying in maudlin regret over the past, stamps the man who is well armored for this world.

And not only well armored for himself, but a good friend and a good citizen to boot. We do not go to cowards for tender dealing; there is nothing so cruel as panic; the man who has least fear for his own carcase has most time to consider others. That eminent chemist who took his walks abroad in tin shoes, and subsisted wholly upon tepid milk, had all his work cut out for him in considerate dealings with his own digestion. So soon as prudence has begun to grow up in the brain, like a dismal fungus, it finds its first expression in a paralysis of generous acts. The victim begins to shrink spiritually; he develops a fancy for parlors with a regulated temperature, and takes his morality on the principle of tin shoes and tepid milk. The care of one important body or soul becomes so engrossing that all the noises of the outer world begin to come thin and faint into the parlor with the regulated temperature, and the tin shoes go equably forward over blood and rain. To be overwise is to ossify; and the scruple-monger ends by standing stock still. Now, the man who has his heart on his sleeve, and a good whirling weathercock of a brain, who reckons his life as a thing to be dashingly used and cheerfully hazarded, makes a very different acquaintance of the world, keeps all his pulses going true and fast, and gathers impetus as he runs, until, if he be running towards anything better than wildfire, he may shoot up and become a constellation in the end. Lord look after his health, Lord have a care of his soul, says he; and he has at the key of the position, and swashes through incongruity and peril towards his aim. Death is on all sides of him with pointed batteries, as he is on all sides of all of us; unfortunate surprises gird him round; mim-mouthed friends and relations hold up their hands in quite a little elegiacal synod about his path: and what cares he for all this? Being a true lover of living, a fellow with something pushing and spontaneous in his inside, he must, like any other soldier, in any other stirring, deadly warfare, push on at his best pace until he touch the goal. "A peerage or Westminster Abbey!" cried Nelson in his bright, boyish, heroic manner. These are great incentives; not for any of these, but for the plain satisfaction of living, of being about their business in some sort or other, do the brave, serviceable men of every nation tread down the nettle danger and pass flyingly over all the stumbling-blocks of prudence. Think of the heroism of Johnson, think of that superb indifference to mortal limitation that set him upon his dictionary and carried him through triumphantly until the end! Who, if he were wisely considerate of things at large, would ever embark upon any work much more considerable than a halfpenny post-card? Who would project a serial novel, after Thackeray and Dickens had each fallen in mid course? Who would find heart enough to begin to live, if he dallied with the consideration of death?

And, after all, what sorry and pitiful quibbling all this is! To forego all the issues of living, in a parlor with a regulated temperature—as if that were not to die a hundred times over, and for ten years at a stretch! As if it were not to die in one's own lifetime, and without even the sad immunities of death! As if it were not to die, and yet be the patient spectators of our own pitiable change! The Permanent Possibility is preserved, but the sensations carefully held at arm's length, as if one kept a photographic plate in a dark chamber. It is better to lose health like a spendthrift than to waste it like a miser. It is better to live and be done with it than to die daily in the sick-room. By all means begin your folio; even if the doctor does not give you a year, even if he hesitates about a month, make one brave push and see what can be accomplished in a week. It is not only in finished undertakings that we ought to honor useful labor. A spirit goes out of the man who means execution, which outlives the most untimely ending. All who have meant good work with their whole hearts, have done good work, although they may die before they have the time to sign it. Every heart that has beat strong and cheerfully has left a hopeful impulse behind it in the world, and bettered the tradition of mankind. And even if death catch people, like an open pitfall; and in mid career, laying out vast projects, and planning monstrous foundations, flushed with hope, and their mouths full of boastful language, they should be at once tripped up and silenced; is there not something brave and spirited in such a termination? and does not life go down with a better grace, foaming in full body over a precipice, than miserably straggling to an end in sandy deltas? When the Greeks made their fine saying that those whom the gods love die young, I cannot help believing they had this sort of death also in their eye. For surely, at whatever age it overtake the man, this is to die young. Death has not been suffered to take so much as an illusion from his heart. In the hot-fit of life, a-tiptoe on the highest point of being, he passes at a bound on to the other side. The noise of the mallet and chisel is scarcely quenched, the trumpets are hardly done blowing, when, trailing with him clouds of glory, this happy-starred, full-blooded spirit shoots into the spiritual land.

APPENDIX.

SPECIMENS OF EARLY ENGLISH PROSE STYLE.

Early Translations of the Bible.

THE LORD'S PRAYER.

Anglo-Saxon Version (about 1000 A. D.).

Fæder ure þu þe eart on heofonum; si þin nama gehalgod. To-becume þin rice. Gewurþe ðin willa on eorðan swa swa on heofonum. Urne gedæghwamlican hlaf syle us to dæg. And forgyf us ure gyltas swa swa we forgyfað urum gyltendum. And ne gelæd þu us on costnunge ac alys us of yfele. Soþlice.

[*Matthew* 6: 9-13.]

Wiclif's Version (about 1380 A. D.).

Oure fadir that art in heuenes, halwid be thi name; thi kyngdom cumme to; be thi wille don as in heuen and in erthe; ȝif to vs this day oure breed ouer other substaunce; and forȝeue to vs oure dettis, as we forȝeue to oure dettours; and leede vs nat in to temptacioun, but delyuere vs fro yuel. Amen.

[*Matthew* 6: 9-13.]

Tyndale's Version (1534 A. D.).

O oure father which arte in heven, halowed be thy name. Let thy kyngdome come. Thy wyll be fulfilled as well in erth as it ys in heven. Geve vs this daye oure dayly breede. And forgeve vs oure treaspases, even as we forgeve oure trespacers. And leade vs not into temptacion: but delyver vs from evell. For thyne is the kyngedome and the power and the glorye for ever. Amen

[*Matthew* 6: 9-13.]

THE PARABLE OF THE PRODIGAL SON.

Wiclif's Version (about 1380 A. D.).

Sum man hadde tweye sones; and the ȝongere seide to the fadir, Fadir, ȝyue to me the porcioun of substaunce that byfallith to me. And the fadir departide to him the substaunce. And not aftir manye dayes, alle thingis gederid to gidre, the ȝongere sone wente in pilgrymage in to a fer cuntree; and there he wastide his substaunce in lyuynge leccherously. And aftir that he hadde endid alle thingis, a strong hungir was maad in that cuntree, and he bigan to haue nede. And he wente, and cleuyde to oon of the citeseyns of that cuntree. And he sente him in to his toun, that he schulde feede hoggis. And he coueitide to fille his wombe of the coddis whiche the hoggis eeten, and no man ȝaf to him. Sothli he turned aȝen in to him silf, seyde, Hou many hirid men in my fadir hous, han plente of looues; forsothe I perische here thurȝ hungir. I schal ryse, and I schal go to my fadir, and I schal seie to him, Fadir, I haue synned aȝens heuene, and bifore thee; now I am not worthi to be clepid thi sone, make me as oon of thi hyrid men. And he rysinge cam to his fadir. Sothli whanne he was ȝit fer, his fadir syȝ him, and he was stirid by mercy. And he rennynge to, felde on his necke, and kiste him. And the sone seyde to him, Fadir, I haue synned aȝens heuene, and bifore thee; and now I am not worthi to be clepid thi sone. Forsoth the fadir seyde to his seruauntis, Soone bringe ȝe forth the firste stoole, and clothe ȝe him, and ȝyue ȝe a ring in his hond, and schoon in to the feet; and brynge ȝe a calf maad fat, and sle ȝe, and ete we, and plenteuously ete we. For this my sone was deed, and hath lyued aȝen; he perischide, and is founden. And alle bigunnen to eat plenteuously. Forsoth his eldere sone was in the feeld; and whanne he cam, and neiȝede to the hous, he herde a symphonye and a crowde. And he clepide oon of the seruauntis, and axide, what thingis thes weren. And he seide to him, Thi brodir is comen, and thi fadir hath slayn a fat calf, for he receyuede him saf. Forsoth he was wroth, and wolde not entre. Therfore his fadir gon out, bigan to preie him. And he answeringe to his fadir, seide, Lo! so manye ȝeeris I serue to thee, and I brak neuere thi comaundement; thou hast neuere ȝouun a kyde to me, that I schulde ete largely with my frendis. But aftir that this thi sone, which deuouride his substaunce with hooris, cam, thou hast slayn to him a fat calf. And he seide to him, Sone, thou art euere with me, and alle myne thingis ben thyne. Forsothe it bihofte to ete plenteuously, and for to ioye; for this thi brother was deed, and lyuede aȝeyn; he peryschide, and he is founden.

[*Luke* 15: 11-32.]

Tyndale's Version (1534 A. D.).

And he sayde: a certayne man had two sonnes, and the yonger of them sayde to his father: father geve me my parte of the goodes that to me belongeth. And he devided vnto them his substaunce. And not longe after, the yonger sonne gaddered all that he had to gedder, and toke his iorney into a farre countre, and theare he wasted his goodes with royetous lyvinge. And when he had spent all that he had, ther rose a greate derth thorow out all that same londe, and he began to lacke. And he went and clave to a citesyn of that same countre, which sent him to his felde, to kepe his swyne. And he wold fayne have filled his bely with the coddes that the swyne ate: and noo man gave him.

Then he came to him selfe and sayde: how many hyred servauntes at my fathers, have breed ynough, and I dye for honger. I will aryse, and goo to my father and will saye vnto him: father, I have synned agaynst heven and before the, and am no moare worthy to be called thy sonne, make me as one of thy hyred servauntes. And he arose and went to his father. And when he was yet agreate waye of, his father sawe him and had compassion, and ran and fell on his necke, and kyssed him. And the sonne sayd vnto him: father, I have synned agaynst heven, and in thy sight, and am no moare worthy to be called thy sonne. But his father sayde to his servauntes: bringe forth that best garment and put it on him, and put a rynge on honde, and showes on his fete.

And bringe hidder that fatted caulfe, and kyll him, and let vs eate and be mery: for this my sonne was deed, and is alyve agayne, he was loste, and is now founde. And they began to be merye.

The elder brother was in the felde, and when he cam and drewe nye to the housse, he herde minstrelcy and daunsynge, and called one of his servauntes, and axed what thoose thinges meante. And he sayd vnto him: thy brother is come, and thy father had kylled the fatted caulfe, because he hath receaved him safe and sounde. And he was angry, and wolde not goo in. Then came his father out, and entreated him. He answered and sayde to his father: Loo, these many yeares have I done the service, nether brake at eny tyme thy commaundment, and yet gavest thou me never soo moche as a kyd to make mery with my lovers: but assone as this thy sonne was come, which hath devoured thy goodes with harlootes, thou haste for his pleasure kylled the fatted caulfe. And he sayd vnto him: Sonne, thou wast ever with me, and all that I have, is thyne: it was mete that we shuld make mery and be glad: for this thy brother was deed, and is a lyve agayne: and was loste, and is founde.

[*Luke* 15: 11-32.]

Sir John Mandeville.

Died 1372.

OF THE HILLES OF GOLD.

(From *The Voiage and Travaile of Sir John Maundevile, Kt.*, 1371).

In the Yle also of this Taprobane, ben grete Hilles of Gold, that Pissemyres kepen fulle diligently. And thei fynen the pured Gold, and casten away the unpured. And theise Pissemyres ben grete as Houndes: so that no man dar come to tho Hilles: for the Pissemyres wolde assaylen hem and devouren hem anon; so that no man may gete of that Gold, but be gret sleighte. And therfore whan it is gret hete, the Pissemyres resten hem in the Erthe, from pryme of the Day in to Noon: and than the folk of the Contree taken Camayles, Dromedaries and Hors and other Bestes, and gon thidre, and chargen hem in alle haste that thei may. And aftre that thei fleen awey, in alle haste that the Bestes may go, or the Pissemyres comen out of the Erthe. And in other tymes, whan it is not so hote, and that the Pissemyres ne resten hem not in the Erthe, than thei geten Gold be this Sotyltee; Thei taken Mares, that han ȝonge Coltes or Foles, and leyn upon the Mares voyde Vesselles made therfore; and thei ben alle open aboven, and hangynge lowe to the Erthe: and thanne thei sende forth tho Mares, for to pasturen aboute tho Hilles, and with holden the Foles with hem at home. And whan the Pissemyres sen tho Vesselles, thei lepen in anon, and thei han this kynde, that thei lete no thing ben empty among hem, but anon thei fillen it, be it what maner of thing that it be: and so thei fillen tho Vesselles with Gold. And whan that the folk supposen, that the Vesselle ben fulle, thei putten forthe anon the ȝonge Foles, and maken hem to nyzen aftre hire Dames; and than anon the Mares retornen towardes hire Foles, with hire charges of Gold; and than men dischargen hem, and geten Gold y now be this sotyltee. For the Pissemyres wole suffren Bestes to gon and pasturen amonges hem; but no man in no wyse.

Sir Thomas Malory.

Floruit 1470.

THE PARTING OF LAUNCELOT AND GUINEVERE.

(From *Le Morte Darthur*, 1485.)

Then came Sir Bors de Ganis and said: My lord Sir Launcelot, what think ye for to do, now to ride in this realm? wit ye well ye shall find few friends. Be as be may, said Sir Launcelot, keep you still here, for I will forth on my journey, and no man nor child shall go with me. So it was no boot to strive, but he departed and rode westerly, and there he sought a seven or eight days; and at the last he came to a nunnery, and then was Queen Guenever ware of Sir Launcelot as he walked in the cloister. And when she saw him there she swooned thrice, that all the ladies and gentlewomen had work enough to hold the queen up. So when she might speak, she called ladies and gentlewomen to her, and said: Ye marvel, fair ladies, why I make this fare. Truly, she said, it is for the sight of yonder knight that yonder standeth; wherefore I pray you all call him to me. When Sir Launcelot was brought to her, then she said to all the ladies: Through this man and me hath all this war been wrought, and the death of the most noblest knights of the world; for through our love that we have loved together is my most noble lord slain. Therefore, Sir Launcelot, wit thou well I am set in such a plight to get my soul-heal; and yet I trust through God's grace that after my death to have a sight of the blessed face of Christ, and at domesday to sit on his right side, for as sinful as ever I was are saints in heaven. Therefore, Sir Launcelot, I require thee and beseech thee, heartily, for all the love that ever was betwixt us, that thou never see me more in the visage; and I command thee, on God's behalf, that thou forsake my company, and to thy kingdom thou turn again, and keep well thy realm from war and wrack; for as well as I have loved thee, mine heart will not serve me to see thee, for through thee and me is the flower of kings and knights destroyed; therefore, Sir Launcelot, go to thy realm, and there take thee a wife, and live with her with joy and bliss; and I pray thee heartily, pray for me to our Lord, that I may amend my mis-living. Now, sweet madam, said Sir Launcelot, would ye that I should now return again unto my country, and there to wed a lady? Nay, madam, wit you well that shall I never do, for I shall never be so false to you of that I have promised; but the same destiny that ye have taken you to, I will take me unto, for to please Jesu, and ever for you I cast me specially to pray. If thou wilt do so, said the queen, hold thy promise, but I may never believe but that thou wilt turn to the world again. Well, madam, said he, ye say as pleaseth you, yet wist you me never false of my promise, and God defend but I should forsake the world as ye have done. For in the quest of the Sangreal I had forsaken the vanities of the world had not your lord been. And if I had done so at that time, with my heart, will, and thought, I had passed all the knights that were in the Sangreal except Sir Galahad, my son. And therefore, lady, sithen ye have taken you to perfection, I must needs take me to perfection, of right. For I take record of God, in you I have had mine earthly joy; and if I had found you now so disposed, I had cast to have had you into mine own realm. But sithen I find you thus disposed, I ensure you faithfully, I will ever take me to penance, and pray while my life lasteth, if I may find any hermit, either gray or white, that will receive me. Wherefore, madam, I pray you kiss me and never no more. Nay, said the queen, that shall I never do, but abstain you from such works: and they departed. But there was never so hard an hearted man but he would have wept to see the dolor that they made; for there was lamentation as they had been stung with spears; and many times they swooned, and the ladies bare the queen to her chamber. And Sir Launcelot awoke, and went and took his horse, and rode all that day and all night in a forest, weeping. And at the last he was ware of an hermitage and a chapel stood betwixt two cliffs; and then he heard a little bell ring to mass, and thither he rode and alit, and tied his horse to the gate; and heard mass. And he that sang mass was the Bishop of Canterbury. Both the Bishop and Sir Bevidere knew Sir Launcelot, and they spake together after mass. But when Sir Bevidere had told his tale all whole, Sir Launcelot's heart almost brast for sorrow, and Sir Launcelot threw his arms abroad, and said: Alas, who may trust this world. And then he kneeled down on his knee, and prayed the Bishop to shrive him and assoil him. And then he besought the Bishop that he might be his brother. Then the Bishop said: I will gladly; and there he put an habit upon Sir Launcelot, and there he served God day and night with prayers and fastings.

Hugh Latimer.

1485(?)–1555.

AN ARRAIGNMENT OF LONDON.

(From the *Sermon of the Plough*, 1548.

Now what shall we say of these rich citizens of London? What shall I say of them? Shall I call them proud men of London, malicious men of London, merciless men of London? No, no, I may not say so; they will be offended with me then. Yet must I speak. For is there not reigning in London as much pride, as much covetousness, as much cruelty, as much oppression, and as much superstition, as was in Nebo? Yes, I think, and much more too. Therefore, I say, repent, O London! repent, repent! Thou hearest thy faults told thee: amend them, amend them! I think if Nebo had had the preaching that thou hast, they would have converted. And, you rulers and officers, be wise and circumspect, look to your charge, and see you do your duties; and rather be glad to amend your ill-living than to be angry when you are warned or told of your fault. What ado was there made in London at a certain man because he said (and indeed at that time on a just cause), "Burgesses!" quoth he, "nay, Butterflies." Lord, what ado there was for that word! And yet would God they were no worse than butterflies! Butterflies do but their nature: the butterfly is not covetous, is not greedy of other men's goods; is not full of envy and hatred, is not malicious, is not cruel, is not merciless. The butterfly glorieth not in her own deeds, nor preferreth the traditions of men before God's word; it committeth not idolatry, nor worshippeth false gods. But London cannot abide to be rebuked; such is the nature of man. If they be pricked, they will kick; if they be rubbed on the gall, they will wince; but yet they will not amend their faults, they will not be ill spoken of. But how shall I speak well of them? If you could be content to receive and follow the word of God and favor good preachers, if you could bear to be told of your faults, if you could amend when you hear of them, if you would be glad to reform that is amiss, if I might see any such inclination in you that you would leave to be merciless and begin to be charitable, I would then hope well of you, I would then speak well of you. But London was never so ill as it is now. In times past, men were full of pity and compassion, but now there is no pity; for in London their brother shall die in the streets for cold, he shall lie sick at the door between stock and stock, I cannot tell what to call it, and perish there for hunger: was there ever more unmercifulness in Nebo? I think not. In times past, when any rich man died in London, they were wont to help the poor scholars of the Universities with exhibition. When any man died they would bequeath great sums of money toward the relief of the poor. When I was a scholar in Cambridge myself, I heard very good report of London, and knew many that had relief of the rich men of London: but now I can hear no such good report, and yet I inquire of it and hearken for it; but now charity is waxen cold, none helpeth the scholar nor yet the poor.

John Lyly.

1553(?)–1606.

THE CHARACTER OF EUPHUES.

(From *Euphues: The Anatomy of Wit*, 1578.)

There dwelt in Athens a young gentleman of great patrimony, and of so comely a personage that it was doubted whether he were more bound to Nature for the lineaments of his person or to Fortune for the increase of his possessions. But Nature, impatient of comparisons, and as it were disdaining a companion or co-partner in her working, added to this comeliness of his body such a sharp capacity of mind that not only she proved Fortune counterfeit but was half of that opinion that she herself was only current. This young gallant, of more wit than wealth, and yet of more wealth than wisdom, seeing himself inferior to none in pleasant conceits, thought himself superior to all in honest conditions, insomuch that he deemed himself so apt to all things that he gave himself almost to nothing but practicing of those things commonly which are incident to these sharp wits—fine phrases, smooth quipping, merry taunting, using jesting without mean, and abusing mirth without measure. As therefore the sweetest rose hath his prickle, the finest velvet his brack, the fairest flour his bran, so the sharpest wit hath his wanton will, and the holiest head his wicked way. And true it is that some men write and most men believe, that in all perfect shapes a blemish bringeth rather a liking every way to the eyes than a loathing any way to the mind. Venus had her mole in her cheek, which made her more amiable; Helen, her scar on her chin, which Paris called *cos amoris*, the whetstone of love; Aristippus, his wart; Lycurgus, his wen: so likewise in the disposition of the mind, either virtue is overshadowed with some vice, or vice overcast with some virtue—Alexander, valiant in war, yet given to wine; Tully, eloquent in his gloses, yet vain-glorious; Solomon, wise, yet too wanton; David, holy, but yet an homicide. None more witty than Euphues, yet at the first none more wicked. The freshest colors soonest fade, the teenest razor soonest turneth his edge, the finest cloth is soonest eaten with moths, and the cambric sooner stained than the coarse canvas: which appeared well in this Euphues, whose wit being like wax, apt to receive any impression, and having the bridle in his own hands, either to use the rein or the spur, disdaining counsel, leaving his country, loathing his old acquaintance, thought either by wit to obtain some conquest, or by shame to abide some conflict, and, leaving the rule of reason, rashly ran unto destruction.

Sir Philip Sidney.

1554–1586.

HER LOVERS DESCRIBE URANIA.

(From the *Arcadia*, 1590.)

It was in the time that the earth begins to put on her new apparel against the approach of her lover, and that the sun, running a most even course, becomes an indifferent arbiter between the night and the day; when the hopeless shepherd Strephon was come to the sands which lie against the island of Cythera, where, viewing the place with a heavy kind of delight, and sometimes casting his eyes to the isleward, he called his friendly rival, the pastor Claius, unto him, and, setting first down in his darkened countenance a doleful copy of what he would speak, "O my Claius," said he, "hither we are now come to pay the rent for which we are so called unto by over-busy Remembrance; Remembrance, restless Remembrance, which claims not only this duty of us, but for it will have us forget ourselves. I pray you, when we were amid our flock, and that of other shepherds some were running after their sheep strayed beyond their bounds, some delighting their eyes with seeing them nibble upon the short and sweet grass, some medicining their sick ewes, some setting a bell for an ensign of a sheepish squadron, some with more leisure inventing new games of exercising their bodies and sporting their wits, did Remembrance grant us any holiday, either for pastime or devotion, nay, either for necessary food or natural rest? but that still it forced our thoughts to work upon this place, where we last (alas that the word 'last' should so long last!) did gaze our eyes upon her ever-flourishing beauty: did it not still cry within us, 'Ah you base-minded wretches, are your thoughts so deeply bemired in the trade of ordinary worldlings, as for respect of gain some paltry wool may yield you, to let so much time pass without knowing perfectly her estate, especially in so troublesome a season? to leave that shore unsaluted, from whence you may see to the island where she dwelleth? to leave those steps unkissed wherein Urania printed the farewell of all beauty?' Well, then, Remembrance commanded, we obeyed, and here we find that, as our Remembrance came ever clothed unto us in the form of this place, so this place gives new heat to the fever of our languishing Remembrance. Yonder, my Claius, Urania lighted; the very horse (methought) bewailed to be so disburdened; and as for thee, poor Claius, when thou wentst to help her down, I saw reverence and desire so divide thee that thou didst at one instant both blush and quake, and instead of bearing her wert ready to fall down thyself. There she sate, vouchsafing my cloak (then most gorgeous) under her: at yonder rising of the ground she turned herself, looking back toward her wonted abode, and because of her parting bearing much sorrow in her eyes, the lightsomeness whereof had yet so natural a cheerfulness as it made even sorrow seem to smile; at that turning she spake unto us all, opening the cherry of her lips, and Lord how greedily mine ears did feed upon the sweet words she uttered? And here she laid her hand over thine eyes, when she saw the tears springing in them, as if she would conceal them from other and yet herself feel some of thy sorrow. But woe is me, yonder, yonder, did she put her foot into the boat, at that instant, as it were, dividing her heavenly beauty between the earth and the sea. But when she was embarked, did you not mark how the winds whistled and the seas danced for joy, how the sails did swell with pride, and all because they had Urania? O Urania, blessed be thou, Urania, the sweetest fairness and fairest sweetness!" With that word his voice brake so with sobbing that he could say no further; and Claius thus answered: "Alas, my Strephon," said he, "what needs this score to reckon up only our losses? What doubt is there but that the light of this place doth call our thoughts to appear at the court of Affection, held by that racking steward, Remembrance? As well may sheep forget to fear when they spy wolves as we can miss such fancies when we see any place made happy by her treading. Who can choose, that saw her, but think where she stayed, where she walked, where she turned, where she spoke? But what is all this? truly no more but as this place served us to think of those things, so those things serve as places to call to memory more excellent matters. No, no, let us think with consideration, and consider with acknowledging, and acknowledge with admiration, and admire with love, and love with joy in the midst of all woes: let us in such sort think, I say, that our poor eyes were so enriched as to behold, and our low hearts so exalted as to love, a maid who is such that, as the greatest thing the world can show is her beauty, so the least thing that may be praised in her is her beauty. Certainly, as her eyelids are more pleasant to behold than two white kids climbing up a fair tree and browsing on his tenderest branches, and yet are nothing compared to the day-shining stars contained in them; and as her breath is more sweet than a gentle southwest wind, which comes creeping over flowery fields and shadowed waters in the extreme heat of summer, and yet is nothing compared to the honey-flowing speech that breath doth carry; no more all that our eyes can see of her (though when they have seen her what else they shall ever see is but dry stubble after clovers-grass) is to be matched with the flock of unspeakable virtues laid up delightfully in that best-builded fold."

Richard Hooker.

1554(?)–1600.

THE MAJESTY AND BENEFICENCE OF LAW.

(From *Of the Laws of Ecclesiastical Polity,* Book I., 1594.)

Thus far, therefore, we have endeavored in part to open of what nature and force laws are, according unto their several kinds: the law which God with himself hath eternally set down to follow in his own works; the law which He hath made for His creatures to keep; the law of natural and necessary agents; the law which angels in heaven obey; the law whereunto by the light of reason men find themselves bound in that they are men; the law which they make by composition for multitudes and politic societies of men to be guided by; the law which belongeth unto each nation; the law that concerneth the fellowship of all; and, lastly, the law which God Himself hath supernaturally revealed. . . . Thus we see how even one and the self-same thing is under divers considerations conveyed through many laws, and that to measure by any one kind of law all the actions of men were to confound the admirable order wherein God hath disposed all laws, each as in nature, so in degree, distinct from other.

Wherefore, that here we may briefly end, of Law there can be no less acknowledged than that her seat is the bosom of God, her voice the harmony of the world; all things in heaven and earth do her homage, the very least as feeling her care, and the greatest as not exempted from her power; both angels and men and creatures of what condition soever, though each in different sort and manner, yet all with uniform consent, admiring her as the mother of their peace and joy.

NOTES.

NOTES.

FRANCIS BACON.

The first edition of the *Essays*, in 1597, contained ten essays, including *Of Studies* and *Of Negotiating*; the second edition, in 1612, contained thirty-eight, including *Of Youth and Age* and *Of Nature in Men*; the third edition, in 1625, contained fifty-eight. In these later editions Bacon revised and enlarged most of the essays already published. The text of 1625 is here followed. In 1638 Dr. Rawley, Bacon's chaplain, published a Latin translation of the *Essays*; whether Bacon himself was the translator is uncertain.

OF TRUTH.

1.—1. **Pilate:** at the trial of Jesus; *John* xviii. 38.—2. **there be that:** understand "those" after "be."—5. **discoursing**=discursive, "passing rapidly from one thought to another" *(A New English Dictionary)*.—9. **imposeth**=lays restraint.—17-18. **masks and mummeries and triumphs:** spectacular theatrical performances, very popular in Bacon's time, in which there was much tinsel and glitter.—18. **daintily**=prettily, delightfully.—23. **vain**=empty, false.

2.—3. "**vinum dæmonum**"="wine of devils"; the father was St. Augustine (354-430).—7. **howsoever**=although.—15. **sabbath work,** i. e., the work of God's one continuous sabbath ever since the great work of creation ended.—19. **The Poet:** Lucretius (96 ?-55 B. C.); the quotation is from his *De Rerum Natura* ("On the Nature of Things"), II. 1 ff., in which he expounds the philosophy of Epicurus.—**the sect:** the Epicureans.—25. **not to be commanded,** i. e., there is none higher (cf. "commanding view"); "commanded" is a military term.—26. **errors**=wanderings.—28. **so**=provided.—**prospect**=looking forth, survey.—31. **poles**=axes.—34. **round**=fair.

3.—3. **Montaigne:** a French essayist (1533-1592).

OF INNOVATIONS.

3.—24. **of course**=by its course, or "running."—31. **admired**=wondered at—33. **round**=rapidly (cf. "round trot").

4.—6. **pairs**=impairs.—13-14. **Scripture saith:** *Jer.* vi. 16:—"Stand ye in the ways, and see, and ask for the old paths, where is the good way, and walk therein."

OF NATURE IN MEN.

4.—18. **doctrine**=instruction.—19. **importune**=importunate.

5.—3-4. "**Optimus,**" etc.=" He is the best liberator of the soul who bursts the chains galling his breast and ceases from grief at once" (Ovid, *Remedia Amoris*, 293); *animi* should be *fuit*. —14. **lay:** so in the original.—25. "**Multum,**" etc.=" My soul has long been a sojourner."—**converse**=live.—26. **affect**=take to, like.—29. **so as**=so that.

OF YOUTH AND AGE.

6.—10. **Septimius Severus:** a Roman Emperor (146-211 A. D.). —11-12 "**Juventum,**" etc.=" He passed a youth full of errors, nay rather of fury" (Spartian, *Severus*, ii.); Bacon quoted apparently from memory, and very inaccurately; Spartian wrote, "Juventum plenam furorum, nonnunquam criminum, habuit" ("He had a youth full of fury and sometimes of crimes"). —14. **Cosmos:** one of the famous de Medici family who ruled Florence in the fourteenth and fifteenth centuries.—**Gaston:** a French general (1489-1512), who won a great victory over the Spaniards at the age of twenty-three.—20. **abuseth**=deceives.—28. **care not**=are not cautious.—31. **unready,** i. e., not ready for use, ill-trained; the Latin version has *male domitus*.

7.—1. **compound employments of both,** i. e., employ both together.—5. **extern accidents**=external effects, i. e., results coming ("falling upon") from without—as in this case, from the disposition of the populace toward age and youth.—8-10. "**Your young men,**" etc.: *Joel* ii. 28.—18. **Hermogenes:** a famous Greek teacher of rhetoric, of the second century A. D., "who became a master at fifteen and an idiot at five-and-twenty" (Saintsbury, *A History of Criticism*, I. 90).—23. **Tully:** Marcus Tullius Cicero. **Hortensius:** a Roman orator (114-50 B. C.).—24. "**Idem,**" etc.= "He remained the same, but the same was not becoming" (Cicero, *Brutus*, 95); Cicero's exact words are, "Remanebat idem nec decebat idem."—25. **magnanimous** = great-souled.—26-27. **Scipio Africanus:** a Roman General (234?-183? B. C.), who won great victories in Africa over Hannibal when little more than thirty years old. 27.—**Livy:** the Roman historian (59 B. C.-17 A. D.).—27-28. "**Ultima,**" etc.=" His last deeds were inferior to his first"; Livy's exact words are, "Memorabilior prima pars vitæ quam postrema fuit" ("The first part of his life was more memorable than the last part").

OF NEGOTIATING.

8.—10-11. **will help the matter in report for satisfaction sake,** i. e., such agents will make a more favorable report than truth allows, in order to satisfy their employer.—11. **affect**=take to, like.—19. **prescription**=former record.—24-25. **the start, or first performance, is all,** i. e., the negotiator who imposes the first and fundamental condition controls the whole situation.—29. **All practice is to discover or to work,** i. e., the object in all practical handling of men is either to discover their natures and purposes, or to make them do something.—33. **fashions**=ways, habits.

OF STUDIES.

9.—7. expert men: experienced, practical men, in distinction from learned men.—12. **humor**=mood, habit of mind.—17. **admire**=wonder at.—25. **curiously**=carefully (Lat. *cura,* "care"). —28. **arguments**=subjects.—29. **else,** i. e., in other cases.—**flashy** =insipid.—30. **conference**=intercourse and conversation.—33. **present wit:** a mind, or wits, always ready for use on the instant (cf. "presence of mind").

10.—2. **witty:** clever, quick-minded, and full of bright notions. 4. "**Abeunt,**" etc.="Studies pass over into manners" (Ovid).—5. **wit**=mind.—13. **schoolmen:** the theologians and philosophers of the Middle Ages, who excelled in analysis and subtle distinctions.—**cymini sectores**="splitters of cummin" (cummin were small seeds); cf. "hair-splitters."—15. **illustrate**=throw light upon, clear up.

JOHN MILTON.

FREEDOM OF THE PRESS.

Areopagitica, selections from which are here printed, was published as a pamphlet, unlicensed, in November, 1644. It was occasioned by an order of Parliament, on June 14, 1643, that no "Book, Pamphlet, paper, nor part of any such Book, Pamphlet, or paper, shall from henceforth be printed, bound, stitched or put to sale by any person or persons whatsoever, unless the same be first approved of and licensed under the hands of such person or persons as both, or either of the said Houses [of Parliament] shall appoint for the licensing of the same." The order merely renewed the substance of previous decrees by the "Star Chamber"; but Milton and other lovers of freedom had expected more liberal things from the reform Parliament, which was waging war against the king on behalf of popular liberty. In form *Areopagitica* is a speech addressed to Parliament. Its name is derived from the Λόγος Ἀρεοπαγιτικός of Isocrates, the Greek orator (436-338 B. C.), who in this oration argued for the restoration of its former powers to the Court of Areopagus (so called from the place of session, Areopagus, or "Mars Hill") as a bulwark of Athenian liberty, then menaced by Philip of Macedon. The outline of *Areopagitica,* in Milton's own words, is as follows:—"First, the inventors of it [restriction of the press] to be those whom he will loath to own [i. e., Roman Catholics]; next, what is to be thought in general of reading, whatever sort the books be; and that this order avails nothing to the suppressing of scandalous, seditious, and libellous books, which were mainly intended to be suppressed; last, that it will be primely to the discouragement of all learning and the stop of truth."

11.—3. **thereafter,** i. e., after they have shown themselves to be bad books.—10. **dragon's teeth:** Jason, directed by Medea, sowed the teeth of the dragon of Colchis, and from them sprang up armed men, (see Ovid's *Metamorphoses,* VII. 121 ff., and William Morris's *Life and Death of Jason,* VIII.).—15. **in the eye,**

i. e., in the reason, man's mental eye.—26. **impression**=edition.—27. **an elemental life,** i. e., a life inhering in the four material elements of medieval physics (Hot, Cold, Moist, and Dry), in distinction from the fifth element, which was ethereal and the very essence of the thing (cf. "quintessence").

12.—7. **those confused seeds:** Venus, enraged with Psyche for having won the love of Cupid, set her the task of sorting a heap of many kinds of seeds, the whole to be done before evening; compassionate ants did it for her (see Apuleius, *The Golden Ass*, Books IV.-VI., for the whole story of Cupid and Psyche).—19. **wayfaring**=traveling along the way; cf. "thoroughfare." (Professor Hales reads "warfaring," on the strength of a written correction of the "y" to "r" in a copy presented by Milton to a friend; whether the correction is in Milton's hand is uncertain. "Warfaring," as Professor Hales says, implies a more active resistance to evil; but "wayfaring" goes better with the figure of a race, in the next sentence, which was perhaps suggested by it.)—28. **blank**=colorless, neutral.—31. **Scotus or Aquinas:** famous schoolmen of the thirteenth century.—32. **Guyon:** *The Faerie Queene*, Book II.

13.—16. **professors,** i. e., professors of religion; here, as often, it means the Puritans, because of their strict and often loud professions of godliness.—17. **lay Papist:** Milton implies that the ignorant laity had more faith in Papist superstitions than the clergy had.—**Loretto:** an Italian town, where were supposed to be the walls (moved from Palestine by angels) of the house in which the Virgin Mary lived.—20. **mysteries**=occupations, trades (Lat. *ministerium*, "occupation").

14.—14. **Alcoran**=the Koran, or Mohammedan Bible.—19. **prelates:** archbishops and bishops of the English church, which the Independents thought too like the Church of Rome.—29. **Typhon:** brother or son of Osiris, the Egyptian god; he dismembered Osiris and threw the pieces into the Nile; Isis, sister and wife of Osiris, sought the pieces far and wide, and whenever she found one buried it.

15.—2. **feature**=shape (Lat. *factura*, "anything made," "a work").—8. **combust:** an old astronomical term, applied to planets when near the sun.—18. **economical**=domestic.—19. **Zuinglius:** a Swiss religious reformer (1484-1531), one of the founders of Protestantism.—26. **Syntagma**=handbook, summary (literally, "collection").—37. **ingenious**=possessed of great intellectual capacity, having genius.—38. **invent**=find out, discover (Lat. *invenire*, "to come upon").—**discourse**=argue, reason.

16.—5-6. **Pythagoras . . . the Persian wisdom:** even if there is any truth in the old tradition that Greek and Persian philosophers learned wisdom from the British druids, it is aside from the point, for the ancient Britons were a totally different people from the English, who did not come to England until the fifth century A. D.; the same remark applies to the reference to Agricola.—10. **Transylvanian:** Transylvania, afterwards a part of Hungary, was then independent.—12. **Hercynian wilderness:** a rather vaguely defined mountainous region between Germany and Russia.—21. **Wiclif:** John Wiclif (1324?-1384), an English religious reformer, sometimes called "the morning-star of the

Reformation"; he denied the doctrine of transubstantiation and renounced his allegiance to the Pope; see pp. 347-349 for extracts from his translation of the Bible.—23. **Huss:** John Huss (1369-1415), a Bohemian religious reformer and disciple of Wiclif; he condemned the sale of indulgences, and was burned at the stake for heresy.—**Jerome:** Jerome of Prague (1365?-1416), a follower of Huss; he was burned at the stake for heresy.—26. **demeaned**=managed.—27-28. **of whom,** i. e., of those whom.—37. **mansion house**=dwelling-house, home, of some largeness and grandeur (Lat. *manere*, "to stay").

17.—14. **the fields are white:** *John* iv. 35.—17. **fantastic**=fanciful.—34. **Pyrrhus:** king of Epirus, Greece, who defeated the Romans at Heraclea, 280 B. C.—35. **Epirots**=men of Epirus.—38. **sectaries**=sectarians, members of a sect.

18.—15-16. **Moses . . . . glorious wish:** *Num.* xi. 29.—27. **maniples**=small bodies of soldiers.

19.—7. **derives**=extends.—9-10. **when Rome was nigh besieged by Hannibal:** during the second Punic War (218-202 B. C.).—15. **to**=as to.—16. **pertest**=liveliest, most agile; cf. "the pert and nimble spirit of mirth" (*A Midsummer-Night's Dream*, I. i. 13).—18. **sprightly:** used adverbially, modifying "up."—26. **methinks**=it seems to me (O. E. *thyncan*, "to appear"; a different word from *thencan*, "to think")—29. **mewing**=renewing by changing her feathers (Lat. *mutare*, "to change").—32. **noise of birds:** figurative for "noisy birds."—**flocking:** because afraid to fly alone, as Puritan England is doing.—38. **engrossers**=monopolizers (from the practice of buying merchandise in gross, or large quantities, in order to get a monopoly; here the reference is to the press-censors).

20.—27-28. **for cote and conduct and his four nobles of Danegelt:** "to resist illegal taxation for clothing and conveyance [="conduct"] of troops and also for the provision of a navy. . . . *Danegelt*=Dane-money, was the name of an ancient land-tax levied to provide means for bribing off or for repelling the Danes. . . . Upon this highly dubious precedent the King's [Charles I.'s] advisers greatly relied in their advocacy and exaction of ship-money" (*Areopagitica*, ed. by J. W. Hales, Oxford, 1894).—35. **controversal**=turned in opposite directions; Janus had two faces, one looking east and the other west.—36. **Set open:** the temple of Janus, at Rome, was open only in time of war; Milton refers to the battle then raging between Truth and Falsehood.

21.—6-7. **discipline of Geneva:** the ecclesiastical system of the Presbyterians, who followed the teachings of John Calvin of Geneva.—11. **the Wise Man:** Solomon; *Prov.* ii. 1-4.—15. **equipage**=equipment.—16. **battle**=army.—19. **dint:** apparently used in the literal sense of "blow"; cf. the martial figure throughout the passage.—29. **Proteus:** a Greek sea-god, who could turn himself into many shapes; cf. "Protean."—32. **Micaiah, etc.:** 1 *Kings* xxii. 15-18.—37-38. **ordinances,** etc.: "Blotting out the handwriting of ordinances that was against us, . . . nailing it to his cross" (*Col.* ii. 14).

22.—8. **linen decency:** "the shallow decorum of surplices and vestments" (Hales); the reference is to the ritual of the Church of England and to its ideals of uniformity in religion.—12-13. **we care not to keep**=we care not if we keep, i. e., we are careless about it.—17. **wood and hay and stubble,** etc.: 1 *Cor.* iii. 12.—19. **subdichotomies**=minor divisions.—34. **neighboring**=near, comparatively slight.—37. **unity of spirit,** etc.: *Eph.* iv. 3.

23.—31. **old Convocation house:** the Convocation of the English Church had been held in the chapter-house at Westminster; the Presbyterian Assembly of Divines now met in Henry VII.'s chapel, Westminster.

24.—1. **his liege tombs,** i. e., the tombs of his lieges.

SIR THOMAS BROWNE.

VANITY OF EARTHLY MONUMENTS.

25.—**Hydriotaphia**=urn-burial (Grk. ὑδρία, "water-pot," "urn," and ταφή, "burial").—1. **These dead bones:** "In a field of Old Walsingham [in Norfolk], not many months past were digged up between forty and fifty urns, . . . some containing two pounds of bones, distinguishable in skulls, ribs, jaws, thigh bones and teeth. . . . That these were the urns of the Romans, from the common custom and place where they were found, is no obscure conjecture, not far from a Roman garrison" (*Hydriotaphia,* Chap. II.).—2. **in a yard underground:** Browne says the urns were buried "not a yard deep."—3. **thin walls of clay,** i. e., the clay urns.—**specious**=extremely fair or showy (Lat. *species,* "form," "appearance"; cf. "sightly").—5. **three conquests:** the English in the fifth century, the Danish in the ninth and tenth centuries, the Normans in the eleventh century.—6. **diuturnity**=long duration.—7. "*Sic ego,*" etc.="Thus I should wish to be buried when I am turned to bones" (Tibullus, *Elegies,* III. 2, 26).—10. **visible conservatories:** such as tombs and monuments.—16. **propension**=inclination, desire for reunion with.—24. **Archimedes:** a famous Greek geometrician (287 ?-212 B. C.).—25. **counters**=round pieces of metal or other material, used in reckoning; cf. *Troilus and Cressida,* II. ii. 28-29: "will you with counters sum the past proportion of his infinite?"—**Moses his man**=Moses's man; *Ps.* xc. 10: "The days of our years are three score years and ten."

26.—1. **one little finger,** i. e., a century; in an old system of counting on the fingers, crooking the right little finger signified a hundred.—10. **Alcmena's nights:** when Zeus visited Alcmena, who became by him the mother of Hercules, he delayed the rising of the sun and made the night thrice as long as usual.—19. **the persons of these ossuaries,** i. e., the persons whose bones are in these urns (Low Lat. *ossuarium,* "a receptacle for the bones of the dead").—21. **wide solution,** i. e., a solution with wide limits.—25. **the provincial guardians:** the spirits guarding the province, or region, where the bones were buried.—**tutelary observators:** guardian watchers of the dead.—35. **Atropos:** the Fate who cuts the thread of human life.

27.—6-8. **the prophecy of Elias,** etc.: there was a Jewish tradition that Elijah, or Elias, prophesied that the world would end two thousand years after the coming of the Messiah; Charles the Fifth, king of Spain and emperor of the Holy Roman Empire, died in 1558; therefore, if the world is to end in 2000 A. D., Charles cannot be remembered on earth more than five hundred years, or two thousand years (twice Methuselah's age) less than Hector's fame had already lasted.—13. **Janus:** see note on **20,** 34; here Browne thinks of the god's two faces as looking to the long past and to the short future of the world.—27. **mortal right-lined circle,** i. e., death; Θ, the first letter of θτοάνας, the Greek word for "death," which came to be used on ancient tombstones as a sign for death, may be described as made up of a circle and a right, or straight, line.—34. **Gruter:** a Dutch scholar (1560-1627), editor of a book of Roman inscriptions.

28.—3. **Cardan:** an Italian mathematician and astrologer (1501-1576); he wrote in his autobiography, "Cuperem notum esse quod sim, non opto ut sciatur qualis sim" ("I could desire it to be known that I am, I do not wish it to be known what I am"). —7. **entelechia**=complete, actual being (in distinction from merely latent, potential being).—8. **exceeds,** i. e., better than. 9-10. **Canaanitish woman . . . Herodias:** *Matt.* xv. 22-28, and xiv. 6-11.—11. **good thief . . . Pilate:** *Luke* xxiii.—13. **to**=as to.—17. **Adrian's:** Adrian, or Hadrian, the Roman emperor (76-138 A. D.), erected a pillar, with an epitaph, to a favorite horse; his own *moles*, or mausoleum, a huge circular tower on the banks of the Tiber, in Rome, was remodeled and put to other uses; the inscription to him, however, still remains in the interior, but it had not been discovered in Browne's day.—19. **Thersites:** a deformed scoffer and reviler among the Greeks at the siege of Troy.—26. **hired**=bribed.—33. **current arithmetic:** the arithmetic of current, or "running," time.—35. **Lucina:** the goddess who presided over child-birth.—37. **right descensions:** an astronomical term, signifying here, like "winter arches," that the sun does not go through the zenith but traverses a shorter arc nearer the horizon.

29.—1. **light in ashes:** "According to the custom of the Jews, who place a lighted wax-candle in a pot of ashes by the corpse" (Leo).—18. **subsistency**=continued existence.—28. **contriving their bodies in sweet consistencies,** i. e., contriving for their bodies a sweet rigidity and permanence by the use of embalming gums and spices.—29. **vanity**=emptiness, i. e., futility. —31. **Cambyses:** Cambyses III., son of Cyrus the Great, conquered Egypt in the sixth century B. C.—32. **Mummy is become merchandise,** etc.: a substance supposed to be made of mummies was in Browne's day sold as medicine.—**Mizraim:** the Hebrew name for Egypt.

30.—5. **perspectives**=telescopes (Lat. *perspicere*, "to look through").—6. **with Phaeton's favor,** i. e., if Phaeton would drive the chariot of the sun near the earth, as he did in the old Greek myth.—17. **only:** the word goes with "Who."—24. **bravery** =show, splendor.—**infamy:** Southey conjectured that Browne wrote "infimy" (Lat. *infimus*), i. e., lowness, inferiority; this reading harmonizes better with the context, in which the reference is not to the moral qualities of man, but to his mortality.— 29. **Sardanapalus:** king of Assyria in the seventh century B. C., who, besieged by rebels in his palace, chose to die on a pyre of precious woods and spices heaped about his throne; see Byron's *Sardanapalus*, Act V.—33. **Gordianus:** a Roman Emperor who was killed in 244 A. D. while warring against Persia; an inscription in Greek, Latin, Hebrew, Egyptian, and Arabic, was placed on the monument erected to his memory at the spot where he died, but it was erased in less than a century by the Emperor Licinius, who claimed relationship with the murderer.—34. **man of God,** etc.: Deut. xxxiv. 6.

31.—3. **decretory term**=decreed ending.—16. **Alaricus:** the Goth, who sacked Rome in 410 A. D. (" By the labor of a captive multitude they forcibly diverted the course of the Busentinus, a small river that washed the walls of Consentia [in southern Italy]. . The royal sepulchre, adorned with the splendid spoils and trophies of Rome, was constructed in the vacant bed; the waters were then restored to their natural channel; and the secret spot . . . was forever concealed by the inhuman massacre of the prisoners who had been employed to execute the work."—Gibbon's *Decline and Fall of the Roman Empire*, Chap. 31.) 17. **Sylla:** Sulla, the Roman dictator, who died in 78 B. C.; by his bloody deeds he incurred the lasting hatred of millions of his countrymen.—23. **taunt of Isaiah:** *Isa.* xiv. 10-17.—30. **angles of contingency:** angles formed by tangents to a curve at consecutive points; they are infinitesmal.—35-36. **Christian annihilation,** etc.: Christian mysticism, in which the soul, while still on earth, transcends the limits of individuality and rapturously mingles with the Infinite Soul: thus " annihilation " refers to the destruction of individual existence, as when a drop of water is annihilated as a separate drop and melts into the sea; " ecstasies " apparently has both the meaning of " raptures " and of " standing-out-of (Grk. ἐκ and στάσις), i. e., escape from the limits of finite being; " exolution " (Lat. *exsolutum*, " freed from," " released ") and " liquefaction " express much the same thought; the " spouse," is Christ, the heavenly bridegroom; " gustation "=tasting.

32.—4. **predicament of chimæras,** i. e., in the state or class of fabulous creatures, talked of but hardly believed in—mere fables and myths.—9. **St. Innocent's churchyard:** " in Paris, where bodies soon consume " (Wilkin).—13-14. " **tabesne,**" etc.= " Whether decay or the funeral pyre consumes dead bodies, matters not " (Lucan, *Pharsalia*, VII. 809-810).

JOHN DRYDEN.

PREFACE TO THE FABLES.

34.—2. **Sandys:** George Sandys, a part of whose translation of Ovid's *Metamorphoses* was made in Virginia, where he lived as Colonial treasurer in 1621-1624.—16. **Godfrey of Bulloigne:** another name for *Jerusalem Delivered*, by Tasso (1544-1595), the Italian epic poet.

35.—2. **Hobbes:** Thomas Hobbes (1588-1679), an English philosopher, who made much of the association of ideas.—3. **Boccace**

=Boccaccio (1313-1375), the Italian novelist and poet, author of the *Decameron*.—19. **Provençal:** the language of Provence, formerly a province in southeastern France; Dryden is in error, the French dialect which influenced English in Chaucer's day being that of Paris.

37.—7. **"Versus inopes,"** etc.="Verses devoid of substance, and melodious trifles" (Horace, *De Arte Poetica*, 322).—11. **a religious lawyer:** Jeremy Collier, in his *Short View of the Immorality and Profaneness of the English Stage* (1698).

38.—34. **were:** an error for "was."

39.—6. **"Impiger,"** etc.: Horace, *De Arte Poetica*, 121.—9. **"quo fata,"** etc.="Where the fates drag us back and forth, let us follow" (*Æneid*, V. 709).—17. **Longinus:** a Greek critic (210 ?-273 A. D.), to whom is attributed a famous treatise on the Sublime.—22. **machine:** the reference is to Iris going as a messenger from Zeus to the Trojans, to rouse them to battle (*Iliad*, II. 768 ff.); such supernatural agency in a poem was called the "machinery."

40.—6. **Persius:** a Roman satiric poet (34-62 A. D.).—7. **Manilius:** an obscure Roman poet, who lived probably at the time of Augustus; he left a poem, *Astronomica*.—15. **Grizild**=Griselda; the subject of *The Clerk's Tale* in Chaucer; Dryden errs—the story was really taken by Petrarch from Boccaccio.—31. **The Cock and the Fox**=*The Nonne Preestes Tale*.

41.—13. **Ennius:** one of the earliest Latin poets; he died in 169 B. C., nearly 200 years before Ovid.—28. **"inopem me,"** etc.= "Power has made me powerless" (Ovid, *Metamorphoses*, III. 466). —32. **Bartholomew Fair:** a play by Ben Jonson (1573-1637).—36. **machines**=contrivances, devices.

42.—3. **had**=would have.—12. **turn of words:** repetition of words, with slight variations; see **87**, 30, **88**, 3-9.—33. **one of our late great poets:** Abraham Cowley (1618-1667).

43.—14. **nimis poeta**="too much a poet"; the passage referred to is in Martial (*Epigrams*, III. xliv.), not in Catullus.—17-18. **"auribus,"** etc.="accommodated to the ears of that time"; the words (says Mr. Christie, in the Globe edition of Dryden's poems) are a misquotation of a phrase in Tacitus's *Dialogue on Orators*. —23-34. The reference is to a reprint of Thomas Speght's edition of Chaucer, in 1687; throughout the passage Dryden is unjust to Chaucer's versification because, like most of his contemporaries, he is ignorant of the correct pronunciation of Middle English.—30. **verse which we call heroic:** the pentameter couplet, used in the so-called "heroic plays" that were popular in Dryden's day.

44.—13. **admired**=wondered at.—26. **Piers Plowman:** not Langland's poem, but a spurious Canterbury tale.

45.—11. **Scandalum Magnatum**="offense against the great"; an old law term.—23. **a king of England and an archbishop of Canterbury:** Henry II. (1133-1189) and Thomas à Becket.—33. **Prior læsit**="He hurt (me) first."

46.—16. **Baptista Porta:** an Italian physiognomist (1543?-1615).

47.—19-20. **"Totum hoc,"** etc.="All this I wish unsaid."—25. The lines as quoted by Dryden afford an additional reason for his poor opinion of Chaucer's verse; the text he used was very corrupt, as may be seen by comparison with some of the same lines as given in Skeat's edition of Chaucer (Oxford, 1894):—

"For this ye knowen al-so wel as I,
Who-so shal telle a tale after a man,
He moot reherce, as ny as ever he can,
Everich a word, if it be in his charge,
Al speke he never so rudeliche and large."

49.—27. **Milbourn:** see **53,** 17.

50.—9-11. "**Multa renascentur,**" etc.: Horace, *De Arte Poetica,* 70-72; Ben Jonson translates:—

"Much phrase that now is dead shall be revived,
And much shall die that now is nobly lived,
If custom please; at whose disposing will
The power and rule of speaking resteth still."

51.—11. "**Facile est,**" etc.: "It is easy to add to what has already been invented."—17. **de Scudery:** a French novelist (1607-1701).

52.—16. **argument**=subject, theme.—23. **Palamon and Arcite** =*The Knightes Tale.*—30. **action:** Dryden loosely uses the word for two things, (1) the action of an epic poem in general, as to the duration of which Aristotle in his *Poetics* laid down no law, (2) the action in *Palamon and Arcite,* the main events of which fill only a year, the other six years or so being passed over lightly. 33. **laurel:** Chaucer, like Dryden, was poet laureate.

53.—1-3. "**Dioneo,**" etc.="Dioneo and the grand lady Fiametta sang together of Arcite and Palamon."

54.—14. **Arthurs,** i. e., Doctor Blackmore's two epics, *Prince Arthur* and *King Arthur.*—19-20. **Dares,** etc.: *Æneid,* V. 400 ff.; Dryden translates:—

"He said: and, rising at the word, he threw
Two pond'rous gauntlets down, in open view—
Gauntlets which Eryx wont in fight to wield,
And sheathe his hands with, in the listed field.
With fear and wonder seiz'd, the crowd beholds
The gloves of death, with seven distinguish'd folds
Of tough bull-hides: the space within is spread
With iron, or with loads of heavy lead.
Dares himself was daunted at the sight,
Renounc'd his challenge, and refused to fight."

55.—7. **Condé:** the great French general's drawn battle with the Dutch, at Senneffe, in 1674, was doubtless still fresh in the memory of Dryden's readers.—8-9. "**ab abuso,**" etc.="from abuse to use is not a valid consequence."—15-16. "**Demetri,**" etc.: **Horace,** *Satires,* I. x. 90-91:—"Demetrius, and you, Tigellius, I bid whine among the easy chairs of your female disciples."

JONATHAN SWIFT.

THE BATTLE OF THE BOOKS.

This satire was begun in 1697, when Swift was private secretary to Sir William Temple. It was occasioned by a controversy among the learned over the relative merits of ancient and of modern authors and over the genuineness of *The Letters of Phalaris*, purporting to be written by the Sicilian tyrant Phalaris in the sixth century B. C. Temple, replying to a French work, in *An Essay upon the Ancient and Modern Learning* (1692) had argued for the superiority of the ancient and for the genuineness of the *Letters*. William Wotton in *Reflections on Ancient and Modern Learning* (1694) took the position that in certain respects, particularly in science, the moderns had beaten the ancients. In 1695 a new edition of *The Letters of Phalaris* appeared, edited by a young scholar, Charles Boyle, who in his preface attacked the great classical scholar, Richard Bentley, librarian of the King's Library in St. James's Palace, London, for his alleged discourtesy in not allowing sufficient time to examine a manuscript of the *Letters*. In an appendix to the second edition of Wotton's book, in 1697, Bentley replied roughly to Boyle, and gave proof of the spuriousness of the *Letters*. At this point Swift came to the aid of his patron Temple with *The Battle of the Books*, which, although worthless as argument, doubtless soothed the feelings of Temple by its vigorous ridicule of his opponents.

58.—36. **their representatives,** i. e., their title-pages.

59.—5. **inform**=animate.—8. **brutum hominis:** a kind of lower soul, with something earthy about it and reluctant to forsake its fleshly habitation; cf. *Comus*, 463-475, and Plato's *Phædo*, § 81.—18. **chains:** in old libraries the books were chained to the shelves to prevent theft.—19. **Scotus:** Duns Scotus, the famous Scotch dialectician and theologian of the thirteenth century.

60.—17-18. **two of the ancient chiefs:** Phalaris and Aesop, whose reputed works Bentley declared spurious.

61.—8. **Seven Wise Masters:** a collection of Eastern tales.

62.—28. **fortification:** the advocates of modern learning argued that the modern art of fortification was superior to the ancient.—37. **expatiating**=walking about.

63.—7. **his subjects:** according to one interpretation "**Beelzebub**" means "god of flies."

65.—24. **turned himself to a thousand forms:** an allusion to Æsop's animal fables.

67.—5. **horse,** i. e., epic poets.—7. **Wither:** a minor poet (1588-1667), little esteemed in Swift's day; Swift doubtless took peculiar pleasure in coupling him with Dryden, who had said, after seeing some of Swift's verses, "Cousin Swift, you will never be a poet." **light horse,** i. e., lyric poets.—8. **Cowley:** an English poet (1618-1667), of great contemporary fame. **Despreaux:** Boileau (1636-1711), a French poet and critic, whose repute was great among the English writers of Swift's day.—9. **bowmen,** i. e., philosophers. **Descartes, Gassendi, and Hobbes:** French and English philosophers of the seventeenth century; the praise of their flights of thought is partly satirical, for Swift had a poor opinion of philosophy.—12. **Evander:** apparently a mistake for Acestes, whose arrow, in the contest described in the *Æneid* (V. 525 ff.), took fire from the rapidity of its flight.—13. **Paracelsus:** a Swiss chemist and physician (1493-1541).—**stinkpot-flingers:** as a means of disconcerting and possibly suffocating the enemy, pots containing asafetida and other offensive materials were formerly used in war.—14. **Rhætia:** a Roman province, including part of the Tyrol, where Paracelsus spent a portion of his wandering life.—15. **dragoons,** i. e., writers on medicine and surgery.—16. **Harvey:** William Harvey (1578-1657), who discovered the circulation of the blood.—**aga**= commander; a Turkish word.—20. **heavy-armed foot,** i. e., historians.—21-22. Guicciardini, Davila, and Polydore Virgil were Italians; Mariana was a Spaniard; Buchanan, a Scotchman; Camden, an Englishman.—23. **engineers,** i. e., mathematicians. **Regiomontanus:** Johann Müller (1436-1476), a German astronomer and mathematician (called Regiomontanus from his birthplace, Königsberg). **Wilkins:** Bishop Wilkins (1614-1672), an English astronomer, one of the founders of the Royal Society.—24-25. **Scotus, Aquinas, and Bellarmine:** theologians, the first a Scotchman, the other two Italians; Scotus and Aquinas were of the thirteenth century, Bellarmine of the sixteenth.—27. **calones** =soldiers' servants; here they stand for unbound pamphlets.—28. **L'Estrange:** a journalist and pamphleteer, licenser of the press under Charles II. and James II.—33. **Hippocrates:** a Greek physician (460 ?-377 ? B. C.), the "Father of Medicine."—34. **Vossius:** a famous Dutch classical scholar (1577-1649).

68.—7. **Momus:** the Greek god of laughter and mockery; according to Hesiod (*Theogony*, 214), he was the son of Night, which is perhaps the main reason why Swift makes him the patron of the benighted Moderns, in contrast to the Ancients' patron, Pallas, goddess of wisdom and light; but there is apparently also an allusion to the supposed satiric spite of modern writers (cf. the spider's "venom" and the bee's "sweetness and light," **65,** 7, **66,** 32), and to the claim that they excel in humor.—37. **Nova Zembla:** the kind of criticism that Swift is satirizing may naturally be thought of as dwelling in polar cold and darkness; perhaps there is a reference also to the fact that most modern literature is the product of northern countries.

70.—11. **Gresham:** Gresham College, in London, where the Royal Society met. **Covent Garden:** an area in London (once a "convent" garden), which abounded in taverns and coffee-houses where the wits and writers often assembled; the famous Will's Coffee-house, where Dryden held his court as king of English letters, was in Covent Garden.

71.—18. **Galen:** a Greek physician of the second century A. D.; for centuries his authority was undisputed, but Paracelsus attacked it.—21-22. **Hic pauca desunt**=" Here a few [lines] are missing."—24-25. **Desunt nonnulla**=" Several [lines] are missing."—33. **his own vortex:** Descartes explained the formation of the universe by a theory of vortices in the matter of which it is composed.—34-35. **Ingens hiatus hic in MS.**=" A great gap here in the manuscript."

72.—3. **Gondibert:** a poem (1651) by William D'Avenant; the "staid, sober gelding" is probably the stanza, which is like that of Gray's *Elegy*.—11. **Denham:** John Denham, best known by his poem *Cooper's Hill* (1642).—16. **Wesley:** Samuel Wesley, father of John and Charles Wesley, and a small poet.—17. **Perrault:** Charles Perrault (1628-1703), a leader in France in the controversy over the relative merits of the ancients and the moderns; he collected and rewrote some charming fairy tales, including *Cinderella* and *Little Red Riding Hood.*—18. **Fontenelle:** Bernard de Fontenelle (1657-1757), another leader in the controversy in France.—38. **the lady in a lobster:** "the triturating apparatus in the stomach of a lobster;—so called from a fancied resemblance to a seated female figure" *(Webster's International Dictionary).*

73.—3-4. **Dryden, in a long harangue:** a reference to the long *Dedication* to Dryden's translation of the *Æneid.*—15-16. **Alter hiatus in MS.**="Another gap in the manuscript."—17. **Lucan:** a Roman poet (39-65 A. D.), author of a spirited but uneven epic, *Pharsalia,* on the war between Cæsar and Pompey.—20. **Blackmore:** see **54**, 9, and the note on **54**, 14.—29-30 **spurs . . . bridle:** Blackmore as a poet needed animation, and Lucan restraint.—31. **Pauca desunt**="A few [lines] are missing."—32. **Creech:** Thomas Creech (1659-1700), a translator of the classics, including Horace.—37. **Ogleby:** John Ogleby (1600-1676), a small poet and a translator of the classics; called Creech's literary father, as being a small author of the preceding generation.—38. **Oldham:** John Oldham (1653-1683), a minor satiric poet.

74.—1. **Afra:** Mrs. Afra Behn (1640-1689), a writer of somewhat loose plays and novels, and some lyric poetry.—5. **imitating:** Cowley introduced into English poetry the so-called Cowley-Pindaric ode, in very irregular metre, which was mistakenly thought to reproduce the form of Pindar's odes.—16. **given him by Venus:** Swift thought that Cowley's love poems were his best claim to immortality, but they have long been out of favor.—37-38. **Hiatus valde deflendus in MS.**="A greatly to be deplored gap in the manuscript."

75.—9. **Etesian wind:** "The term was especially applied by Greek and Roman writers to the winds which blow from the north during the summer months" *(Century Dictionary);* it is used here merely to give a classical effect.—13. **atramentous**=inky.—35. **presumptuous dogs, the Ancients:** for the sake of carrying out the satiric allegory Swift is here outrageously unfair; Bentley was a profound admirer of the ancient writers and devoted his life to the study of them.

76.—3. **Scaliger:** Julius Scaliger (1484-1558), an Italian, and Joseph Scaliger (1540-1609), his son, were both famous classical scholars; probably Swift refers to the elder, for Bentley had recently defended the younger.—23. **Aldrovandus's tomb,** i. e., the place in the library (thought of as a cemetery; see **59,** 7) where stand the books of the Italian naturalist, Ulisse Aldrovandi (1522-1605).—35. **in sphere direct,** i. e., by rays proceeding straight from their source.

77.—17. **in his bull:** the legend is that Phalaris roasted his enemies in a brazen bull.

78.—5. **to rest:** Temple had returned from political life, and was living in lettered leisure on his estate, Moor Park.—28. **the shape of ——:** the allusion is probably to Francis Atterbury, afterwards Bishop of Rochester, who wrote a good deal of Boyle's reply to Bentley, in 1698.

80.—8. **Desunt cætera**="The rest are missing."

SIR RICHARD STEELE.

THE CLUB AT "THE TRUMPET."

The Tatler was started in London by Steele, and ran from April 12, 1709, to Jan. 2, 1711, appearing on Tuesday, Thursday, and Saturday. In the dedication Steele says: "The general purpose of this paper is to expose the false arts of life, to pull off the disguises of cunning, vanity, and affectation, and to recommend a general simplicity in our dress, our discourse, and our behavior." The essay given is No. 132, published on Feb. 11, 1710.

81.—1. "**Habeo,**" etc.="I am much beholden to old age, which has increased my eagerness for conversation, in proportion as it has lessened my appetites of hunger and thirst" (translation in edition of 1764); the passage is from Marcus Tullius Cicero's *De Senectute*, XIV.—23. "**The Trumpet**": a public house in Sheer Lane, near Temple Bar.

82.—32. **bencher of the neighboring inn:** inns of courts are "incorporated legal societies in London, which have the exclusive privilege of calling candidates to the bar, and maintain instruction and examinations for that purpose" *(Century Dictionary);* a bencher was one of the governing members of an inn of court.—33. **ordinaries**=taverns.—**Charing Cross:** the site of an old market-cross, in the center of London; taverns and coffee-houses abounded there, the resorts of "men of the town." —34. **Jack Ogle:** a famous gambler and man about town in the reign of Charles II.—35. **Hudibras:** a poem (1663-1678) by Samuel Butler, satirizing the Puritans.

83.—2. **something**=somewhat.—8. **in Holland:** the new, or Gregorian, calendar was not adopted in England until 1752, long after it was in general use on the continent; it made a difference of eleven days.—18. "**a stick**" . . . "**ecclesiastic**": *Hudibras*, I. 11-12:—

> "And pulpit, drum ecclesiastic,
> Was beat with fist, instead of a stick."

19. **a red petticoat:** Ogle, when he belonged to the footguards, had pawned his trooper's cloak, and at a review carried instead his landlady's red petticoat, in a roll on the crupper; when the order was given "Cloak all!" he was detected, but not abashed, saying that, if he couldn't "cloak," he could "petticoat" with the best of them.

84.—34. **an eloquent spirit:** Belial; *Paradise Lost*, II. 112-113.

JOSEPH ADDISON.

A VERY PRETTY POET.

The essay is No. 163, published April 25, 1710.

85.—1-7. "**Idem,**" etc.="Suffenus has no more wit than a mere clown when he attempts to write verses; and yet he is never happier than when he is scribbling, so much does he admire himself and his compositions. And, indeed, this is the foible of every one of us; for there is no man living who is not a Suffenus in one thing or other" (translation in edition of 1764).—9. **Will's Coffee-house**: the various coffee-houses in London were frequented by different classes of men; Will's was a favorite resort for poets and wits.—15. **Mr. Bickerstaff:** Steele had assumed as his pseudonym in *The Tatler* the name of Isaac Bickerstaff, which Swift had adopted (taking it from a street-sign) in his mirth-provoking controversy with Partridge, an almanac-maker, in 1708 and 1709; and all the *Tatler* papers were supposed to be written by Bickerstaff.—18. **gazette:** a military gazette, containing list of deaths, promotions, etc.—19. **our armies**: the War of the Spanish Succession, in which Marlborough won great laurels, was then raging on the continent.—27. **Waller**: Edmund Waller (1606-1687), who did much to introduce a smooth regularity into English verse; see **44**, 2-4, for Dryden's opinion of him.

86.—5. **gothic**: in Addison's day "gothic" was a term of reproach nearly equivalent to "barbarous," "uncultivated," rude northern art being contrasted with the finished southern art of ancient Greece and Rome.—14. **sonnet**: in the eighteenth century almost any short lyric poem might be called a sonnet.—37. **Roscommon's Translation**: published in 1680, and much in favor with those who could not read the original.

TRUE AND FALSE HUMOR.

The Spectator appeared daily (Sunday excepted), and ran from March 1, 1711, to Dec. 6, 1712; Steele and Addison wrote most of the numbers. In 1714 a new series was begun by Addison, and ran from June 18, 1714, to Dec. 20, 1714, the paper appearing on Monday, Wednesday, and Friday. This essay is No. 35, and was published April 10, 1711.

89.—1. "**Risu,**" etc.="Nothing so foolish as the laugh of fools" (translation in the edition of 1744); the quotation, although Addison attributes it to Martial, is really from Catullus (Carmen xxxix. 16).—28. **Mr. Shadwell**: Thomas Shadwell (1642?-1692), playwright and poet laureate; Dryden satirized him unmercifully in *MacFlecknoe*, but he was not wholly lacking in wit and humor, as Addison testifies.

90.—16. **habit**=dress.—18. **merry-andrew**=clown.

91.—31. **unlucky**=mischievous.

THE VISION OF MIRZAH.

This paper is No. 159, and appeared Sept. 1, 1711.

92.—19. "**Omnem,**" etc.=*Æneid*, II. 604-606; translated in the edition of 1744 as follows:—

"The cloud, which, intercepting the clear light,
Hangs o'er thy eyes, and blunts thy mortal sight,
I will remove."

DISSECTION OF A COQUET'S HEART.

This paper is No. 281, and appeared Jan. 22, 1712.

97.—7. **Pectoribus**, etc.: *Æneid*, IV. 64; translated in the edition of 1744 as follows:—

"Anxious the reeking entrails he consults."

99.—13. **Rosamond's Bower:** there is a tradition that Henry II. built a labyrinth in which to conceal his mistress, Rosamond Clifford, from his queen, Elinor.

100.—9. **admiring**=wondering at.

DANIEL DEFOE.

AN ACADEMY FOR WOMEN.

An Essay upon Projects, from which this plan for an academy for women is taken, shows the restlessness and versatility of Defoe's intellect. It is an "essay," or attempt, to win public favor for various projects or reforms—concerning banks, highways, insurance, fools, seamen, etc.,—and at many points is surprisingly modern, as in the thoughts on the education of women.

102.—35. **persons of quality**=the nobility or gentry.

103.—3. **coin**=corner.—30. **without clergy** (="without benefit of clergy"): "originally the privilege of exemption from trial by a secular court, allowed to, or claimed by, clergymen arraigned for felony; in later times the privilege of exemption from the sentence, which, in the case of certain offences, might be pleaded on his first conviction by every one who could read" (*A New English Dictionary*).

SAMUEL JOHNSON.

SHAKESPEARE.

Johnson brought out an edition of Shakespeare's works in 1765, with a preface, from which the passages here printed are taken.

109.—22. **fable:** what is now usually called the story or plot.—24. **Hierocles:** a Neo-Platonist of the fifth century A. D., to whom used to be attributed a work called *'Ἀστεῖα*, a collection of ludicrous tales and anecdotes, like the one mentioned by Johnson; it was really the work of some unknown person of later date.

110.—15. **every other stage:** Johnson apparently is referring to modern plays only, for he must have known that in Greek tragedy "the universal agent" is not love; in lines 4-9 the same limitation should doubtless be understood.—30. **as**=according as.—31. **exorbitant**=out of its orbit; in contrast to "regular."

111.—32. **Dennis and Rymer:** John Dennis (1657-173[illegible]) and Thomas Rymer (1641-1713), small critics.—34. **Menenius:** a character in *Coriolanus*.—36. **the Danish usurper:** the king Claudius, in *Hamlet*.

113.—14-16. **Pope . . . interpolators:** "For whatever had been added . . . by the actors, or had stolen from their mouths into the written parts, were from thence conveyed into the printed text, and all stand charged upon the author" (Pope's *Preface to the Works of Shakespeare*, 1725).—16-17. **Hector quoting Aristotle:** *Troilus and Cressida*, II. ii. 163-167:—

"Paris and Troilus, you have both said well,
And on the cause and question now in hand
Have glozed, but superficially; not much
Unlike young men, whom Aristotle thought
Unfit to hear moral philosophy."

Aristotle (384-322 B. C.) lived some eight centuries after the latest date assigned to the Trojan War.—17. **Theseus and Hippolyta:** in *A Midsummer Night's Dream*, Theseus, the ancient Greek hero, and Hippolyta, queen of the fabulous Amazons, are made contemporaries with Oberon, Titania, and Robin Goodfellow, of English fairy-lore.—21-22: **pastoral . . . feudal times:** the former in Greek Arcadia, the latter in the Middle Ages.

116.—14. **Corneille:** Pierre Corneille (1606-1684), the greatest French dramatist; his early plays being severely criticised by the French Academy for irregularity of form, in his later works he conformed more closely to the "unities," which thereby gained in popular favor.—31. **dragons of Medea:** Medea, daughter of the king of Colchis, was a sorceress, and in Euripides's play of *Medea* she appears borne through the air in a chariot drawn by winged dragons.—35. **Thebes:** the capital of Bœotia, in Greece.—**Persepolis:** an ancient capital of Persia, far inland; Johnson selects two places a long way apart.

117.—14. **palace of the Ptolemies:** the residence of Cleopatra, last of the royal family of Ptolemy, in Alexandria, Egypt.—15. **Actium:** on the northwestern coast of Greece, where Octavianus and Antony fought the decisive naval battle for the headship of the Roman Empire, in 31 B. C.—19. **Pharsalia:** in Thessaly, Greece, where Cæsar defeated Pompey in 48 B. C.—**Granicus:** a small river in Asia Minor, on the banks of which Alexander the Great won his first victory over the Persians in 334 B. C.

118.—2. **Mithridates:** king of Pontus; in the Romans' third war against him he was defeated by Lucullus in 69 B. C.—17. **moves**=affects [the audience].

OLIVER GOLDSMITH.

BEAU TIBBS, A CHARACTER.

In Goldsmith's *Essays*, published in 1765, he reprinted, with some revisions, articles that had already appeared anonymously in various London periodicals. *Beau Tibbs* had come out in 1762, as Letters LIV. and LV. of *The Citizen of the World*, a series of papers in *The Public Ledger*.

123.—5-6. **temple spectacles:** spectacles having bars on the ends of the bows, to secure a firmer hold by pressure on the temples.—37. **Countess of Shoreditch:** Shoreditch is a district of London; in Goldsmith's day it was on the outskirts of the city, and for many years a great dunghill stood near; the name of the countess is meant to be suggestive of her character and her husband's.

125.—27. **Grisoni:** a Florentine painter (1700-1769), particularly skillful in portraits.—29. **an hundred,** i. e., an hundred pounds.—30. **mechanical:** like a mechanic or artisan, who works for money; hence low, vulgar.—35. **Vauxhall Gardens:** a popular resort in London, the scene of many assignations; cf. the *double entendre* in " horns," l. 36.

EDMUND BURKE.

ENGLAND AND THE FRENCH REVOLUTION.

" It may not be unnecessary to inform the reader that the following reflections had their origin in a correspondence between the author and a very young gentleman at Paris, who did him the honor of desiring his opinion upon the important transactions [the meeting of the States-General, storming of the Bastile, abolition of the privileges of the nobility and clergy, etc.] which then and ever since have so much occupied the attention of all men. An answer was written some time in the month of October, 1789; but it was kept back upon prudential considerations. This letter is alluded to in the beginning of the following sheets. It has since been forwarded to the person to whom it was addressed. The reasons for the delay in sending it were assigned in a short letter to the same gentleman. This produced on his part a new and pressing application for the author's sentiments. The author began a second and more full discussion on the subject."—From Burke's *Preface.*

127.—7. **attention to you:** the letter, if opened by the revolutionary authorities, might have endangered the recipient.—28. **the glorious Revolution:** that of 1688, by which William and Mary were seated on the throne of Great Britain, after the flight of James II.

132.—2-3. **Knight of the Sorrowful Countenance:** Don Quixote, in Cervantes's novel of that title (1605, 1615); in Part I., Book III. Chap. 8, the cracked knight freed from their chains a gang of criminals condemned to the galleys, thinking that he was doing a good deed; they turned upon their deliverer, stoned and stripped him, and fled.

133.—3-4. **the Duke de Rochefoucault's and the Archbishop of Aix's letter:** the duke's letter was a personal one to Dr. Price, occasioned by his sermon; the archbishop, as president of the National Assembly, wrote to Lord Stanhope, president of the Revolution Society, acknowledging the receipt of the society's resolution.

134.—17. **Machiavellian:** *The Prince*, by Niccolo Machiavelli (1469-1527), Italian statesman and writer, has made the author's name synonymous with shrewd and unscrupulous statecraft. —22. **Old Jewry:** a street in the centre of London; so named from a synagogue which formerly stood there.

135.—5. **philippizes:** Demosthenes accused the priestess at Delphi of " philippizing," because she gave oracles in favor of Philip of Macedon, who was threatening the liberties of Greece; Burke says that Dr. Price, similarly, is merely the mouth-piece of the politicians.—12. **the saints:** the Puritans, in the time of Cromwell, who next year executed Charles I.—17. **your league:** the Holy League (1576-1596), formed by the Roman Catholics of France to suppress the Huguenot party and elevate the Catholic house of Guise to the throne.—18. **our solemn league and covenant:** a pact, in 1643, between the reform parties of England and Scotland, in support of Presbyterianism and the rights of Parliament.

136.—25. **hortus siccus**=" dry garden," or collection of dried plants.—29-30. **Mess-Johns**=priests (a term of contempt; " Mess " is a corrupted form of " Mass "; " John," because of its frequency as a proper name, came to be used for almost anything common and cheap).—36. **former blessed times:** the time of the Puritan civil war, 1642-1646.

137.—5-6. " **Utinam,**" etc.=" Would that all the years of his cruelty he had given to trifles " (Juvenal, *Satires*, iv. 150-151); said by the Roman satirist of the Emperor Domitian, after describing an act of folly by him.

138.—9-10. " **Condo,**" etc.=" I store away and preserve, that later I may fetch them out " (Horace, *Epistles*, I. i. 12).

WILLIAM HAZLITT.

ON READING OLD BOOKS.

The essay was first printed in *The London Magazine*, February, 1821, and was republished in *The Plain Speaker*, a collection of miscellaneous essays by Hazlitt.

140.—5. **Tales of My Landlord:** Scott did not make public avowal of the authorship of his novels until February 23, 1827, at a dinner in Edinburgh, although the truth became pretty generally known a year before, upon the failure of the publishing house of Ballantyne, in which Scott was a silent partner. —7. **Lady Morgan's:** Lady Morgan (1783 ? -1859) was an Irish novelist.—8. **Anastasius:** a novel (1819) by Thomas Hope.—11. **Delphine:** a novel (1802) by Madame de Staël.—13. " **in their newest gloss** ": *Macbeth*, I. vii. 34.—17. **black-letter:** a Gothic style of letter, similar to that of modern German, used in the earliest printed books.

141.—22. **rifaccimentos**=" remakings " (Ital. *rifacimenti*, from Lat. *reficere*).

142.—6-7. " **for thoughts,**" etc.: quoted inexactly from *Hamlet*, IV. v. 175-177: " There's rosemary, that's for remembrance; pray, love, remember: and there is pansies, that's for thoughts." —11. **My father Shandy:** the elder Shandy in Sterne's *Tristram Shandy* (1759-1767).—**Bruscambille:** *Les Fantaisies de Bruscambille* (1612), by Des Lauriers; referred to in *Tristram Shandy*, Book III., Chap. 35.—12. **Peregrine Pickle:** a novel (1751) by Smollett.—13. **Tom Jones:** Fielding's greatest novel (1749).—24. " **the puppets dallying** ": *Hamlet*, III. ii. 257.—35. " **ignorance was bliss** ": Gray, *Ode on a Distant Prospect of Eton College:*—

" No more; where ignorance is bliss,
'Tis folly to be wise."

—36. **raree-show**=" a peep-show, a show carried about in a box " (" apparently contracted from 'rarity-show' ") *(Century Dictionary).*

143.—11. **Ballantyne press:** the Edinburgh printing-house which published Scott's novels.—12. **Minerva press:** a London printing-house, which published popular novels.—14. "**when I was in my father's house,**" etc.: "As I was in the days of my youth, . . . when I washed my steps with butter, and the rock poured me out rivers of oil" (*Job* xxix. 4-6).—22. **Romance of the Forest:** a very romantic and sentimental novel (1790) by Mrs. Ann Radcliffe, more generally known by her *Mysteries of Udolpho* (1794).—23. "**sweet in the mouth,**" etc.: "And I took the little book out of the angel's hand, and ate it up; and it was in my mouth sweet as honey: and as soon as I had eaten it my belly was bitter" (*Rev.* x. 10).—25-26. "**gay creatures,**" etc.: *Comus*, 298-301:—

"I took it for a faery vision
Of some gay creatures of the element,
That in the colors of the rainbow live,
And play i' the plighted clouds."

144.—1-3. Characters in Fielding's *Amelia* (1751), Smollett's *Peregrine Pickle* (1751), Sterne's *Tristram Shandy* (1759-1767), Cervantes's *Don Quixote* (1605, 1615), and Le Sage's *Gil Blas* (1715-1735.—17-18. **Chubb's Tracts:** pamphlets on political and theological subjects by Thomas Chubb (1679-1747), a deist, who was a glove-maker and a tallow-chandler at Salisbury.—26-28. "**fate, free will,**" etc.: *Paradise Lost*, II. 561-562:—

"Fixed fate, freewill, foreknowledge absolute—
And found no end, in wandering mazes lost."

—31-32. "**Would I had,**" etc.: Marlowe, *Faustus*, Scene 16.

145.—4. **New Eloise:** a romance by Rousseau (1712-1778), the French reformer and author.—16. **Social Contract:** another work by Rousseau.—18. **Confessions:** Rousseau's autobiography.—**elsewhere:** in *On the Character of Rousseau*, in Hazlitt's *Round Table*.—21. **scattered,** etc.: Wordsworth, *Stray Pleasures*:—

"Thus pleasure is spread through the earth
In stray gifts to be claimed by whoever shall find."

—23. **Emilius:** a work on education, by Rousseau.—26. **Sir Fopling Flutter:** a vain, affected character in Sir George Etherege's *The Man of Mode* (1676).

146.—1. **leurre de dupe**="decoy for a dupe"; the phrase is from Rousseau's *Confessions*.—4. "**a load to sink a navy**": *Henry VIII.*, III. ii. 383:—"a load would sink a navy."—25. "**Marcian Colonna,**" etc.: from Lamb's sonnet, *To the Author of Poems Published under the Name of Barry Cornwall; Marcian Colonna* is a poem by Byram Walter Procter (1787-1874), whose pseudonym was Barry Cornwall.—26. **Eve of St. Agnes:** published in 1820.—28-29. "**come like shadows,**" etc.: *Macbeth*, IV. i. 111.

147.—6. **the great preacher:** Edward Irving (1792-1834), Carlyle's friend; in 1822 he began to preach in a chapel in London and gained great fame.—10. "**as the hart,**" etc.: "As the hart panteth after the water brooks" (*Ps.* xlii. 1).—12. **Sorrows of Werter:** an early work (1774), full of the sentiment then popular in literature.—**Robbers:** a romantic tragedy (1781).—13. "**Giving my stock,**" etc.: *As You Like It*, II. i. 48-49:—

"giving thy sum of more
To that which had too much."

—22. **Lyrical Ballads:** by Wordsworth and Coleridge; published in 1798.—26. **Valentine, Tattle, or Miss Prue:** characters in Congreve's comedy, *Love for Love* (1695).—32. **"know my cue without a prompter"** : *Othello*, I. ii. 83-84:—

"Were it my cue to fight, I should have known it
Without a prompter."

—33. **"intus et in cute"**="inside and in the skin" (Persius, *Satires*, III. 30).

148.—14. **Richardson:** Samuel Richardson (1689-1761), author of *Clarissa Harlowe, Sir Charles Grandison*, and *Pamela*, characters from which are mentioned in ll. 20-21.—21-22. **"with every trick,"** etc.: *All's Well That Ends Well*, I. i. 106-107:—

"In our heart's table; heart too capable
Of every line and trick of his sweet favor."

—23. **Mackenzie's:** Henry Mackenzie (1745-1831), a Scottish novelist of the sentimental school.—24. Hazlitt's memory played him false; there is no such mansion in *Julia de Roubigné*.—28-29. **"that ligament,"** etc.: *Tristram Shandy*, Book VI., Chap. 10.—33. **Boccaccio:** the Italian novelist and poet (1313-1375); the story of the hawk, referred to in l. 34, is the ninth story of the fifth day of his *Decameron;* Tennyson dramatized it in *The Falcon*.—38. **Farquhar:** George Farquhar (1678-1707), one of the four principal dramatists of his day.

149.—2. **"at one proud swoop"** : *Macbeth*, IV. iii. 219:—"at one fell swoop."—7. **"with all its giddy raptures"**: Wordsworth, *Tintern Abbey*.—8. **"embalmed with odors"** : *Paradise Lost*, II. 842-843.—18-21. **"His form,"** etc.: Ibid., I. 591-594.—22-23. **"falls flat,"** etc.: Ibid., I. 460-461:—

"In his own temple, on the grunsel-edge,
Where he fell flat and shamed his worshippers."

—37. **Junius's:** "Junius" was the pseudonym of the writer of a series of famous letters against certain public men and measures, appearing in the London *Public Advertiser* during 1768-1772; they were attributed to several authors, including Burke, but the common opinion now is that they were written by Sir Philip Francis.

150.—6-8. **"he, like an eagle,"** etc.; *Coriolanus*, V. vi. 115-116:—

"like an eagle in a dove-cote, I
Fluttered your Volscians in Corioli."

—18. **Essay on Marriage:** none such is known.—26. **the tables are full:** *Macbeth*, III. iv. 46:—"The table's full."—31. **changeling:** "especially, in popular superstition, a strange, stupid, ugly child left by the fairies in place of a beautiful or charming child that they have stolen away" *(Century Dictionary)*.

151.—4. **"worthy of all acceptation":** 1 *Tim.* i. 15.—12. **Clarendon's:** Edward Hyde (1609-1674), first Earl of Clarendon, wrote a history of the rebellion against Charles I., containing admirable pen-portraits of the leaders on each side.—19. **Froissart's Chronicles:** a history, charmingly naïve and pictorial, of France, England, Scotland, and Spain, in the thirteenth century, by Jean Froissart, a Frenchman (1337-1410?).—**Holinshed:** Ralph Holinshed (died about 1580), author of *Chronicles of England, Scotland, and Ireland;* Shakespeare drew largely from him in composing his plays on English history.—20. **Stowe:** John Stowe (1525?-

1605), author of *A General Chronicle of England from Brute until the Present Year of Christ 1580,* and other historical works.—**Worthies:** *History of the Worthies of England,* by Thomas Fuller (1608-1661), an English divine.—21. **Beaumont and Fletcher:** Francis Beaumont (1584-1616) and John Fletcher (1579-1625), who wrote many plays together.—25. **Thucydides:** the Greek historian, of the fifth century B. C.; author of a *History of the Peloponnesian War.*—**Guicciardini's:** Francesco Guicciardini (1483-1540) was an Italian historian.—29. **" another Yarrow ":** Wordsworth, *Yarrow Unvisited.*

CHARLES LAMB.

NEW YEAR'S EVE.

The essay was first printed in *The London Magazine,* January, 1821.

152.—23. **" I saw the skirts,"** etc.: Coleridge, *Ode on the Departing Year;* in a later edition (Lamb quoted from the first) Coleridge changed " skirts " to " train."

153.—4. **" Welcome the coming,"** etc.: Pope, translation of the *Odyssey,* XV. 84.—19. **Alice W——n:** " identified with Ann Simmons, . . . of whom he [Lamb] wrote his love sonnets " (*The Works of Charles and Mary Lamb,* ed. by E. V. Lucas).—21. **old Dorrell:** probably a real person; a William Dorrell was a witness to the will of Lamb's father; cf. Lamb's poem *Going or Gone,* in which occur the lines,—

" And wicked old Dorrell,
'Gainst whom I've a quarrel."

154.—2. **" other me ":** apparently Lamb is translating the familiar Latin expression, *alter ego.*—8. **Christ's:** Christ's Hospital, a school in London, which Lamb attended; it was founded by Edward VI. in 1552, for children whose parents could not afford to pay for their education.—28. **conceited**=full of queer notions, or conceits.

155.—12. **" like a weaver's shuttle " :** *Job.* vii. 6:—" My days are swifter than a weaver's shuttle."—15. **reluct at**=struggle against.—26. **Lavinian shores:** a reference to Æneas (*Æneid,* I. 2-3), who, after the fall of Troy, sought a new home in Italy (" Lavinian " is from " Lavinium," the name of a city in Italy, founded, according to Virgil, by Æneas in honor of his wife Lavinia).—36. **my midnight darlings:** " I thought how natural it was in C. L. [Charles Lamb] to give a kiss to an old folio, as I once saw him do to Chapman's *Homer* " (Leigh Hunt, *My Books*).

156.—5. **" sweet assurance of a look " :** Matthew Roydon, *An Elegy* (upon Sir Philip Sidney; printed with Spenser's poems):—

" A sweet attractive kind of grace,
A full assurance given by looks."

—17-18. **that innutritious one . . . Canticles:** " We have a little sister, and she hath no breasts " (*Solomon's Song,* viii. 8).—19. **Persian:** the ancient Persians were sun-worshipers.—27. **Friar John:** a fighting and swearing friar in the *Gargantua* of François

Rabelais (1495?-1553), the great French humorist and satirist.—35-36. **"lie down with kings and emperors in death"**: "For now should I have lain still and been quiet, I should have slept: then had I been at rest, with kings and counsellors of the earth" (*Job*, iii. 13-14); some editors think that there is also an echo from Lamb's favorite Sir Thomas Browne (see **26**, 20-21), but the resemblance is not close; a passage in Bryant's *Thanatopsis*, which Lamb might have seen (it was published in *The North American Review* in 1817, and in book form in 1821) although probably he had not, is much more like:—

"nor could'st thou wish
Couch more magnificent. Thou shalt lie down
With patriarchs of the infant world—with kings."

—37-38. **"so shall the fairest face appear"**: *William and Margaret*, by David Mallet (1705 ?-1765), a Scotch poet.

157.—13. **Mr. Cotton**: Charles Cotton (1630-1687), poet, translator of Montaigne's *Essays*, and writer of the second part of Walton's *Complete Angler*.

158.—30. **magnanimity**=large-mindedness.—35. **Helicon**: on Mount Helicon, in Greece, sacred to the Muses, were two fountains, whose water was supposed to give poetic inspiration.—36. **Spa**=mineral spring (from Spa, in Belgium, where is a celebrated spring).

A DISSERTATION UPON ROAST PIG.

The essay first appeared in *The London Magazine*, September, 1822.

159.—1. **My friend M.**: Thomas Manning, who lived in China for some years. In a letter to Bernard Barton, the Quaker poet, dated March 11, 1823, Lamb says, speaking of the essay, "The idea of the discovery of roasting pigs I also borrowed, from my friend Manning." An Italian poem, *Gli Elogi del Porco* ("The Praises of the Pig") published in 1761, a copy of which, it is said, was in Lamb's library, contains many verbal resemblances to the essay. Wherever Lamb got the hint, he evidently worked it up freely in his own way.

162.—17. **Locke**: John Locke (1632-1704), the greatest English philosopher of his day.—30. **mundus edibilis**="world of eatables."—31. **princeps obsoniorum**="the chief of viands."—33. **hobbydehoys**=a youth halfway between boyhood and manhood.—35. **amor immunditiæ**="love of dirt."

163.—20-21. **radiant jellies—shooting stars**: apparently a reference to the old superstition that jellies were deposited by shooting stars.—27. **conversation**=behavior.—29-30. **"Ere sin,"** etc.: Coleridge's *Epitaph on an Infant;* Lamb substituted "timely" for "friendly."—34-35. **and for such a tomb**, etc.: Lucas compares Milton's *On Shakespeare*:—

"And so sepulchred in such pomp dost lie
That kings for such a tomb would wish to die."

164.—25. **"tame villatic fowl"**: *Samson Agonistes*, 1695.—29. **"give everything"**: *Lear*, II. iv. 253:—"I gave you all."

165.—26. **nice**=particular.—29. **discipline**=severe intellectual training, such as that given by the hair-splitting disputations of the medieval schoolmen.—37. **St. Omer's:** a Catholic college in France; Lamb fables in saying he was there, for the pleasure of fabling or to conceal the identity of " Elia "—or for both reasons.

POOR RELATIONS.

The essay first appeared in *The London Magazine*, May, 1823.

166.—23. **a death's head at your banquet:** an Egyptian custom. **Agathocles' pot:** a pot was an unwelcome sight to Agathocles, tyrant of Sicily (317-289 B. C.), because it reminded him of his lowly origin as the son of a potter.—24. **a Mordecai in your gate:** *Esther*, iii. 1-2, v. 11-13. **a Lazarus at your door:** *Luke*, xvi. 20.—25-26. **lion . . . frog . . . fly . . . mote:** *Prov.* xxvi. 13; *Ex.* viii. 3; *Eccl.* x. 1.; *Matt.* vii. 3.—27. **the one thing not needful:** *Luke* x. 42.—

167.—16. **tide-waiter:** apparently used here in the sense of one who waits for something lucky to turn up (literally, a custom-house officer who waits for the arrival of ships, and enforces the revenue laws).

168.—13. **humorist**=an eccentric person.—14. **affects**=chooses. —35. **in the play:** *The Confederacy* (1705) by John Vanbrugh.

169.—9. **Poor W.:** Lamb, in the Key to the essays, says that W. was a real person, one Favel.—20. **blue clothes:** the boys at Christ's Hospital had to wear a conspicuous uniform, consisting of a long blue coat and yellow stockings.—28. **servitor's gown:** a servitor was "formerly, at Oxford University, an undergraduate who was partly supported by the college funds, who was distinguished by peculiar dress, and whose duty it was to wait at table on the fellows and gentlemen commoners" *(Century Dictionary)*.—29. **Nessian venom:** Hercules slew Nessus, the centaur, with a poisoned arrow, and was himself poisoned by a shirt steeped in the centaur's envenomed blood.—30. **Latimer:** Hugh Latimer (1485 ?-1555), a powerful preacher and reformer; he had been a sizar (equivalent to a servitor at Oxford) in Cambridge University; see **354** for an extract from one of his sermons.—31. **Hooker:** Richard Hooker (1554 ?-1600), author of *Ecclesiastical Polity*, had been a servitor at Oxford; see **359** for an extract from him.

170.—32 **artist Evangelist**=Luke; there is an old tradition that he was a painter, and a nearly obliterated picture of the Madonna, painted on wood, now preserved in one of the churches at Rome, is attributed to him.—36-37. **" knew his mounted sign —and fled "** : *Paradise Lost*, IV. 1013-1015:—

" The Fiend looked up, and knew
His mounted scale aloft: nor more; but fled
Murmuring; and with him fled the shades of Night."

171.—2. **St. Sebastian:** taken by assault by Wellington, in 1813, in the war with Napoleon.—25. **Tower:** the Mint is on Tower Hill, near the Tower of London, the historic state-prison.

172.—3. **Grotiuses:** Hugo Grotius (1583-1645), the great Dutch authority on international law, wrote *De Jure Belli et Pacis* (" Concerning the Law of War and Peace ").

WALTER SAVAGE LANDOR.

PETRARCH ATTENDS THE PARISH CHURCH.

The selection is taken from *The Pentameron*, Third Day's Interview.

Francesco Petrarch (1304-1374) is visiting Giovanni Boccaccio (1313-1375), who is ill, at his residence near Certaldo, a town a few miles from Florence.

174.—1. **Messer**=Master.—5. **Ser**: an abbreviated form of "Messer."—8. **missal**=mass-book.—16. **two beans**: a proverbial expression for a small quantity.—18. **semplicetta**: about equivalent to "my good girl" (cf. l. 27).—21. **Monsignore**="My Lord"; used of or to one of the higher ecclesiastics, probably here the bishop.

175.—35. **bestiaccia**="nasty beast."—36. **poco garbato**="little agreeable."—37. **bastone**=staff.

176.—5. **Canonico:** Petrarch was a canon of the Church.—24. **Riveritissimo**="Most Reverend."—27. "**Gnor**": abbreviation of "Signor" ("Sir"), a title above Simplizio's station.

177.—31. **cittadinanza**: a collective term for "citizens"; here it means the women of the middle class. **villeggiatura**: a collective term for "country sports."

178.—11. **crowned in the Capitol:** as poet laureate, in 1341, at Rome.—30. **Padrone**="Master"; the reference here is to Boccaccio.

179.—12. **quattrino**=a farthing.

THOMAS DE QUINCEY.

LEVANA AND OUR LADIES OF SORROW.

This paper appeared in *Blackwood's Magazine*, June, 1845, as one of a series of similar papers; the title for the whole series (which he never completed) was *Suspiria de Profundis* ["Sighs from the Depths"]: *being a sequel to the Confessions of an English Opium-Eater.*

181.—25. "**foundation**": students on the foundation, or endowment, received aid from the funds of the college.

182.—1. **arras**=tapestries, hung on the walls of rooms (from "Arras," the name of the French city where they were first made).

183.—14. **Rachel weeping:** *Jer.* xxxi. 15.—16. **Bethlehem:** *Matt.* ii. 16-18.

184.—3. **Czar:** Nicholas I. (1796-1855), whose daughter Alexandra, nineteen years old, died in August, 1844.—31. **Pariah**=an outcast (the Pariahs are low-caste Hindus and shunned by the higher castes as unclean).—32. **Norfolk Island**: an island in the South Pacific, used by England as a penal settlement.

185.—17. **tents of Shem**: the phrase occurs in *Gen.* ix. 27; Shem, Noah's oldest son, was supposed to be the ancestor of the Semitic race, and De Quincey refers to the nomadic members of that race, such as the Arabs.—26. **turreted like that of Cybele:** Cybele was sometimes regarded as the goddess of town-life and as such wore a crown fashioned like a turreted city wall.

LITERATURE OF KNOWLEDGE AND LITERATURE OF POWER.

This famous passage is part of a review of the poetry of Pope, published in *The North British Review,* August, 1848.

188.—10. **discursive understanding:** the logical, reasoning faculty, which arrives at truth by a process of thought, in distinction from intuition, or the higher reason, which sees truth face to face; De Quincey borrowed the distinction from German philosophy.—17. **iris**=rainbow; white light, passing through moisture (cf. "humid light," l. 16), may be refracted into the colors of the rainbow.

189.—18. **Jacob's ladder:** *Gen.* xxviii. 12.

190.—4. **epopee**=epic.—29. **quamdiu bene se gesserit**="as long as it bore itself well."—34. **Principia:** the full title is *Philosophiæ Naturalis Principia Mathematica* ("The Mathematical Principles of Natural Philosophy"); the work was published in 1687.

191.—1. **La Place:** Pierre La Place (1749-1827), a French astronomer and mathematician.—6. **nominis umbra**="shadow of a name."—17. **Praxiteles . . . Michael Angelo**=the sculptures of the Greek Praxiteles (fourth century B. C.) are characterized by beauty and grace, those of Michael Angelo (1475-1564) by power; apparently De Quincey selected two unlike artists, intentionally, to make his point the clearer.

THOMAS CARLYLE.

BIOGRAPHY.

This essay, preliminary to a review of Croker's edition of Boswell's life of Samuel Johnson, first appeared in *Fraser's Magazine,* April, 1832.

192.—4. **"The proper study of mankind is man":** Pope, *An Essay on Man,* II. 1.

194.—14. **Big-endian,** etc.: an allusion to the Lilliputians' dispute, in *Gulliver's Travels,* as to which end of an egg should be broken before eating it.—20. **"Temple of Immensity":** Carlyle quotes the phrase from his own *Sartor Resartus* (Book III., Chap. 1.), which was still in manuscript.—29-30. **"History,"** etc.: Carlyle quotes from his own essay *On History,* published in *Fraser's Magazine,* November, 1830.—35. **"Philosophy teaching by experience":** a favorite phrase at the time.

195.—36. **Minerva Press:** see note on **143,** 12.

196.—24. **Friar Bacon's Oracle:** Roger Bacon (1214 ?-1294), a philosopher and scientist in advance of his age, one of whose works, *De Secretis Operibus Naturæ* ("On the Secret Works of Nature") contained some remarkable predictions.

197.—2-3. Professor Sauerteig ("Sour-Dough") and his book are characteristic inventions of Carlyle; cf. Teufelsdröckh in *Sartor Resartus*.

198.—25. **Epigoniad:** a poem (1757), sometimes called "the Scotch *Iliad*," by William Wilkie, on an old Greek story.—26. **Lusiad:** the national epic of Portugal (1572), by Camoens.—35. **Shaster:** a Hindu sacred book.

199.—26-27. **Tom Jones,** etc.: Fielding's *Tom Jones* (1749), Goethe's *Wilhelm Meister* (1796), and Defoe's *Robinson Crusoe* (1719) are all realistic pictures of contemporary life.

200.—15. **Pelasgic:** the Pelasgi are supposed to have inhabited Greece in prehistoric times.

201.—31. **Clarendon:** see **151,** 12, and note.—34. **Charles:** Charles II., who was defeated by Cromwell near Worcester, Sept. 3, 1651.

202.—21-22. **jocund or not,** etc.: Gray, *Elegy Written in a Churchyard*:—"How jocund did they drive their team afield."—

205.—22. **Give! Give!** cf. *Prov.* xxx. 15-16.—25. **"snowflake on the river"**: Burns, *Tam O'Shanter*:—

"Or like the snowflake on the river,
A moment white—then melts forever."

206.—23. **Natural History of Selborne:** published in 1789.

207.—27. **Schilderungen**="descriptions."

HEROES AND HERO-WORSHIP.

The lectures on heroes and hero-worship were delivered in London in 1840, and published (much revised) in book form the next year. The passage given is the first part of the first lecture.

209.—10. **These Six classes of Heroes:** the hero as divinity (Odin), as prophet (Mahomet), as poet (Dante, Shakespeare), as priest (Luther, Knox), as man of letters (Johnson, Rousseau, Burns), as king (Cromwell, Napoleon).

211.—37. **Account of his Embassy:** published in 1800.

213.—29. **imbroglio**=tangled mass (same root as Eng. "embroil").

214.—6. **that fancy of Plato's:** It has usually been supposed that Carlyle refers, rather confusedly to Plato's *Republic*, VII. 1-2, and the *Phaedo*, 109. But in Cicero's *De Natura Deorum*, II. 37, is a fancy which corresponds to Carlyle's reference more closely than does either of the passages in Plato, and which Cicero attributes to Aristotle. In the first three editions of *Heroes and Hero-Worship* Carlyle also attributed the fancy to Aristotle, instead of to Plato. It seems probable, therefore, that he really had in mind the passage in Cicero, but later, being unable to verify the reference, decided that the conception was more likely to be Plato's than Aristotle's. Cicero wrote:—"Well, then, did Aristotle observe, 'If there were men whose habitations had been always underground; . . . and they should quit their dark abode to come to us, where they should immediately behold the earth, the seas, the heavens; . . . should see the sun, and observe the grandeur and beauty; . . . when,' says he, 'they should see these things, they would undoubtedly conclude that there are gods and that these are their mighty works'" (Bohn translation). The work of Aristotle from which Cicero quotes is lost.

216.—5. **Jean Paul:** pseudonym of Jean Paul Richter (1763-1825), a German writer; he had a passionate and imaginative love of nature, which he regarded as a symbol of spiritual reality. —16. **Sabeans:** they were inhabitants of Arabia.—28-29. **"a window,"** etc.: Carlyle is quoting, loosely, from his own *Sartor Resartus*, Book I., Chap. 11:—"All objects are as windows, through which the philosophic eye looks into Infinitude itself." —38. **Chrysostom's:** Chrysostom was one of the fathers of the Church, living in the fourth century; called "Chrysostom" ("golden-mouthed") because of his eloquence; of the famous saying (**217,** 2), Professor MacMechan says in his edition of *Heroes and Hero-Worship* (Boston, 1901), "I have found the idea but not the phrase in Chrysostom."

217.—1. **Ark of Testimony:** *Num.* vii. 89.—9. **Novalis:** the pseudonym of Friedrich von Hardenberg (1772-1801), a German poet and mystical philosopher; Carlyle published an essay on him in 1829.

218.—25. **King is Kön-ning:** a false etymology; "king" is derived from O. E. *cynn*, "race," "tribe," "kin," and a patronymic ending, *ing*, and means "the chief man or descendant of the tribe," or perhaps "of noble kin."

220.—31. **Ferney:** Voltaire lived at Ferney, near Geneva, the last twenty years of his life.—34. **Calases:** Jean Calas was broken on the wheel in 1762, the victim of religious fanaticism; Voltaire finally proved the man innocent; in some other cases he secured the release of the wrongly accused.

221.—4. **Douanier**=the custom-house officer.—6. **Maître de Poste**=post-master.—7. **"Va bon train"**="Go fast."—15. **Encyclopedism:** the great French *Encyclopédie* (1751-1772) embodied the sceptical philosophy of France at that time, of which Voltaire was high-priest.

THOMAS BABINGTON MACAULAY.

OLIVER GOLDSMITH.

223.—6. **banshees:** female fairies, believed in in Ireland and parts of Scotland, which attach themselves to particular families, and foretell deaths by appearing to the doomed person.—**Rapparee**=Irish freebooter.—**Baldearg O'Donnell:** an Irish chief who played a prominent part in the struggle in Ireland, in 1689-1691, between James II. and William of Orange.—8. **Peterborough and Stanhope:** English generals who were conspicuous in the War of the Spanish Succession, particularly in the daring capture of Barcelona in 1705.—14. **Carolan:** an Irish itinerant minstrel (died 1738).—23. **Glorious and Immortal Memory:** a phrase used in toasts, etc., in honor of the English Revolution of 1688, which resulted in barring Catholics from the throne and settling the succession on the House of Brunswick, excluding James II. and his descendants.

225.—38. **Fontenelle:** see note on **72,** 18.

226.—15. **usher**=under-teacher.

227.—3. **St. Paul's Churchyard:** the street around St. Paul's Cathedral is so called; the book-shop referred to was Newbery's, for whom Goldsmith is supposed to have written *Goody Two Shoes*.—6. **Life of Beau Nash, which is not reprinted:** it had been twice reprinted when Macaulay wrote.—10. **Sketches of London Society:** the correct title is *The Letters of a Citizen of the World.*

228.—11. **Inns of Court:** see note on **82,** 31.—37. **The Dunciad:** by Pope; the fourth book was published in 1742.

230.—2. **Drury Lane,** i. e., Drury Lane Theatre, where Garrick was manager as well as leading actor.—3. **Covent Garden,** i. e., the theatre there; for the Garden, see note on **70,** 11.—11. **False Delicacy:** by Hugh Kelly.—16. **very best scene:** in Act III.—25. **The Rehearsal:** a play (1671) by the Duke of Buckingham and others, in which the faults of the Restoration dramas are wittily ridiculed; Bayes stands in part for Dryden, as poet laureate.—32. **The finest poem:** the reference is to *De Rerum Natura* ("On the Nature of Things") by the Roman poet Lucretius (96 ?-55 B. C.), on the physical and moral doctrines of Epicureanism; cf. **2,** 19-20.

231.—37. **Kelly and Cumberland:** contemporary sentimental dramatists.

232.—17. **Naseby:** this village (where the Roundheads defeated the Royalists in 1645) is in the center of England, and Yorkshire is one of the northern counties; Goldsmith's mistake is much like saying that New York City is in Vermont.—20-21. **Alexander . . . Montezuma:** the Macedonian conqueror and the Mexican Emperor (died 1520) were separated by eighteen centuries; it was Gibbon who thus trifled with the guileless historian of Greece.—30. **southern signs:** the signs of the zodiac that are on the south side of the equator.—31. **Maupertuis:** a French astronomer (1698-1759).

233.—12. **bulks**=frameworks projecting from the front of a shop.—19. **Beauclerk:** a cultivated gentleman of the day, very intimate with Doctor Johnson; he had a private library of 30,000 volumes.—28. **Horace Walpole:** son of the prime minister, Robert Walpole, and author of *The Castle of Otranto* (1764).—30. **Chamier:** Anthony Chamier (1725-1780), a friend of Johnson and his circle, being one of the original members of "The Club"; he was at one time under-secretary of state.

234.—38. **damning with faint praise:** Pope, *Epistle to Dr. Arbuthnot,* 201:—"Damn with faint praise."

235.—3. **George Steevens:** a Shakesperean scholar (1736-1800); "his life was one of constant quarrels from his habit of making anonymous attacks upon his friends in the newspapers, and his bad temper" *(Century Dictionary of Names)*.—24. **the Temple:** one of the inns of court (see note on **82,** 31); so called from the Knights Templars, who had their headquarters there in the days of the Crusades.—27. **Clive:** Robert Clive (1725-1774), who enormously extended the power of England in India, and was twice governor of Bengal; "Clive returned to England with a fortune of at least £300,000" *(Encyclopædia Britannica)*.

236.—32. **a little poem:** *Retaliation.*

WILLIAM MAKEPEACE THACKERAY.

OLIVER GOLDSMITH.

This sketch of Goldsmith is a part of the last lecture in a series of lectures delivered in England in 1851, and in America in 1852-1853.

238.—1-12. "**Jeté sur cette boule,**" etc.="Cast upon this ball, ugly, puny, suffering, suffocated in the crowd because I am not great enough, a touching plaint issues from my mouth. The good God says to me, 'Sing, sing, poor little one!' Unless I deceive myself, to sing is my task here below. All those whom I thus amuse, will they not love me?"—13. **Béranger**=a French lyric poet (1780-1857).

239.—36. **turf**=peat; used extensively in Ireland for fuel.

241.—1. **Æsop:** an old tradition made the Greek fabulist very ugly and deformed.

242.—1. **buckeen:** in Ireland, a poor young man, without occupation, and aping the habits of the rich; the word is a diminutive of "buck," a dandy.—4. **Temple:** see note on **235,** 24.

244.—2. **Beattie:** James Beattie (1735-1803), a Scotch poet of mediocre ability.—3. **Sterne:** *Tristram Shandy* (1759-1767) made Sterne a London lion in the early sixties, when Goldsmith was struggling for his daily bread.—7. **Newbery:** see note on **27,** 3. —9. **Coleman's:** Coleman was the manager of the Covent Garden Theatre.—10. **his delightful comedy:** *She Stoops to Conquer.*

247.—25. **Yvetot:** a town in France, which, with its territory, was in the Middle Ages a little kingdom by itself, although dependent on the French crown.—33. **Ranelagh and the Pantheon:** Ranelagh Gardens, in a suburb of London, were the scene of rather wild entertainments; the Pantheon, in London, was a sort of urban Ranelagh.—34. **Madame Cornelys:** she was the manager of public social assemblies in London for some time. —35. **the Jessamy Bride:** an affectionate nickname given Miss Horneck.

248.—11. **Hazlitt:** William Hazlitt (1778-1830), the essayist; see **140** for an essay by him.—15. **the younger Coleman:** son of the theatre manager; see **244,** 9; the story is told in his *Random Records.*

249.—10-11. "**I plucked his gown,**" etc.: *The Deserted Village.* 184.—18-19. "**compassion for another's woe**": Pope, *The Universal Prayer:*—"Teach me to feel another's woe."—25. **pensioners**=dependents; see **246,** 13-15.

JOHN RUSKIN.

SELECTIONS FROM MODERN PAINTERS.

Ruskin began *Modern Painters* chiefly for the purpose of showing that J. M. W. Turner (1775-1851) was the greatest of nature painters; in order to demonstrate Turner's truthfulness to the facts of the natural world Ruskin gave elaborate descriptions of natural phenomena, and it is from such sections that the passages here printed are taken.

THE SKY.

250.—*Modern Painters*, Part II., Section III., Chap. I., §§ 1-4. —18. **it is quite certain:** referring to this statement in 1875, Ruskin wrote: "At least I thought so when I was four-and-twenty. At five-and-fifty I fancy it is just possible there may be other creatures in the universe to be pleased, or, it may be, displeased, by the weather."

251.—3-4. **"Too bright or good,"** etc.: Wordsworth, *She was a Phantom of Delight.*

252.—3. **the still small voice:** 1 *Kings* xix. 11-13.

RUNNING WATER.

252.—*Modern Painters*, Part II., Section V., Chap. III., §§ 22-24.

THE SEA.

254.—*Modern Painters*, Part II., Section V., Chap. III., §§ 38-39

255.—7. **the Academy:** the Royal Academy of Arts, London, which holds an annual exhibition of paintings.

256.—14. **sepulchral waves:** the bodies of dead slaves are being thrown overboard.—14-15. **incarnadines the multitudinous sea:** *Macbeth*, II. ii. 60-63:—

"Will all great Neptune's ocean wash this blood
Clean from my hand? No, this my hand will rather
The multitudinous seas incarnadine,
Making the green one red."

MOUNTAINS.

256.—*Modern Painters*, Part V., Chap. VII., § 4.—18. **coteaux**= hillocks.

LEAVES MOTIONLESS.

257.—*Modern Painters*, Part VI., Chap. X., §§ 22-24.

AN IDEALIST'S ARRAIGNMENT OF THE AGE.

In 1871 Ruskin began a series of "Letters to the Workmen and Laborers of Great Britain," appearing monthly at first, and later at varying intervals. In the first letter, on Jan. 1, he explained his purpose as follows:—"But I simply cannot paint, nor read, nor look at minerals, nor do anything else that I like, and the very light of the morning sky, when there is any—which is seldom, now-a-days, near London—has become hateful to me, because of the misery that I know of, and see signs of where I know it not, which no imagination can interpret too bitterly. Therefore, as I have said, I will endure it no longer quietly; but henceforward, with any few or many who will help, do my poor best to abate this misery." In the second letter he gives a fanciful explanation of the title of the series, *Fors Clavigera* ("Chance, the Club-bearer or the Key-bearer "), from which it appears that he wishes his readers to think of *Fors* as Force, Fortitude, and Fortune, and *Clavigera* as suggesting strength of Deed, strength of Patience, and strength of Law.

259.—25. **Denmark Hill:** in south London.—33. **A king's love-song:** *Song of Solomon* ii. 11-13; Ruskin has made a few changes and omissions.

260.—19. **Samaritan:** *John* iv. 17.

261.—25. **pietra dura**=" ornamental work in inlay of hard stones, such as agate and jaspers " *(Century Dictionary).*

262.—23. *Seven Lamps of Architecture:* published in 1849.

263.—12. **Holborn Viaduct:** an elevated roadway in the center of London; it had recently been completed (in 1869), and London was proud of it as a triumph of engineering.—36. **Chaucer:** in *The Flower and the Leaf,* formerly attributed to Chaucer, the superiority of the leaf is shown.—37. **First Psalm:** *Ps.* i. 3:—" his leaf also shall not wither."

264.—10. **Ascidians:** low forms of marine life, popularly called sea-squirts.—19. **my Savoyard guide:** " One of the pleasantest friends I ever had in my life was a Savoyard guide, who could only read with difficulty. . . . But he was, without exception, one of the happiest persons . . . I have ever known; and after lunch, when he had had his half bottle of Savoy wine, he would generally, as we walked up some quiet valley in the afternoon light, give me a little lecture on philosophy; and after I had fatigued and provoked him with less cheerful views of the world than his own, he would fall back to my servant behind me, and console himself with a shrug of the shoulders and a whispered, 'Le pauvre enfant, il ne sait pas vivre! ' ('The poor child, he doesn't know how to live! ') " (*Fors Clavigera,* Letter IV.).—20. **savoir vivre**=" to know how to live."—21-22. **savoir mourir**=" to know how to die."—27. **Cœur de Lion's:** Richard I., king of England 1189-1199, was surnamed " The Lion-Hearted."—**Albert Dürer's:** Dürer was a great German painter (1471-1528).

265.—14. **Buxton and Bakewell:** in Wales, where the scenery is of great beauty.—15. **Vale of Tempe:** a valley in Greece, famous for its beauty; Olympus, the fabled seat of the gods, was near.

266.—25. **a cream bowl:** cf. *L'Allegro:*—

" Tells how the drudging goblin sweat
To earn his cream bowl duly set."

—27. **stilts**=plough-handles.

267.—5. **familiar**=familiar spirit, demon.—10. **Virgil thought so:** *Georgics,* II. 458-460:—" O greatly fortunate, if they had known their good, the tillers of the field, for whom, far from jarring strife, the most just earth itself pours forth from the ground an easy living."—19. **Cumberland:** a county in the north-west of England, containing a part of the beautiful Lake District.

268.—3. **Hesse's:** Heinrich Hesse (1798-1863), professor of painting and director of the art collections in Munich, decorated several of the churches there with frescoes of religious subjects.—7. **Minerva:** as the goddess of wisdom she presided over the useful and ornamental arts, including spinning and weaving.—10. **cinque-cento-fold:** a reference to Italian art of the sixteenth century (*cinque cento* is an abbreviated form of *mille cinque cento*, "a thousand five hundred," by which the Italians indicate the years 1500 to 1599); Ruskin also plays upon "five-hundred-fold" (see l. 9).—20 **"position of William"**: in Letter I. Ruskin has told of a carpenter, William, who borrows a plane of another carpenter, and at the end of a year has to return a new plane, besides giving a plank for the use of the worn-out plane; he calls this situation the "position of William."

269.—22. **German and French**: the Franco-Prussian War was then raging.

271.—16. **I am not rich**: Ruskin inherited a comfortable fortune from his father, in 1864, but had already reduced it considerably by generosity and reform ventures of various sorts; eventually he lost it all, and in his last years was dependent upon the sale of his books.

272.—18. **old potter in France**: Bernard Palissy (1510?-1588). —24-25. **to question the nativity of men**: another fling at the doctrine that men have evolved from lower forms of life; cf. **264,** 10-11,—26. **Magi**: *Matt.* ii. 11.

JOHN HENRY NEWMAN.

THE ROMAN CATHOLIC CHURCH.

Newman, after a distinguished career in the Church of England and at Oxford University, joined the Roman Catholic Church in 1845. In 1864 Charles Kingsley, the clergyman and novelist, published a violent attack upon Newman, accusing him of insincerity and equivocation, and asserting that the Roman Catholic Church favored deceit. The attack aroused Newman to write *Apologia pro Vita Sua* ("Defence of His Own Life"), in which he traced the development of his religious opinions, to show his sincerity and conscientiousness at every step, and also defended the church of his adoption from the charges brought against it in connection with those against himself. The portion here printed is taken from Chapter IV.

274.—12. **Transubstantiation**: the change of the bread and wine of the eucharist into the body and blood of Christ.—18. **Macaulay**: in his review of Ranke's *History of the Popes*, in the *Edinburgh Review*, October, 1840.—33. **the phenomena**, i. e., the external appearance of the bread and wine.

275.—32. **mood and figure**: terms of logic for the various kinds of syllogisms used in formal reasoning.

276.—16. **"lamentations,"** etc.: *Ezek.* ii. 10.—33. **"having no hope,"** etc.: *Eph.* ii. 12.

278.—29. **establishment of religion**: the formation of a state church, such as the Church of England.

282.—4-6. **in his own person . . . living stones**: 1 *Cor.* iii. 16; 1 *Pet.* ii. 5.

283.—37. **St. Athanasius**: a Church father of the fourth century, the foremost defender of orthodoxy in his day.—38. **St. Augustine**: the greatest father of the Church (354-430), who put his stamp indelibly upon the theology of Latin Christianity.

St. Thomas: Thomas Aquinas (1225 ?-1274), an Italian, the greatest of the schoolmen.

284.—4. **ex animo**=sincerely (lit. "from the mind").

MATTHEW ARNOLD.

HEBRAISM AND HELLENISM.

The chapter of *Culture and Anarchy* here printed was first published as an essay in *The Cornhill Magazine*, June, 1868.

286.—5. **Bishop Wilson:** an English bishop (1663-1755); Arnold had already, in Chap. II., quoted this saying from his *Maxims*.

287.—25-26. **"that we might be partakers,"** etc.; 2 *Pet.* i. 4.—36. **Frederick Robertson:** an Anglican clergyman, who had a brilliant career at Brighton, cut short by death in 1853; the sermon referred to (*The Grecian*, preached Dec. 6, 1849) is the more striking as an illustration of Arnold's point because Robertson was comparatively modern and liberal.

288.—3. **Heinrich Heine:** a German poet of Hebrew descent (1797-1856); Professor Gates thinks that Arnold probably took the terms "Hebraism" and "Hellenism" from Heine, and translates as follows from Heine's *Über Ludwig Börne:*—"All men are either Jews or Hellenes, men ascetic in their instincts, hostile to culture, spiritual fanatics, or men of vigorous good cheer, full of the pride of life, Naturalists" (*Selections from the Prose Writings of Matthew Arnold*, Holt & Co., 1897).—17-19. **He that keepeth the law, . . . His commandments:** *Prov.* xxix. 18; *Ps.* cxii. 1.—26-27. **"C'est le bonheur des hommes"**="It is the good fortune of men."—27-30. Cf. *Rom.* xii. 9; *Ps.* i. 2; 1 *Cor.* xv. 31; *Rev.* iii. 12, vii. 9.

289.—5. **capital**=important, forming one of the chief divisions or heads (Lat. *caput*, "head").—17. **patient continuance in well-doing:** *Rom.* ii. 7.—24-25. **"establishes the law":** *Rom.* iii. 31.—34. **Zechariah:** ix. 13.

290.—6-8. *Prov.* xvi. 22; *John* viii. 12, 32.—8-9. **Aristotle will undervalue knowing:** *Nicomachean Ethics*, II. iv.—13. **St. James:** i. 22.—14. **Epictetus:** a famous Stoic philosopher of the first century A. D.—18. **Plato:** in the *Gorgias*.—19. **the Imitation:** *Imitation of Christ*, usually attributed to Thomas á Kempis (1380 ?-1471).—22-23. **"walking in the way of the commandments":** *Ps.* cxix. 32, 35.—23. **"the way of peace":** *Isa.* lix. 8.—26-28. 2 *Cor.* v. 14; *Gal.* v. 24.—29. **Aristotle:** in the *Nicomachean Ethics*, X. viii.—33. **Plato:** in the *Phœdo*.

291.—13. **sweetness and light:** the phrase is borrowed from Swift (see **66**, 32), as Arnold duly acknowledges in Chap. I.; but he puts the expression to new use, meaning by it beauty and intelligence.—18. **the true Socrates of the Memorabilia:** Socrates as portrayed in the *Memorabilia of Socrates* by Xenophon, his disciple, in distinction from the Socrates of Plato's *Dialogues*, in which Socrates is used in part as the mouthpiece of Plato.

292.—5. **Dr. Pusey:** one of the leaders, with Newman, in the Tractarian movement at Oxford University; but he remained in the English Church.—22-23. *Rom.* viii. 26, vii. 24.—36. **Zechariah:** viii. 23.

293.—12. **George Herbert**: the poet and clergyman (1593-1633), one of the saintliest men in the English Church. Professor Gates thinks Arnold is quoting loosely, from memory, a line of the following stanza in Herbert's poem, *The Size*:—

> "Thy Saviour sentenced joy,
> And in the flesh condemned it as unfit,
> At least in lump; for such doth oft destroy;
> Whereas a bit
> Doth 'tice us on to hopes of more,
> And, for the present, health restore."

The stanza and the poem as a whole are less ascetic than Arnold's misquotation would lead one to suppose.—16. **"Let no man deceive you,"** etc.: *Eph.* v. 6.—21. **baptized into a death:** *Rom.* vi. 3.

294.—3. **"entrusted with the oracles of God"**: *Rom.* iii. 2.—6. **foolishness:** 1 *Cor.* i. 20.

296.—19. **Balaam's ass:** *Num.* xxii. 28.

THOMAS HENRY HUXLEY.

ON A PIECE OF CHALK.

This discourse was delivered in 1868 as a lecture to the working-men of Norwich, England, during the meeting, in that city, of the British Association. It was published in *Macmillan's Magazine*, September, 1868. The text here given is that of the magazine; the slight changes which Huxley made in preparing the article for publication in book-form are recorded in the notes.

300.—1. **were to be sunk:** revised text, "were sunk."—15. **Albion**="White" Land.—22. **Weald of Kent and Sussex:** an oval-shaped area in the counties named, marked by an escarpment, or precipitous cutting away, of the chalk ("weald" is apparently an irregular form of "wild"; O. E. *weald*, a forest).

301.—2. **which has precisely**: revised text, "much of which has," and omit "precisely."—7. **runs:** revised text, "it runs."

304.—14. **spoor**=trail.

306.—34. **nature:** revised text, "the nature."

308.—25. **those:** revised text, "the."—27. **those:** revised text, "the."—28. **Radiolariæ:** revised text, "*Radiolaria*," and so throughout.

310.—9. **a most:** revised text, omit "a."

311.—3. Revised text: transpose "at the present day" to a position between "are" and "certain."—32. **is it:** revised text, "it is."—38. **animalculæ:** revised text, "animalcules."

312.—27-28. **Sir Charles Lyell:** by his *Principles of Geology* (1830-1833) he laid the foundations of modern geology.—32. **"The upper valve,"** etc.: the quotation is from Lyell's *Elements of Geology* (1838).

314.—19. **old:** revised text, "whole"; a misprint?

316.—7-8. **"the whirligig of time,"** etc.: *Twelfth Night*, V. i. 384-385: "and thus the whirligig of time brings in his revenges."

318.—33. **And it is,** etc.: revised text, omit "And."

319.—17-18. **Foraminiferæ:** revised text, "*Foraminifera*."—27.

Battle of Hastings: in 1066 A. D.—29. **Ichthyosauriæ:** revised text, "*Ichthyosauria.*"

320.—33. **crocodile:** revised text, "crocodiles."

321.—3-5. Revised text: omit parenthesis; change "Thus" to "But."

322.—2. "**without haste but without rest:**" a translation of the German "ohne Hast, aber ohne Rast."

WALTER PATER.

DIONYSUS.

The essay, *A Study of Dionysus*, the first half of which is here printed, appeared first in *The Fortnightly Review* for December, 1876. The text here followed is that of the *Review;* the new readings of the essay as it appeared later in book-form are recorded in the notes.

323.—5. Revised text: omit "independently."—21. **general:** revised text, "whole."

324.—6. **Galahad's cup:** the holy grail, supposed to be the cup used by Jesus at the Last Supper, in which Joseph of Arimathea, according to legend, caught the last drops of the blood of Jesus; in the search for the lost grail by the Knights of the Round Table, Galahad was successful (see Malory's *Morte Darthur*, Books XIII. and XVII., and Tennyson's *The Holy Grail* in *Idyls of the King*).—10. **compacted together, closing in:** revised text, "presented to the senses, and comprehending."—14. Revised text: omit "those"; insert "that" after "modes of."—21. **Sensitive Plant:** the first three stanzas will show what Pater refers to:—

> "A Sensitive Plant in a garden grew,
> And the young winds fed it with silver dew,
> And it opened its fan-like leaves to the light,
> And closed them beneath the kisses of Night.
>
> "And the Spring arose on the garden fair,
> Like the Spirit of Love felt everywhere;
> And each flower and herb on Earth's dark breast
> Rose from the dreams of its wintry rest.
>
> "But none ever trembled and panted with bliss
> In the garden, the field, or the wilderness,
> Like a doe in the noontide with love's sweet want,
> As the companionless Sensitive Plant."

—23. **culture:** revised text, "lights."—33. **suspicion:** revised text, "fancy."

325.—2-3. **the Homeric hymn to Aphrodite:** the so-called *Homeric Hymns* were written by unknown authors, and are of later date than Homer, ranging from the seventh century to the fourth century B. C., or even later.—12. Revised text: insert "they" before "dance" and before "sing."—15. **nympholepti=**

"seized by nymphs" (νύμφη, "nymph," and ληπτός, "seized"), i. e., inspired by the spirit of nature.—19. **Homer compares to them:** *Odyssey,* VII. 106:—"And he had fifty handmaids in the house, and some grind the yellow grain on the millstone, and others weave webs, and turn the yarn as they sit, restless as the leaves of the tall poplar tree" (Butcher and Lang's translation).—21. **Alcinous:** king of the Phæacians, father of that admirable Greek maiden Nausicaa, who came to the relief of shipwrecked Ulysses (*Odyssey,* VI.).—**Naxos:** the largest island of the Cyclades, famous for its wine.

326.—1. **gush by gush:** revised text, "by little."—**upon:** revised text, "on."—22-23. **dainty-wheeled and dainty-winged spirit of Triptolemus:** "Going swiftly, half on the airy, mercurial wheels of his farm instrument, harrow or plough, half on wings of serpents—the worm, symbolical of the soil, but winged, as sending up the dust committed to it, after subtle firing, in colors and odors of fruit and flowers" (Pater, *Demeter and Persephone* in *Greek Studies*).—25. **in:** revised text, "on."

327.—4. **embodiments:** revised text, "abstractions."—15. **nimble:** revised text, "agile."—18. Revised text: insert "being" after "solace."—28. **he:** revised text, "Pan."—29. **their names:** cf. "satyr" and "satire," and "Pan" and "panic"; but by the accepted etymology now "satire" comes from *satura,* "a mixed dish," "a medley."

328.—2-3. **happiest moments:** revised text, "happy moment." —**Praxiteles:** he came comparatively late in Greek sculpture, living in the fourth century B. C.; see Hawthorne's *Marble Faun* for an interpretation of the statue which Pater refers to.—16. Revised text: add "to Pan" after "hymn."—28. **Marsyas:** Pater specifies this satyr because he challenged Apollo to a contest in flute-playing, and was flayed alive by the god for his presumption.—30. **Theocritus:** the greatest of the classic pastoral poets; he lived in the third century B. C.

329.—13. **Amyclæ:** a town in southern Greece.—19. Revised text: omit "and" after "Florence."—36. Revised text: insert "Eleutherios" after "Deliverer."

330.—3. Revised text: after "there" insert the following sentence:—"There, under his later reign, hard by the golden image of Apollo himself, near the sacred tripod on which the Pythia sat to prophesy, was to be seen a strange object—a sort of coffin, or cinerary urn, with the inscription, 'Here lieth the body of Dionysus, the son of Semele.'"—10. Revised text: insert "then" after "back."—13. **Gozzoli's:** Gozzoli died in 1498, at Pisa, where are his chief paintings, twenty-three frescoes on the walls of the cloister of the Campo Santo, or burial ground (lit. "holy field"). —22-23. Revised text: transpose "now almost departed" to a position between "apprehension" and "of unseen powers."—37. **Titian and Tintoret:** both of these Venetian painters, of the sixteenth century, painted the marriage of Bacchus and Ariadne; see **332,** 1-10.

331.—5. **calpis**=a pitcher.—6. **amphora**=a two-handled jar.—12. Revised text: insert "δεισιδαίμονες" after "sympathies"; cf. *Acts* xvii. 22, where Paul in his speech to the Athenians applies to them the same Greek word, which in the King James

Version is translated "superstitious," and in the margin of the Revised Version "religious."—19. **Aristophanes:** the greatest writer of comedy among the Greeks; he lived in the fifth century B. C.

332.—9. **though:** revised text, "and."—18. **Sophocles:** usually considered the most perfect of the Greek tragic poets; he died in 406 B. C.—20. **Cadmus:** the legendary founder of Thebes.

333.—7. **Callimachus:** a Greek lyric poet of the third century B. C.—34. Revised text: omit "and" after "capricious."

334.—1. **silex**=flint.—2. **lie:** revised text, "are lying."—15. **Aaron's rod that budded:** *Num.* xvii. 8; *Heb.* ix. 4—16. **Tannhäuser is saved:** revised text, "Tannhäuser's repentance is accepted." Tannhäuser, the hero of a medieval German legend, appeals to the Pope for the forgiveness of his grievous sins; the Pope, who holds a staff, replies that Tannhäuser may expect forgiveness when the staff grows green; later it does grow green, a sign that God's mercy is greater than the Pope had thought.—28. **invented**=discovered (lit. "come upon").—31. **mænads**=frenzied female worshippers of Bacchus (Gk. μαινάς, "raving"; "maniac" is from the same root).—38. **spring:** revised text, "summer." **Elis and Argos:** a region and a city in Greece.

335.—4. **the solace of it:** revised text, "its solace."—6. **the prophet Melampus:** some serpents, whose lives Melampus had saved, licked his ears with their tongues and enabled him to understand the language of birds and worms; this gift was the basis of his prophetic powers and insight into the secrets of nature.—11 **Giorgione:** a Venetian painter (1477-1511), who influenced the style of Titian.—12. **Fête Champêtre**="Rural Festival." **Louvre:** the great art museum of Paris.—13. Revised text: insert "and" after "subtle."—16-17. Revised text: omit "of it."—19. **"Acqua frésca!"**="Fresh water!"—26. **Bacchæ:** revised text, "*Bacchanals.*"—28. **epithets:** revised text, "and."—32. Revised text: insert "for them" after "became."—38. **for instance:** revised text, "as it were."

336.—1. Revised text: insert "the" before "human body" and before "human soul"; change "flesh" to "a body."

ROBERT LOUIS STEVENSON.

AES TRIPLEX.

The essay was first published in *The Cornhill Magazine*, April, 1878.

337.—16. **pyramids:** they were built as the tombs of the Egyptian kings. **dule trees**=mourning-trees, under which families or clans gathered to bewail deaths or other calamities (also spelt "dool-tree"; Lat. *dolor*, "grief").

339.—5. **blue-peter:** a blue flag with a white square in the centre, flown when the vessel is about to sail.—29. **Balaklava:** a seaport in the Crimea, near which, in the war between Russia and England in 1854, occurred the famous charge of the English Light Brigade, in which 472 men out of a total of 670 were killed.—32 **Curtius:** a Roman, who in the early days of Rome, so runs the legend, leaped on horseback into a chasm which an earthquake had opened in the Forum and which the soothsayers had said could be closed only by casting into it Rome's greatest treasure.

340.—2. **the Derby:** a horse-race, established in 1780 by the Earl of Derby, which is run every May at Epsom, and is attended by hundreds of thousands from London, many of whom go by coach.—3. **the deified Caligula:** this Roman emperor (12-41 A. D.) had himself worshipped as a demi-god during his lifetime.—5. **Baiæ bay:** near Naples; a favorite seaside resort of the Romans.—6. **Prætorian guards:** the body-guards of the Roman emperors (so called because originally, under the republic, they were the body-guard of the prætor).—35. **Omar Khayyam:** a Persian poet, who died in the early part of the twelfth century; his *Rubaiyat*, or quatrains, have been translated by Edward Fitzgerald.

341.—2. **a vapor or a show:** *Jas.* iv. 7; *Ps.* xxxix. 6.—3. **same stuff with dreams:** *Tempest*, IV. i. 156-158:—

"We are such stuff
As dreams are made on, and our little life
Is rounded with a sleep."

342.—8. **the Commander's statue:** according to an old Spanish legend, Don Juan, the famous libertine, after killing the governor of the city in a duel, broke into the murdered man's tomb and invited his statue to attend a feast; at the appointed time the statue appeared and carried Don Juan to the lower world.—29. **bath-chair**=an invalid's chair on wheels (so called from Bath, the English health-resort, where such chairs are common).—35. **lexicographer:** Samuel Johnson; his English dictionary appeared in 1755.—38. **triple brass:** an allusion to the title of the essay, *Aes Triplex*, which is taken from Horace (*Odes*, I. iii.):—

"Illi robur et aes triplex
Circa pectus erat, qui fragilem truci
Commisit pelago ratem
Primus."

("Oak and triple brass encompassed the breast of him who first entrusted his frail bark to the wild sea.")

343.—38. **mim-mouthed:** "mim" is Scotch for "mum."

344.—7. **cried Nelson:** before one of his great naval battles.—33. **folio:** Stevenson intentionally mentions a book of the largest size.

345.—22. **trailing with him clouds of glory:** Wordsworth, *Ode on Intimations of Immortality.*

EARLY TRANSLATIONS OF THE BIBLE.

THE LORD'S PRAYER.

The Anglo-Saxon version is taken from *The Holy Gospels in Anglo-Saxon, Northumbrian, and old Mercian Versions. . . .* Edited by the Rev. Walter W. Skeat. . . . Cambridge, 1871-1887.

The Wiclif version is taken from *The Holy Bible . . . in the Earliest English Versions made from the Latin Vulgate by John Wycliffe and his Followers;* edited by the Rev. Josiah Forshall . . . and Sir Frederic Madden . . . Oxford, 1850.

The Tyndale version is taken from *The English Hexapla*, London, 1841. Tyndale published his translation of the New Testament from the Greek in 1525; a revised edition appeared in 1534.

347.—1. **þu**=thou. **þe**=who. **si**=be.—2. **Gewurþe**=become, be done (from *weorthan;* same root as Ger. *werden;* cf. "worth" (="come to") in "woe worth the day," sometimes met in poetry). **ðin**=thine. **swa**=so.—3. **gedæghwamlican**=daily. **hlaf**=loaf. **syle**=sell, give.—5. **costnunge**=temptation. **ac**=but. **alys**=release (cf. Ger. *erlösen*).—6. **Soþlice**=truly (cf. "in sooth," "soothsayer," etc.); with the sense here of "may it become truth," i.e., "amen."

347.—8. **be thy wille don as in heuen and in erthe:** the defective form of the comparison is due to translating literally from the Vulgate, which has "fiat voluntas tua sicut in coelo et in terra."—9. **oure breed ouer other substaunce:** a literal translation from the Vulgate's "panem nostrum supersubstantialem" ("our bread necessary to support life").

THE PARABLE OF THE PRODIGAL SON.

In Wiclif's version the peculiarities are often due to translating literally from the Vulgate, as will appear below.

348.—4. **And not aftir manye dayes:** "Et non post multos dies" (Vulgate).—7-8. **a strong hungir was maad:** "facta est fames valida" (Vulgate).—10. **toun:** a mistranslation of the Vulgate's *villam*, "country estate," "farm."—13. **he turned aȝen in to him silf:** "in se autem reversus" (Vulgate).—20. **was stirid by mercy:** "misercordia motus est" (Vulgate).—20-21. **rennynge to:** "accurrens" (Vulgate).—24-25. **firste stoole**=best robe; "stolam primam" (Vulgate).—31. **a crowde:** "chorum" (Vulgate); the Latin word also means "chorus" and is a correct translation of the Greek χορῶν; the mistake was Wiclif's.

349.—2. **so manye ȝeeris:** "tot annis" (Vulgate).—5. **hooris**=whores.—7-8. **alle myne thingis ben thyne:** "omnia mea tua sunt" (Vulgate).

SIR JOHN MANDEVILLE.

OF THE HILLES OF GOLD.

The name of the author is probably fictitious; but there was a John Mandeville who died in 1372. The work itself is mostly a compilation from earlier books of travel in the East. The earliest known manuscript of it is in French, and dated 1371; the English translation was made about the beginning of the fifteenth century. The extract here printed is from Chap. XXX.

350.—23. **Pissemyres**=ants. **fynen**=refine.—28. **sleighte**=cunning (cf. "sleight-of-hand").

351.—4. **or**=ere.—14. **kynde**=nature.

SIR THOMAS MALORY.

THE PARTING OF LAUNCELOT AND GUINEVERE.

Le Morte Darthur, which (says Caxton in his preface), "Sir Thomas Malory dyd take oute of certeyn bookes of frensshe and reduced it into Englysshe," was one of the earliest books printed by William Caxton, the first English printer. The text here followed is that of the Temple Classics edition, which is considerably modernized in spelling. The extract given is from Book XXI., Chaps. 9, 10. The civil war between King Arthur and Modred, his son, had ended in the death of Modred and the mysterious departure of Arthur, sore wounded, into the vale of Avilion. Launcelot, in France, hearing only that the king was hard pressed, came over-sea to help him; being told that Arthur had been slain, he sought Queen Guinevere, who had entered the nunnery at Almesbury.

353.—1. **Sangreal**=the Holy Grail.—12. **gray or white:** Franciscans were gray friars, Carmelites white; so called from the color of their gowns.—26. **Sir Bevidere:** this honest knight, who had carried Arthur to the barge and seen him sail away, had already "taken himself to perfection" and was an inmate of the hermitage.

HUGH LATIMER.

AN ARRAIGNMENT OF LONDON.

The famous *Sermon of the Plough* was preached in St. Paul's Church, London, on January 18, 1548. Seven years later, under "Bloody Mary," Latimer was burned at the stake for heresy. The sermon gets its title from Latimer's thought that the preacher is a plougher in God's field, the world, where the seed of His word is sown.

355.—9. **between stock and stock**=between post and post.—13. **exhibition**="a benefaction settled for the maintenance of scholars in English universities, not depending on the foundation" *(Century Dictionary)*.

JOHN LYLY.

THE CHARACTER OF EUPHUES.

Euphues is a kind of society novel, giving a picture of life and manners in different countries, as Euphues ("Wellborn") pursues his travels. The passage here given is the beginning of the book. The text is that of the first edition, as reprinted in R. W. Bond's edition of Lyly (Oxford, 1902).

355.—29. **only:** to be taken with "she herself," not with "current."—32. **honest**=honorable.

356.—4. **quipping**=uttering quips, or sharp jests.—6. **brack**=